# CHRONICLES FROM THE FUTURE

## The amazing story of Paul Amadeus Dienach

*Based on his Diary Pages*

Edited by Achilleas Sirigos

This Way Out Productions
ISBN: 978-618-82218-1-9
First Edition

Written by Paul Amadeus Dienach
Edited by Achilleas Sirigos

Cover Design by Jeff Brown
Translation by Eleonora Kouneni
Translation Editing by Thalia Bisticas
Additional Translation by Matina Chatzigianni

*For the victims of the Greek depression (2009- )*
*and the millions of immigrants*
*that risk their life in the Aegean Sea*
*seeking a better future for them and their children.*

# Table of Contents

"Άμμες δε γ' εσσόμεθα πολλώ κάρρονες"

**but we shall become much better than you*

*Promissory Oath of the teen Spartans towards the elderly*
*[Ploutarhos: "Lykourgos" 21]*

## EDITOR'S PREFACE

Introductions typically attempt to present the essence of a book, highlighting the most important elements of the story you are about to read. My introduction does not do that. Rather, I will be telling you the story of how this unique text came to be, its journey from the 1920s until today.

This is a book that contains the diary of a man who never intended his words to be revealed to the world. It chronicles an experience that was never shared for fear of ridicule and disbelief. As you work your way through his very personal memoire, the reason for secrecy will soon become clear– the author claimed to have lived in the future and returned back to his original era, 20th century central Europe, to record a detailed account, outlining exactly what happened during his journey.

The real protagonists of this amazing, true story are two persons: Paul Amadeus Dienach, the author and George Papachatzis, Dienach's student of German language studies, to whom he left his notes - the diary you hold in your hands today.

After making the first acquaintances, let's start unravelling their story step-by-step.

Paul Amadeus Dienach was a Swiss-Austrian teacher with fragile health. His father was a German-speaking Swiss and his mother was an Austrian from Salzburg. Dienach travelled to Greece in the Autumn of 1922, after having recovered from a one-year coma caused by a serious illness, hoping that the mild climate would improve his condition.

During his time in Greece, Dienach taught French and German

language lessons in order to provide himself with a minimum income. Amongst his students was George Papachatzis, a student that Dienach appreciated more than any of the others. Papachatzis describes his teacher as a "very cautious and very modest man that used to emphasize the details".

Dienach, as we learn from Papachatzis, was born in a suburb of Zurich and lived his adolescence in a village nearby the large Swiss capital. He later followed humanitarian studies with a strong inclination to the history of cultures and classical philology. It is believed that he eventually died from tuberculosis in Athens, Greece, or on his way back to his homeland through Italy, probably during the first quarter of 1924.

Before Paul Dienach died, he entrusted Papachatzis with part of his life and soul– his diary. Without telling Papachatzis what the notes were, he left him with the simple instructions that he should use the documents to improve his German by translating them from German to Greek.

Papachatzis did as his teacher asked. Initially, he believed Dienach had written a novel, but as he progressed with translations, he soon realized the notes were actually his diary… from the future!

At this point we have to clarify something crucial. Dienach is thought to have suffered from Encephalitis lethargica, a strange neurological disease that develops an immune system response to overloaded neurons. The first time Dienach fell into a lethargic sleep it was for 15 days. The second time it was for a whole year…

During this year that Dienach was in a coma in a Zurich hospital, he claimed to have entered the body of another person, Andreas Northam, who lived in the year 3906 AD.

Once he recovered from his coma, Dienach didn't talk to anyone about his remarkable experience because he thought he would be considered crazy. However, what he did do was write down the entirety of his memory relating to what he had seen of the future.

Towards the end of his life, he even stopped his teaching job in order to have as much time as possible to write everything he could remember.

Dienach describes everything he experienced of the environment and people of the year 3906 AD, according to the mind-set and limited knowledge of a 20th century man. This was not an easy task for Dienach. There were many things he claims not to have understood about what he saw, nor was he familiar with all their terms, technology, or the evolutionary path they had followed.

In his memoires, he claims that the people of the future fully understood his peculiar medical situation, which they called "conscious slide", and they told Dienach as many things as they could in relation to the historical events that took place between the 21st and 40th century. The only thing they didn't tell him was the exact story of the 20th century, in case Dienach's consciousness returned back to his original body and era (as he did) – they believed it would be dangerous to let him know his immediate future and the future of his era in case it disturbed or altered the path of history and his life.

By reading Dienach's unique personal narration page by page, you will be able to decode what he claims to have seen in relation to mankind, our planet and our evolution.

Many may wonder – what happened to the diary in all that time, from the distant year of 1926 until now, almost a century later?

George Papachatzis gradually translated Dienach's notes – with his not so perfect German – over a period of 14 years (1926-1940), mostly in his spare time and summer breaks. World War II and the Greek civil war delayed his efforts of spreading the amazing story that landed on his desk all those years ago.

On the Eve of Christmas in 1944, Papachatzis was staying with friends at a house which was also used occupied by the Greek Army. When the soldiers caught sight of Dienach's notes, which were of course in German, they confiscated them because they considered them suspicious. They told Papachatzis that they would return them only after they had examined their contents. They never did. But by then, Papachatzis had already finished the translation.

George Papachatzis tried to track down information about Dienach, by visiting Zurich 12 times between 1952 and 1966. He could not find a single trace of him, nor any relatives, neighbours, or friends. Dienach, who is thought to have fought with the Germans during World War I, probably never gave his real name in Greece, a country that had fought against the Germans.

After the end of World War II and the Greek Civil War, Papachatzis gave the translated diary to some of his friends –masons, theosophists, professors of theology and two anti-Nazi Germans–

and after that, when everybody realized what they had in their hands, the diary was kept within a close philosophical circle and in the Tectonic Lodge, in which he was a high ranking member. The book was taken very seriously by the Masons, who did not want the information spread to a larger circle. They considered the book to be almost holy, containing wisdom about the future of humanity, and better kept only for the few.

Finally, after strong disputes, George Papachatzis decided to publish Dienach's Diary. It was during the period that Greece entered the hardest phase of the 7 year dictatorship in 1972. Strong protest from certain church circles – who considered the book heretic – and the fall of the dictatorship a year later, condemned the first edition to oblivion. No one was interested in the future when the present was so intense and violent.

All these factors, along with the difficult language and the rough style of Dienach's notes, which mixed together elements of his past, along with his experience of the future, made the diary even more difficult to understand. Only a few had the time and patience to decode the secret knowledge that lay encoded within almost 1,000 pages.

Another edition followed in 1979 in Greece titled "The Valley of the Roses". However, again the book disappeared and it was hardly mentioned again, apart from the few that knew of its existence.

After all the silence, Papachatzis died, and his family did not wish to carry on with his work.

I have to remark that, while Papachatzis was just a student at the time of receiving Dienach's diary, he went on to become a very respectable man of his era. He was a prominent Professor of Administrative Law, Rector of Panteion University of Social and Political Sciences, Founding Member of the Greek Philosophical Society and Vice President of the Council of State, the supreme court of Greece. He was a man of impeccable credibility, who risked a lot in publishing Dienach's work and this on its own reflects his unwavering belief in its authenticity.

Twenty two years passed before the diary was picked up again by the independent publisher Radamanthis Anastasakis, who decided to republish the original diary on a small scale.

That's when I discovered the book for the first time and started to "restore" it, without the sentimentalities that kept Papachatzis from doing something more than an exact translation of the 'holy' scripts of his teacher. Almost a century after the original diary was written, this was a task that had to be undertaken so that a 21st century reader could really understand what a 20th century man wanted to say.

And so I did it, making sure not to change any of the content, but filtering out irrelevant notes pertaining to Dienach's early life and emphasizing his experience of the future, but in a simpler language and without the gaps that Dienach's narration had.

I have tried to keep the true essence of his story intact. This was my debt to Dienach, whose chronicles from the future completely changed my perspective of life. Nothing more, nothing less. My only goal was to make it accessible to all of you, because if Dienach's experience was indeed real, this book contains revolutionary information – something the Masons clearly recognized – and has the potential to radically change your view of the world and mankind.

Now that you know the background to this unique story, I will simply deposit the future in your hands with an abstract from the introduction of the 1979 edition of the book by Professor Papachatzis, the man who personally knew Dienach:

*"The translator of the original texts knew Dienach personally. His belief is that the inspiration and writing of these texts wasn't an imaginary creation of Dienach, based on his education and insightful abilities. It is a true phenomenon of parapsychology that was linked to his life. Maybe he has also added his own things, maybe he didn't see or live all of the events that he so vividly describes and presents. What is certain is that most of the basic elements of his texts are true experiences that he had; he lived in advance a part of the future to come and a metaphysical phenomenon of incredible clarity happened to him - a phenomenon of parapsychology that rarely happens with such an intensity and roughness. Because of him, what is going to happen on Earth starting from the last decades of the 20th century up to 3906 AD, is now known to us, at least in general terms."*

Now, I leave you with Dienach's diary, a chronicle from the future...

Achilleas Sirigos
May 2015

# First Diary

## REMEMBRANCES FROM THE PAST

### December 2nd, 1918

I have decided to write a bit every day so that I can tell my sad story, little by little, from beginning to end.

During the first twenty-one years of my life, you would think I was the happiest person on earth. It's been eleven years since then - eleven unbearable years. The only thing I am longing for now is some solace or something to keep me occupied.

It feels like yesterday, those happy days of craving a never-ending bliss with Anna. It can't be true that this love has had such a sad and irreparable ending, that Anna has been dead for so many years now, that everything has faded away. No, I can't believe it. Nine whole years without her…

"Why do you keep torturing yourself by thinking about all that?" they ask me. I understand. I need closure, but it is hard to find.

You do not know. Our love was no ordinary love. We were still at school when we fell in love with each other. Since then I had been imagining her name next to mine.

That man who brought destruction into our lives and sent her to the grave never loved her! He never considered Anna his one and only, like I did. He never saw anything in her eyes.

When I was young, I would stare for hours through my window, which overlooked hers. And when the weather was foul, that is when I would not budge an inch from there! I saw the people hurrying along, smiling at the thought of a warm soup and a cosy bed at home while I was wishing that the weather would continue so that I'd have a better chance of seeing her.

"What is Anna feeling at the moment? What does this colourless world look like through her eyes?" I would think.

And when I saw her in the lamplight, holding her embroidery, my longing became a life goal vindicated, my salvation from loneliness...

Only on holidays did I wish for good weather because a storm would lessen my chances to happen upon Anna and her family in the park. But still, I became nervous. I would have to greet her and it would be shameful for her parents to see me blush with embarrassment.

How happy were the days that followed! Shortly before her brother left the city to study, I got to know him better. He invited me to his home and I went many a time indeed. I swear to God, my acquaintance with Anna was not the product of my own initiative. I never would have found the courage. Those who have loved purely and vigorously in their early adolescence are well aware of that and deeply understand it.

In the early days, not even Anna had realised a thing; she merely looked forward to my next visit so that she could give me a different present each time: travel books or coloured pencils. I still remember the first time I saw her at church dressed in white. "How did her eyelashes grow so long all at once?" I wondered to myself. I also remember that during my last year in secondary school, all the margins of my notebooks were scribbled with her name.

One day I couldn't help myself and she noticed my teary eyes. We were in the drawing room with a huge book open before us on the table. Her mother was seated right next to her. I will never forget her gaze. It took the form of a huge question mark. It was so serious - too serious for her years.

We exchanged not another word and quickly closed the book. Angry with myself, I wiped my eyes, hastily bid farewell to her mother and rushed out. I cried myself to sleep that night. I would be to blame if I never saw her again.

Eleven days passed. Early one afternoon, on my way back home, I heard noises coming from the drawing room. I walked in and - who would have thought it? - Anna was there with her mother! Before I could gather my thoughts I had to greet the ladies. Anna was completely unabashed, like nothing was going on. A boy could never have disguised himself as well as she did! The visit had been her idea.

Then it was my turn to go away for studies. I was absent for a year or two. By the time I returned, she had become a proper lady. The first times I saw her she did not talk to me the way she used to or look straight into my eyes. And my mind went blank, like a fool, unable to utter a few words to form a sentence. I blushed and answered her every question in monosyllables. But still, I was so happy...

Now I go back to the places where I used to meet her again and again. What else is there for me to do so as to come to grips with my misery? While writing, my tears drop over the fresh ink, blurring the letters. It's ridiculous - I know - for a 32-year-old man to cry like a baby. I've been told so many times by now, enough to know it very well myself. But please forgive me. I'm just a miserable man that has been through too much in life.

Nobody knew about our love back then, no one except her best friend, Amelia. I had not even told my mother, my own best friend, my hero! How much has she been through herself, with my misfortunes and my sickness! And even now, on her deathbed, she is still my shoulder to cry on, instead of me being hers. I remember you, Mother, crying at nights and me not knowing what to do. I remember you going to her house to see her, during her own sickness, and her parents telling you there's nothing else that can be done, no hope whatsoever. And they didn't let you see her. They did not even let me see her.

### December 4th, 1918

Our secret happiness lasted several months. I do not recall what season it was. Did other people talk about us? I don't recall that either. The only thing I do recall is you. My every future plan, my every thought, my every hope was formed by you, and took your form.

Then I was offered the position at that school. I took it as a good sign and was quite happy since I was financially independent and was able to see her every three months. Then another year passed. Her mother died. I had finally saved some money to start my life with her. She used to write to me saying she was very sad. I assumed that her mother's recent death was the reason. I was mistaken.

When that man appeared and asked Anna's father for her hand in marriage, her father begged her to accept, lying to her about his financial situation. He kept pleading with her for months, bending her will little by little. Only after Anna's passing did I learn the whole truth about how her father took advantage of her love and affection for him. Had her mother been alive, she would have sensed the pain in her heart.

Even now Amelia speaks to me about how torn Anna was between making her father unhappy and shattering her own heart forever, knowing how much that would make her suffer. She would cry in her arms for hours and Amelia would urge her to leave home directly, but she could never take that step.

Her mother's last wish from her deathbed - that Anna obey her father - was pinned in her mind and defined her every move. And so, from a misconception of duty, she was consumed by the idea of sacrifice.

One morning I received a letter from my mother. Anna's brother had been looking for me. I met with him. He asked for my help. They still hadn't managed to convince her to marry that man. "Have you ever thought about how you´re going to live, in what conditions? What do you have to offer her?" he asked me. I asked him to leave, cursing him, and then I went home and wept, for I had offended someone she so dearly loved.

I managed to see her a couple of times. She looked happy. "Don't worry, they can't force me to marry him against my will," she said.

For the rest of my life - no matter how long that will be - the memory of her that night, the last time I ever saw her alive, standing in front of me, will always be fresh and vivid in my mind. She wasn't sad. On the contrary, she was full of optimism. She was laughing. I couldn't stop gazing at her. We were on "our" hill. I pressed my lips against her hair. Around us, only blossoming windflowers.

"Enough for today... Let's go back... I have to be home early," she said. "Next time we're here I'll make a wreath of windflowers. Will you place it on my head?"

"Promise me that I will see you again; that they're not going to bend you."

"We will come here again," she promised, "I swear to you that we'll come back."

**December 6th, 1918**

The damned pains never go away... The physicians ordered me to rest. What was I saying? Oh yes! One day my mother asked me to go on a trip. It took me a while to figure out why. It was the period when Anna was supposed to be married. Do not blame her…

Anna died two years after the wedding. She had started losing weight. Her husband said that neither would she listen to anyone nor was she cautious about her health. The physicians had told them that she shouldn't get with child. She died before she could nurse her infant…

When I came back from the trip, I became a recluse for a year without any contact with anyone. My hair and beard had grown down to my chest. The only company I wanted was that of Amelia. Anna was ill, but still alive then. One afternoon in 1909 I heard a knock at the door.

"Open up! It's me. Amelia!"

I ran downstairs and hardly gave her a second to catch her breath.

"What happened? Is she dead? Tell me!" I asked as I shook her. Her eyes were red.

"Listen to me! You have to come with me right now. She wants to see you."

Amelia told me Anna had been asking for me, especially at night-time. And she kept saying she wanted windflowers. But only today did her husband allow Amelia to tell me. Today, because the physicians said the end was very near. He wasn't at home. He had purposely left so that we would not cross paths.

The first thought that came to my mind was that I hadn't seen Anna even once since her wedding. I could think of nothing else. We waited till nightfall. Their house was one of the finest mansions in the state. Amelia and I entered and went straight to her room. Anna was sitting up in her bed. Only sweetness had remained in her otherwise withered face. She was dressed in a silk robe and had arranged her long locks in her favourite hairstyle. The first word she uttered was my name. She smiled, expressing as much happiness as her face could still express. She stretched out her hand. I took it in mine and started kissing it.

"You came, Paul! You came! I'm so glad you came! It's good to see you one last time, now that the end is near... And since my husband allowed it..."

I knelt down beside her bed and asked her to stop. I told her she would recover and everything would be fine. She kept pulling my hand towards her pale face and lips and sighing as if relieved.

"The last time you saw her," said Amelia, "when she swore she would come back, she really believed she could..." Anna nodded in agreement. "But then, she took a turn for the worse and she couldn't. That's been a burden on her soul since then and so she asks you to forgive her..."

I forgave her with all my heart. I kissed her hair just like I used to and suddenly her face lit up with pleasure.

We let her rest for quite a while and then she told me, "When I'm gone, I want you to visit our hill once in a while. The trees and grass might have something to share with you. Do not forget me. If you stay true to our love and don't forsake me, I'll never abandon you. I'll be right by your side, Paul... By your side and my child's. Whenever you need me, I'll be there..."

I escorted Amelia to her house and then went back to mine at midnight, overwhelmed by a strange mixture of pain and happiness. "What is this?" I wondered, "Why do I feel so confident that I will see her again?"

On Wednesday night I saw her. On Sunday she was dead.

**January 17th, 1919**

This morning, at 8:40, was the two-year anniversary of my revival. It was at that time that I opened my eyes and was myself again. I remember it was snowing. My mother was on the floor next to me, crying tears of joy. "What happened?" I asked her. I received my answer from our family physician: "Well, it was about time you woke up! You've broken every record!"

Apparently it was some kind of lethargy. I had been asleep for a fortnight.

The physician, wearing a fancy tie, was trying to cheer me up. Not only did he not succeed but, instead of a smile, a grotesque grin spread over his face.

As the months went by, I began to feel better. I took heart. In the end, man can get used to anything…

"Now that you are familiar with my case," I told the physician once, "I don't need to fear being buried alive…"

**January 23rd, 1919**

It's the fourth misty, cloudy day in a row. What can one do in this weather? No friends come to visit me anymore. I'm reading a history book. Since primary school, history has always had the power to sweep me away. I remember thinking back then that we were all born in a certain place and era out of mere coincidence. We could have easily been born in a completely different country, culture and even century, with completely different friends, occupations and sweethearts. But we wouldn't be able to know any of the things that were to happen later, that is, now.

I'm trying to read, but I'm pushing myself. Back then I used to truly engage with what I was reading. Not anymore. Today, my loneliness has reached its deepest depth.

**February 8th, 1919**

I started seeing the priest again. He never pressured me to talk and that eased my mind. Amelia had explained to him that I needed time. He respected that. That's why I went. He said he liked talking to me. I did as well. The conversation with him was always very interesting. He had a positive way of thinking and clear judgment, free of prejudice and stereotypes. His mind was robust and bright.

I stared at his library. He had almost everything: from the mystics of the East and the Ionian philosophers to the modern philosophers of Western civilisation.

"I see you staring at these worthless books," he told me as if he could read my mind. "Do not expect great things from them. I've read them all. I know all that's been said by the brightest minds of all times. But I will never feel the power that true love has to raise you to the highest point of knowledge. I'll never experience a love like that."

He turned to me. It was the first time that he, such a discreet and considerate man, had made an allusion to Anna, albeit indirectly. He was looking to me for help, for insight. He was hoping to feel what love is, even vicariously.

"She told me she'd be with me, that I'd feel her close to me from time to time. It's been ten years since then. Never, not once, have I had a sign from her. You tell me then, Father, how is the concept of the imperishable soul that you preach about reconciled with the absolute lack of any communication with those who loved us so?"

"If you're looking for shelter from the moments of pain, I have nothing else to offer you other than faith - any faith. But let us focus on you. And I'm talking to you as a brother, not as a priest. If I were you, I would not place my hopes and future in this promise. All these years you've been consumed with overthinking at the expense of your mental health. Why? Do you consider this healthy or right? Have you not had enough experience to know that one should not rely on unrealistic expectations? You need a sign? Why should Creation reveal its secrets to you? And why, with the sole excuse of a lack of signs, do you discard them altogether? And how are you sure that they haven't been revealed to you, but found you too blind to notice or understand them?

I had no counter argument. We sat there for a while opposite each other without speaking and then we left.

That night I prayed after a very long time. I asked the Lord to calm me and show me that my doubts were unjustified. Nothing. But then I cried. I managed to cry! Could *that* have been the sign I was looking for?

**February 24th, 1919**

The thought that I could leave this life, leave once and for all, was very attractive in the beginning. So many people disappear every day, people of every age. Nothing can be ruled out. Suicidal thoughts, however, did not cross my mind. I do not know if my mother or my cowardice was to blame, or rather a pure selfishness created by that open wound in my heart.

The possibility alone, however, comforted me. I was vaguely looking forward to breaking the ties. If she's gone, I'm going with her. As simple as that. That was the thought. And she'd be waiting there for me, unchanged, and everything would go back to the way it was.

# Second Diary

*(the diary Paul Dienach wrote when he came out of his second coma)*

**3 years later**

## THE AWAKENING

**July 16th, 1922**

The preparations for the trip, along with all the forgotten things I decided to get rid of, showed me the way to my old library where, hidden behind the rows of books, was the diary I had kept for three years, from December'18 to February'21. During my illness, some friends had been taking care of the house, especially after my mother's death. Last night I sat there, leafing through it, occasionally skimming over some of its pages. Reading between the lines I rediscovered, for a moment, my old self, whom I had long lost somewhere amidst all the unbelievable things that had happened to me in the meantime. I re-experienced that guileless emotion with such a genuine, pure thrill, inhaling that pure scent of loyalty to the one and only love of my life. Something so rare. I knew back then that it was an exercise in futility, but still, I could not do otherwise.

Many things within me are different now, changed. And at this point, being the old dog that I am, I can tell you that those moments were worth it all. They were precious even if people thought that they were nothing but traces of an abnormal temperament.

Oh my precious Anna... Forgive me. Why don't I think of you more often? Why doesn't your memory overwhelm me like it used to? But these incredible countries I went to changed everything for me. Neither my little hometown nor my first love is big enough for me anymore.

But this is not the reason. It can't be! I wouldn't deserve your forgiveness if it were. This life journey and destiny of mine remind me of a myth I had been told when I was but a boy: the myth of the unjustly killed man. For years and years his soul wandered around in the wilderness of the night. You could still hear the rattling of his chains. But after justice was served, he was never heard from again.

My first days back, two months ago, my fellow villagers welcomed my healthy and changed appearance with utter surprise. Their joy felt genuine. Most of them had taken me for dead. Luckily for me, however, the physicians in Zurich believed differently and therefore let me occupy a bed for twelve whole months - from May '21 to May of this year - tube-feeding me with special liquid foods.

My mother had died before I returned. She departed with a pain in her heart, that unbearable pain of a mother that did not have the chance to see her child strong again. All the excitement and joy I felt, caused by my psychological resurrection, was overshadowed in the beginning by my sorrow over the loss of my mother. My Lord, forgive that holy woman and let her rest in peace.

The priest is away in Italy. I still feel ashamed about the doubts I shared with him, my lack of faith: a terrible sin. On the other hand, he couldn't have possibly had any idea about all the incredible things that followed in my three-year struggle between scepticism and remorse.

I try to drive all these thoughts away using energy as an instrument, an energy I never could have imagined I possess. I'm constantly on the move. I've taken care of all the inheritance issues, sold my land, I work in the fields in my free time and I try to keep my mind occupied at all times. But when the night comes and all my friends are gone, all these memories, so recent, but at the same time so distant, come back and haunt me before I fall asleep. And when these moments come, I can't help but think about what I've lost…

From time to time, it feels like I'm the castaway of a veritable spiritual shipwreck. And I cannot speak of my vicissitude to anyone; I can't even confess it to the priest. The things I know cannot even be conceived of by the human mind. The lifeless paper I write on is not just a lifeless sheet of paper anymore; it is my very self. And my very self knows very well indeed the reasons for my firm conviction. And never, for as long as I live and breathe, will I fear that anyone will laugh about what I've experienced and seen with my own eyes. And I believe them with all the strength I have left in me.

**July 21st, 1922**

The number of my evening solitude companions is dwindling. Perhaps they are right. There isn't much left to say every second night. At this point, most of the times my companions are my books and I am happy with that. Who would have thought that everything that has gone down in history since they were written would justify the value of their contents? My own old childhood loves - Schiller, Goethe, but more recent names as well, such as Einstein, Schweitzer, Bertrand Russell, Thomas Mann and Maeterlinck - I cannot express how strange a feeling meeting them would give me. I - and I alone - could tell them things about the course of the last years of their lives, about how their work would be glorified in history, about their end, things that they never knew and never could have known.

I'm sitting at the foot of a tree, overpowered by the vastness of the existences that I have wandering around me. And yet I feel, from this very spot, as if I could cut the universe in half and squeeze into it!

**August 10th, 1922**

Tonight I went through hell. On one hand, I felt the urge to speak about everything I know, unburdening my soul, but on the other hand I knew I had to push myself to bury everything deep down inside forever!

Where are you, Mother? Were you alive, I'd tell you everything! To you, everything! I know that you would always respect what is now the most sacred thing in my life.

**August 14th, 1922**

Two days ago I happened upon Father Jacob on the street. He had returned from his trip to Italy. I thanked him for all the help and support he had given my mother during my lethargy. I told him I would visit him the day after next, which I did. We sat in his garden. How different it felt being next to him this time! All the doubts I used to have were now long gone.

"Father, I'm not the same person I used to be. If only you knew about the changes I've been through…"

I reminded him of my past thoughts and my disrespectful conclusions and I assured him that I do not share the same point of view with my old self anymore. At the same time, however, I felt I had no right to speak to him in more detail. He seemed very excited that faith had spoken to me.

"I was wrong father. If only you knew all the great things there are." I stopped suddenly. The tone of my voice surprised even me. The priest stared at me with bated breath.

"Even the harshest pain is welcome, both physical and mental. Vindication will come in the end. Never should a sigh come out of a human mouth."

And then came a moment of silence. The priest was now becoming agitated. He looked as if he were trying to make me speak without asking me to. Finally he said, "You see, my son? That is faith!"

"No, Father, no," I replied in a calm and steady voice. "It's not just faith that has changed me. You cannot even imagine what is actually out there. The human mind is incapable of realising the greatness of it."

I revealed no more. But I had already said too much, more than I was entitled to.

At first, Father Jacob patiently waited for me to proceed. Then, he started asking me, in his own casual, indirect way. Then he started begging me. He called me "son", he called me "brother" and he reminded me of our past discussions back in the winter of 1919. Finally, he claimed that it was a sin to believe that something can be exclusively ours to keep, ending with how that something would eventually become a burden on my conscience. I regretted having said all that and having spoiled those sacred truths by giving them the shape of human reason.

Since last night, I've been thinking that something has changed between the priest and me, and that our long-lasting friendship is now something of the past.

**August 16th, 1922**

On summer days like these, the sky is so clear - nearly transparent - and the breeze so cool that midday resembles a crystal clear spring morning. I am joyful that I postponed all my errands for tomorrow, all the paperwork, all the boring seriousness of my everyday routine. Mornings like these are not meant to be spent surrounded by four walls. It should be considered a sin to work on such divine days. Now I understand why we, all the worms of this earth, should think twice before we refer to the divine. I was told that all the great things that surround us are far beyond the capabilities of our finite mind to comprehend. That's why little children find joy in trifles, and based on that, they are undoubtedly much wiser than we are.

Forgive me, Heavenly Father, for my lack of faith.

**August 17th, 1922**

When three people have a conversation on the pavement in the dead of night, naturally someone might overhear them, no matter how low the volume of their voices, especially if that someone´s open window is directly above their heads.

Half an hour ago, I experienced an annoying situation such as this, without them knowing I was listening. At first, they were talking loudly about local matters. I could hear the deep voice of the hotel owner, the characteristic intonation of our family physician's voice and a third person, whose voice I could not recognize. At some point, they realised where they were standing and turned the conversation to me. They asked the physician what exactly was wrong with me and he gave them a short lecture on lethargy. The other two kept on asking more questions while a few "Shhhs" interrupted the conversation every time someone raised their voice.

Then the idea popped into my mind. I remembered the motif from the second part of Ruthemir's *Mass*. Once, twice, three times I played it in my head without any mistakes. I could easily play it on the piano. I sat on my stool, with my window open and then, the divine melody broke the silence of the night, like a storm of happiness, a genuine expression of the knowledge of the future. Then I approached my window. The physician, the hotel owner and the third man were still standing there talking, as if nothing had happened. Unbelievable! I think that even the hordes of peons that used to haul massive stones for the pyramids would be less indifferent to the sound of this melody.

In a few days I'm leaving for Athens. I've already made all the arrangements. I need a more temperate climate - the physicians agreed with me on that. My mind is sound, but my body is ailing; the tuberculosis never went away. I know I haven't got much time left. Maybe a couple of years…

## A NEW LIFE IN ATHENS

### Athens, October 20th, 1922

I feel so ensconced in the white city now. I have become accustomed to the warmth brought by the winter sun, the voices of the street vendors, the scent of chrysanthemums and the dust rising from the carriages. I think I'll fit in just fine here. My greatest pleasure is, however, to go out in the evenings and get lost in the crowded streets, among the bright shop windows and the characteristic, rhythmic churning of the rubber cart wheels. You must be either ill or mad to stay at home at dusk. No one in this city finds pleasure staying home anymore.

The place is poor. It's apparent from the many beggars on the streets and the amiable elderly men with their tormented violins. But the women here are all well-groomed and elegant with an inexplicable air of true nobility.

I just recalled, without really wanting to, the somehow unjust words that Stefan uttered one day in conversation when he wondered what it would be like to "suddenly find ourselves in the heart of the 20th century, among the most proud and rebellious of the underdeveloped and nearly uncivilised nations of the South" in order to emphasise that the cultural hubs had now moved up North. *What ignorant opinions are formed in the absence of any historical knowledge!* I now think, Stefan, my friend from the future, with all his pride and affection for the ancient Scandinavian blood that runs through his veins, easily came to unjustified conclusions about the "uncivilised South". But I, on the contrary, am well aware of all the excesses into which that lucky race was pushed. And I say "lucky" because it could not have achieved anything on its own. They were merely representatives of the other big winning force, by the authorisation of whom they came and re-colonised this tortured continent that was almost annihilated by the fatal war of the year -87 *(our 2309AD).* This is when a medium-scale nuclear war took place, destroying all of Europe with the exception of Scandinavia. *(Europe was then recolonised mostly by the remaining Northern Europeans).*

And as far as the Greek nation is concerned, I think there is not a more relaxed nation under the Mediterranean sun. Unless everyone is pretending, including my landlady that does everything in her power to help and please me, and the little eight-year-old boy that was late for school so that he could take me all the way to the Herod Atticus Odeon on his own, and didn't even accept the tip I gave him.

I don't know about the rest, but I could walk the most remote and secluded streets and districts after midnight, feeling as safe as I would in broad daylight. Here I've met both decent morals and remarkable local culture.

These Mediterranean shores are where civilisation was born and I'm proud to live here now. I feel so light in this foreign, but so beloved country among strangers. I've now settled just fine in my humble room. The only thing I fear, however, is that I am starting to feel the same weight in my chest again, the one caused by the knowledge of my numbered days.

**Wednesday November 2nd, 1922**

In a foreign country the first few weeks are quite difficult. Everything - the morning, the evening, one's habits, the way one plans to spend the day - needs to be redefined. I truly believe, though, that with the passage of time things will get better; and I rely on the reassurance of Mr. De La S that he will recommend me to some of his German language students, whom he has in abundance. After my visit to the archaeological school with the recommendation letter from Mr. M., I have every reason to be optimistic.

During the past few days the weather has been reminding me of home and loneliness keeps flooding my world and my eyes. If I find students to tutor, I will accept them all even if I am underpaid, with the hope of finally meeting someone whom I can actually trust and with whom I can communicate. Hilda, Stefan, Silvia, where are you?

This evening I sat down opposite the Parthenon - on the northern side - and was lost in thought for hours, my gaze caressed by the inscriptions carved into the rock. Suddenly, soft, approaching footsteps interrupted my daydreaming. I raised my head. It was a tall, seemingly cultivated young man. He apologised in French. I introduced myself and he shook my hand, expressing his joy about me not being Prussian. That's all he understood from my accent.

"I understand... I understand you very well," he told me. "When you concentrate your thought entirely on this rock, without allowing your mind to think about anything else, it's as if you're living in that era, two thousand years ago. What more could a person have seen back then, if bent over this spot for a couple of minutes? For those minutes, this rock would have been their world."

I was carried away and answered him, "And after the same number of years it will still be the same. This land has strong and solid foundations. So many things will have happened in the meantime, so much will have changed by then, and yet this piece of rock will remain exactly the same. This is the incredible thing! So, staring at it, and forgetting everything else around us, isn't it like we're living in the future for a moment?

He turned around and looked deeply into my eyes. I fell silent.

"Except," I said after a minute, as if suddenly remembering something, "except then, there would be no bars around it. They would have done away with them."

He looked at me with a strange expression on his face, a questioning gaze. He seemed a bit offended, not by what I had said, but more by the simple and confident tone of my voice.

"I should go now," he said right after, "the doors close at sunset."

## THE TRUTH ABOUT HIS SICKNESS

**March 20th, 1923**

Here we go again. The slight breathlessness and the small but gradual rise of fever every night have returned with the same hostile intentions, with the same malevolent persistence, hints of small and insidious cracks inside me. The end is near; I must deal with it now. The need to unburden my soul grows more imperative by the second. At an age when other people feel young and plan ahead, I am dying with a mercilessly intolerable moral onus inside me.

Everyone in my hometown knows that the physicians were wrong to believe that the disease that tormented me for fourteen days back in 1917 would not come back to torture me again. It returned once more, not for a couple of weeks like before, but for approximately twelve months. They remember rushing me to Zurich in mid-May 1921 and me looking like a dead man. Everybody there knows it. What they don't know, however, is that the first time I recovered I didn't remember anything from the time of my illness: for me it was as if I had lost touch with myself and the world just for a second, not for two weeks. On the contrary, the second time I opened my eyes, I was filled with fresh, crystal clear memories of a real 360-day life, so recent and so vivid in my mind!

You can give whichever explanation suits you best - medical, scientific or whatever else - and I will accept them all. Just do not tell me it was a dream or a figment of my imagination because you will never have been more mistaken! There are things that the human mind does not know or comprehend. Only if someone put themselves in my shoes could they ever feel my absolute certainty. God be my witness, and I say God because he and he alone can see into the depths of my soul. And he knows how much I respect and cherish his name.

Listen to me, the truth cannot be concealed. The signs are innumerable: first and foremost the passing of time. When one has lived a certain reality for a certain amount of time, when one has seen and touched all these tangible things and their embossed details, it's very difficult to assert that it was all a dream and not an actual part of one's real life. The same applies to my experience. It has now been months since I re-found myself and the logical thing would be for these "memories" to have blurred or faded away. Well, I assure you that, never, throughout this period, have I doubted my firm conviction that all these things that happened to me were incidents of actual live experience and that I spent 360 days of real life in the distant future!

**March 21st, 1923**

I am not feeling better. I think my condition has been exacerbated by the surprising temperature drop over the past few days. This cough, which in the beginning I thought would pass, continues to rack my lungs. I didn't like the look on the physician's face yesterday. But what else is there to tell me? If I am to die, so be it. After what I've experienced what else remains for me to see? For as much life I've got left, that will be my prayer and that is what my soul will await.

**April 1923**

I remembered the myth of the white-haired hermit: back when he was young, his beloved took him out of the monastery after many years, and made him spend some time with her. Before she left, she put her emerald ring on the middle finger of his right hand. The hermit woke up again in this life among the shrubs where he had lain down, believing he had been dreaming and that everything he remembered - the golden lampposts, the thick carpets he was walking on, her sweet kiss - was part of that dream. But after looking at his hand, he shuddered; the ring was there. The other hermits later confirmed it.

I'm sitting here, staring at my empty hands and I wonder: *Why can't reality, no matter how distant in time, leave behind the slightest tangible sign, when a dream once could?* But these things only happen in myths and legends. If, however, I could choose what tangible sign I'd like to find on me last May, surrounded by the physicians of Zurich, it would be neither her emerald ring nor her picture nor any other of her precious little presents. You can make all the assumptions you want about me, but what I'd really wish to find would be my original manuscript that I wrote when I lived in the future. That's what's been constantly befuddling my mind. What happened to that diary? It took me a great amount of time - almost a year - and many sleepless nights to finish it. With true joy and genuine passion I put down on paper every single detail of what I had experienced during each day in the future. The memory of Andreas Northam, whose body I lived in, and of my manuscripts, "The Diary", which I left behind, burns a hole in my heart.

No, no! I must at all costs dismiss these disturbing thoughts from my mind: the belief that nothing is truly irreversible in this universe and that we have no right to measure everything with the finite capabilities of our human mind. And after all, what do I have to worry about? One day, in a couple of thousand years' time, Andreas Northam will write these pages himself!

My judgment is still clear enough to point out to me that these mistaken ideas are pushing me towards idleness and submission to my fate, my doom drawing closer by the second. But I won't fall into the trap. My heart might be ailing and challenged and pained but, thank God, my brain is still strong and working properly. You, my Lord, chose a humble, unimportant man, a man that suffered and is still suffering from a severe illness, to show him a small shred of your eternal secrets. It is you who decides what needs to be done on every occasion; I know it, I believe it. So please, give me the strength to finish what I started and relieve my burdened heart. Let the paper become my confessor and my saviour!

**Tuesday, April 24th**

A while ago, my landlady, an amazing woman, knocked on my door to see if I needed anything and make sure everything was all right. Well, you won't believe it, but I felt this sudden urge to take her in my arms and deliver to her the great news: that now I most certainly can write everything down! Because once again, I was given the chance to verify how excellent my memory skills are. After all the hardships and the suffering, it's still here! I managed to put down on paper, word for word, complete stanzas of poems that I had never read or heard in my life before Silvia recited them to me that unforgettable night under the stars.

So what can possibly keep me from re-writing my lost pages, my memories from the future? I can definitely do it now! Any doubt I might have from here on will merely be an unsound hesitation that I will have to fight against.

I don't mind this cough tearing my insides apart or this fever burning this obnoxious carcass of a body. All this is not sufficient to cast a shadow over the excitement that the prospect of completing my work gives me! Time might be limited - perhaps only a few months - but this will be my "future" from now on; and it will be the joyful re-writing of the manuscripts that were once ready but left behind. The same fate that doomed me has given me, now, in the end, this unique chance and I'm convinced that I can remember it all, page for page, if not word for word.

I stayed up late tonight and savoured my newfound happiness. I'm ecstatic! Nothing will be lost; from now on my short life will be empty no longer. I have a new reason to live!

My case has nothing to do with inspiration and creation. I was never blessed with such gifts and you cannot lose what you never had. My case is that of a traveller who never spoke about his adventures and who has finally decided to break his silence.

I have no friends; my mother is dead. I'm completely alone in the world. So, whoever you are, you who somehow, one day, will end up with my manuscripts, be my friend and feel me. Do not laugh and do not mock me. I've been tried and tested a great deal in life. Everything you read I've seen with my own eyes; I've lived it, I've touched it, I believe and I worship it all!

I will not return to my homeland; I have made my decision. I don't need any obligatory, superficial relationships with the neighbours. I just want to tell my story in the most precise way possible; and I want to tell it to the end!

## REBORN

### August 17th

It's the twelfth day today and I've already commenced writing about it! Whatever happened to that combination of astonishment and horror of the first week, that religious awe in the sight of everything that, in the beginning, I considered supernatural? Where has the fear of losing my mind gone? All these mixed feelings lasted much less than expected. Here you have it then; man can, indeed, get used to anything! One can become accustomed to the most unbelievable things and will eventually return to one's everyday routine.

### (After a while)

Almighty God, the course that my life has taken was always planned by you and your desire. All these days and nights, only my faith has kept me from losing my mind over this incredible reality that I've been living. Have mercy on me, my Lord, and don't deny forgiveness to your unworthy servant!

### (At night)

It's been three days now since I managed to drag myself out of bed and noticed something unexpected: my pains have vanished and I was able to walk even during the first few hours. The mirror is now the only reminder of the bandage that I still have wrapped around my head. And if what they say is true? They are to remove it the day after tomorrow. Have I recovered then? Can it be true? Am I not dead? Who could imagine and believe a miracle like this?

### (Three hours later - dawn)

I even feel much better psychologically, after the soothing words of the physicians and my meeting yesterday with Johannes Jaeger. Before, my days and nights had been excruciating. The pain was nothing compared to the mental torment I was going through due to the inner conflict between a world of unbelievable things happening around me and the existence of another world inside me, one of different memories, but nevertheless complete and lucid.

My mature judgment, the result of my age, had taught me how to distinguish the real from the unreal and my exceptionally good memory was flooding my mind with images and events from my past, in sharp detail, exactly as I had lived them. I was functioning perfectly, as I remembered myself. But so did all the mad things around me...

I was certain it was me; on the verge of a nervous breakdown, yes, but it was me! Once, when I was in the presence of the *Ilectors*, I broke down and started to weep, that's all... And in any case, I don't think that anyone could confidently say that they'd be able to control their nerves in such a situation.

These last few days I haven't seen anyone else apart from the two physicians. The nurses were being kept away from me following the episode with the mirror, when I first saw my new face and went berserk. The new physician stood by me as a kind and skilful healer, but also as a silent partner, who always avoided looking straight into my eyes whenever we were alone and who always had a hint of agitation in his gaze.

The day before yesterday, the chief physician, Professor Molsen, unexpectedly came to my chamber in the afternoon. He seemed more excited than usual. He told me to stand up and, holding me by the arm, helped me walk to the adjoining drawing room. I realised at that moment that a whole new world was opening up before me. Sometimes I find myself overpowered by a newfound, child-like eagerness. I hadn't felt so impatient since I was a young boy!

I stood at the entrance for a while, looking at the drawing room. It was a strangely large room with all kinds of bizarre - for me - things and that tall, transparent door that offered a panoramic view of the lush countryside, the mountain slopes and beyond. Then I started walking again, but not for long. Every two steps I stopped and peered about. At some point, I turned around and saw the physician looking at me with a curious expression on his face. I'll never forget that look, but at that moment I cared about nothing.

It was neither the fairytale-like gold nor gems that amazed me. Everything there was made of a beautiful type of crystal in perfect combinations of pastel colours; sky blue, emerald green, milky white and rose red. Everything, from the tables and chairs to the stools and the frames, seemed to be made of a colourless metal on which a soft light flowed incessantly in harmonious waves. Everything was bright and clear, even the flower pots and the crystal sprigs of blooming flowers. However, if you came too close, like a curious child, believing you would find something in that transparent kaleidoscope of colours, the sense of touch would correct that first impression because the surfaces of the seats would prove soft and warm.

The physician didn't rush me. Passing through the drawing room we found ourselves in a large hallway. That is where I finally saw people again after the isolation of the past days. It was a spacious vestibule that led directly to the enormous main terrace. It was afternoon and the place was filled with light. Physicians and nurses stood around quietly chatting to each other. At the sight of the chief physician they discreetly stood aside and made way for us to pass. While walking past them, I heard them whisper that name again, the name that everyone kept repeating all these days when in my presence: "Andreas Northam." I shivered. "Who is this Andreas Northam?" I wondered. Reality mercilessly unfolds before my eyes in every direction. There only remains for me to accept, along with the physicians, this unprecedented thing happening to me, which exceeds even the wildest dreams of the most overactive imagination.

## MEETING THE LEADERS OF THE FUTURE AND REVEALING HIS TRUE IDENTITY

Across the hallway, in front of an extremely tall door stood six boys and girls who, judging from their apparel, probably did not live in the institution. They had just arrived. I only saw them for a couple of seconds and didn't have the chance to observe them meticulously. They were adolescents, all of them with long pageboy haircuts, wearing almost matching uniforms, in the same pastel shades as the drawing room, and all of them wore belts embroidered with silver thread and short silk scarves tied around their waists. Though strangers, they were the ones to open the door for us to enter the small sitting room. Suddenly, the door shut behind us and, without anyone having told me anything, I found myself face to face with two *Ilectors*.

They looked at me in silence. Nobody else was present. To my surprise I saw Professor Molsen - who had brought me here - standing respectfully poised.

I felt my body and stamina failing me. I didn't know if they were priests or kings but, these venerable figures, dressed in white, with their imposing appearance, impressed me from the start. I viewed them as a peaceful harbour for turbulent souls. I wanted to tell them everything immediately.

I fell at their knees and in a quivering voice told them everything in amongst sobs. I was struggling to breathe every so often, but my fervour and yearning were so intense that I carried on. I had never felt like this, not even during confession. I was so shaken and upset that I couldn't keep my narration in chronological order, but I managed to tell them the whole truth, little by little; and I think that the tone of sincerity in my voice, in my nonlinear, but otherwise coherent narration, my apparent emotional upheaval and the steadiness of my tearful gaze did not escape the grasp of the two elders.

While staring at me, their peaceful faces started to turn pale. No words could describe the expression in their eyes. I begged them to believe me. They gradually started asking me in broken German - the language in which I was speaking to them - a storm of questions concerning the place where I lived and my time. I explained everything without circumlocution. I could see them growing more preoccupied by the minute by my foreign tongue.

I remember that for a moment I lost heart and almost broke down, but then I resumed answering all their questions as precisely as possible. I kept reassuring them of the truthfulness of my words, weeping with emotion, but also sorrow, for not being able to provide them with tangible proof.

In the end, these wise men believed me! Oh my God, they believed me! They lifted me up, sat me next to them and with that inexplicable air of profound blessedness and utter benevolence they looked at me and spoke to me as equals.

God bless them! Only he can repay them for the good they did me in those extremely difficult and bizarre moments.

I didn't make out very much from their insights on "the narrow limits of human cognition" or "the relativity of time and the potential existence of simultaneous time intervals". Neither did I fully comprehend the concept of "the great and unified reality lying beyond the human perception of the past, present and future".

But the rest of what they told me about divine and human matters calmed me. They conveyed to me such a profound serenity, such consolation, which made me feel more at peace than ever before. They were a balm to my troubled soul. Later, of course, I achieved a deeper understanding of their version. In their view, they had before them "one of the rarest metapsychic phenomena", a peculiar manifestation of a mental state, not entirely balanced - at some point they even called it pathological - but not something supernatural that escapes the confines of the laws of life and of the physical world.

## ANDREAS NORTHAM'S ACCIDENT

The two elders left. I hardly realised how quickly the time had passed and it was now dark outside. Valleys and mountains surrounded me. I could now hear the familiar celestial melody *(their evening prayer)*, sung by children's voices as if coming from afar, from another, otherworldly planet. Truth be told, I never wanted it to stop.

### August 18th

### (After midnight)

It's two o'clock in the morning. I am surrounded by complete and utter silence and I arose from my bed to write. My day was painless and my nervous system free from the tension of the first days. If they are telling me the truth, there's still hope for me to recover from the shock.

Today was the thirteenth day of my new life, thirteen days full of newfound experiences and emotions. My thoughts are always with God. Only he can show mercy even to the sinner.

Yesterday morning I went out to the terrace and enjoyed the sun. I spent a long time by myself. I sat down and re-read what I had written the previous night.

Later, Professor Molsen joined me and kept me company until noon. He was different with me today. He was talkative and we communicated quite well, except for the times when he tried to talk to me in his own German. Yearning to know more, I accused him of having experimented on Andreas Northam, without being sure that such a suspicion had any right to cross my mind. He vigorously denied that allegation with apparent sincerity.

The day before yesterday, *Ilector* Jaeger told me that they had brought Northam to Molsen, having suffered fatal head injuries in a crash. He died in Molsen's arms and only after fifteen minutes and after having frozen him did Molsen manage to bring him back to life. I didn't mention any of this to the physician. I asked Jaeger why they didn't let me speak to everyone freely, like the rest of the patients did, and he assured me that this would only last for a few days. He also told me that my insomnia would not harm me as long as I spent most of the night lying down.

As far as my life was concerned, he didn't ask me about anything other than the illnesses I had been through. I talked to him about the incident of 1917 in as much detail as possible; "a kind of lethargy" I called it.

In the afternoon, Jaeger paid me a second visit. Both times he was sent by the *Ilectors*. He told me so much... His company is a great consolation to me. He speaks in such a different way from the physicians; he puts his heart and soul into our exchange.

## THE TRUTH: FAINTING IN THE PAST (1921 AD) AND WAKING UP IN THE FUTURE (3906 AD)

At night I felt extremely nostalgic. Everything I had ever loved, everything I had been accustomed to my whole life triggered torturous memories that made me weep inconsolably. If only I had something here from my own place and time, anything, even an inanimate object, to keep me company and make me feel at home.

The awareness of the incredibly long time-gap weighed heavily on me. It gave me a feeling of a moral abyss that proved much more frightening in my internal world than in the external one. The idea of an intentional escape from life entered my mind. The unbearable image that penetrated my thoughts at all times was that of my beloved grey-haired mother, desperately crying over the lifeless body of her child in some hospital in Zurich. "Mother!" I'd cry out sobbing, "Mother, I will never see you again!"

That first night before I woke up here, while lying in bed half asleep, the vivid memory of Anna once again conquered my mind. I had spent the evening on our beloved hill with the windflowers. When the darkness of the night fell, it found me there. I returned home walking through dark and deserted streets so I could hide my tear-filled eyes from the world.

I lay down on my bed, careful not to make the slightest noise that would wake my mother, who was lying sick in the adjoining room. She had been exhausted lately. When I switched off the light and it became completely quiet, I could hear her breathing, I remember. Her presence, the feeling of being in the company of my mother, somehow sweetened the misery caused by the loss of Anna.

I was burning up with fever. My eyes hurt when I blinked. I knew I had a bowl of water beside me and a towel to dampen and put on my forehead if I needed to. But I was so fatigued that I couldn't find the strength to get up, so I tried to cool my eyes and forehead on my cold pillows, changing positions all the time. Then, I remember the sensation of slowly falling asleep, and I thanked God for that sweet salvation even if it lasted only for a few hours. My last thought before I fell completely asleep was that the next day I would go sit under the two fir trees.

Waking up, however, was tremendously painful. I realised I had a very high fever. My mind went straight to the bowl of water and the towel. Without opening my eyes I tried to reach it, but I couldn't even move. After a while I fainted from the fever.

These alternations between consciousness and unconsciousness lasted for several hours. And the moments of consciousness were excruciating for me. I felt like I was free-falling into an unfathomable abyss. The agony of the abyss never left me.

Amidst the dizziness of fever I remember seeing, as if in a dream, men and women standing over my head. I was aware of my situation, that is, I knew I was ill and I thought that they had moved me to a bigger city, to another hospital and that all these people were physicians and nurses. Nothing else was clear in my mind. Oh! And my mother! I felt that my mother was no longer by my side.

Then I thought I was having nightmares. "Why are they dressed like that?" I wondered. The setting around me looked completely different and unfamiliar compared to what I was used to. "No," I thought to myself, "it can't be a hospital." I blinked and caught glimpses of the countryside, the sky, shades of blue and green blended together and a pink light reflecting on the crystal walls, so bright and so beautiful…

I also recall breathing the scented spring air and sometimes, a celestial melody wafting to my weary ears. It resembled a prayer sung by children's voices. I could distinguish the sound of the harp. I had never heard anything more melodic and more extraordinary in my life and I wished it would never stop. And then I wondered, "Am I dead?" But if I was, why would I feel ill and feverish?

Another mad thought crossed my mind: when I was still at school, I had read that our beloved Earth might not be the only planet in the universe. But I ruled that possibility out after remembering the people I saw standing over my head. They were humans; they were our kind. And I had also caught a glimpse of the familiar light of our earthly sky.

All these tangled and scrambled thoughts dominated my tired mind every time I somehow opened my eyes in the midst of the feverish daze. And the truth is that they didn't leave me with an unpleasant memory. But it's impossible to describe the surprise that awaited me one morning when I had completely recovered and managed to get out of bed - I get shivers down my spine even writing about it. "My God! This body! This body isn't mine!" A young man looked me in the eyes with a face distorted with terror. I thought I had lost my mind. I cried out for help. I sensed someone running towards me. I choked and fainted.

## THE LANGUAGE: ENGLISH AND SCANDINAVIAN BLEND

When I came to, I saw two physicians standing next to me with a strange look on their faces, anxiously waiting for me to regain consciousness. It was if they were hanging on my every word. Everybody else had left the room. I was so nervous I could barely breathe.

"What happened?" I asked with a trembling voice, "Have I gone mad?" And I could hear my voice fading away, but I managed to utter, "Where am I?"

Then I remember crying out several times "Mother, Mother!" as though I was asking where she was.

And instead of answering my questions, these men of science just stood there, stunned and pale, as if my simple words had rendered them speechless. One of them was young, in his late twenties-early thirties. I reached out for his hand, I begged him in the name of God and his own mother, but he was shaking and obviously trying to avoid my touch.

Shortly after, the older physician turned to him and said something. "They're foreigners," I thought. For a couple of minutes I just looked at them talking, abashed, and struggling to reach a logical conclusion. A faraway land… Yes… Yes… That must be it. Their clothes, their manners… Look! And now the foreign language! I wasn't familiar with that tongue. I remember that the man's accent had struck me. Some words sounded somewhat similar to ours and had Anglo-Saxon roots and some others resembled Scandinavian words - quite familiar to me - and thus I understood the gist of what they were saying. The older physician, still pale and unsuccessfully trying to force a smile from what I could see, told the other physician that he had lost his patience. The young physician denied it by shaking his head. The former seemed deeply puzzled. He repeated my last words, stressing each syllable: "Mo-ther… Mo-ther…" Nothing else. "Mut-ter… Mut-ter…"

He grasped my hand. He spoke to me. I understood that he was asking me if my head ached.

"Now less," I replied, "I'm better."

Physically speaking I was telling the truth; but I didn't say a word about what was going on in my mind…

"I want to see my mother," I added.

I noticed that, once again, I was having some difficulties articulating words. But I blamed it on the illness.

On top of everything else I was thinking about, I was also quite convinced that if I couldn't help myself and started crying for help, they would treat me as a lunatic who talks to himself and then I wouldn't stand a chance of finding out more about them. But if I could just see my mother - I told them - she would help me see things clearly.

And then I noticed something about them, something that made a difference and explained much: what made them look so stunned was not what I was saying, but the *way* I was saying it and the language in which I was saying it. While they were talking to me, their wide-open eyes revealed the incredible thrill they felt!

The older one leaned towards me once again and, in a quivering voice, he slowly uttered a sentence in my own tongue, "Andreas Northam, don't you recognise me anymore?"

The last words he managed to pronounce with evident effort and some difficulty still resonate in my ears, "Nicht mehr?"

"I want to pray," I managed to reply in a fading voice.

And then I fainted again.

It's been thirteen days. The younger physician came to my room this evening and saw my pillow soaked with tears. He tried to console me but, unintentionally, he did me more harm than good. I talked to him about my mother, who would be mourning the death of her child and he spoke to me with a completely misplaced smile about some kind of a story buried deep in the past, saying that there's no need to fret now! Dear Jesus! I can't believe any of this! I don't want to see that man ever again! I simply won't let them drive me mad! Tomorrow morning I'll talk to the older physician and demand they tell me the whole truth!

## THE NORTHAM-JAEGER RELATIONSHIP

### August 20th

This morning they removed my bandages. When *Ilector* Jaeger visited me, my face lit up! He gave me a firm handshake and with obvious joy he praised and congratulated the older physician. I didn't know that eighteen years ago, Jaeger had been Andreas Northam's teacher. From what they explained to me, this now famous and widely celebrated spiritual man, this "eminent thinker", whose work has now been widely read and whose lectures at the *Reigen* are attended by thousands, back then was still unknown to the public. He contributed towards young Northam's education for four years, wholeheartedly offering him the care and affection of a spiritual father.

Then they became caught up in life's responsibilities and they each went their separate ways.

When the superior *Ilectors* discovered who had stood by Northam's side as a teacher and a guardian in his early years, they called upon him and asked him if he could dedicate some time to him again in the afternoons. And it was very moving to see the now middle-aged thinker coming alone, without the escort of an *unge*, a young aide, and devoting his precious time to convey the same childhood learning to the same person - now a twenty-eight-year-old man - who, physically at least, resembled his spiritual son of two decades ago. What's more, as they informed me, he had unexpectedly been resurrected - but as a completely different man, disturbed and half deranged - after his fifteen-minute trip to the land of the dead. Jaeger confessed to me how delighted he was, when Professor Molsen told him that the freezing process had been done hastily but just in time. His brain hadn't suffered the slightest impairment.

## CONFESSIONS

### August 21st

Today, for the first time, Jaeger was accompanied by Stefan, Andreas' closest friend and three years his senior. He is an earnest young man; I truly took a liking to him.

Jaeger let him observe the lesson for a while. Then I showed him my first writings. I had already started to write and I continued writing in his presence. I thought he'd be impressed by the fact that I had recovered my writing skills even from the first days, but Jaeger had already informed him about my past research on Ibsen, about which I had talked to him as well.

"This is not Andreas' handwriting," was the only thing Stefan said.

Apart from the superior *Ilectors*, only four other people knew about Northam's unique case: the two physicians, *Ilector* Jaeger and Stefan. I pleaded with Jaeger to keep it a secret and not to let me become an object of curiosity in the eyes of the whole world. He promised, but he also added something that I didn't understand: "The Valley of the Roses will have the last word; it's up to them to decide how long this will be kept a secret from the rest of the world."

As for Stefan, he will start coming regularly in a few days; he has much to teach me about Northam and his life. He says that I need to know all that before I expose myself to this new world. The words that Jaeger said, shortly before Stefan's departure, come to mind: "In any case, Andreas Northam's family and friends will seek him out. Since the news of his recovery has become known, what's going to stop him from going back to his normal life?"

When we were left alone, I asked Jaeger to tell me what the *Ilectors* had been saying about all this and I told him what happened that night when the young physician saw me crying at the thought of my mother. "Try to put yourself in my shoes for a moment because, trust me, in such a bizarre and horrible situation it's worth considering both sides. Your course of life flows normally and unobstructed, at the same pace as always. For you, Northam is the one who's changed. For you, this is a case of 'personality shift' of a man who was revived after fifteen minutes of clinical death, a very rare parapsychological phenomenon associated with xenoglossy.

Your friend is a man who once was one of yours and now speaks a dead language. But I haven't changed at all. What I see is a piece of the future. Taking that into consideration, how can I not think that I've lost my mind? That I've gone mad?"

I was sobbing uncontrollably. I was utterly at sea because I could not believe that in there might be the slightest rift in the solid axes of time and space that I knew. The rift had to be somewhere inside me. I had to be the paranoid one!

"Only you can tell me the truth. If it's been two thousand years, like the young physician told me, then I'm going mad. You can't imagine how fresh, how recent the memory of going to sleep is in my mind; it feels like yesterday. I could hear my mother's breathing; she was sleeping in the next room. I can almost see the basin of water next to my bed and the fringed towel with the blue-green embroidery on it. It's as if she is in front of me right now."

I stared at him in agony, but Jaeger made no attempt to avoid my gaze. He could understand most of my German. "I don't think," he said holding his gaze steady, "that hiding even the tiniest vestige of truth from you will help to still your heart but, trust us, we know much more than you do. We don't live in the times of Descartes and Kant anymore. Many things have changed. But not everything can be measured solely on the basis of the intellect and constricts of the mere human brain. Are you absolutely sure, for example, that at the time you went to sleep, as you say, Andreas Northam did not yet exist? And are you absolutely sure that, right at this moment, your mother has ceased to exist?"

His incredible response struck me less than it would have a few days ago when it would have seemed inconceivable for me to process. Now, what brought tears to my eyes was the way this great man spoke to me, in such a different manner from the physicians. And he talked to me in my own tongue…

## SLEEPLESS

### August 23rd

Yesterday and today were two very quiet days. I spent the day writing or talking with Stefan in the mornings and Jaeger in the afternoons, and the night-time reading. I've turned into a voracious reader, a proper bookworm!

The physicians believe that trying to induce sleep artificially would be futile. Moreover, lack of sleep is neither fatal nor very harmful in my case, according to them.

At night they let me read, provided that I do it resting in bed or an armchair for at least half of the hours, and in the morning I wake up so fresh, as if I've slept for seven hours. Little by little I've started picking up their language as well, the "universal tongue" as Stefan calls it or, as I call it, "broken Anglo-Scandinavian". This language does, however, have a certain consistency between pronunciation and writing as I can now read much more comfortably though I often need the help of a small dictionary.

My long conversations with Jaeger are like a spiritual and mental cleansing for me. Under his tutelage I have ceased to seek shelter in the memories of my old life. This man has managed to sow the seed of faith deep inside my soul and has given me a new brand of confidence of which I had never thought myself capable. Because of him I've stopped feeling that I inhabit a foreign body. Because of him I can now look at myself fearlessly in the mirror and, strangely enough, somewhere beneath all these foreign features, I can distinguish my own expression as I have known it my entire life.

Without having mentioned anything myself, I heard Stefan share a similar opinion on the subject with me the other day. "The man I see in front of me is, indeed, Andreas Northam but, by his accent, the tone of his voice, and even the way he expresses himself and looks at me, I can tell it's not him."

### August 24th

Today, like every other day, Jaeger tutored me in articulation, elocution and pronunciation. Next, we will start learning about the world around me. This incredible man spends a great amount of his time patiently explaining every little thing, its use and function. When I go out into the world, I will have to be able to get around by myself and not look lost.

Whenever he gets tired, we take a break and I tell him all kinds of stories: about my hometown, my life, my mother's love for me… And he raptly listens to me, taking interest in the ways of the 20th century, asking a myriad of questions about our schools and our habits in general, even taking notes every so often. He seems delighted with my outbursts of nostalgia.

I've told him that I, too, used to be a teacher in my time and I've spoken to him about my preference for history. With these conversations I have been overwhelmed by a great spiritual thirst; the thought of an immense prospect suddenly opening up in my field helps me temporarily forget my situation and makes me quiver with anticipation. And this thirst in my heart, only some steps away from this new and unexpected El Dorado, only I can feel.

**(In the middle of the night)**

I'm tired. I've been walking around on the terrace for hours on end in the divine serenity of the night. I feel a hint of joy springing up inside me, as if I could hear my heart beating. Am I feverish again? The prospect of the new emotions welling within me meets the permanent turmoil of my mind. Will I stop obsessing over this incredible experience and slowly become accustomed to it? Will I become a normal person that finds interest in everyday life again? Will I be worthy of new excitement? I feel like an avid philatelist who has just been offered the King of England's stamp collection and can't wait to examine it; or like a Classics scholar who has just gained access to the Library of Alexandria.

**August 25th**

Jaeger said to me tonight, "Trust Stefan. He'll lead you through everything, step by step." I kindly requested him to give me some more history books for now, and he promised he would. He also suggested the *Reigen-Swage*, something completely new to me, a type of narration that consists of a simultaneous combination of sight and sound, which you do not even need to read! A voice narrates them and you see pictures come to life before you.

"Listen to me," he told me - and I recount his words not as he spoke them but as I understood them - "When the time comes in a short while and I will no longer be by your side, rise to the challenge and do not let your thoughts be nourished only by facts. Delve more deeply into the great spiritual paths that have now been opened to humankind. You won't benefit much from hard facts. Try not to be dazzled by them and end up spending your hours watching them unfold on the *Reigen-Swage*. After all, whatever happened has happened before. History repeats itself. Try to read between the lines and see beneath the surface of mere events."

He made an allusion to the "new, bright paths" that will lead to "quenching the thirst of the longing of centuries" and to the alleviation of "humankind's metaphysical pain".

Nevertheless, I am not entirely in a position to know if I've interpreted correctly all that this wise man has patiently taught me. It is *us*, he says, who pass by, not time. We, the human creatures with the short-lived biological destiny, come and go. The dimension of depth eludes us. Our antennas have a very limited capacity. They only form subjective impressions that are totally irrelevant to the true and objective "Great Reality", the *Samith* as he called it.

**August 26th**

There come times when the idea of that huge, unknown world out there frightens me. I'm becoming accustomed to living the same, unchanging and unsurprising life, day by day in the institution and I find some joy in it. But Stefan tells me that I have to fight against my shyness and face the life that's out there, waiting for me.

**August 27th**

Today Jaeger remembered young Northam again. Then, looking straight into my eyes, he murmured, "I know Andreas is not with us anymore; but I will always call you by his name."

Stefan told me the same thing the other day: "Let me call you Andreas..." And such was the tone of his voice that anybody would be jealous of Northam, of that rigid faith in the concept of friendship (so foreign to us) that was so strongly connected to his memory.

**August 30th**

A few days were enough to change everything around me! The environment, the people, the circumstances; all so different! Who could have imagined…

## NORTHAM'S CIRCLE AND THEIR SOCIAL CODE

### 1-IX-MDIX

***(The dating system changes. It is our 3906 AD, but according to the future calendar it is 1509)***

And once again, everything is crumbling inside me. A great part of the expectations and the dreams of recent days have proven futile. The famous environment of my new life, Andreas Northam's social circle appears to be nothing more than a playful and carefree bevy of young people. I am, however, starting to enjoy this whole story. Who knows, it might be just another defence mechanism of my mind…

The plan for this morning was to take a walk along the nearby lake, where there were boats for hire. Youth, laughter, fuss, singing. Stefan struggled to marshal the group at every turn.

"Hilda! Hilda! Wait! We can't catch up! Andreas can't run!"

He looked somewhat annoyed by the fact that his sweetheart happened to be the one who was far ahead of everyone else and that she was the reason why the whole group had to speed up. Walking between him and Silvia, his other friend, it was difficult for me to keep pace.

"Forgive me, Andreas," Hilda later said. "My mind was elsewhere…"

I felt that I had to say something nice to her as well. I looked at her. Truth be told, she was very pleasant to look at. With an awkward smile I said that it didn't matter and that I was now feeling strong enough, which was not true. Stefan noticed my fatigue and suggested we took another break. Luckily, the rest of the road was downhill.

I sat next to Stefan on a stone bench and we listened to Axel and Eric, who were talking about the beauty of spring mornings while picking poppies. Silvia was chatting with Aria. Juliet and Hilda were chasing a couple of blue butterflies.

"So this is the group of Andreas Northam's friends then?" I pondered in disappointment. "I think that no one could expect to learn very much from this bunch of overgrown children".

These two twenty-five-year-olds, along with the four young women and Stefan, had stormed into the institution three days ago as soon as the physicians allowed visitors. They surrounded me full of joy, whooping and laughing and asking me a thousand questions! They could hardly contain their excitement seeing me strong and healthy again - at seeing Andreas Northam, that is.

I was impressed by their manners that would be considered rather childish for their age. It seemed very strange for Northam to have such a circle of friends since I knew that, before the accident, he had been a respected young scientist, who had worked in some sector of applied physics - I don't remember which exactly - and with quite good results for that matter. In fact, the institute for which he was working had called the Molsen Institute several times asking about his health.

Unintentionally, I looked towards the North, behind the high mountains, with a vague sense of nostalgia for my old homeland. I felt a tear trapped in the corner of my eye. I didn't say anything to Stefan at that moment; he was pointing to some villas far in the distance, innumerable houses clustered together, almost like entire states. He told me that in many places they had kept the same archaic names like Waren, Cernobbio, Belano, Menaggio and others, names that now sound peculiar in a language that has changed so much.

Hilda had the idea of singing a song with the rest of the girls. It was a spring song that they sang all together, verse by verse. It was a cheerful song to sing amongst friends. Out of the blue, a window opened, a girl appeared and started accompanying the song on her violin. Right next to her, a painter, who, up until then, had been struggling with his palette and his brushes, pulled out a flute and, in turn, accompanied the melody.

How did that happen? How could these people drop what they were doing and attune themselves to our pace and gaiety? I was immensely impressed by that spontaneous and facile joy, their positive attitude and their desire to identify with us! The sense of camaraderie spread as if the melody of the song became an invisible bond uniting us! Before heading to the lake, we applauded our new friends and they applauded us, as if we were old mates.

Then the chaps started pinning flowers on the girls' lapels. Stefan pinned one on Hilda, Axel on Juliet and Eric on Aria. Silvia was looking at me with a hint of a smile, waiting for my move. With trembling hands I pinned the flower on her lapel like the others did, and we sauntered downhill holding hands, like little children. The four boats were ready. Most of the other groups of friends had already taken position and greeted us, the "late arrivals", raising their right hand and waving to us from afar. The white sails were already set.

I stop and observe their codes of behaviour. As Stefan explained to me, in this new world people are not strangers to each other. You talk to people you have never met open-heartedly, as if they are old friends; and they, in return, respond in the exact same way. They all have the same kind and relaxed attitude, the same naivety in their manners, the same benevolence, the same tact, the same warm camaraderie, as if they had all together attended a big, universal college in their childhood.

I wanted to ask Stefan so many things. But how? It would have to be just the two of us if I were to do that. He had promised he would show me a typical image of modern life. He knew that what I wanted to see and experience was not the countryside and the holidays but the exact opposite: the large urban centres, the world of work and the everyday people. And I knew that these things existed somewhere.

I would also like to know whether this shared behaviour, which was highlighted by strong and obvious characteristics of childhood purity, was the result of the purely economic factors that Stefan had talked to me about, which, with the passage of time, managed to raise this equality, this homogeneity, to such a high level. But without first seeing it with my own eyes in all its manifestations, I am not about to believe this universal fairy tale with its flawless and refined manners and its genuine brotherhood of man lacking in any ulterior motives.

## 3-IX

The odd change I'm going through all these days should be investigated, if anything, from the psychological point of view. My heart is calm and I'm becoming accustomed to all that I see around me. That has not been easy. I remember the first days when even the way people dressed seemed strange to me. I now find my life increasingly interesting. Every little thing intrigues me and I ask Stefan about so many things that it would take me ages to write it all down. But why do I not have the power to express all that I feel with precision? Wouldn't it be more suitable for a craftsman of writing to be granted with this unique fate instead of someone like me, a poor and sickly teacher? So many new and different things and experiences! How wonderfully better a writer would transcribe them...

Every day I think of my mother, the only source of affection in my life, and I wonder how it would be if she could be next to me and see it all with me. Anna still pops into my mind from time to time, but I feel that my old wound has somehow started to heal in my heart and doesn't hurt as much anymore. My mind then takes me elsewhere: Oh God, how light is the weight of my twenty-eight years! How light! From this perspective, it's as if I've turned back time! Looking at myself in the mirror, something that terrified me and almost drove me insane in the beginning, now gives me untold pleasure!

Everyone treats me as if I were Andreas Northam. And I am sure that none of them - excluding Stefan - knows the truth. From what I've understood, the old Northam was a bit superior to the rest in his circle of friends. The same goes for Aria if I judge by the way they treat her. Aria is twenty-five years old but, when she speaks, the rest fall silent. And another thing I noticed: last night when she entered the drawing room of the villa where we were, the ladies of our group stood up, like we men used to do - something that in our time and our social circles the ladies would never have done.

**5-IX**

In the meantime, I've learnt a great deal from Stefan regarding my new companions. Axel's relationship with Juliet is only two months old. She is very young, nineteen or twenty years old, brunette, pretty and somewhat frivolous. She's always a bit scruffy and enthusiastic about life and when she's by herself, she often hums. Axel is her first love and their acquaintance began one day when they were in a garden and Juliet's muslin dress was soiled and Axel hastened to hem it with pins in a makeshift way before it became dirtier. Axel plays the violin quite well, though if you ask Juliet, she'll tell you that he'll soon become a virtuoso! Nevertheless, they both have hearts of gold and the group can't live without them.

As for Silvia, I learnt that Andreas Northam loved her very much for a period of two-three years, but she never felt anything for him beyond a simple friendship and appreciation for the man and his work. Her heart might belong to someone else, who knows? Stefan doesn't know anything on the subject since nobody cares for gossip here. However, when I saw her for the first time I got the feeling that I had seen her before. Then, when I was alone, I realised: I remembered because of my blurred memories from the hospital. She was among the nurses and even in the midst of my feverish daze I had noticed her. There was something very gracious and noble about her figure and she stood out from the others.

Stefan told me again yesterday, "This love was very painful for Andreas. There were nights that his eyes constantly welled with tears."

I replied that he should, however, appreciate the honesty and principles that characterised Silvia, who never even thought of reciprocating without having feelings for him. "Somebody else in her place," I said, taking into account Northam's reputation, "wouldn't really mind feigning love and affection in order to be with him."

Stefan, startled at first by my words, replied, "Why would you say that? That would be vulgar! No woman would do that!"

I should not have opened my mouth. I quickly changed the subject and asked him what the others had to say about the "new" Northam. He told me that Silvia had mentioned me several times over the past few days. In fact, this morning she had asked him if he had noticed my changed gaze and if he remembered Andreas having such an expression before the accident. She also told him that Andreas was acting very strange, that he seemed unusually quiet, hesitant and timid, that his accent had changed and that he even found difficulty articulating words.

I asked Stefan what to do since it was impossible for someone to make sense out of countless new things, obtain a new mentality, new manners and speak the language fluently, from one day to the next. He encouraged me with a smile and said that things would get better. An old friend of theirs happened to suffer a dreadful car accident and, after his recovery, he temporarily struggled to regain his mental capacities; that's the impression they have. Would that ever be a reason for them to love you less? No. "You can see for yourself that they're always by your side showing you such affection."

I'm sitting on the terrace and all these thoughts and discussions flash before my eyes like moving pictures. I can hear the girls talking and laughing below. They tease me and ask how on earth I can read and write in such a ruckus. The sun has almost set and soon it'll be time for "The Prayer of the Dusk" they hear every afternoon. I hear them call out for Stefan before I sink into my thoughts again.

Here's the peculiar thing about Stefan. It appears that we share a bond, a bond that he didn't even share with his closest friend, Andreas Northam: the same love for history. His main occupation was the study of history in general and the art of the past millenniums in particular. And so our friendship evolves effortlessly even if there's nothing in me to remind him of Andreas - neither their shared memories nor their dreams…

As for Stefan's bond with Hilda, it's something that has stood the test of time. They've been happily together for over four years now and it looks like it'll stay this way for the rest of their lives. Here is a truly happy couple! In fact, they have decided to have a baby and they have already handed in their legal statement to the Office Partners, the executives of the demographic services, to whom those wanting to have the one child they are permitted must submit their application. It'll be their turn in roughly a year.

Hilda also helps Stefan with work sometimes, reading aloud or copying, although Stefan himself says that he's not made for big things. All he wants is to learn and that's all. He knows he's not meant to make any great contributions to the world of research, the exact opposite of Aria who, at twenty-five, has already published papers that took five or six years to complete and made a name for herself.

As for the other three–Hilda, Silvia and Aria–they are bound together by a special friendship, different from their friendship with Juliet, which is a very recent one. The latter, of course, knows it, but she doesn't mind in the slightest since she sees how much they care for her.

They met on Christmas Eve eight years ago, in the Valley of the Roses in one of the palaces of the *Lorffes* - another ruling class similar to the *Ilectors* - where they, according to Hilda, along with many other teenage girls, carefully hand-picked among thousands for their natural beauty, dressed in white and holding torches, were welcoming the *Ilectors* to the reception after the great evening mass. They describe it as their best childhood memory, like a dream that was later hard for them to believe came true.

Eric is finally coming! He's holding some sort of racket and some other smaller paraphernalia needed for a game or sport I haven't yet bothered to ask about. He's wearing sandals and he is naked from the waist up. He looks fresh and excited. The acquaintance between Eric and Aria was a fateful one. They've been together for fourteen months and no one knows how long this relationship will last. This special girl, with her early inclination to study what she believed in since childhood, has managed, in her twenties, to be present at excavations in America together with great experts and who, based on a bold intuition - almost like an inspiration - argued for her own conclusions on the life of the Incas, findings that were later to be proven true! This inherently wise young woman, whose views were vindicated in so many aspects, who made her own statements before an audience of thousands in the megacity of Norfor two years ago, who lately had a whole crew of young people to help her with her research, had given up everything for this dark-haired young man, who might have an exquisite heart, but could not bear to hear a word about her job. A while back, Stefan heard him say, "Talk to me about sports, talk to me about travels, about swimming or whatever else you want, but don't say a word to me about God and all these ancient treasures!"

They're ready to go. It's time for the prayer. I won't be writing till tomorrow.

## THE TWO-YEAR GLOBAL SERVICE, EVERYDAY LIFE AND DEMOGRAPHIC REGULATIONS

### 6-IX

I asked Stefan to leave me alone for the day so I could rest. I need to think about many things. "Stefan... Stefan," I say to myself every so often, "I think you're wrong about Silvia's feelings towards Andreas Northam."

I constantly criticise myself and the feebleness of my character. "What are you doing to yourself, you poor lunatic?" I think, "You'll be very sorry one day…"

I feel the insidious and deceitful attraction of chaos. "Silvia… Silvia..." I keep repeating in my head. What a strange name… I like saying it out loud. The fact that she's from another, more superior race from a different era gives her an extra, metaphysical charm.

The voice of reason whispers in my ear: "Be careful, you poor wretch… The serenity of the heart is as important as the health of the body; you will only appreciate its value once you've lost it." And the truth is that I must not forget how essential the absolute serenity of the heart is in my case, and it is my duty to protect it. The infinite horizons of knowledge that lie ahead demand my undivided attention and constant meditation.

At the same time, however, I take pride in realising that on no occasion should I lack confidence. Not only have I got the looks but also the heart and inner wisdom, so, based on what I've seen from all these people, they are no better than me. I could easily be one of them without being subject to comparison. I feel like I'm entering their world for real now!

### 7-IX

Stefan was avoiding taking me to cities and showing me the life there. One day, when he was standing silently on the terrace, I pointed to the exquisite nature before us and said, "It's a happy life you have here… You've got everything. You lack nothing." Immediately after that, I made a vague reference to the duration of this holiday. At first he looked at me, puzzled. Then he smiled and, with feigned fatigue and supposed indifference, he let his head drop on the back of the armchair. "Oh yes…" he said, gazing far into the distance. "I was lucky. From seventeen to nineteen, I happened to find great job opportunities and do good business back then. 'So young?' you might ask. Yes, so young, strange though it may seem to you. Within two years, not only did I manage to pay back my parents for all the money I had cost them up until then, but also save enough money to secure a comfortable life for the rest of the days I am destined to live."

I detected a note of sarcasm in his last sentence so I showed him, in my own way, my disbelief in every word he said. I smiled and asked him why someone would give up such profitable work so prematurely.

"The profits I had made were sufficient," he replied gravely. "It was someone else's turn to replace me."

"And what sort of job did you do?" I asked, adopting a similar gravity of tone.

"Oh, I used to do something beautiful," he sighed nostalgically. "Part of my good fortune was that I was given one of our more artistic jobs: we made combs. Mostly for women. I worked there for two years. Millions of combs passed through my hands. I remember thinking about how much hair that had been combed by them, the millions of young girls that had looked at their reflection in the mirror with pleasure while wearing them, the millions of plaits that had become tangled in them. If combs could talk, each one of them would tell me incredible stories. And I'm proud of my creations, which were the product of two of the most fertile and memorable years of my youth."

His final words were filled with true emotion. But I stayed faithful to the cheerful tone of the beginning of his monologue: I didn't want to show more credulity than I should. "That must have been interesting," I said, awkwardly smiling again. "This story of the lucky and prematurely retired industrialist is definitely an interesting one, to say the least. Did our other rich friends have a similar fate, perhaps even starting from their early school years?"

"In the beginning, when I talked about luck, I was just joking. It's not about luck; it's an institution. You see us now, living a life of comfort, but all of us, men and women have been through that.

Every single person you've met and everyone you'll meet in the future, including Silvia, Aria, and Hilda, were 'partners' from the age of seventeen to nineteen. After finishing their basic education at school they went and earned their living. They worked in construction, in food, furniture and clothes manufacturing, in public transport, in utensils, machines, in everything you see around you and everything you can imagine. And if their lives are easy now, it's because they dedicated themselves wholeheartedly for two years, and that required a great deal of effort. Thus, neither did we burden our parents financially, nor will our children burden us. Before our 'service', the previous generation worked for us, we did the same in our time and now, it's the youngest generation's turn to work for everyone."

If I was sure that Stefan had stopped joking, I'd have a thousand things to ask him. But I'll have time to judge if all this is true. For the moment, I just wanted to somehow switch the conversation to what I intended to say. "In any case, given my situation and my justifiably great curiosity, I think it's not too difficult for you to understand that this air of relaxation and well-being is becoming almost agonising for me. So I was thinking if we could somehow exchange this holiday atmosphere with a typical image of modern life… As for the people, I find them all more and more lovable with every passing day - especially you and Hilda. I wish I could have you with me all the time." Silvia's name kept echoing in my mind. It so happens, sometimes, that we avoid talking about what interests us most…

"A typical image of modern life…" Stefan repeated, gradually speaking louder in a cheerful manner. "Did you say 'a typical image of modern life'? Well, for the majority this is pretty much the most common way of life now. Simple life, surrounded by the beauties of nature, carefree, cheerful, among friendly faces and our loved ones... It is a life without ambitions or the slightest desire for posthumous fame, without the need to perform great deeds. To give the *Ilectors* and the *Lorffes* their large palaces with all your heart without any secret desires; to live free and, above all, unfettered from all sorts of projects that will, gradually and without your realising it, enslave you for your entire life; to stay away from any contact with the institutions of our times, few though they may be; to see your life flow in obscurity among the treasures of the heart and of nature, happy in your anonymity, and to occasionally lose yourself in reading or in the pleasure of being a sensitive admirer of the fine arts; that's the image of modern life you're looking for!"

You could see that he was thrilled by his own words. It was obvious that for years he had been building his lifestyle around the imperatives of his own psyche and temperament and he wouldn't let anything and anyone change that.

"You don't understand me, Stefan," I continued. "It's not as much about the way of life as it is about the world as a whole and its people. After entering this developed community with its extremely cultivated and sophisticated - and "superior" for that matter - people, with their impeccable manners and civilised lifestyle, isn't my need to see how most people live justifiable?"

"But we *are* 'most people'," he claimed in amongst peals of laughter - and this time his laughter was genuine, that of a child. "Does it seem so absurd to you? Yes, we are those who you, in your time, would call 'working class'. Listen, because you don't seem to understand: so what if we have everything in abundance daily and, literally, not one bit less than the greatest *Ilector*? We deserve all these 'consumer goods'. We worked hard for them in our youth. And, in any case, there is such an abundance that we never run out. Travels, entertainment, sports - whatever we want - are at our disposal. However, all kinds of moral satisfaction like respect, fame, recognition, accolades and generally all honours are reserved for others." And lowering his voice, he added in a serious tone that struck me, "The common perception about us is that we 'do nothing'. And it's true…What can I say?"

"What?" I spontaneously interrupted him, affected by the sincerity of his bitter confessions, a product of his self-consciousness. "This perception is not fair. You've carried out your duty; you've paid off all your debts to society!"

"And they've carried out theirs," he replied in the same low voice. "They worked in their time too. They ran with the same fervour to the *glothners* and were appointed to our modern construction sites, laboratories and *werksteds*. They faced temporary spiritual and intellectual malnutrition and lived the disciplined life of active 'partners'. They endured the unbearably long shifts and the torturous - for the free spirits - tedium of their labour. They gladly completed their two-year service like everyone else. Nevertheless, coming out into society with the title of *Cives*, they didn't choose to sit back, relax and enjoy what they had earned from their service, like we do, like most people do; they had every right to. Instead, and without the slightest hint of thirst for recognition and rewards, they tried to make something out of themselves, to leave something behind."

"Most of the times," Stefan continued, "this 'something' was based on dreams and pure ambitions that had already started to emerged in their teenage years, insights born in their final years at school. But quite often one's inclinations manifest themselves at a more mature age. But in any case, no one forces them to do anything. That's what they like, that's where they find happiness. Some derive pleasure and satisfaction from taking care of children and sick people; others dream up inventions and technical applications that will make our lives even easier one day; others want to become physicians and open up new avenues in science.

All these millions of people who go to our major spiritual centres to study know that there isn't the slightest material gain or professional prestige to look forward to after finishing the course they have chosen. Many of them just sit there and listen to the same things for many years, just out of sheer love for their subject. Many are old but no one can be under nineteen years of age because our higher education always comes after the 'service' without exception."

Stefan told me that, the majority of these young men and women come to listen to the great masters, about whom they had been hearing great things since their early teenage years and whom they had always admired from afar. In fact, some of these young people are lucky enough to become, even for a short period of time, members of the crew or followers of these wise men, called *unge*, an honorary title.

He also told me that he cannot entirely agree with what almost everyone believes, that is, that, at the highest level, above the wise scientists, leading thinkers and teachers, are the great artists. "They are the ones that attract all the attention, recognition and acknowledgement nowadays. They are the ones who now electrify the crowds. They are now the idols of the wider, anonymous public, according to the modern meritocratic beliefs. But I think that these two categories are incomparable, to say the least."

He emphasised how valuable the contributions of the men that stood out in the sciences - especially physical sciences - were to humankind. I also remember him wondering why only the philosophical sciences are now considered equivalent to art.

"It is said," he added softly, almost as if talking to himself, "that only these sciences share the element of 'transcendence'. But don't the physical sciences too, at their highest level, take on the same transcendental aspect, leading to philosophical thinking?"

At that point I decided to interrupt him, arguing that the fervour with which he spoke about the 'upper class' somehow contradicted his previous description of his simple, carefree life in obscurity as 'perfectly satisfactory'. In fact I reminded him of what he had said earlier:

"Now more than ever, people like us, who do not wish to pursue professional 'success' and do not need to make a living, have to arrange our lives around our capabilities as conceived by each of us individually. I'm perfectly happy with the way I am because I know that I wasn't born for greatness. The truth is that creators are born, not made. If, however, before I was born, I was given a choice, I think I would sacrifice this calm and carefree life for the agonising world of creation."

He fell silent for a few moments and then, touching my hand in a friendly and confidential way, he continued with a hint of a smile. "I won't lie to you; neither Eric nor Axel agrees with me on this subject. Eric, with his heart of gold, would choose the exact opposite. As for Axel, he continues to saw on his violin, unwilling to realise that he will never reach that level of excellence that would even justify devoting one's whole life to it."

He then added, "This candid approach, which was true for the arts since the beginning of time, now also applies to the world of science. And the reason is what I told you before: one's involvement in science is not a professional need that justifies mediocrity for the sake of one making a living. Our universal socio-political community needs high quality rather than quantity. It all comes down to this: either you say something actually worth saying or say nothing at all!"

I asked him if it were true that the content and purpose of the current class distinction was purely spiritual and if, apart from the honours that these people necessarily - as he claims - accept, there is no other material gain for all those prestigious wise men and great artists, or any special power over the others.

"You will not see any further distinctions beyond the ones I've told you: love, respect, enthusiasm and gratitude. That is, unless you consider material gain the few palaces and artworks that were given to The Valley of the Roses *(their hub of learning)* and our other great intellectual centres. These things have more of a symbolic significance than anything else. In fact, these immense buildings even tire them sometimes."

"On the other hand," Stefan added, "there are many more joys in life: youth, travels, requited love - joys that we enjoy to the fullest every day and of which they are deprived, choosing sacrifice and creation to quench their thirst for knowledge. They're not made for our way of life; they don't receive enough satisfaction from these things. What could quench their thirsty minds cannot be found in this 'environment'."

"I think that nothing could quench their thirsty minds; the constant feeling of dissatisfaction and unfulfilment is part of their destiny," I added, wanting to show him I understood his point.

"The only thing that could," said Stefan in a tone of profound faith, "is the Great Reality, the *Samith*... But it is inaccessible down here. Every worthy conception and form in art is nothing more than an attempt to touch it, an excruciating endeavour, full of desperation and, at the same time, frenzied hope! Every worthy conception and form in art was, is and always will be generated by the longing for the *Samith*... If that did not exist, neither would artistic creation. And if even the greatest artists are never satisfied by their works, that's because the *Samith* is the quintessence of the greatest arts, just like infinity is the ultimate of the largest numbers we can imagine. But now I'm talking to you about *Volkic Knowledge*, something you're not familiar with..."

"When are you going to talk to me about this type of knowledge? Will you give me some books on the subject?" I asked him impatiently.

"That is a subject that will take many hours to discuss. We don't have enough time today because Hilda will be here shortly. I will only answer the last part of your previous question. Material superiority is unknown to the contemporary ruling class and so is any type of power over others. Twelve or thirteen hundred years ago, when still under the rule of the leading physical scientists, the concept of 'power', in its original sense of penalties, enforcement, coercion was still in force. But corresponding legal relations and property disputes were almost inexistent back then, as they are now. The implementation of private laws and institutions had proven largely unrealistic. But the rights and responsibilities between citizens and political authority still needed to be defined by a multitude of modernised and efficient institutions, enacted by those wise people in accordance with new needs. Eventually, with the passage of centuries, any form of compulsion and penalties became obsolete.

This socio-political phenomenon is not recent. It occurred at the beginning of the *Eldrere (Old times, Eldrere began in our 2396 AD and lasted for 986 years until 3382 AD)*. Scientists accomplished it using the notion of abundance and an unprecedented progress in the education of children as their tools. The 'service' lasted twenty years then and before that, thirty years, but never did it cross anyone's mind to wrong one another or steal from anybody, since no one lacked anything."

I also asked him if something else was true, something that I happened to hear when I had my accident - or rather, when Andreas Northam had had his accident. I wanted to know whether even in case of an accident if the authorities only take into consideration the technical and medical variables without assigning any responsibility.

"That's where education comes in, as I mentioned to you before. First of all, the likelihood of a car accident or any other kind of accident occurring is extremely low nowadays. But suppose that something like this happens and the driver of the *linsen* survives; there would be no need to assign blame, because such a possibility would be completely ruled out."

There is a saying here, as Stefan told me, that says that the man of today, the *Troende* as they call him, 'can do no wrong' as the British used to say about their king. This reality was made possible as a result of the deep respect they have for the value of the human life, which is implanted in their conscience from an early age. According to the current 'Volkic perception', each and every one of 'thy neighbours' is a 'whole inner world' full of dreams about life, affection, love and sacred human suffering, high ideals and a wide range of spiritual values, all reflections of the *Samith*, about which he had talked to me earlier. Their attention to detail and their foresight, which sometimes reaches the point of exaggeration, is incredible. They are extremely careful not to insult this 'whole inner world' in the slightest, either in terms of its physical or its moral existence. These people have followed, to the highest possible degree, the commandment of 'love thy neighbour'.

"The same goes for the extremely rare occasion of someone illegally having a child," Stefan continued. "The state does not envisage such a thing happening out of intention or carelessness because the respect for our demographic institutions precludes such possibility. In such matters, statistics are our infallible guide: such low percentages of illegal births cannot affect or disturb, even in the slightest, either the process of population screening or the rhythm of life. The compulsions and penalties have been replaced by domestic laws. Truly civilised people, people with 'inner culture', cannot do something that is wrong. Even if you force them to, so to speak, they cannot! Let's look into the matter of signing up for the 'service', for example: if you search among the millions of young men and women, you won't find a single person that would try to avoid it! Quite the contrary, in fact. Our leaders and educators are forced to fight, with proper instruction and arguments, the feeling of inferiority and unjustified remorse for those few children that annually, due to health problems, are not accepted into the *glothners*. Their great misery comes not from their illness or disability, but by the feeling of being a burden to their fellow men..."

He again stressed the simplicity of the existing institutions, assuring me that there were no other ones, apart from those concerning the 'service', population screening and traffic control.

"So few constraints," he said with some obvious pride, "so few institutions and this lack of authority and enforcement in an individual's life creates a great deal of space for individual freedom - always combined with self-discipline, of course. Nowadays no one stops you from travelling to the other side of the world, from saying and doing whatever you want, believing in whatever you want, the way you see fit. Education - from the most basic to the highest - the *daners*, the 'temples', the *Reigen-Swage*, the theatres, the parks, the beaches, the museums, the hospitals, all sorts of institutions, the walks, the malls, the *larinters*, the countryside, the exercise centres and all sorts of sports, all these and so much more that you cannot even imagine, are all open to us, especially from the age of nineteen and onwards. And the help of statistics is also miraculous when it comes to 'distribution': they keep a balance between supply and demand making everything abound by monitoring all global needs and making early and precise predictions."

I asked him how the lack of any form of enforcement, as he says, is compatible with the work of the *Ilectors* and the *Lorffes*.

"Their role is more of a regulatory one," he replied. "It's more a duty than political power. Some of these wise men will decide, for example, if the application of a new technical or technological development would prove beneficial to the production of consumer goods, like food and other things; others will take up the job of regulating traffic; others will decide the pace of the coming of a new generation and so on. They haven't invaded, however, personal lives and haven't dealt with individual cases for centuries; there hasn't been a need to. Sometimes, in the past, they had to intervene and that's when they had true power. On the rare occasion, let's say, of someone being 'too fertile', they would forgive any violation of the order of priority or the number of children they were allowed."

I couldn't help myself and told him, "You speak of individual freedom, Stefan, but you seem to be forgetting your unnatural demographic limitations..."

"Because, as I told you, these are general rules and not interventions in individual cases. According to this regulation, those who desperately want to have a child will get their turn in good time. And don't worry; everyone is entitled to have children! The purpose is to meet the current demographic 'rate of replacement', so that the next generation doesn't end up being more populous than the current one throughout the whole earth. Essentially, this restriction is not as terrible as you think. It is a matter of order and understanding for the sake of humanity."

"In my era, which you call barbaric, we were much closer to nature and to individual freedom."

"The need wasn't so urgent back then. Also, the division of the earth into rivalling political and economic powers engendered, in turn, a corresponding rivalry in terms of population. The danger of overpopulation had increased dramatically in the old days. After that, the world was in desperate need of regulation and now, as a result of that regulation, we're at the point where it's not about the quantity of people anymore, but about quality. In your era, the world population balance was effortlessly restored by your wars and epidemics; people died and people were born every day. But in our world these two 'solutions' have long become obsolete. So what choice did we have? If we stopped keeping track of the demographic indicators, all the flourishing science and technical applications could only maintain these high living standards of the international community for a short period of time, and, in the end, they would not be able to prevent its fall."

That's when, from what I remember, Hilda walked into the room holding a bunch of flowers. Stefan abruptly stopped talking and, shortly after, we changed the subject.

## ROMANCING WITH SILVIA

### 8-IX

I stayed in all afternoon today. Since earlier in the day I haven't been feeling so well, but Hilda took care of me and brought me a hot beverage. Now I feel much better. The books Stefan had ordered a while ago arrived with yesterday's "distribution". I sat with him and went through them to pass the time.

### 9-IX

I don't know what's wrong with me again today, but, once more, I feel the anticipation of great joy. Something tells me I might see her today... Throughout the night I felt wonderful. I left very early, with that fresh breeze of the dawn, and took a walk in the gardens and the forest. I don't know why, but I often feel the urge to go out and walk by myself in uninhabited places like these.

Stefan was wondering where I was and, when I returned, he asked me. I didn't mention anything other than how well I was feeling. What's the matter with me? One second I'm happy and the next tears are filling my eyes. Now, for example, I feel like crying. And to think that this morning I was filled with inexplicable joy. Even the sight of a single sun ray made me smile.

What does destiny hold for me tonight? Am I going to see her? Is she going to join the group? I'm counting the minutes again... Counting the minutes...

**(At night)**

Nothing... Nothing... Once again nothing! I don't understand... She knows exactly where we get together every evening... All these days...

### 10-IX

I last saw her a couple of days ago, crossing the park with a big group of people I didn't know. They were chatting with each other as equals, with an apparent comfort and composure. I thought that if I were one of them, I would hardly be able to keep talking so tirelessly for so long. I felt a bit jealous of them...

They were approaching the edge of the park, where I was sitting, and I didn't know if I had time to pull myself together a bit. I was bedraggled and I was quite sure my complexion was ashen. Among other things, I was afraid she might think that I was sitting there with the sole purpose of seeing her. While passing, she turned and looked at me, as if she had just seen me. She barely greeted me, as if I had done something to her, and she didn't look very thrilled to see me but, when our eyes met, just for a single second, I felt the happiest person alive for absolutely no reason. And then I knew right away that her behaviour had nothing to do with me. She was just moody or angry at herself. I could tell from that hint of agitation in her eyes.

Angry at herself… There are times when I think that maybe I'm the only happy member of the group. Should I stop being so aloof? Could it be that it's my fault? All this timidity, lack of courage and unjustifiable attitude…

### 11-IX

I'll ask Stefan to postpone the trip to Norfor that he mentioned last night. And to think that, a little while ago, only the sound of this glorious location would have made me jump for joy!

### 16-IX

Stefan knows everybody here. He managed to find some old acquaintances of his who are interested in science books and so we traded a big part of Northam's book collection with some history books of great significance, which would have taken ages to arrive with the "distribution". Among them, a basic history book for children, ideal for beginners like me, a Dupont edition, a true miniature of three thousand glow-in-the-dark, green pages, with stereoscopic illustrations, tiny print that successively became enlarged only at the part that you're reading and full-page panoramas.

I returned to the villa late at night. With the heavy bag tucked under my arm, excited about my new possessions, I locked myself in my room and emptied my treasure on the table. At the sight of it, a multitude of cheerful and magical memories of my childhood came to life, like a colourful parade before my eyes!

**17-IX**

Today, it was meant to be... Today, destiny had a beautiful surprise in store for me: I unexpectedly ran into her on my way back home. We spent a whole hour together. At first she cried. Then I told her I loved her. She then placed her hand on my heart. I kissed her and, finally, we stared deep into each other's eyes... No one will ever know what happened between us! Thank you, God, for this moment! And I had a feeling since this morning that it would be a big day today!

She told me that she had been suffering and crying herself to sleep for days, due to the doubts that tortured her. She didn't know what to do. She was reserved due to her earlier behaviour towards me. But my unwavering love, plus the fact that, after the accident, I looked purer and gentler and with a more romantic attitude - something that excites women - had struck her. I'm happy! She told me she wants to go everywhere with me. All the places she has visited, she wants to see again with me. Only then, she says, can a mere visit be transformed into true experience; otherwise only the eyes are satisfied and not the soul...

**18-IX**

I've been sitting here for hours, thinking about what happened yesterday. I can't even read. I look like I'm daydreaming. There is no way that Stefan hasn't figured it out. Yesterday was an outburst of emotions; reason and judgment had no place in it. Today, after so much stress, I feel so weak and exhausted that I can hardly write. I have so much to think about. I just remembered something that Stefan said, that as human beings, that is, forms of life with limited capacities, we are unable to define the borders of the "real" and the "unreal" or assess the actual scope of the Great Reality. It is impossible, he says, to know what lies beneath appearances and even less through the prism of our "child-like" temperament that frequently blows simple, human psychological reactions out of proportion. As he explained to me, they now believe that the old interpretation of the "idealisation of human instincts" merely seems to be so, and that the dimension of depth escapes us humans. The current global community wouldn't hesitate to view an insignificant person who has made no apparent contribution to life as a harbinger of great things and erect a statue in their honour in the Valley of the Roses, their sacred city.

**4-X**

The most exciting thing for me is riding their flying vehicles, the *linsens*. Today we went to Orta, an experimental nursery spanning a thousand acres, surrounded by elms, at the centre of which were six ancient marble seats. There we sat, in "our own living room" as Silvia jokingly called it. She now regrets having refused Andreas' love and affection in the past. She felt that, because of her, they had wasted too much time and missed too many precious moments. And on the other hand, look at the position I am in: she's opening her heart to me and I can tell her nothing. So I just sit there, answering mechanically and using the few things I know about Northam from Stefan to answer her. And, in the end, in order to escape her constant questions, I keep saying, "Silvia, believe me. I don't remember anything else."

I'm ashamed of myself. But Stefan told me a few days ago, "There is no other way for now. Remember, it was you who asked for it to stay a secret. But, apart from that, Rosernes Dal - the Valley of the Roses - has not yet reached any conclusion regarding your case."

## TRIP TO THE WEST COAST OF ITALY: AN ENDLESS, GLOBAL HOLIDAY RESORT

### Salerno, 6-X

We've only been here in the South since last night. We delayed it a little on purpose to avoid the huge crowds flocking here for the "summer celebrations". We're staying on the third floor of one of the huge hotels of New Youthsmile. We booked the whole floor because six more friends are coming. Among them is Diseny, one of the most famous young physicians, and the painter Syld, Aria's friend, a nice, quiet and modest blond man in his thirties dressed in dark clothes that contrasted with his blue, day-dreaming eyes.

From what I understood from the others' behaviour towards them, they must consider the physician and the artist as the "stars" of the group, but the latter seem to have no clue about it. They always talk in a simple, down-to-earth way about various things, but never about their work.

Seeing the west coast of Italy from above, I noticed that it is now, from one coast to the other, built with huge hotels that make it seem like an endless resort. The place names change every so often and in many areas they've kept the ancient names that now sound rather strange next to the newer and more poetic ones: Scarlet Rivershore, Seaside of Joy, Small Blomsterfor, Blue Lily, Diamondstones of Midnight, Resenfarvet. Yet, neither the form nor the consistency of this vast state changes anywhere; it stretches eternally into the horizon. There were thousands of gigantic palaces for travellers, but not a trace of residential homes or churches or institutions or schools and industrial and scientific facilities - only these huge hotels and youth centres (*larinters* and *civesheims* they're called), built between *quays* and parks, vast sandy beaches and harbours. Each of these palaces of the *Cives* - the citizens - was a separate rectangular building adorned perimetrically with a type of bright crystals that reflected the rays of the sun, gathered throughout the day. And they were so bright you could see them from the night sky.

The architectural styles varied, but the whole was perfectly harmonious. Yes, here I do feel like I'm in one of their largest urban centres. Even when I'm alone in my room, in complete silence, I can almost hear the hustle and bustle of millions of travellers visiting this vast, seaside resort every day.

**7-X**

And whilst here you feel the pure joy of life to an incredible extent - compared to our time - the things they do and the way they do them do not differ that much from ours. At sunrise, I saw thousands of people standing outside their gigantic hotels holding crystal mugs filled with water and fruit and gazing at the incredible view. Below us, in the courts and fields, you could see young people playing sports and ball games. Close by, at the parks and beaches, people were strolling, swimming and having picnics, exactly like us.

Silvia and I took quite a long walk. Stefan and Hilda were further ahead. She told me that for the first time, these days, she has come to know herself in all its depth. She discovered a kind of peacefulness inside of her that she never thought she had. I didn't know how to reply to that so I just clasped her hand and kept walking.

"I can finally appreciate songs! I can finally identify with their meaning!" she added. Even the changes of the seasons bring me an inner sense of joy. I remember I felt this only up until the age of fifteen. Then it disappeared. Until now."

I still haven't touched her, nor do I think about her naked body. We're both still in that first stage of deep and true love, where feelings manifest themselves purely in the heart and not in the flesh.

## THE ESSENCE OF SAMITH AND "DIRECT KNOWLEDGE"

### 7-X Again

### (After midnight)

In the evening, the whole group left the *linsens* behind and, walking through the pines, headed inland. There were fourteen of us in total. Around midnight and after the walk was over, the women of the group suggested that we go to one of the large terraces to watch the big dance performance from above. Silvia had told me that it would be impossible to find time for just the two of us tonight.

We joined the rest of the crowd that wasn't taking part in the happening and sat above the enormous dance floor, watching the spectacular and slow moves of the big, communal dance.

I whispered to Stefan that all this reminded me of a very unique ballet troupe, but he shook his head no. Shortly after, he explained to me the meaning of the symbolic dance and the communal silent prayer that followed it. He said that, if we were in the possession of the appropriate clothing, we could all take part. I believe that such a spectacle, such harmonious coordination and magnificence would be the utmost dream of even our top choreographers. Only in our time, this dream could never become reality.

The male dancers were dressed in black and the female ones had wreaths of flowers on their heads and wore the official silk, draped, monochromatic, floor-length *kjole*. They passed before us, each one with their choreographed moves, like a perfectly synchronised whole, offering me newfound, indescribable emotions.

They even engendered a feeling of pride and euphoria in me for being present at this unique, ceremonial environment that had, however, nothing to do with any official religion or religious coercion. The music itself spoke to you, the sounds, the dance moves too… You'd think they too were capable of feelings and nostalgia, just like the human heart. They spoke of true love, the kind of love that can make you sacrifice yourself... They also spoke about another kind of love, a love that can conquer time and make you live forever, for you wouldn't care about death or about yourself, just about the other person. They spoke of love in a thousand different ways, in countless tender movements and turns as if they had the gift of human speech!

On the other side of the terrace, which looked like an expansive square, a large crowd, dressed in the typical costumes of the *unge* - who always escorted important people - had surrounded an elderly man whose name, as I was told, was Nichefelt, and who was one of the most prominent painters of the time. "He has just come back from the Valley of the Roses," I heard people saying. Syld, the painter of our group, who used to be Nichefelt's student, said that the *Lorffe* had changed dramatically since the last time he had seen him.

It was time to go. "We'll come back tomorrow," I told Silvia before we separated. "It's worth seeing all of this again, just the two of us, isn't it?"

She smiled at me and nodded in agreement. Oh God, how many years this nod took me back! It reminded me of Anna; every time she nodded, a gentle breeze rippled through her hair. I confess with remorse, but this coincidental, instantaneous similarity made me think of Anna again. This name used to mean so much to me…

**8-X**

Stefan made me smile today by giving too much weight to a simple observation of mine on modern morals. I was quite upset that Silvia had gone off on her own despite having told me that we would spend the whole day together. Instead, she chose to sunbathe on a different terrace with the rest of the girls. So, the only thing I said was that in older times, people used to be closer to nature and enjoy the gentle caress of the sun, the air and the water all together - men and women.

Stefan said nothing at that moment. Lying on his back, with his eyes half shut and his muscles relaxed, he was enjoying the morning breeze as if he had never heard what I said. Doctor Diseny, who was also present, waited for a while to see if Stefan would say anything and then decided to speak.

"That is so true, my friends… We seem to have forgotten nowadays that nudity is nothing but the truth of nature. I wish we could go back to those blessed years when the world was ruled by the masters of Science. Every time I read those old books I remember how special and enlightened those people were, the ones who bequeathed us with all those perfectly organised laws and customs. Back then, young people looked at life in a positive and rational way rather than in a romantic one. And I wonder: have we followed the right path? Is this torrent of sensuousness and emotion the right way to look at life? I don't know… If you look closely at these girls who now run away from us like wild beasts, I'm certain that up close they would be as beautiful as paintings. But let's not share these thoughts with our friend Syld's teachers and the poets of the Valley, who managed to plant the idea of 'the charm of hidden beauty' in peoples' heads."

And it was with these words that Diseny left our company for a while. Close by, a group of teenagers, who paid us no heed, were taking a break from water skiing. Thousands of people had chosen the seashore as a place to rest and enjoy the wonderful breeze. Most of them were women, the majority of whom were wearing clothes surprisingly warm for this weather.

"I didn't want to start a conversation in front of the physician," Stefan said, interrupting my daydreaming. He leaned towards me so that we could hear each other and added, "But I could have asked him if, in those blessed years he feels nostalgic for, feelings had the same depth they have now, if they could reach the uniquely high level they reach now."

He spoke slowly, avoiding looking me in the eyes, and I had a hunch that he was being careful not to say anything that would hint at my feelings for Silvia. I was sure that he had figured out what had happened between us; but he was the only one, nobody else. But as I've said before, they don't care for gossip here, nor do they show it when they know something.

"Then he would tell you, Stefan," I said, "that it really wouldn't be a great loss if the world was deprived of all the pain and suffering of the heart…"

"He wouldn't say that," said Stefan. "No matter what he tells people, deep down he knows, like all of us. Like a real *Troende*, he firmly believes in the Volkic preaching. He couldn't, therefore, deny that the *Lipvirch*, this 'gentle illness of the heart' , as you once called it, is one of the main reflections of the *Samith*, as is pure religious emotion, art, the great ideals and eternal spiritual values. It is the legacy of our ancient civilisation and the old dream for universal love. And while some might support that the sight of a naked woman might not diminish the *Lipvirch*, 'the pain of the heart', historical data and past experiences suggest otherwise. Remember, Andreas, the female dancers, their divine figures and stature… I know most of them and I know that they don't only have divine bodies but also divine souls that are worthy of being loved to the maximum degree. Didn't they look impressive in their full-length *kjoles* under the moonlight? Syld, himself told me that looking at them revived some of the happiness that he used to derive from fairy tales when he was a child. Wouldn't the charm and majestic presence of these women be lessened if they lay down or walked around naked among us?"

I left Stefan without an answer. His words about the "reflections of the *Samith*" haunted me, reminding me of something similar that Silvia said the other day. I remember asking her, "Where does this whole thing lead? It's such a shame for our love to go to waste, not to last forever…"

The look of satisfaction on her face was beyond words! It was a mixture of joy and pride!

"Whatever happens, keep this in mind: it's wrong of you to say that it's a shame for our love to go to waste; this is the whole purpose of it! That's when you can truly call yourself blessed! This love has now become our possession, no matter what is to happen next. It's something that can never be taken away from us. It's a part of another life, of another world now; it's a part of the *Samith*."

I turned to Stefan and in a voice louder than I intended I told him, "Tell me, then, Stefan. Is this whole world with all its truth, which the physician talked about, just a microcosm?"

"There is no person that believes the opposite," he answered calmly. "And he's not wrong about what he said, that the nudity of a young and beautiful body is a pure truth of nature; but it's not the only truth and it's definitely not the greatest one. I told you that the *Lipvirch*, the pain of the heart, is a reflection of the *Samith*, the Great Reality we now know to exist; we're not making assumptions anymore, we know! So, nature, in turn, is another different reflection of the *Samith*. But the *Samith* itself is something superb;

much greater and much more powerful than all its reflections. Even today, if someone spoke to us about how extremely great it is, we wouldn't be able to conceive it. But nobody talked to us about it; we saw it with our own eyes! And that's our main difference."

We were sitting far enough from other people that no one could hear us. Stefan kept silent for a minute, staring far into the open sea. He looked moved but he carried on. "We saw it and that explains the, unknown to the older generations, feeling of immense happiness that has filled our hearts since then. We saw it thanks to the *Nibelvirch* - the supreme *Virch* - after thousands of tormenting doubts, many tears, many moments of moral weakness and despair, and after being prepared for centuries by the Valley of the Roses. And you cannot say that Alexis Volky was some demi-god who was the only one that possessed and could convey all this wonderful direct knowledge. He was a mere mortal like the rest of us; only, before him, the *Oversyn* was something unknown to the world. He was the first one to withstand the 'new vibration' that had proven fatal to many others; he was the first survivor."

Doctor Diseny started heading towards us right after Stefan had given his word that the next day he would bring me some books about the *Nibelvirch*, the *Samith*, Alexis Volky and the *Oversyn*. Oh God... I couldn't believe all the incredible things I had just heard...

**(Back in Stefan's mansion)**

**12-X**

**(Midnight)**

So that was it. No more sea. We all returned to Stefan's mansion yesterday morning and are already yearning to go back. They wanted to depart early in order to avoid the heat, so everybody arrived tired; everybody except me that I've now become accustomed to sleepless nights.

While on our way to the villa, Stefan talked to me about how tiring the lifestyle of those who currently live in the big urban centres is. It seemed as if he was trying to give me an explanation although I could never understand this kind of modest and apologetic tone he sometimes assumed when he spoke. Was it a sign of modesty? Or was it a sign of guilt for being one of the members of the majority who just "rested" after his two-year service? I don't know. But he told me that other people too, including the "*Cives* workers", often gave up their cities and lived for a long period of time in the countryside. It wasn't only a habit of the "unemployed". No one, he says, could live in the modern, massive and populous cities for ever.

Look at that! Who would imagine that I would miss my little room? I'm so well settled here that I've started to love this familiar table, the small orange chest of drawers of books, my deep and comfortable armchairs, my glass vases and my few other possessions - few, but clearly mine.

We rested a bit in the morning and then, as agreed, went for an afternoon walk with Silvia having told Stefan and Hilda that we were going for a tour above the lakes.

We flew over the old Bignasco, looking from above at the huge rectangular, crimson palace, the *Civesgard* that rested on the western mountain slope. I had seen many other buildings from above, in various places, but this one made a strong impression on me because of its bold colours that completely contrasted with the usual pastels that prevailed in this land.

From the terrace on which we landed, I could see the hanging gardens. It felt very refreshing and relaxing to be near them. Further away, on the horizon, young men and women in individual flying machines that resembled huge, mechanical wings were flying over and around the opposite mountains. I do not know why I'm so happy when I'm near her. Even this quick switch, from the sea to the mountains within a few hours, filled me with joy.

There are very few people, not even twenty, on this huge terrace and the adjoining large central hall with the immense aquarium. That's a tremendous contrast to the thousands of visitors on the beaches, with their shouting, their laughter and their games.

Suddenly, Silvia turned to me and said, "I think about those places, behind the mountains, and that there are more lakes there, just as beautiful as ours."

My heart was beating fast. The place behind the mountains was Switzerland. I didn't say anything; I let her finish.

"We'll go there, right? It'll be so beautiful. I don't know what happens to me, Andreas, but every time I travel to Switzerland, I don't feel any particular joy. I feel as always. But when I look at these places from a distance, only from a distance, I feel melancholic, almost nostalgic…"

I had said nothing to Silvia or even Stefan about my old love for Anna. Every time I talk about my old life, I am extremely careful not to let anything slip out regarding that person, as if she is a secret charm that I want to protect from any foreign, profane human heart.

Silvia's last words became a pretext for re-evaluating this discovery of mine. I feel like my old secret is still inaccessible and well-guarded in my soul and that nobody knows anything.

"So, what do these places remind you of?" I asked her.

"Nothing special. That's why I don't understand where this inexplicable melancholy is coming from. I was fourteen when I first visited these places," she replied while pointing to the snow-capped mountain ridges on the horizon. "And not only do I not have any special memories tying me to that trip but also, because I was in the awkward phase of adolescence, I remember dealing with a thousand worries and problems."

"And who tells us that, in another life, powerful memories did not connect you to this place?" I asked her, averting my gaze.

"Well, no one can know that for sure," she said without looking at all surprised. "Maybe yes, maybe no… Within the scope of the *Samith*, everything is possible. But we are humans, Andreas, and we will never know everything."

She seemed entertained by the conversation. The fact that she seemed to consider it neither heavy nor pointless, made me dig further into the subject, momentarily losing my control. "Do you believe, Silvia, that it's possible for a person to suddenly recall incidents from a previous life? Have you ever tried to?"

It was the first time I ever talked to her in this voice trembling with emotion, gazing into her eyes with an expression of love and loyalty, almost as if possessed by a divine inspiration. I then remember telling her, "Who knows? It could be that we just met again after being separated for centuries…"

At first she looked somewhat puzzled by my rambling on "memories of pre-existence", but soon she smiled with an expression of joyful surprise and eager acquiescence. "Do you think so, Andreas? That would be nice… But, I would prefer to remember everything that has happened to me in this life before I get to the memories of pre-existence. Because I think that there still are some incidents of my childhood buried somewhere in my mind. I'd like to remember those first…"

Obviously, her words did not satisfy me. They were somewhat irrelevant to my point. But I insisted, "What would you say if someone suddenly happened to remember incidents of a past life very clearly?"

"What do you mean 'what would I say'? I'd call it exactly what it is: a rare metapsychic phenomenon."

I was quite befuddled by this whole conversation, unlike Silvia who, as I said, dealt with it in a completely natural way, so I decided to change the subject. We kept on walking hand in hand in the woods.

I feel like our love is growing, day by day. The signs are too many to ignore, on both sides. We can no longer spend even a single day without seeing each other. Our loneliness grows heavier than ever when we do. As I had now read in the books that Stefan had supplied me with, one of the basic principles of Volkism is, for the *Troendes*, the "nostalgia of the *Samith*", "the pain of the heart", which is caused by the lack of it and which pervades the entire human existence without us being aware of it. In our species, this nostalgia presents itself in the form of "noble pain", such as the anticipation of a great and true love.

"A voice inside me," said Silvia interrupting my thoughts, "has always been telling me that there would come a day when someone would give meaning to my solitude and my sensitivity; so I had to wait. There were days when I sat, dressed up, in front of the mirror in the morning and thought to myself, 'Maybe today…' But I feared that I wouldn't recognise him, that I wouldn't be able to tell who he was. In the end I was right; it was you! Why did it take me so long to recognise you?"

She then started asking me questions about my childhood, meaning, of course, Northam's childhood, questions quite difficult for me to answer. She remembered the first time she met Northam, at the Tebelen, during "The Prayer of the Wildflowers". He was about to write his name on one of the windows, fogged up by breathing and she stopped him.

"I was so indifferent towards you back then… I think, though, that the first time I *really* met you, was in the Molsen institute, where I had come as a nurse, when I saw you wounded and helpless like a little baby. But enough of that. Now tell me one of these ancient stories that you like to read together with Stefan, the ones about the dashing princes and beautiful princesses…"

I started to tease her, saying that when she was young she must have been addicted to the *Reigen-Swage* and their three-dimensional spectacles. She admitted it. As for the fairy tales about princes and princesses, she has loved them since she was a child.

I have realised that these ancient, for them, stories exert a very strong appeal on the people of this contemporary Universal Commonwealth. In my view, the reasons why they appeal to them so much are the depictions of youth and beauty, fate and destiny, the ideal of "happiness", and all that combined with the extra charm that huge temporal distance gives. The notion of "political power", which is completely alien to them, is certainly not one of the reasons.

I talked to her about some of our great names, such as Goethe and Pasteur, and found out that she knew them very well. Then we wondered what the great creators must have felt while creating. This subject brought to mind the painter Nichefelt, the *Lorffe* we had seen a few days ago. They told me that, as a child, feeling the sacred flame within him, he had mythologised and idealised all the great personalities of the famous artists of the past generations. His dream was to be like them one day and the happiest day of his youth was when he was accepted as their student. If someone could have shown him back then the position he would hold thirty years later, he wouldn't have been able to bear such boundless happiness. For years he couldn't escape the feeling that his works were mediocre, no matter how much others admired them because they didn't meet his own expectations and couldn't quench the thirst of his heart. But there came the day, after working for decades, when he finally reached his much-coveted dream. Then, the already mature man, burst into tears in front of his finished composition. That work of art brought him recognition and endless praise from "the Palace Boulevard". The new *Lorffe* was then offered the same position that his teachers once held in the Valley of the Roses, but at a much younger age than them.

It was obvious by the way she talked about them that Silvia worshipped these truly great men. And as for Nichefelt, she strongly believes that he owes his incredible artistic creation to the thirst and longing for the *Samith*. She claims that if that longing did not exist, he never would have reached the point of artistic greatness that he reached. Everything seems to be connected to the *Samith*. I don't completely understand it yet. It looks as if it were their God, but then again it isn't. It seems to be the "source of everything".

"I wonder," I commented, "when he walked through the Palace Boulevard and saw your Sacred Arch, did he find the salvation he had been seeking for thirty years? Or perhaps not?"

"Of course not," she replied. "What he wanted to touch was untouchable… But he did enjoy it whole-heartedly."

Nowadays, the prevailing view is that you should authentically rejoice and celebrate the spiritual happiness that this era has to offer, for it is a gift! People need to think about how many challenges the world has faced and how many obstacles and dreadful dangers it has overcome. They no longer believe that it is temporal distance that embellishes things, persons and situations and what makes difficulties and problems fade away and be forgotten. They don't believe in psycho-physiological interpretations in general or, to be more accurate, they consider them very superficial; even shallow. They say that the '*Nibelvirch*' was what gave them the true, deeper explanation. Through the acquisition of 'direct knowledge', they saw the *Samith* and, therefore, the Truth. They clearly saw that that light didn't belong to this world…

She talks to me, thinking I understand everything completely, not knowing my true situation; and this confuses me even more. Sometimes I am truly myself and other times I impersonate Northam; for how much longer?

"Silvia, have you ever thought that I might disappoint you? That I might never completely recover, never remember and never regain my old self?"

"You know better than I do that I didn't love the old Northam," she said with a smile. "As for your research and your papers, they mean nothing compared to the person with this enormous heart that I have now here, in front of me!"

These words of hers had nothing to do with the words of hope and encouragement of the early days when she kept asking Stefan why I didn't try harder. I remember when, one day, Stefan caught her crying alone, following a discussion they had on whether or not it would be beneficial for me to go to Markfor for a course given by the very simple and understandable Astrucci, former student of one of their great educators, Gunnar Bjerlin, and continuer of his work in their educational institute. I think it's something akin to the special schools of our era, for people with mental retardation, something very demeaning for the old Northam. Stefan told me to go see what was wrong with her and, when I found her still crying, I clasped her hands, kissed her and told her, "I won't go if you don't want me to… I just don't want to see you cry… I can't bear it."

We arrived at the terrace around the time the sun was setting. At some point, for some inexplicable reason, all those who were sitting on the terrace, stood up and started heading towards the second balcony. Everyone had stopped talking and the only thing you could hear was the twittering of the birds. We hadn't yet arrived when Silvia beckoned me to go closer. We joined them and I was impressed by the religious devotion that characterised everybody's behaviour even though we were outdoors, not in a church. But suddenly, I heard a melody, a very familiar one indeed. "It's ours! Ours! Of our time!" I thought. I then realised it was a part from Beethoven's 9th Symphony. No matter how much time has passed, it hasn't been forgotten! I felt the need to say something to Silvia; a word, a name, something. But I barely managed to stifle a cry of joy inside me. Only a castaway who sees the vessel that will save him approaching, after days at sea, can feel the way I felt at that moment: a feeling of salvation and incredible pride. I wished that Stefan was there to tell me why, if such a strange barbarity characterised my time, modern culture now takes its works of art and turns them into prayers. "Listen, Stefan!" I would say, "This comes from an era that you call 'prehistoric'!"

The symphony played for quite a while. The dusk had already fallen, when I noticed the tear-filled eyes of two of the people next to me, who were devoutly listening as the prophetic words of the chorus faded out, words that cried faith for the great destiny of humanity, words that were written more than twenty centuries ago…

Froh, wie seine Sonne fliegen
Durch des Himmels pracht'gen Plan
Laufet, Bruder, eure Bahn,
Freudig, wie ein Held zum Siegen

*(As joyously as His suns fly*
*across heaven's splendid map,*
*follow, brothers, your appointed course,*
*gladly, like a hero to the victory)*

As soon as night fell, the environment around us changed completely. We were about to leave because we had told the group that we'd have dinner all together, when we heard the first young voices and saw the first bonfires on the nearby mountaintops and in the clearings of the woods on the opposite slopes. Little by little the songs multiplied and so did the fires and the phrase "The new *Cives*... The new citizens!" was chanted by every mouth. We learnt that thousands of young men and women had just completed their two-year service yesterday and would stay here tonight, in the "palaces of the foreigners". They had already put spare tables and chairs all over the ground and first floor and had made many preparations that we hadn't even noticed. If you looked around, you wouldn't find a single unhappy or dissatisfied person, as though everyone was possessed by the charm of the old beloved tradition. Even older people were singing along to a few songs they remembered from their time of service. The "partners" on the other hand, the future *Cives* - still children - bubbled with excitement, enjoying in advance the bliss of the "great day" which, for them, was due in a couple of years, but still, today it had at least interrupted the monotony of work.

The new citizens are burning their deep green, silken work-suits. The ritual will soon be over and several of these young men and women will spend the night at our *Civesgard*. But we need to go. As we leave, I see all the *gestels* together for the first time; these majestic hotels must number over 100 in the whole area. I hadn't realised how many they were during the daytime but, now, as I see them glowing from above, they look like an entire state of hotels that spread further than the eye can see!

## THE ESSENCE OF SAMITH AND THE GLIMPSE OF THE GREAT BEYOND

### 14-X

Stefan and I went for a one-hour walk in the Albiel forest, just the two of us. It was another precious day and the whole thing reminded me of my first walks in the company of Father Jacob. At the time, I was overcome by bitter scepticism and lack of faith. How many great and incredible things have happened to me since then! This time, I might have not had a very educated clergyman by my side, but then again, the people of today seemed to know much more and at a younger age than any of the educated men and women of our time; it is as if they are redeemed from doubt.

"Stefan, promise me that you'll take me to the Valley of the Roses when the time comes," I urged him in a warm voice. "I think I more than deserve to come with you. Please promise this to me! You know how much I've suffered… It's only fair that you satisfy my request."

My words left him a tad pensive. Avoiding my gaze, he gave no answer. I continued, "Think about it! Not even Jaeger would object to this. I remember his words: 'Trust Stefan; he will lead you through everything.' And then he stressed that I need to look more into the great spiritual paths that have now been opened to humankind."

"But who would object?" asked Stefan in complete honesty. "It's just sad to realise that you still believe that the *Nibelvirch* is a question of place and that the Valley of the Roses has some kind of magical power. You will be disappointed. Do you too think you're ready? If only you knew how many of us think we're ready and how few actually are…"

He then asked me, changing topic, "Did you take a look at the books I gave you?"

I had to tell him the truth, that is, that I had understood very little on the subject of Volkic Knowledge. It wasn't that their modern, rich in Anglo-Saxon and Scandinavian roots, universal language - a corrupted mixture of Danish and American, I would call it - was too difficult for me to understand. On the contrary; the problem was in the meaning and in the very specialised terminology mentioned in these books without the slightest explanation, as well as in a few completely unknown words of the old language used by the *Ilectors* of the Valley.

I was overwhelmed with enthusiasm and eagerness in anticipation of finally discovering this "knowledge", which I now knew existed and was widespread among people after so many centuries. That's why Stefan's words about my upcoming disappointment jolted me back to earth. I saw him looking at me initially with surprise and immediately after with a light-hearted smile, like an adult who's realising the naivety of a small child.

"Now I see how useless the books I gave you to read were. And it's normal to have felt and understood so little of what you have read. Did you truly believe that we have conquered the pure essence of these great things and have actually managed to make it our own? Do you belittle and undervalue the essence of the Great Reality so much that you would think that it's so accessible to our cognition and mental abilities?"

"It isn't *my* belief," I replied in a voice that faded along with my hopes. "Everybody shared the same belief in my time. And to think that the main supporters of this belief were the world's greatest minds of the era, who are still being cited and referred to nowadays. Each of these spiritual leaders analysed how the biggest questions about the world, life and the origin of God and reality could be explained. And they seldom agreed with each other. Each of them had their own interpretation. But there was one thing they all agreed on: that the substance and texture of the Great Reality is not impenetrable to human perception. The Indians, Chinese, Egyptians, Greeks and other Europeans after the Renaissance believed that they had found the explanation or, at least, that they were very close to finding it. And of course, everybody thought that their own theory was the correct one."

"You're right," said Stefan. He didn't say anything else for a while, as if he was contemplating the past. "You're right, that's how it was back then; and not only in your time but even for a great while after it, until the time of the first *Nibelvirch*, a couple of centuries ago. The world lacked so many wise teachings until then. But only when the *Oversyn* came, along with the acquisition of direct knowledge, did we realise that reality is so incredibly great that our poor perception and rational organisation and our 'antennas' in general are in no position to capture its essence."

"So the *Nibelvirch* didn't really offer you the knowledge of the Great Reality…" I murmured.

"The knowledge of its essence, no—only a 'superhuman' cognition could perhaps understand it or at least conceive of it. But it did offer us the knowledge of its existence in a direct and obvious way, completely different from the teachings of your time. And that's what ultimately rescued and redeemed us, putting an end to our metaphysical doubts once and for all. Because it's one thing to have people telling you and trying to convince you that something bigger than you exists, but it's another thing to see the light within you and feel its existence yourself!"

"So were we and all our teachings wrong about everything, all those years? Was no part of our knowledge right?"

"On the contrary; we consider them the first attempts of humankind to approach the Light and therefore we greatly appreciate and honour them! But all this surfaced only because of the *Nibelvirch*; it all originated from the nostalgia and the thirst for the *Samith*, as were the greatest works of art and all great human accomplishments. This thirst of spirit and soul for a godlike destination and proof of our superhuman origins is what makes us idealise and beautify thousands of aspects of our everyday life in this poor earthly environment: virtue, forgiveness, friendship, humanism, youth, beauty, justice, happiness, freedom, affection. The lack of the *Samith* is the deepest source of all great works of intellect."

And the truth is that man's destiny in our time was to be born, to love, to hurt and to die. Seemingly, at least. But because man's consciousness intuitively knew that something bigger was concealed behind appearances; it couldn't tolerate this explanation and rebelled.

"We could not explain it," I said, "and we secretly wished to have been born robots without the ability or the need to conceive of all these things since they are so alien and inapproachable anyway, so incompatible with real life."

"They're only incompatible in the poor and temporally finite environment of this world and life. But if nothing bigger existed, none of our thoughts and concepts like eternity, infinity or God would exist either. The innate mental propensity for perfection would not exist and neither would the Platonic world, Buddhism, or even Christianity - to speak in your own language. Acts of self-sacrifice such as Socrates' refusal to flee, the 300 of Leonidas or even the crucifixion of Jesus, never would have happened in human history."

I didn't want to speak or listen anymore. I had entered another dimension, a different, more empirical world of questions and answers. There were already far too many concepts I needed to contemplate. However, I felt that a gap had somehow been filled inside me, that many questions had been answered and many doubts resolved; yet more were born out of their ashes.

# INFINITY, AFTERLIFE AND THE ORIGINS OF THE ETERNAL IMPULSE TO DO GOOD

## 14-X Again

## (Late at night)

From yesterday's conversation with Stefan I saw why these people are concerned with the major "historic" cases of the least famous and low-profile altruist: unknown people who did not go down in history, such as convicts serving long sentences, who changed their inner world, or random parents with stories of incredible acts of sacrifice. People here believe that, although such acts haven't been registered in the collective memory of mankind through history, once recorded, they are equally as important as any famous act and that they haven't been lost.

Stefan told me that they had known about the sanctity of human suffering since the era of Christianity and that the *Nibelvirch* had simply helped them realise how significant this moral value was. I asked him his opinion of Christianity and he told me that it was a very comforting religion that worthily stood in for direct knowledge for thousands of years. His words made me feel very good and boosted my faith that had begun to falter with everything that I have seen since I woke up here.

"Not that we have now grasped the meaning of life. On the contrary; but even the fact that we know how indescribably great the reality objectively is, and the fact that we know it exists for everyone, sooner or later, is enough to free us and grant us salvation. The time-space continuum, you see, is not exactly as imagined by human perception. Infinity and the ever-present are one and the same. Objective reality is multi-dimensional. Numbers, matter, the spirit, individuals, ideas or infinity do not exist separately, but all together. If we could penetrate the true meaning of each of the aspects of the *Samith*, the Great Reality, then we would also feel God. We would be able to understand the purpose, texture and meaning of life. We would acquire a wisdom superior to that of humans. But that just can't happen, my friend... Direct knowledge, the *Nibelvirch*, showed us that the physical universe, creation, God, infinity and all these notions, are mere aspects, mere sides of the Great Reality. And there is a multitude of other sides, inconceivable to humans."

According to Stefan, after the *Nibelvirch*, man's attempt to reduce all phenomena of the world and life to a single "principle" has remarkably decreased. Now people see many aspects of reality as components of the *Samith*. He kept reiterating that only a small part of it can be sensed by our antennas. That's as far as our "knowledge capabilities" go. "I know, my good friend, and you understand how much more difficult that makes my life. My own antennas are even smaller than yours", I thought to myself.

I was, however, encouraged by the view that in the Great Reality nothing goes to waste and nothing is ever lost. Even if everything else is destroyed, our spirit will find a way to manifest itself - probably somewhere else - but what matters is that it will. Today, it is argued that the purpose of life is clearly the self-cultivation of the spirit - particularly for our species and for life on our planet - and that's as far as humans can go. As Jaeger told me, man's life purpose should be the steady upward course towards an increasingly spiritual culture. People will never understand the larger purposes of life, no matter what they do.

The big difference is that, nowadays, the anonymous hero, the martyr of everyday life is never forgotten and that's because they understood the sanctity of human suffering: the acts of love for your fellow man, forgiveness, patience, sensitivity, compassion and self-sacrifice bring the person one step closer to the divine. In their eyes, inner man is a whole new world. And that's because they believe that the real world lacks the secret of the almost symmetrical composition of the individual and the universe, the microcosm and the macrocosm, the aspect, that is, of the natural world, which is also one aspect of the *Samith*.

All this was not completely unfamiliar to me. I was surprised, though, by the fact that Stefan was talking in a way as if he weren't another simple person like everyone else, but as if he were standing on the other side, on the side of the laws of creation. Anna inadvertently came to mind again, the memory of our last meeting on the hill with the windflowers.

"Stefan, it has happened to me before, in my normal life, to hear a person speaking the way you speak, as if standing higher on the human scale than the rest of us."

He replied, almost offended, that he wasn't speaking from a position of superiority, but it was just that the human standards were higher and more enlightened now than in my days. I fell silent…

"It's alright. You don't have to say anything if you do not wish to. What was the name of this "precursor" that you came across? If we go to the Valley you may see their statue along with the others."

"No, no, she wasn't famous... She was nothing but a noble existence that died young and unknown."

This time we both stopped talking. Stefan was the first to break the silence. "Why are you so surprised by the way I think? After all that we have seen, how could we possibly think in the same old way that you did? Now we have a tangible reason to keep our soul more serene."

I couldn't help myself and said, "You mentioned before that nothing is ever lost. Did you see that too or is it just an assumption? What difference does it make for me how big reality is if I'm no longer here to see it? Tell me, Stefan, what did you see about the afterlife? Is there a better world beyond this one?"

"That's how it used to be divided and defined, I know: the past, the present and the future. But we do not divide it like that anymore. Now we know that life is one as is the world; one entity, one essence. Reality is fluid and the environment of our life, including us, is a small subdivision of the *Samith*. Reality is everything, and nothing that exists in it can ever be lost; and this certainty, as I told you, this inclusion in the *Samith*, is sufficient to keep us away from all the pain and past doubts."

He talked to me about the voluntary return to organic life, to fight again, to gain new experiences, to be challenged, to love, to hurt, to give ourselves unconditionally, to learn to do good, not because we have to but because we want to, because of an internal impulse. With all this as our tools and guardians, we can accomplish our mission and shorten the road to our godlike destination. "To some extent, we create our own destiny," he said verbatim, much like a theosophist of our time. He also talked to me about "the barrier of oblivion", which isolates this life from the knowledge and recollection of former ones. He then asked me how it is possible to not have heard, in our time, any teachings or interpretations that even vaguely resembled the principles of Volkic knowledge. I told him that there were a few similar views and ideas on the subject, but they were relatively tentative and too weak to be heard outside of certain intellectual circles.

He respectfully spoke of the great figures of the past, whom he described as "precursors". He mentioned the names of Pythagoras, Socrates, Plato, Aristotle, Jesus, several Eastern figures I do not remember, Plotinus, St. Augustine and Origen, Bacon, Descartes, Spinoza and Kant. From the 19th century he spoke of Engels and Kierkegaard, who are now considered among the greatest. Beyond that, he said the era of one-sided technological prosperity that followed and lasted for about five hundred years, created a climate that was not conducive to the emergence of great spiritual figures and teachings. The next names he mentioned were of some great intellectual minds of the Valley of the Roses and especially Chillerin from the Aidersen Institute.

I asked him again about the major differences between the new and the old knowledge - if what we had in our time could be called knowledge.

"The first difference," he replied, "is the spreading of knowledge. The Volkic perception of the major issues of life and of the world is not only localised in the intelligentsia or certain ethnicities. The people of today are impregnated with this knowledge and they believe in it so much that it has become part of their everyday life."

The truth is that I have observed several times that, even in their daily occupations, these people often incorporated principles from Volkic knowledge in a way that showed deep understanding.

"Then," he continued, "it has to do with the way knowledge is transmitted. Thanks to the *Nibelvirch* we have access to direct knowledge, which is free of any external teachings. And last but not least, compared to the reality that revealed itself to us through the *Oversyn*, all that had been said in the past by the formerly great mystics of religion about disappearing in our own spirit and becoming aligned with the divine seemed like children's words to us. We still honour them, of course, because they are the spiritual heritage of our ancestors. They had been alleviating human suffering until the *Nibelvirch*. Direct knowledge had to come for the comparison to be made and for the tremendous difference to show. Only the comparison to what really exists out there could demonstrate their childish naivety, and it did. But now, all this is only of historical significance."

Stefan stopped speaking for a few minutes, as if he were trying to remember what he had seen or read, trying to put his thoughts in order.

"That's how everything revealed itself. And that explains that horrific hit of the *Roisvirch* that, if you saw it all at once without being prepared, it scared you to pieces and which, at first, was fatal to thousands of unprepared human hearts. This sudden and impetuous torrent of such unprecedented spiritual happiness was more that the human soul could endure. They say that older generations could not imagine and believe how much objectivity there is in what we call 'spiritual worlds'. Back then, we thought that if the human race did not exist on Earth, then beauty, art, religion, poetry, philosophy and other moral values wouldn't exist either."

He stressed again how metaphysical the spiritual sciences ultimately proved to be. "Just as the man watching the dust and stones could not imagine the true composition and structure of matter, so too the spiritual world is merged with the material world in a transcendent way. It's just that our mind is too finite to comprehend it and our sensors are faulty. But this does not mean that it doesn't exist."

He stopped talking again and concentrated on his thoughts. "*Nibelvirch's* arrival brought to mind something similar that had happened in the past, concerning the awareness of the natural world. Two thousand years ago, around your own twentieth century, there was a boom in the natural sciences and their technical applications, a huge, unprecedented leap forward, within a very short period of time. One after another came the inventions, human knowledge was significantly upgraded and somehow the borders of the natural world expanded to an incredible extent. In a few decades' time they came to understand that the earth was, in fact, a nothing in the middle of nowhere, instead of the centre of the universe as they had previously believed. Something similar happened with Volky - though not only regarding the natural world

- and then we realised that the truth was completely different from the way theological tradition and the exact sciences presented it."

I sat and watched him and thought about how much faith these people have in them, how much they believe, not in our time's narrow-minded, absolute way but, instead, with an absolute certainty that what they've seen is right. I asked him whether he believed that people would have managed in some other way to obtain the knowledge they now have, without the *Nibelvirch*. He said that he seriously doubted it. He claimed that the gap between the knowledge of the past and that of the present was huge and the human mind couldn't cover the distance by itself. But even if somebody managed to see it or learn about it and then tried to convince other people, they would find it impossible to believe. They would first have to break free from the selfish, anthropocentric mentality that clouded their judgment; and this mentality was very difficult to escape from.

"But how was it possible," he wondered, "for men to believe that they and their planet, a dot in the universe, were the centre of everything? That they were 'chosen' by destiny among trillions of other stars, of other dots? Was it so hard to believe that, under any law of probability, there might be other major centres of intelligent life elsewhere, and that organic life and the famous 'law of adaptation' could exist in a million other worlds, older but more evolved both from a biological and an ethical perspective?"

"And how can this incredible greatness tolerate all this filth and injustice within it?" I asked.

"Precisely because it's so big, it easily accepts such pettiness. The worst human evil doesn't stand a chance before this blizzard of wonderfulness, trust me. Not to mention that this part, of sorrow and pain, directly related to our finite biological fate, gives us an element of reality, without which we would be incomplete."

He then took some time to explain to me that, in the time of the first *Nibelvirch* and the *Roisvirch* that followed in the world, Volky himself stood up and raised his voice along with the other great men of the era, because they had faith in the desirability and necessity of this progressive form of existence, and their words, full of peace and hope, managed to calm down the crazed crowds and stop the stampedes and the onslaught of collective suicides.

But in no way could I comprehend and accept what he was telling me. It was inconceivable: how can something so extremely wonderful have a part of it steeped in pettiness, ugliness and evil, and still remain flawless?

He asked me if I had had a chance to read Tinersen's book and I told him the truth: that I hadn't. It was one of the books he had recently given me and I hadn't managed to read it. The only thing I knew about this book was that it was approximately from the MCC century and that it was one of the hundreds of simplified and popularised books of Volkic Knowledge.

Once I replied negatively he started telling me an imaginary story, a kind of parable from the book. He told it simply so that I would understand it. And the story went like this:

Millions of small beings are born and die in a closed, dark, dirty place. This place, which for us humans is nothing other than the inside of a flute, is for these little creatures their whole world, their entire universe, their natural habitat and they don't imagine that there might be something else outside of it. Suppose now that they are endowed with an element of intellect and are aware of the ugliness and darkness of their world. Their very brief lives - about seventeen human minutes - flow monotonously, generation after generation; it is a constricted life of endless boredom.

Every now and then, however, some extremely distant echoes of a harmony, which they never could have imagined existed, reach their weak sense organs. And in surprise, the small creatures wonder where such wonderful harmonies could be coming from.

With the passage of time, some of these creatures, their "spiritual leaders", managed to see and feel that their dark prison was not everything and that their world was something minimal compared to the 'whole' that existed. Very few of these creatures saw and understood this at first and the rest of them considered the few crazy. But in the end, the existence of other worlds and realities became common knowledge and became a shared faith. These tiny little creatures finally realised that what really exists, objective reality, was far bigger than their dark world.

And according to Stefan, this is the most important point of the parable: "You explain to them that their natural environment is only a part of this Great Reality, this great harmony, and that it's even essential for its completion," writes Tinersen, "but it is impossible for them to believe it. They argue that there is nothing wonderful about this bit they live and this place they live it in and that it couldn't possibly be part of such incredible beauty since it would spoil it. These tiny creatures were unable to understand the meaning, purpose and mission of a life that is committed to the whole."

I'm thinking that these people have either reached a whole new level of knowledge and spirituality or they are in desperate need of a cure for their childlike gullibility. Nevertheless, I understand the joy and the incredible spiritual happiness that fills these people's lives. As Stefan reminds me all the time: "We don't just believe in it; we've seen it!"

Oh, how I envy them! How I wish that the *Nibelvirch* would come to me as well! Although I think that, no matter how strong my faith, I wouldn't be able to keep that happiness pure and unadulterated in the face of this reality full of suffering.

This is only a small part of what Stefan told me that night. The fatigue and the late hour forced me to stop. Stefan was very patient with me and didn't leave until a quarter to midnight. After he left I sank into my armchair. Once again, I had much to ponder; and once again, late at night, I got up and resumed writing…

# THE WORK OF THE AIDERSEN INSTITUTE AND THE SUPERIOR INNER LIFE AS A PATHWAY TO HUMAN EVOLUTION

## 16-X

If I'm not mistaken, the theories and principles that spring from the Valley of the Roses, the wondrous Rosernes Dal, bear the stamp of a newfound spirituality, unprecedented in the entire modern civilisation, a stamp of superiority compared to those of their previous cultural peak. Especially the Aidersen Institute, also located in their spiritual capital, has global prestige and a unique influence throughout the world.

Remarkable progress in the human intellect had also been made in previous times by previous generations. However, none of them can compare to the major leap forward that the Aidersen Institute made regarding the spiritual and intellectual path of our species. Up until then, for thousands of years, all the historical achievements were in relation to the psycho-spiritual abilities of a certain type of man. That's why, until the last years of the *Eldrere (their old era)* the spiritual journey of man moved more or less along the same lines. From our intellectuals to their own, such as Runerborg from the Valley of the Roses, *Lorffe* Esterling of Aidersen and more importantly Chillerin, the greatest, by far, of the Aidersen institute, our species had not changed. Human intellect, despite the different "schools" and views, had always headed in the same direction, a direction which was defined by the bio-capacity of our species - our biological fate.

The great accomplishment of the Aidersen Institute was that it opened up new perspectives for intellectual human history and, after long preparation, endowed mankind with a new "antenna", thus taking a decisive step towards the transformation of the old type of human being into a new, intellectually superior version.

It didn't create a superhuman, of course, but it did give us a significantly "advanced human being". Thanks to the Aidersen Institute, *Homo sapiens* gave way to *Homo Occidentalis Novus*, the current "enlightened man" of the *Nojere*, the New Era *(the Nojere started in 3382, on the 6th of September according to our calendar, which is when Volky survived the Nibelvirch. When the ascendance of Volkic*

*Knowledge was complete circa 3430 AD, this day was labelled the "start of a new era in history").*

The Great Men of the Valley had said it from the very beginning of the Valley's establishment, the very first centuries of its operation in the middle of the *Eldrere*: the superior human being is not going to be given to us by the computers or the brains of technology. We can't expect anything from the lifeless devices. If such an evolution ever occurs, they said, it won't be due to or by means of technological progress. If humankind ever succeeds in surpassing its very nature, that can only be done through our inner cultivation. Only this could ever make us capable of experiencing a superior inner life.

The noble and well-intentioned aspirations of these first great men were limited to this realisation. That's as far as their ambitions went. They couldn't see that there are vast realities, separate and unrelated to the human-inspired religions, worldviews, ideologies and discoveries; they had no idea about them. The new era, the *Nojere*, showed everyone that it wasn't reasonable to consider man as a "small, earthly God". True reality would exist regardless of the contribution of our own species.

I asked him if what we thought back in my day, that is, that in accordance to the anthropocentric version, humans, and more specifically their spirit, are the only species that regards both themselves and the entire universe as an object of observation. Everything else that exists in the natural world, whether animate or inanimate, is always the object of observation and never the subject.

"Do you not even acknowledge this?" I asked.

"Yes, we do. But the current philosophy considers this truth applicable only in the context of our planet, which, as you may have realised, is something minimal compared to the inhabited planets of cosmic space."

So what do the Aidersians argue? They argue that true objective reality exists independently of the sensory capabilities of each species. Its existence became known to the people of *Nojere* thanks to the *Nibelvirch* when they felt direct knowledge coming not from the outside anymore, but from within, if we are to believe Jaeger, Stefan and the rest. Therefore, the *Samith* proved to have this indescribable greatness described in the Volkic preaching. Thus, the

*Oversyn*, the "new antenna", was acquired, and everything that seemed transcendental before, had now been proven to be within the grasp of human capabilities. The scope of the cognitive capabilities of humans expanded, something that allowed the *Homo Occidentalis Novus* to see the *Samith* and accept its existence.

As for the element of spirituality, it doesn't only exist within humans. It is the wonderful fruit of long-term biological evolution, unrelated to natural forces. The acquisition of this element of spiritual entity is what unites millions of intelligent, rational and emotional beings in the universe. It's what unites the gifted, by destiny, species that are separated by astronomical distances from one another and which, biologically speaking, differ enormously from one another due to the natural environments in which each developed over millions of years.

Thanks to this element of spirituality, these thinking species, including ours, escape the confines of the nature that surround them and, with the passage of time, gradually enter into other, higher stages of development.

They gave me an incredible description of our species in the depths of time; I felt as if the whole history of humankind flashed before my eyes like a film. At first, they said, we were a simple part of the fauna of this planet. Once we eradicated most of our animalistic instincts, inner life and external culture began to develop. This is when the self-consciousness that now separates us from "the rest of the fauna" made its appearance.

After several stages of biological and spiritual development, humankind began to be possessed by an intense feeling of living in a foreign environment, by an inner need to find answers to its origins, a need that proved to be the source of man's greatest cultural and intellectual achievements. This thirst of the soul manifested itself through worshipping of invisible forces, capturing the secrets and laws of the physical world, depicting ideal beauty, imposing a moral order that regulates social life and through allowing justice, humanity, liberty and equality to prevail. They argue that the concepts of good defeating evil and morality defeating immorality are innate in humans. And the reason why people suffered was exactly because none of these "innate laws" was kept or respected. That's why people so impulsively pursued the worldly forms of the *Samith*; in the finite environment people lived, they dreamed of the infinite...

And when the *Nibelvirch* came, everyone understood why. Everyone understood where all this nostalgia and faith in something much greater and brighter stemmed from. It explained all the struggle and sacrifices of thousands of people for purposes that had no practical usefulness for them whatsoever. In a nutshell, as I understood it, the source of all spiritual cultures in the history of the earth is none other than the metaphysical, human suffering, the deepest bitterness of the human soul caused by the absence of the *Samith* in our world. That's how all the human achievements are interpreted nowadays: as efforts to overcome the barriers of physical nature and redeem the "real people" from this suffocating environment.

**17-X**

I returned this morning. I took Stefan with me as well. He was trying to convince me not to go, but I made him come with me to my old Switzerland, the place where I grew up. I wish I had listened to him; I wish I hadn't gone. There was nothing left to remind me of my hometown. In the place where my house should have been, there were now only piles of stones, ruins... There was no sign of smoke or light on the horizon, nor did you hear the sound of crying babies or voices of adults. They had given way to countless pasture lands with thousands of animals, all part of the collective of the partners. There was nothing more. Once I managed to find my bearings, I sat down on a rock together with Stefan, facing the opposite mountain slopes, the companions of my childhood heart; at least they hadn't changed in the slightest.

I quickly went back to my room. Silvia had sent me a message. Now, not only could I hear it but I could also see her through a screen; her eyes, her lips. She was cross for not having seen me for two days, but the sweet kind of cross...

We stayed in at night, listening to Liszt's *Hungarian Rhapsodie*s and two more wonderful pieces by one of their own composers named Wesley. I hope that in a couple of months I'll have a piano exclusively for me, and it'll be just like the pianos of our time! Stefan promised that he would do everything in his power to get me one. Yesterday I heard him talking on the phone with the *Consumfiorinin* and the Partners, who hold the archives in major centres around Blomsterfor.

## COMPLETION OF HIS RELATIONSHIP WITH SILVIA

### 22-X

Over the last few days my life has been a dream. Silvia and I have consummated our love! I constantly feel inebriated—that's how happy I am. There is a whole ritual around the sitatska, their purple, silk, wide ribbon which they stretch over dozens of flowers, which they've made sure to grow in abundance in the place. Following the ancestral custom of centuries, Silvia herself tied the ceremonial ribbon to the entrance. Before we entered I took one last look; it was as if I had entered a little paradise. And then…. oh God, thank you for allowing these hands to touch that divine body without taking away the magic from our relationship! I couldn't have imagined it better. It was the ultimate completion! Don't worry, my beloved, with me you will never regret it!

### 22-X Again

### (Late at night)

Her nod, however, once again reminded me of Anna. With Anna it hadn't even crossed our minds to consummate our relationship. And I believe that if it had happened, Anna would have burst into tears and I would never have seen her again. She would have thought that our love was tainted.

## TRIP TO THE NORTH: THE SUPERCITY OF NORFOR

### 5-X

I was unable to resist the temptation of a new, short trip to the North. Once we were there, I asked Stefan, who continued to be very patient with me, to go to the western part. I was attracted by the colours of the settlements. I think that at no time in the history of civilisations had the dream resembled reality as much as here. Lengthy platforms made of synthetic marble shed a white light along the lakeshores. Consistency in architectural design and evenly distributed blocks of mansions across the whole area had made my familiar sights unrecognisable. You couldn't tell Vevey from Clarens or Montreux anymore; they have all become one, or rather, have ceased to exist. A modern Babylon has taken their place, inhabited by millions of people if we judge by the innumerable mansions that almost reached the mountaintops.

There was nothing left of the age-old fortress of Chillon either. In its place, hanging gardens, scaly roofs, ball fields, hostels, *Civesgards* and *Civesheims* now spread over an area that would seem unbelievable in our era. And opposite, across the pond, were the eternal snows; the artificial air conditioning they had invented was not needed this far north. At the nearby lake there was an endless feast going on. I don't know if it was an everyday occurrence, but from above you could see its waters studded with hundreds of colourful sails for hundreds of kilometres - a delightful view to look at.

### 15- XI

It's been three days now since I've returned to Stefan's, and I've returned to my writing after this sensational week. We engage in new, interesting conversations even more often lately. You don't know what to expect here, from one day to the next. The long-planned trip to Norfor has now been postponed until the beginning of next week, though I was never asked. I seriously couldn't believe their haste or even indifference to a certain extent. I think they might have miscalculated the impact that sudden change of scenery could have on me. And of course, it was doomed to fail, considering what they had been expecting of me. They had brought me back within two days.

They are now forced to come to me to conduct their strange and pointless interrogation. This happened yesterday and the day before, when Jaeger brought two of the big names of the Valley to our villa, late at night, when everyone else was sleeping, just so that they could have the pleasure of hearing about the past in all kinds of detail. I did it just for Jaeger's sake in appreciation of all his help. If it wasn't for him, I wouldn't even have agreed to see them.

I had been dreaming about and looking forward to this trip to Norfor since I learnt about the existence of this "super-city" and heard people describing it as a "trip to fairy-tale land". Everything I had read about the position of this fourth largest city in the world, combined with what Stefan and Jaeger had told me about its great influence on global lifestyle, made me long for this trip to the so-called "Flower of the North" with fervent desire.

Apparently, I had to miss the forests, the lakes and the light for a few days in order to deeply appreciate the serenity and bliss they offer and to realise that I wouldn't change them for anything. It seemed obvious; it was not. The famous "Flower of the North" and even Skane and Artenfor, New Helsinburg and Riegen, Tholosi and the Garden of Lilies, Svendoni and the hectic city of Sgelen, and further south the Grand Torneo, the Lesley Gate and the Star of the Dawn, New Göteborg and the majestic Enole with its enormous old streets and palaces: all the current vast states of central and southern Europe, where Stefan took me from the sixth to the eighth of this month, are not for me. I do not fit in there.

I felt like my soul couldn't breathe in those colossal, overpopulated cities that looked more like states with their massive roads in the middle of which, despite their width, you could barely find an empty square meter or see a bit of sky, with all the flying or street-moving vehicles gliding every which way. It was the apotheosis of the titanic: a continuous hustle and bustle that drains your heart and dries your mouth. This explains why, sometimes, I curled up in the *linsen* and didn't want to get out even when we had reached our destination. I did not do this advertently and I think they realised this as well.

The first thing that disappointed me was the journey. In a large avenue of Markfor, on the outskirts of the giant, nearby garden city,

I was distracted for a few minutes among the crowds of travellers constantly going to and fro waiting for the *daner*. I was filled with joy, anticipating the vehicle that would take me to the truth of their city centres. How I had looked forward to this trip! Imagine my disappointment when, only a couple of minutes after departing, Stefan told me we had arrived! I thought he was joking! Was that it? Yes, that was it.

In every place in this world, blessed by God and nature, the further you travel, the more things there are to see. Here the opposite happens: you might get stuck between four walls made of colourless metal, but if the trip is short, you can see the whole world parading before your eyes. However, if you are travelling a bit further, the only thing you'll see is the place to which you are heading. In the meantime, you can spend your time walking around the facilities of the vehicle: the gardens that host rare flowers from around the world, the pools, the shot-put fields, the vast lounges and shops of the flying state, or you can just relax in your armchair, watching the latest news and current affairs on your *Reigen-Swage* or glancing at the young people dancing below the artificial light coming from the side, like a morning sunbeam that lengthens the shadows on the floor.

Norfor!

From the plateau of Vikingaand, which means the spirit of the Vikings, with its enormous *quays* where we docked, for the first time I saw before my bedazzled eyes a never-ending ocean of long boulevards and parks and alleys and squares and those, unfamiliar to me, gigantic buildings, which continued interminably up to the mountains and across the valley of Lyseblaa.

Holding Stefan by the arm, in the midst of a vertigo attack, I gazed in awe at this densely populated area that hosts twenty-eight million people, twenty-three of whom are permanent residents, and spanning the city a mesh of bridges, pitch black with all the people on it. And high up above, at an altitude of about three hundred kilometres, I could scarcely see the island-observatories, floating in the air, almost hidden behind the countless *linsens* that were incessantly coming and going. Stefan was trying to convince me that not only was this the everyday image of this city, that it's always overcrowded and ridiculously busy, but also that, beneath our feet, deep inside the earth, there also existed another gigantic, illuminated city, similar to this one, full of life and awash with a soothing, pale green light that greatly soothes the eyes and soul. Well, I could not believe that!

Huge streams of people, endless crowds with the same cheerful expression on their faces that every time makes me wonder if they have been given a gift or something. Frightened and bewildered by the crowd, I grabbed Stefan by the shirt to prevent him from taking me through the main road. Truth be told, I was completely at sea; my heart was beating like that of a frightened baby bird. Thankfully, Stefan once again proved extremely patient with me and let me look upon it from a distance.

In the crowd there were many young people with the badges of their universities sewn on their clothes. As time passed, I started to become more daring and joined them, getting the chance to observe them up close for the first time. What would it be like if I actually were Andreas Northam? These people might be in my circle… I was indescribably excited by this thought!

The very young, those in their early twenties, weren't yet characterised by the comfort in manners and kind naivety of the rest, which will become a habit to them too after a few years. They seemed as if still dizzy from the recent fulfilment of their "duty" and the early acquisition of the "*Cives* rights". It was as if their facial expressions were kept in place by a restrained pride that would soon give its place to the pure joy that comes at the age of twenty-three to twenty-five.

You could see them standing somewhat stiff and awkward in groups of two or three, not able to see beyond their noses, dressed in their university uniforms for the first time, with a serious look, unsuitable for their age, talking about their chosen fields of study or about the new professor - who, as Stefan learnt, was a very famous expert coming from the other side of the ocean to teach a summer course. And as expected, they were paying for their choice to isolate themselves with the indifference shown to them by the girls that passed them by.

The majority of the adults were in the company of others or with their companion. You saw all kinds of races: Tyrolean, Tuscan, Spanish women strolling gracefully down the street, wearing either the *skulderbind* or the *skaerf* of the North, and African women, whose complexion was fair, however, because, as I was informed, the entire black Continent was now inhabited almost exclusively by whites who originated from Latin America and settled in Africa centuries ago *(as a result of the nuclear wars that took place circa 2309 AD and the recolonisation that followed in the years after that).* You saw children from Cyprus and Malta staring in astonishment at the polar excursion advertisements on the big, self-luminous billboards. All of them had a purity and kindness, qualities that were difficult to find at these ages in our time. This is something that, in my view, is definitely connected to the existence of the "Source" that is now common knowledge among all people.

I was told that all of them have been taught history and are aware of all the different beliefs on the theme of love that prevailed in society in the past. They have heard about the sexual freedom that started from an early age and the materialistic upbringing of young children and they considered our time as "the dark ages". They believe that everything that happened back then in matters of sexual morality is not suited to the morality of their times. They were surprised by how primitive this era had to be to degrade love and intimacy so much by reducing it only to its animalistic side and portraying it as a merely sexual instinct. They feel that the value of relationships had been disgraced and that they had reached a very low level. They don't agree with the "scientific sexuality" of our times as they consider it superficial and deprived of the precious emotions of love and pain that a relationship with another person has to offer.

I think that these people wouldn't last a second in our world; they wouldn't have enough air to breathe. They're much more emotional and sensitive than us and face life with more admiration and more hope. They wait for the years to come with joy and immense faith. And mainly because of that, the intense eroticism of our time, materialistic pleasures like group sexual encounters and the sexual delirium of our ancestors in general, would be unbearable for them. They believe in "living life as a dream", and our lifestyle would most certainly spoil that dream.

The thing that leaves you speechless in Norfor is the massive districts-cities that, fringed with vast green spaces, succeed one another. Each of them is bigger than the Rome or Venice of our time. When I was there, I felt like I was a peer of Aristotle who suddenly found himself in an American metropolis. There was, however, a harmony and a balance between the quaint ambience and the incredibly enormous architectural constructions that surpass human imagination. College campuses surrounded by gardens, theatres, museums, libraries, and thousands of, unknown to me, institutes stretching for mile upon mile.

No matter how hard I strive, I will never manage to get the point of this vast metropolis or grasp its deeper meaning and that's because my soul lacks guidance and a preparation of whole generations. Unlike them, the voice of their ancestors doesn't echo in my ears and their spirit doesn't live in me.

## THE INTERROGATION: VISIT TO NORTHAM'S WORKPLACE

I think that my first contact with Norfor, that panoramic view of it from the hill of Vikingaand was the most comprehensive of all my impressions of this vast state. The very few days that I stayed there, Stefan looked baffled and distracted by the endless debates with Jaeger and four other foreigners. They actually seemed more like interrogations than conversations since poor Stefan had to answer everything and in as much detail as possible and give explanations over past "reports" on me and my case. So he didn't even have the time to show me around the city. I have the feeling that this whole trip was planned exclusively for these foreigners, so that they could satisfy their curiosity.

They made me spend almost my entire time in the scientific lab where Northam used to work, up until a few years ago. At least I felt comfortable in there and got used to it quite easily, so I didn't have to chase Stefan around all the time. They used to take me there after the personal labs of the researchers had closed and leave me for quite a while in Northam's long-abandoned office among the piles of his old papers in the event that I remembered something.

I spent many hours locked inside those huge walls of the amphitheatre. Standing in front of me with some kind of a notebook were the foreigners, taking notes and trying to make me remember. And the more it became obvious that these places reminded me of nothing, the more sceptical became the blond forty-year-old who was wearing the official toga and the *Tilteys*' belt, signifying his place as a mid-ranking official in their spiritual hierarchy. Both he and his companion, whose name was Stirlen as I heard, were unsuccessfully trying to hide their disappointment. This was in sharp contrast to Jaeger's kind, patient smile and to the serene expression of faith of the others.

On the last day, a few hours before departure, they brought me a young, pale and slim, grey-eyed man, around twenty years old. His name was Alex Wettel Smith and he had just come from the Baltic countries on Stirlen's invitation. Even though he looked tired, the second he arrived, he came and stood next to me, smiling and ignoring everyone else. I remember his name so well because I had heard that, without him, Northam wouldn't have survived the accident. The damage would have been much worse if Alex hadn't been near him. He had realised what was about to happen and in a fraction of a second he had thrown himself in front of Andreas in order to save the scientist he regarded so highly. He had just been discharged from the orthopaedic-surgical clinic on the shores of the Baltic a few weeks ago, where he had been hospitalised for months. It was a miracle that he survived. Yet another miracle…

Since the morning I had been hearing that the wise man with the toga and the other one, Stirlen, were basing their hopes on my "reunion" with Alex Wettel Smith. They were hoping that his image would work as a shock that would restore part of my memory since it was the last image that Northam had seen before the crash. Of course, he didn't remind me of anything… It was the first time I ever saw the man. They made him stay with us for over an hour and a half to talk to me about past incidents and that fateful trip.

Then, they asked me if I could remember among whom I was sitting directly before the accident. I reassured them that I didn't remember anything before waking up in the Molsen Institute. The next thing they obsessed about was my lack of sleep. They said it was impossible that I had been awake since then and kept asking me if, even for a couple of seconds, I had slept. They were pushing me to do my best to remember a dream, any dream I might have had, even the silliest and most insignificant one. I calmly replied to them that I knew full well that I had not slept at all, not a wink.

I realised that my case had become known to a somewhat wider circle over the last few weeks although only a few people had been added to the initial "insiders". If Stefan was being honest, not only had the Valley respected my request to protect me from becoming an object of curiosity in the eyes of the world, but also disliked the prospect of things related to my case coming out in public, especially since they still had no clue themselves about what exactly was going on with me. Moreover, this circle of "insiders" comprises very serious and positive figures, with sharp critical thinking and judgment, predisposed to being sceptical, who like to take their time and weigh everything carefully. These very down-to-earth people believed that it would not take long for Jaeger and the others to find out where their assessment of my situation had gone wrong.

There was even one person who had only been present at a couple of the discussions and who argued that my accent had nothing to do with an accent of a dead language, as Jaeger supports. In this man's opinion, it was the result of a post traumatic shock combined with the severe cranial-cerebral trauma that Northam had suffered and had nothing to do with "ancient German-speaking Swiss."

I also overheard Stirlen at one point telling Jaeger to stop looking in ancient times for the secret to my personality, but to start focusing in a positive manner on treating my amnesia so that I could unveil my personality once more. "We know that he is Northam, now we must convince him to come out of the world into which he has locked himself in order to avoid facing real life after the accident."

I realised that they were discussing a possibility similar to what we would call "split personality" or "personality change" and they support that Northam is still alive somewhere inside me. They think that my memory has been locked at the point of the accident, like a metal door that's blocking the way of the rationale, rendering it impossible for me to remember anything from the time of the accident and, obviously, all that preceded it.

Nevertheless, two of the wise men, Esterling and Erlander, kept speaking of some sort of "out-of-body knowledge and experience". I heard them mention the term "out-of-consciousness memory", although, unlike Jaeger, they've ruled out the possibility of reincarnation.

On the other hand, the version of another wise man, Valdemar Esklud, was completely opposite. He believes - and he truly poked and tired me these past few days - that if I make a real effort I might remember moments from the first days of my short illness back in 1917. I was vainly trying to convince him that my memory has never betrayed me until now, and that I had never remembered anything from those two weeks when I first fell into the lethargy.

However, he and Ms. Coiral with her silver hair and her heavy, ebony cane with the platinum handle, were the only ones who respected my outburst into tears and didn't start shouting at me when I revealed to them my firm conviction that one day, I will return to my time and place, even if it's for a few seconds before I die.

Apart from that, Esklud and Coiral lean more towards Jaeger's view, that is, that they are witnessing one of the most unusual and rarest parapsychological phenomena - or "metapsychic phenomena" as others called them" - that has ever manifested itself with an unprecedented clarity of memory and remarkably heightened sense of consciousness.

As for the information they asked me to give them, I was surprised by the fact that they were more interested in the conditions of our everyday life, our way of thinking, habits, institutions and beliefs, more than the great wars or political events perhaps because they knew the latter very well from history. And what was of particular interest to them was the century before ours. They always led the conversation to that topic. And what intrigued them the most was not the man who lived in 1921, but the man who was in adolescence at the changing of the century and learnt about the recent past from school and books. As a matter of fact, they explained to me that the 19th century was marked as a "suspended century" that stood out between the previous and next several centuries. Especially the end of the 18th century and the beginning of the 19th, was for them a very unique era, that harboured many precursor figures and works that could even be argued to be equivalent to the ones of today.

More specifically, the fact that the ideas of freedom, equality, brotherhood and love for nature were introduced and nurtured in that era drove them to distraction! They spoke highly of the struggles of the nations for true liberation and freedom and, of course, of the peace pacts of Europe.

The events of the 20th century did not seem to excite them very much, nor did the Great War, which I hope is never repeated *(Dienach is not aware of the Second World War and most probably, the people of the future did not inform him of it, thinking that he might return to his 1921 self)*, or the huge losses that the nations worldwide suffered. They didn't know how many people swore to give their lives - and did - so that at least their children could live better and free… I did…

I realised that the passage of time and everything that has happened in the last 2000 years up to their time made them forget all those watershed events that once shook our own lives and changed the course of history. Past leaders, who went down in history as saviours of humankind and whom we considered immortal, are now characterised as “petty people”, “unworthy local leaders”, “opposed to commonwealth and progress of our species”, “deniers of culture” and “anti-humanists”. And I am speaking of leaders who, for decades, played a significant role in history. The only things they asked me when I told them that I was Swiss, were, firstly, if I knew any details about a global child protection organisation, based in Geneva, and secondly, if I had ever met any of the two famous “Alberts” of the era, Schweitzer and Einstein, or Bertrand Russell and Bergson. The latter is considered as another precursor here, since it’s because of his observation on tuition that they managed to “see” the prophecy about the *Nibelvirch*. The same goes for Maurice Maeterlinck and “Blue Bird”… They claim to have seen the true “Blue Bird”...

The last memory that Norfor left me with was also the best. I said goodbye to Norfor by visiting the old town of Blomsterduft that had kept its old institutes and its alternating fields of green spaces and tree-lined streets, where you could almost feel the ancient Scandinavian spirit floating in the air you breathed. It was one of the few areas of the former Norway and Sweden where some national memories had managed to survive in this most devastating global melting pot of their times…

One of the first things done by young students who come to Norfor from all over the world in the millions is to pay homage to the old city, the cultural hub of their ancestors for 32 generations. Every nook and cranny is a memento of their culture of the last few centuries. As I learned, two great teachers from two-three hundred years ago were called Holberg and Eilensleyer and the traditions these two spiritual figures left behind have not faded in the least.

If the Valley of Roses - which is not even a quarter of the population of Norfor although the two places cover about the same area - is today considered the “Heart of the Earth”, Norfor, starting from Blomsterduft is the “Ark of the Spirit”, according to Stefan and Jaeger, because of the direct link it had to the development of Western civilisation, giving Europe a place next to the North American and South African cultural regions that for hundreds of years had been the centres of spiritual culture, from California and Florida to Boston and New Orleans, Cape Town and Pretoria.

## PRIVATE MEANS OF TRANSPORTATION AND THEIR OPINION ABOUT WORK

### 17- XI

On our way back we travelled through the western, coastal Alps to another state that was unknown to me, which was awash with an artificial pale white light, with palatial buildings that continued in endless symmetrical rows up to the Mediterranean Sea. We went down avenues at least one mile wide. I only managed to take a quick glance before we boarded on our individual means of transport heading back to our villas. While we descended, Stefan showed me a vast complex of buildings that looked as if made of children's toy blocks, strewn across the whole country. At first I couldn't understand what it was but I remember thinking that those blocks must have been of immense size. Stefan explained to me that we were flying above the production centres of Ragrilia: an entire industrial city, one of the largest in Southern Europe, with colossal production units where millions of enthusiastic youngsters worked nonstop in shifts.

People of today know that the existence of industrial states such as Ragrilia was a prerequisite for the existence and maintenance of Norfor, the Valley of the Roses and their other spiritual centres. They are well aware of the fact that these huge state production units with the endless electronic devices are the foundation of the current spiritual culture.

"The fact that we live in such comfort, that we have plenty of free time for inner cultivation and that freedom and happiness are now truly possible is owed to these states," Stefan had admitted.

And just like Stefan, they are all convinced that there is no likelihood of humans returning to their previous condition. They believe they are now on their way to writing true history and that no generation will ever allow this incredible social edifice crumble again.

"We've paid for those mistakes too dearly to make them again. Rivers of blood and tears were shed in order to escape the mire. People will not return to living in hunger or being exploited by other people ever again. You might not have given enough importance to those things back then, but such history of pain and shame has not and will never be forgotten by us."

I told him that such extreme situations in our time were rare and not a daily occurrence as they may think. He shook his head incredulously and told me that I had to admit that during the "prehistory"-my time- *(people of the future consider the time before Eldrere, that is 2396 AD, as "prehistory")*, rationality was completely absent in social and economic life. And he knew much, so much that he put me in the difficult position of becoming an advocate and an apologist for our era.

But there were also moments when he spoke with pure naivety, telling stories with amazing plots and exaggerations about arms manufacturers and landowners who took tall and blue-eyed European women as "loot".

"Just like the old barbarians of the North, who once drowned Europe in blood, so did your own barbarians lack any moral, spiritual and aesthetic values."

The pride that people of today took in the current situation was evident in Stefan's every word. "Don't think that the individual *linsens* or the privilege of not working again in your life after nineteen years of age were always a given," he told me. He then explained to me that it all started on a winter day of 427 of their new calendar *(in 2823 AD of our time)* on the ground floor hall of the Binenborg Palace, on the eastern side of the large central square, when the four leaders of that decade were the first to accept the free individual means of transportation of that era, which they would, from that point on, always have throughout their professional and private lives.

It was then when one of them, Torhild, a leading figure in natural sciences and later governor and leader, posed a symbolic question: "Aren't the people with disabilities or other problems going to need them more than us?" The rest then assured him that everybody had already received their own means and that there was no shortage anymore...

Stefan, evidently moved and excited, paused for a second and then told me, "You can't imagine what moral satisfaction you derive from working for the common good instead of individually hoarding or putting money aside so that your grandchildren can enjoy the boredom and tedium of not being able to find a purpose in life."

What could I say? I admired their amazing system that allowed them, with only two years' service, to secure the rest of their lives. I asked him why, however, they did not raise the service to five, ten or fifteen years to provide them with even more wealth.

"Because our life's objective is not untold riches," Stefan answered. "One is wise when one knows when to stop. And trust me, it is not always easy to tell where sufficiency and comfort stop and absurdity and extravagance begin... We don't need excesses. Our goal is to never be accused of putting barriers in the spiritual way of the *Cives*, the citizens. The job of an industrial worker for example doesn't satisfy any innate need of the human soul. Hard work is not a need of the heart; it's nothing like scientific, artistic or intellectual creation. We consider it as a new individual right for the born scientist, artist or philosopher to be left alone and unencumbered to create."

"That's no excuse," I remarked, "to leave the *glothners* in the hands of those kids, especially when you know how much better production would be if left in the hands of more mature people."

"There's no need to fret about that. The current partners are much more mature than you'd think, considering their age."

His last words reminded me of an observation I made regarding these people, everywhere I went, since the first day. On the one hand, these young people seemed to have an admirable maturity that I wished our adults could have. On the other hand, however, all of them, adult men and women, sometimes looked and behaved as "big children".

I was thinking that if I managed to learn how exactly they achieved abundance in consumer goods and means of transport, if I could find out the details about the service plans and the method of enlistment, their universal confederation of trade unions, the commonwealth of the *Cives* and their rationalistic institutions and could return to our time one day, we could implement all this as well. But first we'd have to transform humans, build them from scratch. Because here, for the last centuries, there hasn't been a single instance of one person approaching another person with the purpose of benefiting from them or exploiting them for any reason. This phenomenon has vanished from their interpersonal relations. And I'm ashamed to admit it but, in the beginning, even *I* happened to take advantage of their naivety in order to make exchanges that would prove beneficial to me. I would achieve any exchange the way I wanted to, in less than two minutes, by first showing excessive enthusiasm about something of theirs and then appealing to their friendship and good nature. The thought that I wasn't being completely honest, never crossed anyone's mind. Then I stopped doing it.

You could easily do them irreparable damage by taking advantage of their naivety, but the most terrible thing is that, afterwards, they wouldn't talk about the damage or try to claim responsibility; they would just wonder how there could be so much cunning in the world, and how their love and honesty was repaid with such malice.

One day I asked the Office Partners of the sector of technical resources for a second *Reigen (a 3D screen)*, claiming that I had lost the first one. The next day they sent me a new one without even checking if I was telling the truth and without verifying the order or the serial number.

The Valley of the Roses itself gives directions to the *glothners* so that there is abundance and variety of consumer goods in order for the *Cives* to have the privilege of choice, but only for the standard goods. The officials of the spiritual hierarchy, however, even the *Tilteys*, are entitled to personalised products and can make specialised orders. As for the sufficiency of the products in number, it is ensured by statistical demand; the types, variety and quantity of production are determined by the previous year's statistical data gathered from the consumers.

## TROENDE: THE NEW HUMAN BEING

Stefan doesn't know anything about my aforementioned behaviour in the beginning of my stay here, and in any case, it is a thing of the past. Their childhood purity of heart and mind is so moving that it makes you want to be like them. Their intellectual and moral purity and clarity has such a power to relax and alleviate me that there are times when I feel love for the whole world... They don't suspect anything bad about you and you, in turn, feel the need to get rid of even the slightest ugliness inside you. In their eyes you look so much better than you really are and that urges you to actually become better. They see so much sincerity, love and selflessness in you and something inside you makes you want to justify this idea they have for you, as much as possible.

That's how it is: the current *Troende*, the man of the new era, is a social and psychological type of human, successor to the human-robot, the "practical man", who wore the blinders of his daily struggle for survival, who was always on the verge of anxiety, deprived of any inner life and free time look after himself or nature, the man-product of the soulless techno-culture, the materialistic man of the era of mechanistic philosophy that was completely out of touch with any spiritual foundation.

Furthermore, now they are also capable of distinguishing the intellect from the soul. Today, more than in any other moment in the history of mankind, the spiritual culture burdens the consciousness of the contemporary man, regardless of the achievements of the intellect, knowledge, scientific and technological progress.

But the most surprising difference between the old and the new social history is arithmetic; the *Troende* is now the most common type of social man worldwide. Here, the commandment of "love thy neighbour" is the prevailing way of living - it is the rule not the exception. These people have managed to turn the "unbelievable" and the "impossible" into the "possible" and "real". They are following the preaching of Christianity without being Christians.

## SEX, MATERNITY, RELATIONS AND THE ESSENCE OF LOVE

### 25-XI

Lately it seems that someone has cast the evil eye upon our group and two out of the four couples have split up. Axel and Juliet, who appeared even more in love than Stefan and Hilda, after a lot of whining and misunderstanding, decided to go their separate ways. Nobody knows what the exact causes of the separation were since nobody here talks about them. They were probably too young for a long-lasting commitment. After a short farewell party, in between sobs and laughter, she left, heading north. Shortly after, Axel left too. He first went to Sicily but was planning on leaving after two months' time to continue his violin studies.

A week ago, Aria broke up with Eric with unexpected and remarkable determination and went to live with her folks in her second homeland, Norfor. This separation was seemingly sudden. For a long time it was obvious that their cohabitation and coexistence wouldn't last long. They split up in a completely civilised manner and with a few clear words.

We went to see Eric on the first night after Aria left and we kept him company for hours. He felt sad that he couldn't keep her and he said that he had always known that if they ever broke up it would be on her initiative, as it eventually happened. He accepted it, however, with a relaxed and slightly sad attitude and lack of cheerfulness.

"I wish I could have made her happier," was his last sentence.

As for me, I was still staying at Stefan and Hilda's and near them I was experiencing every day the one thing I had truly missed in my life: brotherly love.

Even if we had lost our two friendly couples, our meetings with our wider circle did not dwindle. Quite the opposite, in fact; the high temperature of the past few days made Stefan take a break from his morning occupation for a while and now he very often takes us on one-day trips to the swimming pools of Mendrisio, the flower gardens of Verbania, Lake Lugano, Bellinzona and other times to the coasts of the Italian Riviera, west of Genoa.

Now, as far as Silvia is concerned, she hadn't come to our meetings in a long time. She said she wanted us to be alone when we met. Both Stefan and Hilda were now aware of what was happening and so, with tear-filled eyes, I confessed everything to them.

They were very happy for us and told me that we made a great couple. I told Stefan that we were planning on going to the Pyrenees for a few days and he whole-heartedly agreed that it was a good decision.

We then talked about how frequent an occurrence "love" was in their age and he told me that the majority doesn't experience it more than once in a lifetime, or even never, on some rare occasions. I asked him if they consider love-making that isn't a result of love as unethical. He replied that in no way do they consider it unethical, but it cannot be compared to the true union of love, which is a bit like the *Lipvirch*. During the old days, throughout the whole era of the *Eldrere*, when the sense of the *Lipvirch* was still non-existent, physical relationships were based solely on the attraction between the sexes and the assessment of character. But even back then, just like now, many changes of sexual partners weren't applauded. Then they were more interested in liking the person; the tenderness and spiritual bond came after the natural attraction and appreciation for the human being, whereas here, during the last few centuries, the Valley of the Roses has been arguing–even if some of the *Ilectors* disagree–that abstinence, especially when it's a conscious decision, increases spirituality, something reminiscent of the ascetic principles of our times.

Overall, they no longer see love as a battle in which the most cunning wins and the most naïve loses, but as an alliance between equals, without secrets or ulterior motives, an alliance that provides you with the necessary peace of mind to live your life.

"So your morality is only opposed to the very frequent changes of partners," I remarked.

"Something like that. Too frequent changes are neither common nor applauded in our time. The balance always exists. But ethical issues aren't always generated by these changes alone" Stefan replied.

He asked me how I would think of Juliet, for example, if now that she has broken up with Axel, she found a new love and went to live with him.

"I'm not referring to a couple of random instances," I replied. "What would *you* think if you saw her spending her whole youth changing partners every six months?"

"Even then," he said, "we wouldn't consider her unethical or socially inferior. One could characterise her as careless, unlucky, frivolous or very much unable to tame her urges. One could argue that she'd be better off being free and living alone. In any case, if she didn't have any intention of fooling anyone, her way of life wouldn't be considered antisocial or immoral. Besides, look at all these young men and women who live alone and seemingly unmarried –and who have officially been *Cives* for decades now. Does anybody know or has anybody asked them how often they change partners? They may socialise with each other and speak in front of others with the utmost dignity as if nothing is going on between them, but that's not always the case. And of course, I'd be the last person to blame them. It is not a matter of hypocrisy but a matter of moral superiority of people who do no evil, but, by nature, are not yet capable of making permanent unions. Nobody here goes about revealing their secrets. But I can't really argue that each and every one of us waits for the *Lipvirch* patiently, for years and years."

"Is there something that you do consider immoral? Are you familiar with the concept of immorality?"

"Of course! And whatever is truly immoral is exemplarily punished. In such instances we're firm. But it's just that they're so rare. The people of today get a certain satisfaction from being ethical, without being forced to feel that way. Unlike you, who, if I remember correctly, had a saying that said "the forbidden fruit is always sweeter."

"That's easy for you to say," I replied somewhat miffed, "since essentially nothing for you is forbidden."

"You're wrong there," he responded quietly. "Our society also has certain moral restraints. If, say, when Juliet was living with Axel, she secretly met with another man, that would be considered immoral. But neither Juliet nor someone much more flighty than her would do something like that. All she would have to do is tell her partner. Why should she hide it? People tell each other how they feel and whatever the outcome - acceptance or separation - they have told the truth. In fact, most of the time, acts such as these are forgiven, especially if it's an infatuation, a moment of passion or a loss of self-control. While, if they hide it, things become complicated and people are plagued by a guilty conscience, which in our times is very difficult to handle."

I was wondering where he was going with this and very curious to find out.

"Never would a woman be with a man, or vice versa, out of self-interest, just to benefit from them later and not out of love or strong physical attraction," Stefan said. "Dishonesty is inexcusable and unforgivable. What we want most is to have a calm heart and a calm mind, far from moral uncertainties like jealousy, suspicion or fear. On the other hand, our leaders have put up stricter ethical barriers for young people. Normally, until they become *Cives*, they're not allowed to have sexual relationships. And it's incredible and of great significance how the *Ilectors* succeeded in establishing the concept of sexual abstinence in the minds of young people at the both tender and difficult age of nineteen. Today, a partner should appreciate directness, love, honesty and respect some moral values - even if it is with some deprivation. The service is therefore simultaneously a test of self-discipline and of sexual abstinence. Only a few violations occur each year and, of course, there is no penalty."

I asked him at which stage of life a woman decides to become a mother.

"I couldn't possibly answer that accurately. The same as in your time, sometimes sooner, sometimes later. It depends on their temperament and on luck... There are many factors involved. Our case with Hilda is among the most common. Most of the times it takes three to four trial partnerships, born either from the *Lipvirch* or from strong attraction in order to find "The One". Usually the first partnerships are shorter and may not even last year. Then they become more stable. With a little luck, three or four switches between freedom and cohabitation with someone are enough for the person to acquire a more mature mentality, which enables experience and knowledge to do their job and maybe give their later relationship the form of a lifelong bond."

He then spoke so derogatorily about our time and its "values": adultery, lack of straightforwardness and loyalty, everyday dishonesty, fraud, prostitution, the exploitation of weakness and poverty, perversions, violence, crimes of "honour" and sick passions. I didn't know where to hide. He even considered the wedding ceremonies of past times as indecent: the gathering of the people, the fun, the comments, the teasing and… well… what came after: the more intimate moments of the couple.

"Our conscience and our innate moral compass complement the gap of those abolished institutions very efficiently and so, every partnership and cohabitation is based on and defined by pride and honour. Whether a great disappointment, a new love or unbridgeable differences in beliefs and characters can sever the bond is irrelevant. Besides," he concluded, "didn't the same thing happen in your time, regardless of legal limitations?" I had nothing to say.

I then asked him what happened the first night that the partners become *Cives*-citizens. That must be the night when they totally go wild, I figured, and reasonably, after so much restraint. I was wrong.

"That is indeed what used to happen… Several hundred years ago, though. Physical attraction still played the most important role and that night was seen as the call of nature for the young. But it's been a long, long time since then. Things have changed. I'm not saying that nobody makes love that night, but those who do are mostly the couples who met during their service and decided to consummate their love on their first day as citizens. The vast majority, however, doesn't. Some wait months, even years, until they find a suitable mate, long after they burn their white stole, the symbol of their purity, on their night when their service ends."

Stefan stared into space as if pondering the past.

"I, too, had a night like this, you know…" he said. "Such a thrill! On the one hand the whole world is opening in front of you that night, and on the other, you finally become entitled to the magical sense of love-making. Unforgettable years…"

His eyes filled with tears. I was startled. He continued, obviously moved. "Even that song that we sing that night means a great deal to me… to us... All the inhabitants of the earth have been singing it for over thirteen hundred years. We all learn it at school, boys and girls. I know that it hasn't got great lyrics but still, have you got any idea how that simple and somewhat flat old melody echoes in our ears, in our souls? Have you paid attention to the lyrics? 'In the light of your nineteen years, the swallows come and the flower buds opened early'. Or the other one; 'Life's a rosy dream that now begins. Sing it'."

He was now speaking with utmost enthusiasm. I didn't interrupt him of course. "A relatively few generations after yours, after the puritanical movements began to disappear and Flessing and Kirchof found the remedy for your terrible illness, the nightmare ended and things started to change in the way in which parents spoke to their children about love and sex. There was no longer need to speak to them about risks and precautions. Instead, they spoke to them about the anticipation of a great happiness which, if they were patient enough to wait for the right time and the right person, would be theirs to enjoy - in moderation - for the rest of their lives.

As the generations passed, the idea that this level-headed, ethical and unmarred happiness is better to come after the fulfilment of duty, became part of their social awareness. That was after the service had been considerably reduced. That's when they started giving the white stoles to the adolescents. In fact, they were told: 'No one will force you to fulfil your two-year service in the *glothners*. If you refuse there is no penalty. Just consider that the Universal Commonwealth needs you.'"

And indeed, as Stefan told me, no one left. And that way they corrected the injustice of our time that associated the "fulfilment of duty" with retirement, which came at an age when happiness could not be bought with the finest gold.

They considered the age of fifteen as the key stage in one's life. They believed that it was then when the new horizons in human esoterism are opened. It was then when everything changed in the eyes of a person since, from that point on, the soul took over and saw things differently. In fact, he told me that "the eyes start to well up more easily".

I told him that if they think the same didn't happen in our time as well, they were very much mistaken. He answered me that he was referring to the rule and not the exception: "The exceptions don't define an era… the rule does."

"Yes, but you just told me that the limitations helped in our time because otherwise the situation got out of hand and reached the point of promiscuity. You said it yourself that we needed restrictions since we were 'practically uncivilised'."

"Sometimes I'm under the impression that you and I cannot communicate, that we don't speak the same language. And yet that's normal since we come from different eras, different cultures, and different ways of thinking. I wonder how much of what I'm telling you, you truly understand. You talk about 'the justifiable' and 'the necessary', without thinking about the effect they all had on humanity, regardless of their appropriateness at the time. They had created for you a world that was surrounded by a grey sky and inhabited by dead souls. Did you ever think about how many innocent people of the minority had been constantly - and for thousands of years - paying for the laws designed by the majority, just because your leaders couldn't enact individual laws? And are you sure that you'd be truly happy in the absence of laws and restrictions? Or is there something else to blame for your unhappiness; something deeper, something hidden that was actually the reason why laws became necessary in the first place?"

He told me more, much more: how love wasn't a humble and insignificant thing and how we were too inferior for it, too insignificant to grasp its beauty and superiority. "Just as the work of Valmandel or Larsen will always be monumental, no matter if there come dark times when people won't understand and appreciate poetry and music." And he hadn't finished...

"The worst thing about your spiritual leaders back then - and by spiritual leaders I mean your teachers, parents, lawmakers, priests and writers - is that they had no problem blocking your sources of pure spiritual joy. And do you know what that means, Andreas? Do you know that these "enthusiasms" (and he used the Greek word for it) are manifestations, aspects of the *Samith*, nearly as important as art? What would you say about someone who destroyed Praxiteles' *Hermes* or our own *Nostalgic Green-eyed Lady* by Nichefelt? There was a systematic tendency to suppress any form of joy in your time."

I struggled not to smile with his childlike way of thinking. "I wish that was our only problem, my dear Stefan... We had so many things that troubled us, so many responsibilities, privations, unnecessary worries: dependence, poverty, addictions, and uncertainty about the future… There were millions of problems that couldn't be solved and millions of needs that couldn't be satisfied just by smelling the flowers and looking at the stars. You may now have all the time you want to observe, think about and analyse everything, but back then, we couldn't even tell they were missing…"

But he wouldn't agree with me.

"Don't say that," he complained "and don't say that you didn't think about them and that you couldn't tell if they were missing. Joy is the food of the soul. Can you realise that? The violent, everyday suppression of any spiritual or emotional inclination, even if you couldn't see how harmful it was, was gradually and cumulatively breaking every chord of joy you had in you. So no, letting your soul die before it's time, little by little, is not acceptable. This artificial, premature inner aging of yours was a great and unjust loss for our kind, a lot greater than you can imagine. The conditions under which you lived your daily life and the social conventions that prevailed were bluntly stealing what was given to humans by creation and whose complete meaning we just felt and realised: the smile of God."

He once again made an allusion to the findings of the Volkic Knowledge and to the "timid glimmer" of the *Samith*. Strange as it may seem, this is their view of the *Lipvirch*: it is the experiencing of a higher spiritual life and the access to the divine - on the path to the *Samith* - but via a whole different way from meditation, religion, art or world view.

"That's why no elderly person would ever mock the ideals of the youth, nowadays; because older people have their own ideals and wouldn't want anyone to come and insult or disrespect them. Besides, we ultimately know that there is one, common origin and source of all ideals, despite the vast - but superficial - differences amongst them."

Later, however, he admitted that the spiritual wealth of their youth was not only due to heredity or tradition and that it was not entirely inherent either; proper guidance and education from the family, schools and the *glothners* stood as a very helpful assistant.

## OLD AND NEW LOVES: THEIR WAY OF SEPARATION

### 26-XI

Sometimes I wonder if their current perceptions and new social conditions are really capable of protecting their hearts from pain and they have truly managed to attain true happiness through them. From what I've seen, not only have they not acquired the long-sought "serenity of mind and soul", but all too often they also seem to come across the same problems in their emotional lives, the same profound pain, the same dramatic dilemmas and internal conflicts that we suffered in our own time. And let's say I believe what Stefan said, that is, that the old, violent passions and the "dramatic solutions" of our time have completely ceased to exist. I've heard with my own ears about cases when a strong, new love has come into conflict with long-standing partnerships and strong emotional bonds, disrupting the affection between the couple, their shared memories and dreams and their shared lives

What happens then in such cases? There is no rule, no penalty, no apparent solution. It seems that in such matters there is no "must" or "mustn't". There are tears and emotions on both sides. And then they sit and wonder what they are doing. Stefan argues in that incidents like these the most frequent thing is each party leaves the decision-making to the other. But is this a product of altruism or an attempt to avoid responsibility for the happiness of their loved one? Stefan says - and it'd be very nice if it were true - that very often in such cases the companions feel for their loved ones what parents feel for their children: the same love and emotion. Putting themselves and their feelings aside, they try to see what's best for their partner and act in such a way so as to avoid getting in the way of their happiness. "Nowadays, we have a highly developed sense of caring and understanding for our fellow men." he said, "It's one of the most distinctive features of our mentality. The exact opposite, that is, of the selfishness and the instincts of primitive times."

If, on the other hand, you ask the Valley, they'll tell you that the most important thing is the stability of the partnership. They strongly disprove of fervent passions and love affairs that bluntly and hastily come to break long-term and refined emotional bonds. However, they advise the "old loves" not to be afraid of a true, genuine *Lipvirch*, if they ever happen to come across it… It can do no harm to civilised people with spiritual courtesy who, above all and everybody else, respect themselves. They advise them to embrace it and see where it takes them. Of course, the final outcome of such a conflict, with thousands of different factors each time, differs from case to case. Sometimes the new love ends up only testing the strength and resistance of the old one and soon fades away defeated.

Less often - especially in cases of very long partnerships with already grown-up children - it so happens that new love and old affection compromise and reconcile themselves without displacing one another. Each one holding a special place in the person's heart, they last and evolve alongside each other for many years.

At times, however, the new love proves stronger and breaks the old bond. And even if such an outcome is not applauded, insomuch that there are no other deeper discrepancies in the partnership - because normally the phase of experimental partnership aims to bring to the surface such latent incompatibilities and not to open the door to new affairs - things turn out like they did in our times.

Generally, their argument is that the current relationships, being completely free from and alien to any old convention and based on unrestrained choice, mutual love and the pure intention for a lifelong bond - without the legal barriers of our time - should be immeasurably stronger and more stable than ours.

You could say that these scarce separations along with the instances of unrequited love are, if not the greatest, some of the greatest troubles of their current carefree and happy lives.

"Are we completely free from pain? No, we have succeeded no such thing…" Stefan was telling me yesterday. "There is no poverty, dependence, violence and matters like that, but the pains of the heart, no matter how intense, are welcome. They remind us of the nostalgia and the thirst for the *Samith*. We still suffer up to this day, and even more profoundly than you used to, but at least we know why we suffer…"

I have observed how they suffer in silence and with dignity, how they hide the pain coming from a loss of a loved one or by an unrequited love with a perseverance that reflects the old Christian perception of inner pain. They believe that this inner pain elevates the soul so much that it can become an acquisition even greater than love itself! While the one is transient, the other can never be taken away from you…

In a book I was reading by their Jonas Geerlud it that said that in a true *Lipvirch*, which was, however, one-sided and remained unrequited to the end, the person one should pity was not the one aching in loneliness, but the other person who was never able to reach that level of almost metaphysical pain. "Because the former stands higher and sees unique things that the latter will never lay eyes on."

Another writer, Alex Rogen, writes that deep down inside nothing is ever lost. Appearances shouldn't lead to wrong conclusions: "Everything you have ever dreamt of and everything you have cried over is stored for you and will not be forgotten, you kind old souls…", he writes, alluding to the imperishable of the Source and the beatific Volkic preaching of the universality of the *Samith* that contains everything…

Everybody here says that "the past is not as past as it seems…" reminding me of my own destiny. "What *you* used to call happiness only exists in our dreams," Stefan told me. "We didn't come to this world in order to find tangible happiness, something that is impossible, but in order to grasp the true meaning of it and find out what its source is in order to be able to recognise it when we see it!"

At this point he recited the words of one of their poets: "For why else were we born, why else do we live, except to see our own lives go to waste?" What he meant by this was that the noble thirst of their souls that never ceased throughout their lives was the painful evidence of the superiority of this advanced species that never tires of looking for the *Samith* in all its mundane forms (art, religion, metaphysical concerns, self-sacrifice and so on) and never gives up or becomes frustrated by the obstacles and disappointment on the way…

"So, if, let's say, Hilda found someone new that made her feel more complete. Wouldn't that bother you?" I asked Stefan.

"It would definitely not be pleasant, but it's not like I could stop her. But deep love is a fiery, internal process that makes us better. In the beginning of our relationship I suffered a great deal of pain myself; that sparkle I saw in her eyes the first times she spoke to me and which I hadn't seen for a long time, I saw it while she spoke to someone else. I prepared myself for the worst, but nothing happened. It was something completely transient. But I was more concerned about whether she would be happy wherever she went and whether that person could really complete her as a person than I was about her leaving me. A friend of mine forgave her companion when he confessed his infidelity, just because she remembered how happy he looked during those days and how happy it made her, as well, to see him happy. In fact, during those days, she had told him: "Whatever it is that gives you so much strength, joy and creativity can be nothing but good."

So here's another manifestation of the *Troende*, the Volkic person of today, the shareholder of the new wisdom, the not-so-stable and not completely normal in our own eyes…

Now, as far as our concept of marriage is concerned, they have kept the part of the affection, the interest in the other person, the loyalty, the reciprocity and the altruism and have integrated them into today's life. But the part that they don't understand is the element of the abrupt and premature internal aging that came with marriage in our time. They believe that society pushed people towards early marriage, depriving them of the opportunity to live their own lives first, to experience spiritual and other types of joy along the way. Social and political expediency demanded this sacrifice.

I told him the struggle for survival showed us from the beginning how difficult life was going to be and so it was easier to adapt by yielding to the routine of having a permanent partner. We had to share all those troubles and concerns with someone…

"Fortunately this abrupt and unnatural sterilisation didn't unconsciously give birth to true hatred for your partner," he replied.

What can I say? In any case, these people manage to stay young at heart forever, combining family happiness and its entirely human nature on the one hand, and on the other, the new enthusiasms and the pure spiritual joy of divine origin. I have no idea how they do it…

## SOUTHERN EUROPE

### Loikito, 30-XI

The Pyrenees welcomed us with three-day, non-stop rain and massive canyons filled with fir trees that leaped out of the fog. Two days ago, though, the sun reappeared and it looks like it's here to stay. The lifestyle here is quiet, peaceful and relaxed, quite similar to the one that we came across half a month ago around Bignasco and the beaches of Salerno. But this place is much more crowded; every evening, at dinner time, it's impossible to find a free table at the restaurants. The partners with the silken, snow-white robes work all day long - the opposite, that is, of what we saw in Bignasco.

### 1-XII

It's just Silvia and me this time and I feel blessed for every single day that finds me next to her. Today, I was patiently waiting to see her wake up, to see her first blinks under the morning light. When she woke up and saw me looking at her, she laughed. I don't know what she thought of me at that moment.

I think that I made a huge blunder yesterday, while at one of the *Civeshostels* of New Tarracona, located on the opposite side of the mountains, where we had gone with a whole bunch of people and stayed until late at night. I had been dancing with Silvia all night but at the end, they told us that the ribbon that they had given us would determine out next dance partner. I happened to have been matched to a very rare, for the night, girl: a blond among so many light and dark brunettes. My mistake was that I rushed and asked her name in the middle of our dance, but then I remembered that nowadays you are supposed to talk to everyone as if you've known them for ages.

At first we talked about a thousand things, while dancing. Her conduct was very simple and unpretentious. I don't know what came over me and I asked her name. "Stella Cadens," she answered in a witty manner. It was obvious she was joking so I laughed and changed the subject. I noticed, however, that from that point on she replied in monosyllables. I thought that my asking her name had upset her, but I was wrong. Soon she started making jokes again and when I called her "Miss..." she completed my phrase with the same name that she had given me before, and in the same witty manner.

Perhaps her mind was focused on her partner, a tall dark-skinned lad, who didn't seem much delighted to be dancing with the chubby girl he was matched with and whose gaze was constantly fixed on his girl.

I just remembered another odd thing. Two days ago, when the rain stopped and we all went out for a walk in the woods, I noticed a great many men and women who were observing ants for hours, with no apparent reason! They said they enjoyed watching them live and work under the light of day. They had fixed their eyes on two massive lines of ants, one going to work and one coming from work, carrying their burdens. They were even commenting that when an ant wasn't able to carry its load, it searched for three or four other ants and, touching their antennas, clamoured for help. Two days ago, they also started giggling at the sight of the first, fresh grapes of the year! And if you asked them: "Haven't you ever seen that before in your life?" they considered *you* strange. But that's how people are here; I've started becoming accustomed to them. They get excited about the simplest of things: the moon rising from behind the tree foliage, the bleats of the animals in a silent night, a cordial greeting.

An image filled with natural beauty is not just an image to them; they don't only see it, they feel it as a unit that vibrates with the sheer joy of creation. Their antenna is not vision, like ours; they truly "experience" what they see! Plus, the ability that their individual vehicles - the *vigiozas* and the *linsens* - give them to go anywhere they want fills them with joy. "Just think of a place and you can fly to it," they say, and they literally mean it… They have their own way of not letting the "inebriation" of new experiences fade away.

Even the changes of weather make a huge impression on them and become a topic of conversation. A phenomenon as simple as the change of seasons is a great source of happiness for them. And if you tell Stefan that the people of his era have rather lost their grip on reality, he won't admit it. "It's unbelievable," he told me, "how much potential happiness is hidden in our inner world. You had no idea about it in your time, but just because we can't grasp it doesn't mean it is non-existent. The sensors of our souls have been dulled and are no longer adequate receivers. So all these things that you view as strange, who is to say that they are childish instead of divine?"

Living among them long enough one begins to feel unwittingly influenced by their lifestyle. Personally I see it as a type of mental detox and consider it good for me. Stefan considers it necessary! Here they manage to maintain the adolescent state of mind for many years. They try to keep their early years and the mentality they had back then unadulterated and the Valley urges them to keep the eyes of their souls open until they're old and grey if they can.

### 1-XII Again

### (During the night)

Today, Silvia told me that when she's with me she doesn't miss her family. Then she told me that she had always known that nobody can be happy when alone, without a loved one by their side whom they can love and cherish.

She then added, "But if I hadn't found you, I don't know if I would ever be able to imagine how great a thing love ultimately is." She also said that she wants to have my child, a child that would inherit my heart and my way of thinking and perceiving the world around us.

What else could I ever ask for?

Before I met her, such a creature with so many talents in soul and spirit and so much emotional wealth, existed only in my imagination. I remember thinking that the mere acknowledgement of the existence of such a person somewhere in the world would more than satisfy me. I didn't dare to imagine anything more... That is her mere existence is the greatest moral and emotional rewards I've ever received. And this realisation is enough to make me happy; my life seems like torment no longer...

### 2 to 3-XII

### (Very late at night)

How many times has there not been talk about pain being the dominant essence of life and of the world? I believed it for a long time myself and I experienced it more deeply than anyone, and now that I've recovered and can see life clearly and live it more profoundly, I can't recognise my new self!

Don't rush to argue thoughtlessly that the true essence of life is only pure and tangible in adolescence and that after that the psyche inevitably begins to become distorted in a way that it makes the old joy impossible to be found again, no matter how successfully you match your surroundings to the circumstances in your life. I have spent endless hours squirming in my armchair at night to no avail, every inch of my body awash with joy and anticipation for a million wonderful things to come, a joy and anticipation that persistently keep my eyes open and prevent every possible attempt for concentration and meditation.

"O fate! The greatest of all people's dreams are nothing compared to what *you* are capable of!" The awareness that these people are so much more enlightened than us fascinates me! A sense of gratitude makes my heart swell. I think about their certainty in the "multiplicity of life", their faith in the "afterlife", their thoughts on the successive existences of the same personality, their knowledge that the failing in consciousness is temporary and relatively rare and that long distances, and the time-space continuum in general, do not constitute barriers for the spirit, and finally, I think about their firm conviction in the eventual justification of the human soul and I am overwhelmed with such an enthusiasm as if I had seen all that with my own eyes!

I also remember something else that Stefan had told me a while ago, in reference to the realities that are beyond human comprehension.

"There is no way that our minds could understand what happens to us after the so-called "death". It's one of the facets of the *Samith* I talked to you about, inconceivable by human cognition and rationality. Don't forget what Matjei Svanol said about some of the greatest and most sacred parts of the human psyche after he saw the *Nibelvirch*: "It was all lies, indeed. But who could have known what great Truth was concealed behind those 'lies'…"

The Aidersian tradition is, as I found out, cautious and does not go beyond the *Roisvirch*. It doesn't state anything more apart from what the *Oversyn* had shown. However, many internal, personal experiences of people, taken from a wide range of circles, have shown that in the soul of the *Troende* there is a multitude of existences in superimposed layers. Sometimes they even speak of a corresponding multiplicity in modern and parallel lives - that surpasses human nature - until the Ego gains full consciousness, the sense of unity and the unbreakable continuation of individuality. One whole life dedicated to knowledge, one to emotional wealth, another one to great love experiences and a separate one for spiritual or artistic creation…

"In your era," Stefan told me, "you dreamt about and longed for eternity, even though a rainy afternoon was enough to make most of you feel bored and lonely." Once again I noticed their condescending tone when talking about the era of "unilateral techno-culture and mechanistic life" in which people lived, the era of which I will be a part again if I ever return…

Explaining it as best as I can, this is how they perceive the emotional attraction of the human spirit to the "infinite" and the "eternal": as a matter of "space" or "duration" although it is something incomparably higher than that.

I remembered Anna now… How much you went through! Can you hear me? Are you listening right now? All that we had imagined and dreamt of, my dear Anna, all that made our eyes water, they exist! They're all real! It wasn't our imagination! They all exist here, in real life!

## CITY LIFE IN WESTERN FRANCE: COMPARISON WITH THE 20TH CENTURY

### 9-XII

I savoured the fresh air of the mountain altitudes again, tonight, after this week's getaway, off the coast of the ocean. A few days' trip to the coast of our own western France, so different from the grand centres of production and the luxurious beaches of the South, is enough to give you a fleeting but typical image of the - now identical - states everywhere: successive, immense…

For a traveller coming from my time, the place is unrecognizable. The life of the harbours, the quaint images of the commercial and naval traffic, the typical local colour of this part of rural France, even the lagoon complex that used to prettify the place: they're all gone! Even the climate has changed; it has become milder, sweeter and more… transparent, free from the humidity brought by the sea, more… Mediterranean if I might say. The old glorious "worldwide" language had now been replaced by the vernacular, which I now have almost learnt by listening to it at the villas and in Salerno, during my brief visit on our way to the cities of central Europe and the big capital of the North. Contrary to what I had noticed while in the outskirts of Salerno, here, no place names have been salvaged, not even the most historical ones.

Only their fruitful vineyards are reminiscent of the old days. Across the country, however, there was no inch of land untended. Perhaps the population could become a matter of debate and one could argue that some places could afford more or fewer inhabitants, but that was it. They had transformed the swamps into huge garden cities. These once indifferent rural areas had now acquired the air and charm of a vast megacity and had turned out to be more striking than even old Paris! Now you don't see misery next to beauty… You wouldn't come across any works of art anywhere else except in places where they can be self-conserved. They can't bear ugliness and decay, not even on the smallest scale. What I saw was a unique sense of beauty and uniformity generously scattered everywhere, as if it was artistically done by a rational spirit. That, of course, was a result of the current economic conditions and their incredible technological capabilities.

Away from the coast at about sixty kilometres inland there is a place called the Flowery Nest, which spreads all around the huge town of Denia Vallia with its crimson flowered terraces and the incredible number of spaces designed for plants and flowers. They were literally everywhere: on every column, every balcony, every roof, every arcade, on the facades of the palaces... I remember wondering how these people managed to grow and preserve all these flowers year-round so as to always look so fresh and incredibly beautiful and, above all, why all this excessive flower-flood, which ultimately doesn't benefit the residents here, who are mostly former students.

Another thing that struck me was the existence of big and shiny butterflies, which, as Silvia informed me, had this place as their natural habitat and were one of the biggest and most beautiful species in Europe. There were times when, walking through the city, you were startled by swarms of hundreds of light blue butterflies that leapt out of clusters of white roses!

But I was more taken with the statues. As soon as I saw one, I'd go straight to study it. I could see the pedestal and read the inscription, but, unfortunately, the names meant absolutely nothing to me. These people may have changed the course of history and I didn't have the slightest idea who they were. At moments like these, the distance and my difference from Silvia, Stefan and the rest felt greater than ever. I was and always would be the man from a different era.

I cast these bad thoughts out and wandered in the crowd feeling as if I fit in again, like I belonged in their world. At least that's what my physical appearance said - without betraying anything of what was happening inside me - and that made me swell with pride! I did, however, wonder whether the joy and happiness I felt was ultimately non-existent, whether it was nothing more than mere enthusiasm.

Further down, I saw little boys and girls inside the flower beds, who, dressed up like poppies and cyclamens, were running uncontrollably around and singing out of tune, each one in their own rhythm. The health and whole-heartedness of these dishevelled children, who lacked for nothing and were given the freedom to express their pure and unadulterated joy so effortlessly through songs, laughter, games and funny voices, was incredible.

On the outside, life in the city during the morning was more or less the same as in old times. Thousands of people flooded the streets each with a different destination. Except, they, the prematurely "sacked" from the *glothners* and their service, had nothing to fear in terms of redundancy, boredom and other symptoms of our time. Most of them went to the ball fields or to the fitness centres, some painted, others studied but, no matter how long I waited, I never saw any labourer in a flat cap, any employee in a stiff white collar or any businessman in a suit with briefcase tucked underarm.

## SOCIAL CLASSES, HIERARCHY, MANNERS AND THE DEFEATED BEAST OF BUREAUCRACY

From a social point of view, the modern perception of the Flowery Nest was that of a lower-class state, that is, the opposite of Waren, the Garden of Lilies, New Göteborg, Soonval in the South and, above all, Norfor. I thought about Aria who, as she said, chose it for its aura of spirituality and its overall attractiveness.

As time passes, I get deeper into their meanings and evaluative beliefs. The class hierarchy here has a purely intellectual and cultural content. The Flowery Nest, for example, hosts very few spiritual leaders, who live there only temporarily. The people there are educated by following the spiritual guidelines and the ideological trends that come from the large centres of the North.

There are also some old graduates of the schools of Norfor living there, truly enthusiastic people and passionate art lovers who might not be great artists themselves but know how to distinguish the good and beautiful elements in an artistic creation. True receivers, they're capable of even bursting into tears at the sight of a work of art.

We had so few people like this in our era. Here there are infinitely more. Plus, there's only a handful of the type of people who, lacking any esoterism, simply accumulate knowledge so that they can show it off in corresponding circumstances. These people confuse knowledge with education but are, in actual fact, truly uneducable.

And yet, this majority of cultivated people with this exceptional inner refinement, who would be more than welcomed and highly estimated in our era, in this era simply constitute the relatively lower class and I've often heard them being accused of doing nothing. The most mediocre physician or the most humble nurse are considered socially superior than Stefan, Hilda and the rest of the neighbours of the villas, provided that they, too, can "experience" nature and "be moved" by the high art, which I understand to be the case with nearly everyone from the Volkic generation and onwards.

Therefore, concerning the masses, the established social perception of today challenges the correctness of spending decades on studying, concerts and spectacles, courses and lectures, exhibition visits and travels, sports and other recreational activities that leave them no time to do something for their fellow human beings.

And all that is completely unrelated to the service. I remember the first days of my new life in the Molsen institute, which itself was a microcosm of society: an entire, small community with all the characteristics of the current social structure. The office partners were doing their service there. I still remember their leader, a dark-skinned nineteen-year-old boy who bowed to all the patients, the *Cives*, that is, who were being hospitalised there, as if they were going to tip him.

The nurses were considered socially superior to their *Cives* and, of course, to the office partners, the partners whose job was to assist them in keeping records and other general administrative matters. The nurses, therefore, were not doing their service; they were all mature and treated by everyone like priestesses.

Leaving the Molsen institute I became more aware of all the different steps of the current social hierarchy. So here's how it works: the *Lorffes* from the Valley of the Roses, all kinds of *Ilectors*, the "leaders" of the Aidersen Institute and all its branches and, last but not least, the great Maîtres of Norfor are the ones who rule. That's who the masses have as their idols. All these people, according to today's meritocratic perceptions, now in 3906AD, hold the positions that a thousand years ago were held by the scientists who, in turn, had been chosen by the great men of our era - from CC to D *(from 200 to 500 according to their calendar, that is circa 2600-2900 AD)* - and who in our own terms were something like the tycoons of America, the Supreme Court Judges, the great politicians, the self-seekers, the generals and the aristocrats. Besides, I had verified for myself that the few existing administrative positions were covered by the partners who were doing their service. And to think that ordinary *Cives* like Stefan were considered immeasurably superior to them.

In fact, the exemption of the *Cives* from any mandatory intermingling with the office partners - similar to our own public servants - or at least the reduction of this contact to the minimum possible was a right that had been definitively won centuries ago by their Universal Commonwealth. And it is actually considered to be one of their most valuable and enviable achievements, something like the securing of civil rights and individual freedoms was for us. Of course, such a right wasn't won from one day to the next, but gradually, over hundreds of centuries. And it's a very promising thought that the monster of bureaucracy will one day crumble to the ground, defeated by logic.

The administrative approvals that are required nowadays are very few - mainly of a scientific nature - and are willingly brought ready to the *Cives* by the partners. This willingness to serve is one of the most fundamental elements of their culture.

The demographic and traffic regulation and control is always done in a certain way and is always communicated directly to the *Cives*, so that they are aware of it. That is all. There are no violations but, even if there are, the intervention of the partners in individual cases is unjustifiable. For example, Stefan's *linsen* is in constant need of tune-ups but he is not required to remember anything or keep records. The partners are the ones whose responsibility it is to keep records of the dates and details and to ask when they can come and get the *linsen* and return it fixed without bothering him! In fact, they have even been taught how to stand with respect not only before Stefan, but also any other *Civis*. And all this respect stems merely from the fact that the latter have fulfilled their "social duty"; their service.

Now, if one focuses only on the *Cives*, one will realise something else that we didn't have in our time: the current class distinctions, from the *Lorffes* to the rest of the population - the masses, that is - do not stand in the way of all social classes obtaining the same inner cultivation, the same air of "high society", the same joy of life. And this is something that we never achieved, not even during the French Revolution.

These people have managed to achieve - and I don't even know how - that the mass be a soulful receiver, have the same courtesy and the same manners as the top intellectuals of Rosernes Dal. And, as they informed me, they all consider themselves descendants of the old working class!

It seems incredible how this class managed to evolve to such extent since that decisive moment in history - over twelve hundred years ago, circa 2600 AD when the technocrats and natural scientists undertook world governance - when the political leadership was abandoned and replaced by the Marie Curies and the Max Plancks of the time. And I remember how surprised I was when Stefan told me that the great ancestors of today's *Ilectors* used to be industrial workers.

For a social observer of our time, a walk through the streets and the gardens of the Flowery Nest would surely be of great value, to see with their own eyes how everyone, without exception, knew how to dress, how to talk, how to enter a group for the first time, how to walk and stand in any given circumstance. It is perhaps surprising that a world so advanced in its inner culture, doesn't consider this commitment to "good manners" as something superficial, something too formal and conservative, too unworthy a social convention for the "superior people" to engage in. But they argue that something that reflects a real emotional and moral wealth cannot be classified as shallow and superficial.

Seeing them give this tone of joy and happiness to everything they do is truly delightful. You see them socialise with each other and the current perception that has passed from generation to generation from a very young age comes to mind: this guileless and selfless love combined with courtesy and good manners: a true masterpiece!

And I wonder: is it the property of each person individually or is it another admirable achievement of their current upbringing and education? In my opinion, it's neither of the two on their own, but rather the two combined. This unpretentious finesse and courtesy of theirs, their typical nervousness, their morality and modesty and their complete indifference to cheap humour, to the instinct gaining the upper hand and to following some pre-planned strategy in their everyday social life are not things that come out of the blue or that are earned only through persistent exercise.

The same goes for their salvation from the old ancestral inferiority complexes that used to manifest themselves through selfishness, arrogance and vanity. So many generations before this one had spent their entire life in such an atmosphere of love and true nobility, that it gradually became their own and was transformed into a natural and effortless way of life.

I imagine how uncomfortable these people would feel if in the presence of some of our own, clever professionals, whose essential purpose was to seal profitable business deals and weren't even close to interested in the delicacy of manners or subtlety of style and expression. They would be completely consternated from the very first second. They would conclude that they had to do with boorish, primitive people. And they'd be right. On the contrary, they might have been able to communicate with a "good" man of our time for a couple of minutes. And I'm saying a couple of minutes because after a while, our "good" men would get bored, think there was nothing to be gained from that conversation and get up and leave since even I was tempted to take advantage of their naivety and gullibility in the beginning.

Now you can see that men and women cannot tolerate even the slightest "politics" and expedience in their social interactions even when it comes to a handshake. Any calculating behaviour - if, of course, it comes to their attention - causes adverse reactions. These people do art for art's sake and never for profit, otherwise it stops being art. They make friendships for friendship's sake and for the spiritual nourishment it offers, away from utilitarian objectives.

## THEIR RENAISSANCE AND HUMAN EVOLUTION BEFORE THE FIRST NIBELVIRCH

### 9-XII Again

### (Late at night)

As far as their inner cultivation is concerned, Stefan had told me a while ago, "Our teachers have their ways. For each of those children there comes a time, even before they enter their adolescence, when they feel such an attraction to our culture that, learning about it in school and gradually coming to a deeper understanding of it, makes the voices of the generation of 876 *(3272 AD)* come alive in their heads! That year, millions of people stood in endless queues for months, day and night, to see the newly completed then 'Temple of Love and Peace' in the Valley of the Roses. They stood in such awe that they thanked God for not having been born in a different era. In that same awe and with that same inner need our youths stand before the spiritual edifice of our civilisation."

As I learnt, a hundred and ten years before the first *Nibelvirch*, Alicia Neville added the Temple of Love and Peace to the sea of the Valley's masterpieces, which was considered to be the greatest marble creation of all times. They too had their own Renaissance, around the turn of the seventh century of their own chronology *(circa 3100 AD)*, the starting point of which was marked by the building of the Valley of the Roses. This century went down in their history as incomparably higher than the 5th century BC of Athens or the 19th of Western Europe.

One night, I searched in the *Reigen-Swage* for this incredible building located in the outskirts of Markfor which, as I noticed, manages to combine the symmetry and harmony of ancient sculptor Ictinus with the majestic way in which the peoples of the North expressed the soul in their architectural masterpieces.

Sometimes, the information I have to process is so much that I get lost and confused. I go back and forth from subject to subject that I often forget to mention the most important parts. I'm really trying to record as much as I can and in the most precise way possible, but I don't always succeed.

Now I remembered something else, a bit irrelevant: the first one to foresee the evolution of mankind was an ordinary biologist of the Valley named Jansen, who at the time wasn't among the best in his field but got luckier than his teachers. After centuries of life in this vast spiritual capital and drawn out initiation of several generations into long-term self-cultivation that had refined the psyche of the people and had transformed them into more sophisticated human beings - and everyone here verifies that no interventions were ever made on infants by the biological institutes of the Valley - he, Jansen, was the first who, with great confidence, announced from his lab to the whole world that he had proof that supported that there had been tiny but extremely significant anatomical changes in the most delicate and important neurons of the brain, changes that were directly connected to the quality of spiritual life of the residents of the Valley. Everyone agreed on their existence, but they had never managed to prove if those changes were indeed a result of the quality of the spiritual life or vice versa.

Regardless of the differences of opinion and ways of expressing them owed to the different time periods, another wise man, Jacobsen, had made a vague statement regarding the possibility of a new, eminent flourishing of culture. Twenty-five years later, if I remember correctly, the aesthete and philosopher Close and Lelia Nopotkin called the attention of their generation to the need to keep their eyes open, have faith and be prepared for something unexpectedly great: the "century of secret promise", for what "is today invisible."

The specialists of each field had their own theories and opinions on the subject. In the various observatories in the faculties of the Valley, each of which had the size and structure of a small town, the two Ferids, father and son (astronomers and thinkers), along with many other faithful followers of the venerable elder, a great lover of the universe, were looking for spiritual influences and messages from distant, kindly beings.

Before the year 830, Aloisius Nilson, an intellectual and recluse from Flambia, wrote from there, in the midst of his solitude, about the "great events that are dozing in the depths of the future" and that "they may not be as distant as they seem". He said that "the day is not far when the dialogues of Plato may be rewritten; when new

Parthenons may be built and new 9th symphonies may be composed."

None of them, however, was able to predict - neither then, nor later in history - the arrival of the *Nibelvirch* a hundred and fifty years later.

Those hopeful and promising sermons lasted for decades. In fact, the last years before the arrival of the *Nibelvirch*, a few *Ilectors* - mainly Bearen, Tatiana Baclyn and some fellow named Gunnar whose last name I don't remember - spoke to their generation about many things related to this, both general and more specific, things that they later were lucky enough to see with their own eyes.

Humanity waited for "that which was to come" for decades. The conditions of life had improved so much that they had reached the level of making prediction possible. But there were many who said that people would be better off without the ability to predict with such confidence a spiritual revolution that would happen sixty years later, the way they could formerly predict a natural phenomenon like the coming of a comet. So intense was the thirst of their hearts that they couldn't wait.

Those people who had a more philosophical approach could more easily compromise and accept their fate. There were many, however, who couldn't, and would blame their luck for not being born later in time so that they could have the chance to see what's coming. They believed that "he, who dies in these times, dies a thousand times". They considered it a great loss to miss the coming of such an immediate future reality. In the end, they found consolation in the thought that at least their children would have a serious chance of being present when it happens and that they'd see the great days of the future through their eyes.

Indeed, a few decades later, the promised flourishing of culture finally came. It first influenced the European nations, which for fourteen hundred years had fallen into obscurity, caught in between warring giants. And the reason why this new wave of spiritual civilisation hit Europe first was the establishment of Norfor as a spiritual centre of the world already since the year 450 *(circa 2850 AD)*, and of course the establishment of the Valley of the Roses.

In terms of duration, this boom in arts, letters and intellect had many similarities with the old "Greek miracle", but in terms of space, this new European spirit did not stay localised in one place. Its initial outbreak may have been in Europe, but it rapidly spread across the whole world.

Dozens of names of cities and regions and of great figures of the new civilisation are listed in the history pages: great, wise men, spiritual leaders, artists, educators, philosophers, researchers, heroes of the human intellect and apostles of humanism, who worked and taught generation after generation, during those unforgettable sixty to seventy years in Gran Torneo and Gled, in the Gate of Lesley and Blomsterfor, in Ossen and Vikingegnist, in Leag-Aud and New Upsala, in Roselukin and, especially, in the Valley of Roses.

Their current history says that particular era - their 9$^{th}$ century - was the first one in the entire history of humankind that managed to depict so precisely people's ideas and dreams and make them come alive. They told me that it was as if a divine spell was cast upon earth while those two blessed generations lived on it. Those years seemed like a dream to the world population of the time: countless immortal and everlasting artworks, secrets of the physical universe decoded, unique pieces of writing, new unheard ideas, musical harmonies that exceeded those of the ancient, for them, Germans.

But regardless of the vast differences in style and character from those of ancient Greece, the common aesthetic consciousness had risen to a level similar to that of Classical Athens. Except then the population was 10,000 and now it is millions…

## THE GIANTS OF ART: LARSEN AND VALMANDEL

I remember the names of a few artworks. I hope I'm spelling them correctly: Melsam's *Marble Braids*, up on the hill of Spring, the famous painting by Dora Vilen *Back to the Old Path*, and another highly mentioned artwork, *Among the Roses* by Svansen. But the true gods of art were two: Larsen and Valmandel: their equivalents to Homer and Beethoven.

Larsen, the "Homer of lyric poetry", who with his magical lyre made the "masterpiece of poetic creation of all ages" and who left this world in 857 in Skanes, passing into immortality, showered with endless fame and deep love from his fellow citizens. Two and a half million people stood around his scented, hexagonal pyre - I saw pictures of the mournful ceremony myself on the *Reigen-Swage.* I remember that when the body was burnt and the ashes gathered, the crowd spontaneously broke out into endless cheers, crying full of gratitude "Larsen, Larsen," in unison.

And three years later, on one of the first days of the summer, during a concert in the Garden of Lilies of Valmandel's oratorio *Prayer Among the Stars' Golden Spheres*, something unexpected and unprecedented in the history of symphonic music took place - something that no one had ever thought would happen: the music of leading figures such as Bach, Beethoven, Mozart and Wagner was surpassed!

Unfortunately, I can remember only a few of the names, events, ideas and works of art that changed the history of human culture. I seriously should sit down one day and put everything I remember on paper. I'll rack my brain in order to remember, I promise!

## COMPARISONS WITH THE 20th CENTURY

Stefan told me something else that made me rejoice: that they accepted that this incredible spiritual and intellectual creation was not solely a product of the past few decades. The foundations were set by our ancestors four and a half thousand years ago! At first in the Mediterranean and then all around the world, in every corner of the world, every generation made its contribution, whether small or big, depending on their strength and capabilities, to this incomparable achievement that the human race now considers as its most valuable ornament. From the self-sacrifice of leader-heroes and the unparalleled preaching of Christ to the millions of humble and anonymous hearts within which lived the spirit of selflessness and altruism: they all contributed to this miracle! That's what they believe.

Nowadays, the great majority of those people who don't possess the gift of creation in any specific field find their life purpose in feeling and experiencing as intensely as possible the most important cultural acquisitions of their times. They want to make it their own and are extremely obsessed with self-cultivation.

Naturally, they have elevated their values and ideals to a great extent. They literally adore them: religion, the planet, freedom, family, humanity, education and justice echo in their hearts like the trumpets of the Revelation! And along with the old ones, they have their own, new ethical systems as well: the current perception of beauty, the spiritual sermons of the past centuries, the new waves of ideas, their institutions, their new meritocratic beliefs and their amazing achievements in the field of humanism. All these make them very sensitive and I think that's how they have earned the faith, loyalty and trust of their fellow men.

I'm positive that every each and one of them would gladly give their lives in order to defend the global brotherhood and protect the coherence of the Universal Commonwealth. I believe that the Volkic idea and the new and wonderful meaning they have given to the deeply human moral saying: "All this pain cannot and will not go to waste, but will be justified sooner or later," are the basis of their mentality.

They "live" the joy of nature, the joys of travel, love, music and dance, of kindness, friendship and the thrill of beholding the aesthetic. They enjoy the unimaginable, for our times, pleasure of working on what they really want, on what their souls desire, without anyone pressuring them! In this way, their inner world becomes enriched. They say that when you follow your inclinations, the aversion to evil is created automatically inside you. And the more you climb this spiritual mountain, the clearer you see life.

If one is to accept what Stefan says, it seems that this high level of inner superiority that these people have reached through their exquisite civilisation may even justify the childlike cheerfulness I have written about so many times.

They say that there is nothing simpler and easier than this happiness. Life is full of it. Creation has generously spread it everywhere: in the sunbeam that emerges after the storm, in the colour and the odour of the flowers, in the whiteness of the clouds, in the purity of thought, in the singing of the birds, in noble intentions, in good deeds… Life is a priceless, divine gift! And every aspect of our existence overflows with unadulterated joy and grace.

"Who's blame is it that you tore your souls apart with you own hands?" Stefan asked me.

I think I just now realise how wrong the road that we had chosen was, how different from the real, simple and straight road that leads to happiness. The conditions of our lives in the 20th century were coming back to haunt me in the form of a dirge that echoed in my mind. The everyday activities and chores that killed the spirit, the routine that blackened our mood, the selfish thirst for profit, the struggle for supremacy, the eternal fear of an upcoming disaster, enemies, worries, deprivations and this whole economic, political and social anarchy that prevailed. How they harmed us! They ended up constantly poisoning our soul until they made it atrophy and gradually become disabled. And thus we stopped enjoying the treasures of the heart.

Stefan continued. "As the years went by, you bitterly regretted it, but it was already too late. The reflections of the Great Reality, of the *Samith*, had definitively ceased to exist in your life. They had fallen into oblivion. Your nerves were frayed by the everyday anxieties and by suppressing the finest things you had in you for so many years you allowed your inner world to run dry."

I told him that there was also a good side to our spirited temperament and personality, all the rivalry and the war for supremacy because they were the only way for a new day to come, the only way for a step forward, for a better life. "There was creation in those battles too, not only blood and pain", I told him. He wouldn't even hear me out…

"Progress and improvement in your narrow living environment, yes, maybe there was, but in the context of the *Samith*, there wasn't," was the answer. "Creation sees life as an alternation between creative work, joy, inspiration and love. Life is a journey among winsome and joyful travellers."

They don't feel like we felt; that "you only live once". They don't feel that repetition makes impressions fade. "New day-new joys" is their motto. They rejoice with everything, every little thing, without expecting to gain anything from it. A simple chat with clever and pleasant people is enough to make them happy.

I remember one morning, about two months ago, when they organised a dance of thousands of people up in the mountains, just because it was the summer solstice. And I'm not talking about farmers or small children. Hordes of serious men and women started out at dawn from the villas and Orta, Varez, Arona, Streza and Luino, dressed in antiquated, traditional costumes that they had dug out from God knows where especially for that day: red socks and colourful head ribbons for the girls, embroidered waistcoats, loose white shirts and shoes with coloured laces for the boys. I saw them setting up poles adorned with garlands of fresh flowers and then dancing around them to the rhythm of their ancient, ancestral songs, celebrating the sun and the good weather, as if it were something rare on the Mediterranean coast.

I was even told that there were people who, before they died, thanked God for giving them the chance to spend the nights of May walking through the Roads of Jasmine under the stars, something that I did myself in Norfor and I have to admit was wonderful.

I think that our youth would look very old in soul and spirit compared to their mature adults. Here, even if you're elderly, you're still considered young. People here, along with keeping up with the serious aspects of their lives, also achieve a remarkable preservation of their child psyche. This is their secret. And it is no coincidence that one of the fundamental principles of their psychological life is summarised in the phrase: "Back to the early joys of our childhood!"

If you talk to them about resting, they'll laugh at you! You see them feel like that and you can't help but think: haven't they learnt yet? Haven't they realised the falsity of the world yet? Do they still live in a pink little bubble? Haven't the years that have passed opened their eyes? Constant eagerness and excitement to live and travel, hopes and childhood dreams as if they're still fifteen years old. And yet, yes; their enthusiasm is permanent and lasting! Age for them doesn't matter. The anticipation of the end does not cause them bitterness or sorrow.

I remember seeing the new Planetarium being built, not long ago, in New Göteborg, an entire state in the forest. They said that upon entering what would be the largest of its kind in the world, you would be able to travel to infinity, so far from our solar system that it would make our sun look like a star. In special *Reigen-Swage* you would be able to see real landscapes of other worlds, with double and triple orange, blue and greenish suns. I heard a lot more talk like this about this future, magical state, for which the name planetarium wasn't suitable anymore, but was still used as a figure of speech. It was being built mainly for educational purposes, for both children and adults, and it would be ready in about 20 years. A colossal project!

On the occasion of the Planetarium, I came to the conclusion that, along with the adolescents of twelve to fifteen, who were looking forward to the day they'd see it finished, the same joy was shared by the old people who had no chance whatsoever of making it to that day; a carefree, genuine joy, as if they had never grown old.

Jaeger and Stefan attribute this new mentality and temperament mainly to Volkic preaching and not as much to the material prosperity of their times since, as they told me, during the *Eldrere*, all their economic problems had already been solved and yet, happiness was not at all secured. The youth of the era used to rush to grab what they thought of as an opportunity for happiness very early in life, and then they realised that, what they had ended up with was not what they were looking for. For true happiness cannot exist without basic, moral values that operate as the base for a person's inner balance and give life meaning and a higher purpose. Jaeger and Stefan likened *Eldrere* to a long, thousand-year-old era, waiting to find its saviour - its own Confucius, Christ or Socrates - which eventually found him at the Aidersen Institute.

## A UNIQUE CONCERT

### Majorca, 13-XII

Silvia and I went to Majorca for Olaf Ledestrem's concert, the great maestro of New Loria, who came all the way from Norfor for this express purpose. It is scheduled for tomorrow night at the Temple of Idea, at midnight, when the whole state will be asleep.

Seven thousand loving couples came from all the surrounding Mediterranean coasts to hear this exquisite maestro. Many are already here, but there are still many more coming. In fact, Hilda and Stefan will join us as well.

I heard that Ledestrem had chosen to perform the second part - the shortest one - of Ruthemir's glorious "Mass" and Beethoven's entire "Ninth Symphony".

Meanwhile, Silvia and I wandered around the whole state with its characteristic floral gardens high up on the roofs and the ornate railings on the balconies which, for some unknown reason, made me rejoice. The flowers here, however, are much less than the ones I saw in the coastal towns along the Bay of Biscay, on the west coast of France, from old Biarritz up north to the regions of Bordeaux. But what truly moved me and left me speechless was neither the flowers nor the crowds, but the existence of horse-drawn carriages, visibly different from ours, but still horse-drawn! You get on one of them and the partners of this romantic transport consortium take you on a tour to the beautiful parts of the island with the palm trees, beaches and orange groves as if nothing had changed from the times of my youth.

# SILVIA'S WORLD VIEW

## 13-XII Again

## (Late at night)

Silvia told me how lucky we are that our planet, an insignificant stone in the crown of the universe, happened to be hosting species endowed with the element of spirituality. When I told her that beauty does not exist without life, she replied that I was wrong because today they knew that only a few planets are inhabited, but all of them are beautiful...

She said that it's not only about the existence of life on a planet, but that a percentage of that, a minimal percentage where organic life exists in the universe, evolves at more advanced stages of biological evolution and spiritual growth. And at some point of this stage of evolution, the "thirst of the soul" emerges and manifests itself through the tendency to reach and achieve things that are "incredible, inexistent and unfeasible" for many. "Then," she said, "comes the most significant turning point in the history of spiritual culture of any kind. In the old days we thought of them as creations of the human spirit, but we now know that these manifestations stem from elsewhere and would exist elsewhere - possibly in different forms - regardless of human habitation on the planet. Similar types of psychic life would have made their appearance on other planets apart from our own. "

She also said that one of the features of this turning point is that it generates a "common conscience and faith for the purpose of individual life", which escapes the constraints of prosaic, rational reality. She spoke to me about sensitivity, selflessness, sentimentality and voluntary sacrifice, about the inclination of the soul that can go so far as biological self-destruction, which is not a human creation. She completed her phrase by saying, "Before, the Volkic dimension of depth eluded man as a receiver."

What she was trying to tell me was more or less what Stefan and Jaeger were trying to explain to me all the time. When I asked, she admitted that of course she didn't know the ultimate, overall purpose of life, but that, in her view, the immediate purpose of life for every biological species with spirituality is to build, during their lifetime, the highest possible personal culture. And that's what gives value to the lives of our own humanity. "Truly," she said, "it's worth being born human. First we had to go through all these tests, of course, but I think that, ultimately, they were worth going through."

It seems to me that her sole purpose was to impress me, make me pay more attention to her and maybe even to prove how fresh in her mind everything she had learned at school still was. Besides, I already knew from Stefan that that's what they learn about at school: moral perfection rather than material prosperity, and not only in terms of the individual, but in terms of the race overall. Ultimately reaching one's destination had nothing to do with gaining power over nature, unlocking its secrets or enslaving it, nor with technological evolution, riches and assured prosperity. They claim that those are the means, not the ends.

Silvia added that they are aware that humankind won't live forever, that it will be erased at some point or another. And they believe that only if our species chooses "a path towards the *Samith*" will we not have lived in vain.

"Whatever we achieve in this life is only worth it because it takes us one step closer to the *Samith*; it's an attempt to feel it, to touch it. That's the only way something can last after its disappearance or after death. That's the only reason why nothing ever goes to waste. Without the *Samith* neither the perfect institutions, nor the Universal Commonwealth, nor the abundance and the amenities we enjoy would be of any value."

Finally she told me that, without the quality that defines our love, we would have been deprived of the "magical knowledge" that we all share today. It's the quality of it and not its intensity or the power of physical attraction that helped us deepen our relationships so much. And such a heart-to-heart-connection is something completely different from a fierce passion. She then added - if I understood and convey her words correctly - true love can be compared to a religious experience or intuition. So incredibly creative is its power!

She talked to me about many things, like other cultures and their strengths and capabilities, explaining to me that the greatest and highest values of inner culture do not differ from world to world; they're one and the same no matter if one culture is intellectually and spiritually superior. The same divine spark still exists.

## POETS OF THE NEW ERA

### 14-XII

### (Dawn)

It was one o'clock in the morning when Silvia opened the book of poems and started reciting them to me. She went from Larsen to Goethe and from Schiller to Sulsnik, whose verses she remembered by heart:

Poets, don't cry over your long-lost inspirations,
They had the most deserving fate.
They stayed pure, genuine and true,
Just as they were within your heart.
Without being betrayed by expression
Or externalisation,
Or being reduced by dressing them in human words…
Poets, don't cry over your long-lost inspirations,
For nothing is lost within the *Samith*…

And then she resumed reading randomly. I remember one ancient poem about the wind and then a couple of Munsven's poems in a row, which were written about three and a half hundred years ago in fluent French, a language quite rare to find in oral tradition in the poet's era. Both were inspired by the Volkic preaching.

I still remember two verses from the first one:

Dechira le voile du Temps et fit preter
L' Oreille les siecles étonnés du Passe

They talk about the *Nibelvirch* and about the "cry of ecstasy and awe" and with the word "étonnés" they want to emphasise how so much had been said and "predicted" by each one of all the different religions, theories and philosophies, but none had ever imagined that human expectations could go that far, that the longing of thousands of years and the hopes and desires of every human heart would eventually be justified!

From the second one I remember these verses:

De diverses lueurs fuyantes de la même
Realité suprême

Now, about Pradelli *(3rd century of their chronology)*: I had been told that he wasn't one of the top ones. Indeed his era was a time of recession in arts and creativity. For a long time his name and work had been forgotten but, in the beginning of their new era, the *Nojere (their year 986 or our own 3382 AD)*, he was rather lucky since the people of that era were obsessed with searching among the old intellectuals for things they had "predicted without being aware of it". And the main cause of that obsession was the fact that the "Great Revelation" they witnessed reminded them that past generations had many a time predicted and expressed - though faintly and vaguely - enough relevant things and clues whose importance and meaning their contemporaries could not and did not grasp.

The same can be observed in these verses of his that I heard tonight - the only ones that have survived:

Passai la mia vita qui piangendo
Da nostalgia di Qualche Cosa
Che on questo mondo non existe

They don't owe their survival to their value, but to the fact that they were written 700 years before the *Nibelvirch*.

Silvia recited them all in one fell swoop, piously and with a voice full of joy and enthusiasm even though a Parisian wouldn't be able to bear her pronunciation.

Who would have known, however, where all the old hopes and sorrows of those sensitive human beings were aimed? Who would have thought how timid all those expectations would prove compared to what "truly exists"?

I believe I have already mentioned that, nowadays, they are strongly convinced that the one and only, the root cause of the entire historical culture of the world, is the yearning for the *Samith*; this sacred thirst of the heart and soul, this "metaphysical pain", as the past generations used to call it. Without its existence our life would be the same as that of an animal or a robot, they say.

From the purist Volkies, the most popular ones were not necessarily the greatest ones. Selius, from the era of the first *Nibelvirches* - or the period right after them - is a typical example: he became popular with his "verse-cry", in which he beautifully caught the atmosphere of astonishment that prevailed in the midst of the "holy horror" and skilfully revived the cry of ecstasy that was heard before the miracle happened. "*Samith* efir! *Samith* ves gret efir!" It was the cry that was heard from the Valley and more specifically from the Aidersen Institute, followed by the torrent of the unrestrained *Roisvirch* that came to conquer human life. Silvia knows all of these verses by heart. As she comes across the page, she recites it almost without looking at the text, while her moistened eyes prevent her from reading.

There it is! There's the amazing flame,
that made everything sparkle!
You can finally see it from up here!
After a climb of centuries,
through countless tribulations,
we finally reached the top,
and we can see it from up here!

That's what happened back then in the Valley - what is now considered as "the greatest event in human history". It was followed by the unprecedented preaching: "Something exists, something so great that it's impossible to grasp it with our human minds, something so great that the mere expectation of it will be enough to fill the world with endless happiness!"

Silvia continues to read. I'm sitting next to her and looking at her. The book jumps in her trembling hands. She's trying to suppress her emotion. The last words she managed to utter, before she burst into tears, I think were of our own Lamartine:

Deux mille ans sont passés, je te cherche aujourd'hui.
Deux mille ans passeront et les enfants des hommes
S'agiteront encore dans la nuit où nous sommes.

It looked like her whole existence was protesting and crying out "no!"

Her voice, charged with emotion, faded while she read the last sentence. She mumbled the name of Volky and of the Valley and told me that if it hadn't been for him, the pessimistic prophecy of the poet could have been verified. She wiped her eyes and stood up.

"It's time to go, Andreas," she told me.

## GRETVIRCH AARSDAG

### (At night)

Silvia and I were in the temple when, after midnight, Olaf Ledestrem directed one of the greatest parts of Ruthemir's glorious *Mass*. Stefan and Hilda, who had arrived two days ago, were sitting next to us.

The first part of this magnificent work was played in the midst of complete silence, without the slightest sound being made from the 14,000 souls who were present!

I remember listening avidly and devoutly, feeling like I was hovering somewhere between the earth and sky, thinking to myself how helplessly impotent human hearing is to appreciate such a miracle and hoping it would never end!

At the same time, however, I was proud that I was born human and that one of my peers had managed to speak to God thus, in his own language. With eyes and mind in the stars, I was listening with devotion to the perfectly harmonious voices that, at that moment, in my heart, seemed identical with the harmonic laws that govern the universe.

It was the first time I ever heard the glorious *Mass* and I truly felt it touched the purest and kindest side of me. I felt deep faith flooding my soul after listening to their own Bach of their 11$^{th}$ century. And I admit that they were right: he had surpassed our own...

The music was now over but no one from that sea of people moved from their seats for a long time. During those approximately ten minutes that passed, I wondered what they were waiting for. One could think that they had been petrified or that Ledestrem didn't even deserve a single round of applause today… And those colours in the twilight...The women, all seven thousand of them, dressed in silk mantles, in different light colours, and the men dressed in black, wearing the traditional costumes of the Valley of the Roses. They even made us wear the short trousers with black, silk leggings that reach up to the knee. The women who had the standard for such circumstances strict, uniform hairstyle, looked like flowers of the same family, incredibly and equally beautiful! I realised that, inside the indoor auditorium, there were seven thousand different love stories!

In the end, I wondered whether Ruthemir's *Mass* could still be heard up there, or rather if now there was a real, secret Mass going on instead under the moonlight that lit up the whole sky.

**(Half an hour later)**

When, after the concert, Silvia and I were alone, she pulled her favourite ring out of her things, the one with the green stone - one of the very few pieces of jewellery she possessed - and after she kissed it, she put it on my finger "to commemorate our joint prayer tonight", as she said. She stood silent and looked still influenced by what she had heard. At that moment I happened to notice that on her left wrist she was wearing her one and only bracelet with the colourful gems. Emeralds, rubies, sapphires, diamonds and amethysts, ten in total, were sparsely distributed and set in gold.

After a while I asked her, "When do you think fate decided our union?"

But she, despite her deep sentimentality, is still an educated, down-to-earth woman with critical and positive thinking.

"Do you think that destiny has nothing better to do than plan our union?" she replied smiling.

I didn't want to continue the conversation. I have never said a word about my past, my other self. Nor does she know about Anna, of course. She knows nothing about her life, our life…

I asked Stefan if those who are not young and in love have no place in this big anniversary, the *Bigvirchstag*, like we do. Plus I hadn't seen any of the great *Ilectors* and the *Lorffes* either. He told me that this midnight found the whole humanity kneeling down. Everyone throughout the entire land was praying last night. But the Temple of the Idea had been reserved for these seven thousand couples and only them. The rest of the world prayed elsewhere and the Great Leaders had their own congregation in the Valley.

That is where the first successful *Nibelvirch* - *Biglys* and *Storlys* they call it in their language - took place, he said, five hundred and twenty-three years ago, at midnight. Volky was the first one who saw it and survived or rather who survived after seeing it. And after that came the redemption of human life. Such redemption could not have come unless humanity had gained consciousness and mastery over its existence.

**(Very late at night)**

The meeting with Stefan and Hilda before the concert - with a warm handshake and the girls kissing and hugging each other - gave me the opportunity to catch up on all the news of the past twenty days that we hadn't seen them. Among other things, I was struck by Aria's triumph in Norfor where her courses had sold out! You couldn't even find standing room, let alone and empty seat even though bad rumours said that more seats were reserved by the admirers of her beauty than by the lovers of intellect.

Stefan had heard about all that from visitors of the North. He also told me that the top archaeologists and historians had paid tribute to her and that a great wise man - whose name escapes me - who had initially disagreed with her, recognised his mistake and actually admitted *she* was the one who was right. And that made her even more popular among the public. Aria told two of her friends in Norfor: "With great sorrow it was that he sent me the chain of rubies that he had possessed for four years, with great sorrow but also quite excited to get rid of it!"

Does her work have such significant value? I knew that she had a very unique personality, but from the little acquaintance I had with her, she hadn't given me the impression of such great worth. Of course, she never talked about her work. She had never dropped the slightest hint about the colossal superiority of her work in relation to Stefan and his own poor engagement. I just found out from Hilda that her classmates at school used to make fun of her "love affairs with the Incas" and of her habit of writing her ideas down everywhere: on the margins of her books, on her desk, she even wrote on her lap once, so that she wouldn't lose her inspiration!

It is said that, after her break-up with Eric, she is never escorted by the same person more than once, since there are many who would be glad to label anyone her fiancé. It seems that this kind habit of people not to intrude in other people's personal lives only applies to mere mortals. And I praise God for making Andreas Northam one of them.

Anyway, this incident with Aria and my mistaken first impression of her made me sceptical about how many things I can truly perceive and understand around me. Today has been a hundred and thirty days and nights since I started my new life and I still wonder to what extent I have grasped any of the concepts, beliefs and habits of this new world. And, of course, quite a remarkable part of my life and attention revolves around Silvia…

I query whether I perceive everything I see around me in the right way and therefore, whether I capture it correctly…

At midday today I had a conversation with Stefan about the concert. He had the nicest things to say about the maestro, the orchestra and the choir that he had brought with him from Norfor. The soloists were the top of Blomsterfor, Norfor and New Göteborg. Now I only remember the name of the blue-eyed soprano Hilda Diran. I changed the subject to our own Beethoven, since the entire 9th was played at the concert last night, right after the second part of Ruthemir's composition.

I finally got a chance to tell him what I had thought to myself a long time ago, but never had the courage to say to him: "We must have had some strange 'barbarity' in our time, for you to take our works of art and turn them into prayers…" I uttered, looking forward to his answer. Last night, despite his discretion, I noticed that he was watching me while the 9th Symphony was being played. When the drums entered and played their part and my eyes filled with tears, he firmly gripped my hand. I felt touched and proud throughout the whole time the 9th was being played, a feeling slightly different from the one I had during Ruthemir's composition. It was something "mine" this time, something from home!

But Stefan didn't seem at all shaken by my statement. From what I've heard, I take it that they consider Beethoven "one of them", same as they considered Christ and Socrates "their brothers who were wandering in the darkness of prehistory". He said that we understood very little of what they said and tried to convey through their work, and that they didn't deserve to have been born in those times. Finally, he rhetorically asked how we managed to spare Beethoven's life and didn't poison him or crucify him too and then added that culture isn't made by certain people and their work, but by the impact and appeal they have on those around them…

He also told me something very nice about the deafness of Beethoven: that today they liken him and his impairment to Prometheus, who was punished by the Gods because he stole fire. Just like Prometheus, he too was punished for having given this divine music to the primitive, immature and astonished humanity by being imprisoned in a soundless world!

For them, Beethoven and Ruthemir are precursors and evangelists and it is no coincidence that their works were played together.

Today the 9th is seen as some kind of a universal the national anthem that preaches love and loyalty to humanity and its divine destiny. Indeed, they find that it is improper to listen to it sitting down...

## MARKFOR *(EX-ROME)*: THE MEGACITY
### Visiting the Reigen-Swage Palace

### 16-XII

**(At our villas at dawn)**

I'm writing these few and hasty words in the dawning light: the news of last night made me very happy! Tonight we're leaving for Markfor, where the four of us will be staying for the whole autumn, perhaps even for the winter! Regular, permanent residence in a big city with all its wonders! Walking the Roads of Jasmines! I'm extremely excited!

**(Sunrise)**

All night I was squirming in my armchair with impatience. I remember the very first time I visited Markfor with Stefan, late one night, about three months ago; it made me the same wonderful impression that Paris did the first time I saw it, with all its feverish joy and lights, and it revived in my sub-consciousness the memories and freshness of my youth! Stefan didn't feel like sleeping that night so he came into my room and found me reading a history book. "Why on earth would you sit and read at such a divine hour?" he told me and pulled me towards the window to show me the magical starlight...

And so began the journey, if it can even be called a journey. It was rather a dip into infinity, so silent and quick that I didn't even realise it! It only lasted four minutes and it felt like we were in a vacuum!

Lombardy spread beneath our feet, the Lombardy of today, that is, this massive, vastly populated city-country inhabited by millions of Scandinavians, or rather, their dark-haired great grandchildren, which, however, has kept the same ancient name. It looked like a gigantic human beehive that stretched into infinity! Imagine that the entire plain, from Gallarate and onwards, is now an immense settlement that stretches continuously as far as the eye can see!

I don't know what happened to Stefan and he suddenly - for the second time - gave the vehicle a straight upward trajectory. My instinct and reflexives pushed me to grab him in order to hold on.

In response to my reaction, he gave me the "We're almost there" look...

There came a moment that I thought would be my last one but, ultimately, my faith in their technological advancement mitigated the fear in my heart.

From up above, you could see countless milky-coloured floodlights coming from the South. One of them started getting closer and closer at the point where it looked like a piece of evening daylight sank into the deep darkness of the night... This unburning, cool light they have managed to create is, in my opinion, one of their greatest achievements.

"Look! Look! It's Markfor!" Stefan shouted, pointing in the direction of the city. And instantly the "State of the Temples" revealed itself below us: this exquisite megalopolis, the centre of modern art and literature, which I had heard so much about from *Ilector* Jaeger.

We slowed down, entering the normal flow of traffic along with the other mechanical birds that crowded that part of the sky, silently passing by each other. In a few minutes we were landing inside the powerful white light.

Seeing how excited I was, Stefan told me that he wished his own mental world were a tabula rasa like mine, ready to welcome new impressions without being influenced by any previous memories.

You didn't see houses here - only palaces, parks and temples. Various incredibly large terraces and plenty of architectural works of art, strongly influence by the Roman order, I would say. Enormous gardens and squares, and many sculptures, including a huge marble statue I saw, depicting Christ with a halo on his head which, however, wasn't made of marble but of an invisible source of light instead!

Many times that night I heard Stefan utter the phrase "another day"... He was so narrow-minded that he couldn't understand that for me and my impatience there was no "another day"; I wanted to see everything now! Among other incredible sights, I saw a very leafy tree, something between a fir tree and a cypress, huge in size and very different from ours.

After a while, in the Reigen-Swage Palace, the partners walked ahead of us, leading us through the building. Those kind young ladies and willing young lads, all with the same, typical pageboy hairstyles and dressed in their white and light green uniforms adorned with silver belts, appeared behind some enormous columns to welcome us, before we had even finished going up the great exterior marble staircase. I remember asking a seventeen-year-old blond with grey eyes, who ended up being our guide, if having to stay awake so late at night was tiring for her.

"Why, of course not!" she replied smiling hesitantly, as if she were surprised - whether from my question or my accent is unknown. "Each of us only has to stay up at night once a month, but still, we switch every few hours."

Stefan had entered the Reigen-Swage Institute to inquire and, for a little while, I waited alone and slightly lost, observing the scenes from modern history captured by the big boards on the walls. There were no inscriptions on the bottom and so the subjects and contents of them remained unknown to me. Suddenly, Stefan came out and my heart leapt excitedly. It is incredible how even seeing this man makes me so cheerful, considering that a few months ago I was completely unaware of his existence. What's wrong with him, though? He doesn't look so pleased.

"Some other day," he says, "we'll be able to see things that interest you and matter to you more. Today we came without any notice and they are displaying things you are already familiar with. What would you like to see?"

For now it didn't really matter to me what I saw, as long as I saw something. I told him to go inside anyway because I couldn't wait any longer; my impatience was killing me!

They led us to one of the small doors along the corridor. We opened it and entered…

Oh my God! The feeling of entering a place with a secret expectation of joy, the feeling of hearing the door closing behind you - as if forever separated from the world - and suddenly facing the void is breath-taking! It wasn't pitch-black darkness that we stood before: I wasn't afraid of the dark. Something frighteningly endless spread out around us that gave me a crystal clear impression of a colourless abyss surrounding us from everywhere… Shaken and sputtering, I grabbed Stefan who, however, appeared reassuringly calm.

"You have no reason to be afraid," he told me. "Keep walking."

I took a tentative first step. Indeed, one could stand and walk very securely in this chaos. Stefan patiently walked me through the small room and made me spread my hand and touch the walls until my mistaken first impression - this terrible optical illusion - had been corrected. I realised that we were simply inside a room like any other, with a ceiling, a solid floor and walls of a colourless metal. I also observed that two steps away from the walls were sufficient to re-give you the impression of absolute chaos.

Somewhere in the middle of the room there were some comfortable seats, which we sank into.

"Now listen," he whispered to me. "Don't be scared, because from now on we won't be able to keep talking to each other. Here…" he grasped my hand, "I'll be right next to you… I'll hold your hand…"

And then with my own eyes I saw things which seemed incredible. I suddenly found myself with Stefan in the countryside and a soft light began to rise out of the distant horizon, an ambiguous light that increasingly grew brighter. At first I couldn't clearly see the shapes of things, but gradually everything started taking shape and form, like a new creation! And finally everything came to life: the countryside and the meadows, the grazing herds and the watermill, the storks hovering above the surrounding mountains.

In a blink of an eye a whole world had been created around us. Without moving a finger, we became spectators not from the outside, but from inside that world! Stefan and I found ourselves sitting on a rock on a hill, when in reality we were still nestled in our seats.

Beside us and before us, the village: streets, fountains, the typical cross-beamed framed houses with the old triangular roofs and the square to the right. On the other side of the square they were changing the horses of the mail coaches. On another side there was a gathering of farmers in the characteristic outfits of the French villages of the 18th century. The farmers were gathered around someone who, standing up on a table, was speaking while animatedly gesticulating.

That was not a mere spectacle then! That was life! Real life of the past, drawn out of history pages!

What I was seeing and experiencing was so plausible that it had made me forget where I really was. It looked so real that it kept your interest undiminished at all times and to an incredible extent! If you tried to speak, your voice would not be heard, no matter how hard you tried or how loud your scream was. If you tried to stand up and walk, then this whole miracle would instantly disappear and you'd be caught in the darkness once again. If after that you returned to your seat, then you'd start seeing again, but you'd have lost a part of the story.

There! A man was now coming panting from afar. He was heading directly to the city hall. Shortly after, big news was announced in the square. That man was the postman Droue and he had seen a carriage outside the town coming this way. He was very surprised by the incredible resemblance of the passenger of the carriage to the man depicted on the banknote that he happened to be holding in his hands. Now I understood!

"We were in Waren! Isn't that right, Stefan? We're in Waren during the great French Revolution! It's the day when the king fled and they caught him! There! The citizens are now running to get their weapons! Oh God, everything's so real! So, so real…"

On the way home I did nothing else than talk to Stefan with great enthusiasm about my impressions. My mind was working incessantly. I knew that for others all this was very common, but for me it was the first time. I knew that on the *Reigen-Swages* one could virtually go back in time and see the events of bygone eras unfold before their eyes like a giant dramatic spectacle, but I never thought that it could look so perfectly real!

I remember that, even when we had long left the Reigen-Swage Institute and we were on our way to the Stella Maris Park to get our *linsen* and head home, I was still so affected that I was naïve enough to ask Stefan to what extent all that we had seen was authentic.

"How *could* they be authentic, since we're talking about an era so far back in time?" He said, looking at me noticeably puzzled.

He also said - if I understood well and transfer his words correctly - that what some scientists wanted to prove still remains an unfulfilled dream, that is, that some day in the future we, humans, will be able to capture the images that had, in the meantime, run towards infinite space with incredible velocity. Now, however, their technological progress has begun to decline and there are no big visions for new technological advances like there were in the past. From this perspective their culture has begun to wane. He explained to me that of course all this was but a representation, though from a certain era and onwards they were indeed authentic.

We arrived at the villa very late and Stefan, who wasn't used to such late hours, seemed worn and exhausted.

"You didn't sleep again tonight because of me…" I told him.

He replied kind-heartedly that he felt fine and that the evening breeze had revived him.

**Markfor, 27-XII**

For eleven days and nights I didn't write a single word. Hard to find the time and mood for writing or even for a little meditation and undistracted thinking.

Lately, I hardly ever set foot in the house, a big and comfortable new apartment given to us four when we arrived, located in one of the six cities that constitute Markfor. In fact, the men said that it is much bigger than the one Stefan and Hilda had last year in the old city.

I spent our entire first night here outside the city, wandering through the nearby neighbourhoods and looking mainly for monuments and statues with inscriptions. Stefan was persistently trying to convince me to stay for a few hours at home and rest, but I was adamant.

Now every day I walk from morning till noon around this vast state, and then again in the evening, either with Silvia or by myself. Never before in this new life of mine had they let me go out by myself so often and for so long, but now Jaeger had told them that there was no longer need to prevent me from doing so. In fact he's staying here as well, in his own little palace, and two days ago I went to see him.

I cannot describe how much joy it gives me to be able to freely go wherever I want, to have the liberty to choose any route and destination and explore this dream-like state on my own terms! I stop and stare for however long I fancy without anyone pressuring me and dragging me around. And trust me, it's one thing to come here as a guest and another, quite another to stay here permanently for a while. The latter has given me such great self-confidence that I can walk around the streets of Markfor and see thousands of pairs of eyes around me instead of *on* me and say, "I'm one of you. I belong in your world. I'm a part of your circles. I'm another drop of water in this river!"

They have some odd-looking bicycles here called *velos*, very different from ours, and almost everyone uses them to get around when they're not walking.

What I want to say is that, if you are like Stefan and the rest of our group, redeemed from crazy ambitions to climb up the social ladder or be famous, free from any class or individual aspiration to stand out, from any obsession with original, creative spiritual work - which here is the only way to stand out, equivalent to our "success-in-life" notion - then you really feel and are happy and complete. In this funnel of a world, dreams and aspirations, individuality and toils and sacrifices are obliterated.

## STATUES FROM THE FUTURE

### 28-XII

### (Midday)

Today I wasted all morning at home. Silvia wanted everyone's opinion and help - including mine - to sort out the thousands of things that had arrived yesterday along with the carpets and the furniture for the new apartment. This distribution was for the whole winter and there wouldn't be another one. Among all sorts of useful things, there were also quite a few curious things made of synthetic ivory, picked out a few days ago by Silvia from the Partners' Exhibition in Monza, and some other little figurines made of something like porcelain, from New Cristiana.

I spent hours staring at the latter today. The material they're made of looks a lot like our porcelain but the colours, the style and what these little sculptures represent - something I had to ask to find out - were completely different.

Such objects or ones similar to them had been sent to every country of the world. Only the *Tilteys* have nowadays the privilege of "uniqueness" in works of art. Only *they* have rights to artistic works with personality, without the mediation of the machine. Only *they* can make them "theirs" even if it is for a little while and in a limited number of copies, provided, of course, that they make their orders on time.

### (At night)

Nothing is like the first time. There was none of the traffic fever and feeling of doom that permeated the air and my body whenever I did not feel Stefan beside me. It's easy to find your bearings in this endless garden city with its impeccable layout and urban planning and its rational arrangement of motorways – no other type of roads exists here. The most striking and characteristic element of this city are the immense parks and green spaces and the monumental temples, larger and far more impressive than any other that I've come across in my travels around today's world.

The traffic and overcrowding in motorways and sky is only unbearable during the early morning and the late night rush-hour, but even then, everything moves calmly and silently, without unnecessary anxiety and noise. There is great symmetry governing the lined up flocks of these wingless, fusiform, flying vehicles, which all have the colour of the grass directly hit by sunlight, and a thick, dark olive green tape on the bottom. You can see countless of those vehicles travelling in the same direction and on parallel tracks over the domes and arches of Santa Virgo, in eastern Markfor.

The faces of the people passing by are characterised by an incredible serenity, the exact opposite of the hurried travellers queuing up for the *daners* at the airport *quay* in Norfor, the "Flower of the North".

They're all so peaceful that it makes you wonder whether they all go somewhere and pray in groups. Maybe they go to one of their myriads of temples: the temple of the Universal Spirit, the Socrates, the History Temple, Ars Poetica, Divine Wisdom, Mercy, or the Temple of the Heart of Jesus. This last one with the twin belfries in the front strongly reminds me of the towers of our own Grossmünster in Zurich, though these are much taller. Their temples are extremely large and can hold up to about forty thousand people each. I feel that someone else, more experienced than me, would be better at feeling and appreciating their history and their style and deeply understanding their true meaning. I think that I'm the wrong person for the job…

I'll try to write down some names in the inscriptions of the statues I saw, names of distinguished contributors of the new era: Inge Borksen, Spinelli, Rodersen, Axel Jenefelt, Tinersen *(the one with the parable)*, Felix Torquay, Erlander, Rudelin (a mountain of fresh laurels surrounded his monument), the famous cultural critic Anerholm, the historian Esterling, the aesthete Nimotti, Dimagia, Larsen and Mary-Lea Volky, whose statue was lying ecstatic on the golden sand, with her hair wet by the sea and her forehead shining under the sunrays. She had been Alexis Volky's student and after she died, she almost achieved sainthood. From our own familiar men, I saw the statues of writers Friedrich Schiller and Victor Hugo, poets Edward Young and John Keats, Saint Francis of Assisi, philosopher Jean-Jacques Rousseau and statesman Lorenzo de Medici. It was as if the statues had added a new spiritual beauty to their faces. They all had a hint of a smile drawn on them, as if they knew exactly what was mapped out for humanity…

**(Half an hour later)**

Sometimes I wonder if someone has cast some kind of spell upon this place that makes everyone becomes so happy just by breathing its air and staring at its sun! Eleven days here I haven't done anything other than wander around from place to place with a map in my hands, thirsty for exploration. Museums, palaces, art galleries - I can't get enough of them! I always need more time to enjoy them. I could spend my whole life in this city studying until the end of my life. What I wouldn't give to have grown up here and have experienced as a child all the past years and all the joys of childhood first hand…

And then there is that charm of the place name: the great Stella Maris Park, the Little Anolia, Rosenborg (a simple district of Markfor, no relation to the great state of central Europe), the two Fiammes - the east and the west - Fiammarosa and Fiammazzura, the seven-lane Roads of Jasmines (parallel and numbered motorways), ancient Magenta… I get drunk at the mere mention of the names… And strange as it may sound, I felt a pang of jealousy when I heard a ten-year-old boy that I ran into on the street two days ago so naturally talking to his mother about their coming back from Smirilud, on the west side of the town. I was jealous because he was born here, he speaks with such ease about all kinds of things, he mentions with such naturalness the name "Smirilud", he lives among them, he remembers names from his earliest years. As for me, who knows how long it'll take for these places to accept me as "one of their own"?

**(Later)**

Stefan finds all this impatience, thirst, enthusiasm and overall "fever" of mine normal. It's the same thing that Jaeger had told me about five months ago: that if I could get used to the idea of my unbelievable, personal destiny and could finally let my heart breathe, incredible images and experiences were awaiting me, unattainable by any other man of my era. And he was right. I never forget how much my mature friend helped me tame my nerves and anxieties and calm down, look my destiny straight in the eye.

## PROMINENT INHABITANTS OF MARKFOR

### 28-XII Again

### (At night)

This spiritual El Dorado has no end! At some point, when you get out of the settlement and into the open spaces, you feel like you arrived at the outer regions of this giant state. And suddenly, behind the dense trees of the large park, you see another city popping out of nowhere and the lure of the unknown flares up again inside of you.

"Markfor is for all of us who were born in this ancient Italian land, and share its pride and joy," Stefan told me tonight. "It is proof that, no matter how many misfortunes Europe had suffered due to the criminal naivety of its own children, the human mind never faded under the Mediterranean sky."

At some point I asked him how it would be if people from my era and of my generation came here. Would this place change them? He told me that it depended on the mentality with which they arrived. Would they arrive with the mentality of the old times?

He considers this matter for the most part as a purely internal one. He sees it as a question of preparation. Then he said something - I don't know if he did it to make me feel better - that gave me courage: "In many aspects, your heart was quite prepared for us. And yet, think how long it took even for you to detoxify from the poisons of your time."

His way of thinking made me smile.

"It's not a compliment," he said gravely. "Jaeger is the one who first said this about you in his closest circle in Norfor. And you know well enough that Jaeger doesn't pay compliments."

Then I opened my heart to him and talked about all that I had seen in the forests of Filiatura with its freshly washed, light-coloured pine trees, about the crowds that flocked to the docks of the Transportation Cooperative, where they drank iced and sugared mineral water in the shade, about the happiness that fills my heart every time I see couples on the street. I told him that it feels like I have found the right climate for my soul to grow.

"I feel like all this is mine too," I told Stefan with a chuckle. I was laughing at myself since I was speaking with the naivety of a child, avoiding his gaze.

Stefan grasped my hands, trying to make me look at him, and told me, "Of course they are yours too! They are yours if you feel them yours! That's how you *should* feel. You have become one of us; that's why I'm now holding your hands. That's exactly what wealth of heart is all about: being worthy to rejoice with everything and live everything. The landscapes, the sky, the songs and all the divine messages of the *Samith*. That is true richness of life and not spending a lifetime toiling unnecessarily in order to make everything yours! Woe to those who wait to first buy something and have it in their name until they can start enjoying it and feel it is theirs."

"That's how it worked in my time."

"I know... You even had individual 'land and property registers'," he chortled somewhat sarcastically. "How did you manage to bring so much misery into your lives? That's some perception of happiness you had back then!"

I remember that at that exact moment he raised his hand and pointed at something outside the window. "How would these gardens and those flower beds make us happier than they do now if they were our property? Would the relief that they offer to the eye and soul be any different? Trust me... Rich is the man who can enjoy them; not the man who possesses them."

Regarding the pride they felt about Markfor, he told me that it had as much to do with the beauty and wealth of this megalopolis as it had with the soul of the city; Markfor had grown exclusively because of its intellectual life.

In fact, I remember him telling me that the populations of the production centres in the neighbouring Ragrilia, in southern France, was a lot bigger. "But those are production centres", he said.

"All you have to do is think about your Oxford with the population of your New York or your London."

I noticed that Stefan avoided comparing Markfor with the big cities of the North that were also dedicated to the intellect. But the story of the North was old and different. Markfor was born *from* the intellect; it wasn't constructed on the ruins of an old industrial and commercial centre.

There was, however, a significant difference between Markfor and Oxford that made Stefan's comparison inaccurate: in our time, those who went to Oxford were almost exclusively students, while today, all those who come to Markfor are normal, everyday people. They don't study the spirit and the intellect; they live it!

It must be over a month now that the permanent population has come back from their summer holiday along with thousands of travellers from the southern states and all the auditoriums, halls, museums and venues have opened to host poetry competitions, sculpture and painting exhibitions, festivals and conferences for art lovers and music events. This is their daily routine!

They told me that in their meetings and symposiums they don't have a single bite and that in their festivals no music that even slightly resembles the Italian music of the 19th century is heard. Opera is not really their cup of tea... In the theatrical plays, however, which are countless, they play everything from Shakespeare, Schiller and the great dramatists of New Göteborg to Evelyn Cornsen and Borodin's trilogy *The Ethereal Paths*, inspired by the astonishing Valmandel's work *Prayer Among the Stars' Golden Spheres*. I heard many people speak with respect about this oratorio that is described as being an entire "musical universe" in itself.

Foreign thinkers hardly ever come to Markfor to teach anymore. This gigantic state has its own maîtres, half of whom are born and raised in the city and extremely proud of it. You may happen to run into some of them on the street, walking by themselves, undisturbed, without anyone bothering them with excessive effusiveness. The good old notion of discretion governs this city that knows how to recognise and respect the intimate moments of a person and not bother them by taking it further than calling out a cordial greeting. And I'm talking about names unknown to us, yet very famous nowadays, real stars! Stars that have not risen in the night sky of our times...

Here is where Axel Engelmeier, the mathematics philosopher, has worked all his life and still teaches now, at a very old age. Here is where Kershey does his winter courses on the philosophical approach to culture. Thousands of people gather every night in the temple of Lysborg in Altona for the religious sermon of the beloved Knut Dieter, with the snow white hair and the soul of a child, to hear him recite so exquisitely the "Love thy neighbour as thyself" commandment and listen to his speech on the Mount of Olives. And the list is very long; Rudelin, Brigita Luni, Lestrem and Kirsten Nymark. The latter is famous in the field of history of art. Her annual schedule is this: four months of travelling and studying, four months in isolation, writing and doing research and four months giving lectures. She says that this alternation of time and occupation is enough for her to rest.

My old teacher Jaeger is the only "interpreter" of the work of Alex Jenefelt, who now lives in the Valley. I was very disappointed, though, one day when I went to listen to his lecture. I hardly understood a thing. Granted, Jaeger himself had told me only to go to the lectures of Lain and Astrucci, because there I would understand more.

I understand the phrases and expressions, because I am now very well used to their corrupted Anglo-Saxon, but I can make no sense of them whatsoever. Very well then, I'll go to Astrucci's class, to see what this educator of the future has to say. Or better yet to Lain's. That's what I'll do. I just have to make sure that Silvia doesn't find out and starts crying again for the fall of Andreas Northam...

Koralsen, Jaeger's very close friend, had fallen behind with his work a long time ago, as Stefan informed me, because of a great love. When Jaeger had asked him whether it would have been better to have missed out on this love, he had replied that "if it was something common then maybe yes, but when it comes to something so unique and beautiful, it's worth giving up everything to gain this wealth of soul that the memory of it leaves you with." Koralsen was an expert in analysing and interpreting Larsen's songs and especially a particular type of his songs.

Dalia Keetly is as famous for her gorgeous, silky hair as she is for her method of classifying the history of music.

Endless crowds lined up to participate in Felix Diemsen and Duilio Markmatt's series of courses about the $19^{th}$ century and I attended as well! I also went to hear the critic Oaken, whom we met in person a few days ago when he was giving a lecture on the great dramatist of their $9^{th}$century *(3300 AD)*, Inias Valmin. Lucifero had constructed a whole series of courses as well, based on the renowned painting *Nostalgic Green-eyed Lady* by Nichefelt.

And there are plenty of other leading figures in all fields; study of ethics, philosophy and history, cultural criticism, philosophy of nature and science, whose names I didn't even try to remember because I think it would be pointless and futile since I don't even understand the subjects of their fields of study, spanning from Volkic ontology, epistemology, the new cosmological approach and other, unknown to me, spiritual sciences.

Others take on the analysis of major works of art throughout the centuries; Shakespeare, Dante, ancient dramatists like Virgil, and lyric writers of the Renaissance like Victor Hugo and Alessandro Manzoni. They also analyse books like *Faust*, Dostoyevsky's *The Brothers Karamazov*, novels by Dickens - mainly *Great Expectations*– and Knut Hamsun's *Hunger*, Tolstoy's *War and Peace*, Thomas Mann's *The Magic Mountain* and several more works by our writers.

It struck me, though, how small the creations of our time are, compared with the great works of their 9th century: a huge gap.

Truth be told, the ancient spirit hasn't been washed away by either the scientific or spiritual advancement of the new era. On the contrary, I would argue that their 9th century has rather rekindled it, breathing new life into it. Just like the Volkic preaching didn't prevent the survival of the ancient and Christian values, but rather gave them another interpretation, another depth, another meaning. Freedom, justice, honour, democracy, love, pain, homeland, ideals, struggle for eternity, thirst for knowledge…More or less the same concepts but in new, more integrated forms.

It was no coincidence that I saw the statue of *The Gracchi Brothers* by Feinrich, the marble sculpture *Jesus Praying in Gethsemane* by Levertin, and *Ethics* by Gutorp Nilsen, all in central Markfor, a few kilometres from each other. The latter was a work of incomparable beauty, made of synthetic ivory, a work that manages to artistically capture and portray pain as inextricably linked to mental happiness. The same goes for the masterpiece *Towards the Light* by the sculptor Pradelli, who is said to be a distant descendant of the poet of the 3rd century. I happened to see all four of them in the same day and in the same area; in the heart of the city.

The other thing I wanted to mention is the respect with which everyone in Markfor treats the old Rome, which still exists but occupies only one fifth of Markfor and is now a new, different city, rebuilt from scratch after the Great Destruction of their -87 *(our 2309)*, which nearly wiped out all the temples of Europe, as they say. I haven't found out any more details about it yet.

So that's how I spend my days. Nylienborg, Almetta, Aurizio, Aarl, Rho, Legnano, Arona, Notiburg and Sesto Calente are the next on my list of destinations. And I will visit them all! I'm so happy. Actually, I don't know what I've done to deserve such joy...

## LANGUAGE AND ART

### 29-XII

### (At night)

Another reason why I'm so happy is because I see that my language skills are improving day by day. Back in the villas I hardly ever used the knowledge I had obtained from the language and pronunciation classes that Jaeger and Stefan had given me in the beginning. Markfor, however, is for me a field of infinite opportunities to practice conversation. You can widen the circle of your interlocutors very easily, as long as you can pass for one of them and hide deep inside you any hint of "previous life", any thoughts on pre-existence and afterlife.

Talk to them about neutral things: the weather, the new advancements and facilities in urban air transport, yesterday's mass in Santa Virgo, last year's maquettes of flower gardens whose construction was delayed so much… It's the best language practise ever, and it's definitely working.

As a consequence of the modern, collective type of living with this universal character, the old languages of our time have disappeared from everyday life. They haven't become obsolete in written texts and studies, but they no longer constitute the common vernacular.

The sense of belonging to one single ethnicity dominates everywhere on earth: "our country" as they call it. Yet the historical memories have survived as has the feeling of moral obligation to the greats of the past.

The intellectual culture has become one throughout the world, but there still exist some individual forms of literature, music, history of science and philosophy of consciousness.

All the different languages that we had, had ceased to exist as a result of the intermarriage of the peoples over the years, as they told me. They became extinct when mainly the European nations became entangled in a terrible civil war and were nearly annihilated *(in the medium-scale nuclear war that broke out in Europe in 2309 AD).* There had been an alarming reduction of the population due to the perpetual wars, in the past, before the Universal Commonwealth emerged, and humanity was in decline. But the law of history is always one: progress always comes, despite back-stepping, times of darkness and decline. But they say that the "New Dark Ages" - as they call the era starting from our 1914 and onwards - were not in vain. Thanks to that era, humanity took an upward course of evolution. As Soren Kierkegaard, a wise man of our time had prophesied, those dark years were necessary for the progress that came after.

Based on their theory, everything happens for a reason and everyone plays their own special role in the course of history. Nothing and no one is useless or unnecessary. Even the most seemingly insignificant persons are useful in some way or another because the whole is comprised of mere individuals and that whole is the axis of progress and evolution.

## INTERROGATION AT HOME

### 30-XII

I didn't go out until late today, because Stefan welcomed me very early in the morning with very disturbing news. Sabba, the sceptical blond in his forties with the outlandish theories, Stirlen's companion, would come to see me and I had to be at home at a certain time because he was very busy and couldn't wait long.

As soon as he came in, he started asking me dozens of questions about my life in Markfor and my impressions and if I remember ever being here before. He was accompanied by Alex Wettel Smith, the young saviour of Northam at the time of the accident. I really liked the behaviour of the latter towards me. He had a serene look on his face and seemed quite indifferent to the thoughts that troubled the professor's mind. A hint of irony in his eyes suggested that he did not agree with his methods. His gaze suggested something like: "If you had believed him from the beginning things would be simpler…" If Sabba hadn't been present, I would have shaken his hand and thanked him.

These "wise men" of the North are truly unfair to themselves. If they could overcome their selfishness and re-examine their prejudgment that I was merely a case of "split personality", they would be more human and able to realise and admit their mistake…

I spent the whole afternoon inside. I didn't go anywhere. I sat and meditated instead. I was wondering how many more new dawns I'm meant to see before I die. No one knows.

## NEW YEAR'S EVE

### (Just back from Santa Virgo, Markfor)

Tonight we will all stay awake until midnight to welcome the New Year.

I'm standing by my window, looking at this wonderfully lit state. It's the only time of year that all the lights are on at night. I raise my eyes and look high up above, praying for God to make me worthy of seeing my own world again for I had visited Rome in my former life and that is where Markfor is built. I feel my eyes well with tears. Night had fallen for good.

Three hours before midnight we went with Stefan and the girls for a short but very moving Mass in Santa Virgo. I noticed that everyone on the street was carrying candles as if it were Easter Resurrection. "New year, a new leaf in life" was their motto. Isn't that what *we* used to say as well?

Markfor is the city with the most intense Christian spirit and all the churches stayed opened and functioning until midnight so that they could please all the millions of people that had arrived. The last day of every year, everyone thinks about their year in retrospect, in terms of morality and other inner factors. And when I say everyone, I mean everyone, with no exceptions and not out of obligation. This is their New Year's Eve. White candles, devoutness and silence. No colourful balloons, no fireworks, no celebrations. And yet you can't believe the incredible amount of happiness that this day offers.

## DEATH AND SPIRIT

### 1-I-MDX

I date it as the first day of the year, but that was yesterday. Yesterday I couldn't write even if I wanted to. Nobody does. They spend all day concentrating, meditating and praying. I didn't see Stefan or Silvia at all yesterday and the truth is that I got tired of being on my own. I couldn't even read. I was still over-stimulated by the climate of yesterday's solemn evening.

These people seem to see things totally different from us. About death, for instance, we used to say: "Everything must come to an end. Say goodbye to everything. Life is something unique and unrepeatable. You will not see any of it again. You're leaving everything behind."

Now they have different beliefs: they feel that, when you depart from this world, you leave behind all the good deeds that you have done and all the work that you've completed and that the only thing you take with you is your inner cultivation and the improvement of yourself, depending, of course, on the path that each spiritual life has followed.

With this logic and mentality, and because of this belief, they don't mind carrying the weight of another year on their shoulders.

Their metaphysical faith is also completely different from ours. We believe that you're only born once, while they believe that even if the human body didn't exist, the spirit would find its way to manifest itself in some other world.

In any case, Stefan had told me to be upstairs on time, just before midnight. And so I was. I was looking outside my window when suddenly all lights went out in the entire city and the bells started ringing! Simultaneously, the artificial light - this time light blue instead of white - began to gradually envelop each and every district of the city. The magical part was that the light emanated from the earth! It was as if the city was being born out of nowhere! The Heptagon with its statues and its arcades, the eight parallel avenues Lambarene, the domes of Grazie Dei, the endless gardens of Serinaio, Chilisprin, Gretatria, the lawns of the Alexiad, the cloisters of the Novum, the Roads of Jasmine, the Central Gallery, Santa

Virgo, the temple of *Gretlys*, the hanging Tuplin Park, the Artificial Hill of Noghera, the artificial lake of Viborg with its famous Japanese cherry trees - wherever you turned your gaze you saw semi-circular arches in vertical position emitting light in such a way as if they were pulling it from insides. Veiled in that transparent, blue, glimmering light, the city welcomed the start of the New Year for half an hour. I was enchanted!

**3-I**

**(Late at night)**

It's my 150$^{th}$ day today and my heart is overflowing with happiness and excitement. Today there was a beautiful morning sun after ten hours of light drizzle that had forced me to keep my windows shut. This sun reminds me of my city and my mother. Mother, let me lean my head tenderly on your shoulder like I used to… Remember? Let me tell you my story about the great happiness I've found, a happiness so big that I still don't know what I have ever done in my life to deserve it…

**4-I**

Back to first joys of our childhood! Back to the time when even the slightest little thing was a source of joy! It's a nice, clear morning and we're off to Jaeger's small seaside mansion!

# GOING TO SCHOOL
## Lessons by professors Lain and Astrucci

### 4-I Again

### (Midday)

Stefan and I just got back a little while ago from Professor Lain's, where we spent about two hours this morning. For the first time Jaeger came along. I enjoyed seeing this affable, white-haired teacher with the bright eyes again after about three months, and all these little children who, surprisingly enough, all called him Father. He is simple and easy to understand, I like the way he talks and I might be coming to hear him teach, whenever I have nothing else to do. Plus, Silvia has finally made peace with Andreas Northam's condition. And Jaeger has talked to both Lain and Astrucci about me. I think we're slowly becoming great friends, the venerable *Ilector* and I.

### 6-I

I think that when the people of our time reach maturity, they get trapped in a routine and slowly become enslaved by it. They become seemingly "knowledgeable" and "down to earth" and start walking with their heads bowed down from the pressure and the stress of everyday life, losing any interest in the colour of an autumn sky, like the one I'm looking at right now. No, Mother, it's not a lie! Believe my words: "The great state with the trees with golden leaves" did not only exist in the dreams of a simple, naive and gullible child's heart...

### 9-I

It's the third morning that I go to hear Lain. This man has his way not only to convey knowledge, but also to speak directly to your heart. And how nicely he explains and simplifies everything! There is not a thing I didn't understand any of these three days.

This afternoon I went to the big boulevard that runs along the central park. I didn't look for its name but it's parallel to the middle road of the Roads of Jasmine and, in my opinion, it's the most beautiful part of this entire state. On my right-hand side, I had that enormous park with the artificial lake I've mentioned before, and on my left-hand side, on the other side of the boulevard, I had the 130-meter long row of palaces, which looked as if inhabited by Titans.

The light drizzle was falling on me and bouncing off my shoes and I remember that I thought that in my previous life I would have already fallen into melancholy with such weather. But now I'm happy! I know I repeat it all the time, but this psychological contrast of mine surprises me and I can't help pointing it out over and over again.

# THEIR MONTHS AND FESTIVE DAYS
## Teachings by Lain

### 9-II

It's the ninth again, but the ninth of the next month. I didn't write a single word for thirty whole days this time. I'm so absorbed in Lain's lessons in the mornings, in my endless walks around the city in the evenings and on the *Reigen-Swage* at night that I haven't had time to write.

Nowadays, each month has exactly thirty days. They now mark them in Roman numerals instead of the old names we used to distinguish them. The start of each New Year is marked by the autumn equinox. It has been that way since the top scientists took the political authority in their hands and obtained the power to legislate and handle all political matters of everyday life.

Each year consists of five intercalary holidays: New Year, Christmas, one dedicated to human altruism and two of anniversaries. The first is to mark March 5th 2396 *(according to our calendar)*, the *Aarsdag* of the *Retsstat*, which is the anniversary of the day that the whole world was united into a Universal Commonwealth governed by law and order. The second is commemorate of September 6th 3382, the *Aarsdag* of the *Gretvirch*, the day of gaining access to direct knowledge from Alexis Volky, who led the human species to the next stage of evolution.

They have a sixth holiday every four years, which had occurred the year before last, the MDVIII *(3904 of our chronology)*. The ancient division of the week is not used anymore, perhaps because the two-year service, without any exceptions or days off, putting an end to the distinction between working days and Sundays. As for the citizens, the *Cives*, such as Stefan and the rest of the people, they adjust their individual timetable depending on their mood and the work to which they have dedicated themselves, if they have any...

Now on the subject of Lain and his lessons. In the classroom you hear things that aren't just for children. Even adults could complete their education there. He teaches almost everything, from philosophy and history to social sciences and their own, mainly spiritual, sciences: a breadth of fields though not in so much depth, but still, something like that would never happen in our time during our years of basic education. And so these mature sixteen- and seventeen-year-old adolescents have perfect knowledge of at least the basics of each field of study when they graduate and therefore can, after completing their two-year service in the *glothners*, choose to specialise or just receive training in any field they feel they are inclined towards.

Nowadays they truly appreciate and honour the spiritual sciences, not the ones designed to describe and interpret the external world and life, but the ones that pay special attention to inner depth, the ones that penetrate into the deeper meaning of existing things. And they argue that these sciences are not so much connected with the abilities of the human intellect, but mainly with feelings and emotions. And what they use as "means to capture and interpret" that part of the human existence is nothing else than the experiences and delights that shake the human soul to its core.

This man speaks in a very strange way and it becomes even more interesting when he, himself, teaches about the great men and women of the Aidersen Institute and the Valley.

"Nobody ever expected," he says, "such an incredible justification, such a catharsis of the human tragedy." The "smart" and "knowledgeable" people of earlier eras, the "experts" of the *Eldrere*, let people be perpetually bombarded with moral values just to facilitate their own lives. The more people were bound by ethical principles and feelings, the more difficult it was for them to compromise their conscience and the more the "specialists" benefited from all this. They used the honest hesitations of ordinary, good people to their own profit.

And the powerful leaders of the planet said the same things; political, social and ecclesiastical leaders advocated maintaining that "code of conduct and ethics", because it helped their plan. And so these ideals were being recycled over the years and kept manifesting themselves over and over again in identical or similar forms, pushing the evolutionary course of life of mankind to maturity, and yet serving individual and collective interests at the same time. Especially the promise of an afterlife as a reward for virtue was one of their major tenets!

"The people of prehistory," said Lain, "and even of our *Eldrere* were fascinated by the unstoppable advent of high ideals in the form of love of freedom, social justice and humanism. However, nobody before the *Nibelvirch* knew the true Reason for them. They called them ideals, dreams, protests of downtrodden crowds for the degradation of human dignity and life. But then they saw what great truth was hidden behind them..."

## 13-II

"Up until the generation of Mary-Lea," said Lain today, "one of Volky's students, everything transcendental or metaphysical was considered and dealt with as a form of faith, not knowledge. It took a while until they realised why this simple distinction between good and evil existed and understood that they weren't just some man-made rules of expediency, useful only for the smooth functioning of society."

## THE ESSENCE OF THE AIDERSIAN KNOWLEDGE: THE UNITY OF THE MATERIAL AND SPIRITUAL WORLD AND THE EVOLUTION OF RELIGIONS

### 14-II

Lain said again today that the greatest realities are the ones we're unaware of. Our eyes cannot see them and our intellect cannot conceive them. There are no words familiar to human reason to describe their divine substance. The awareness of our existence might have been given to us as a gift, but, for as long as we stay simply human beings, its substance and structure will remain transcendent and beyond comprehension to us. Then he said something that I didn't completely understand: that the path towards knowledge is a "relative idea" we approach it, at times more so and at others less, but we can never possess it.

Only after the Aidersen Institute pointed it out did people realise that the distinction between the physical universe and the spiritual world is completely subjective and human-generated. There are no material and spiritual worlds; there are only genera of living beings, organic, rational, biological species, others with stronger antennas and others with weaker cognitive abilities. The Great Reality is single and uniform and this was proved and demonstrated by the great visionary minds of the Aidersen Institute. And so the "cognition" of our race became enlightened and its limits expanded enormously, something that in the era of the *Eldrere*, nobody could have ever suspected or expected; not even the ancestors of *Homo Occidentalis Novus*, the next evolutionary stage of humans after *Homo Sapiens*.

Lain continued that there are no miracles and supernatural things; there are no things that break the laws of nature. All these things that we call supernatural are nothing but laws that are inaccessible to human cognition, logic and way of thinking.

Their history and chronology only consists of two eras: the *Eldrere* and the *Nojere*; the old and the new era. The first one is the genuine heir of our 19th and 20th centuries, infused by the spirit of technical culture and the achievements of science, dazzled by the technological achievements of man, science, reason and the mind. The second one, the *Nojere*, revealed the true depth and meanings of existence and gave the correct interpretation to the mental tendencies of man. It revealed that the world and life have a divine meaning and purpose, completely different and unrelated to the narrow and finite human destiny. The natural sciences were not and did not offer true knowledge. Science was practical and very useful to our lives, but did not contain the absolute truth. Only the new experience of *Oversyn* or *Oversynssans*, as they also call it, in conjunction with the *Nibelvirch* give man pure knowledge and deliverance from pain and doubt and terminate his metaphysical anguish. This "new experience" is the miraculous achievement of the Aidersen Institute.

Just writing about all this gives me goose bumps. Every single time I hear them or think about them, they seem unbelievable to me. All the knowledge that stemmed from science and the metaphysical beliefs of the ancient - to them - times has been concentrated, adapted and reshaped to create something single and united: Volkic preaching. Dogmatic faith - or rather the dogmatic part of all religions - has been replaced but without tampering with its substance. Quite the opposite, since religions were exempt from the age-old burden of simplistic details that had obviously been inspired by the human mind. As a result, the moral and emotional elements and treasures of every religion then came to the surface and were finally highlighted. So here, religion no longer becomes subject to criticism or questioning after each scientific progress and breakthrough. It doesn't get "refuted" every now and again and it's no longer forced to constantly and desperately defend itself.

He continued, citing as an example the fact that cremation was now more widespread and that those alive no longer expected "to be caught up together with them in the clouds to meet the Lord in the air." He quoted the Bible word for word! I couldn't hold back my laughter when the words came out of his mouth... This man has his ways…

He says that maintaining the self-consciousness of the ego is now enough to save them from the threat of the old narrow and finite biological destiny of humans. So the death and decay of the body doesn't matter to them anymore.

"Did man of the ancient, unenlightened years," he asked, "mind the findings of biological research, which showed that every seven years there remains nothing of a human's material self since all our body cells are renewed?" At this point, even the youngsters laughed.

He mentioned familiar names, like Nietzsche who, in Lain's words, tried to "destroy every spiritual value and affect the validity all previous spiritual victories", and Darwin whose mistake was "his excessive belief in the cognitive abilities of man."

"The Darwinian Theory is indeed compatible with the divine gift of life," he said, "but only if you see it as a separate, individual point of view instead of the absolute truth. Because, in that case, you ignore the millions of different species of rational living creatures that inhabit millions of other planets. But I guess that's how it goes... Just like the *Homo Sapiens* spent thousands of years until he finally gained consciousness, the same thing happened in the next stage of human evolution: Man's world was rocked by hundreds of manifestations of this incredible thirst of the soul and spirit, but he didn't know that all that came from the *Samith*. He had no consciousness or knowledge. We needed the arrival of the *Nibelvirch* in order to gain consciousness of ourselves and the world and interpret, belatedly, all the emotions we felt as a species."

He also said that thanks to this divine element of undiagnosed texture, all the species of the universe tend to rise higher and higher, both spiritually and intellectually speaking, having managed from a bestial state of organic matter to end up creating a whole history of culture. Coming to the end of the lesson, he spoke again about the "self-cultivation of the spirit" that goes together with overall biological evolution.

## HOW TO LIVE ACCORDING TO PROFESSOR LAIN
## Comments about Prehistory and the unity of time

### 16-II

I remember Lain saying yesterday that in every era young men and women are thirsty for ideals because the young soul is made that way. While speaking to the youngsters, he made a distinction between the "ideals of a people" and their personal ideals. For the former he said that their objective is the maintenance and improvement of the historical course of humanity and spiritual civilisation. He added that culture, as an ideal, doesn't have a beginning or an end and is not limited to our planet.

Now, as far as their personal ideals are concerned, I recall him saying that the highest personal ideal one can have is the ideal of freedom, namely the attempt for everyone to become a free, moral and spiritual personality, to the maximum possible degree. And also that true education is not necessarily defined by knowledge as much as it is by the inner cultivation of the person and the mental urge to act based on and led by high moral standards.

"Get rid of your passions, the vices, all things vulgar and base. Free yourselves from the shackles of the material human nature. Be free, moral personalities and try to enlighten your lives with all that is beautiful and meaningful."

These last words of his reminded me of several of our religious sermons. But then he spoke about how, after the youth is over, people drift away from the reflections of the *Samith* and how this ends in moral pain and anguish, causing a type of depression that often touches post-teenage souls.

"But you," he said, "won't let your youthful enthusiasm fade away. You won't be brought abruptly back down to earth like older generations. You won't become "knowledgeable" no matter how many years go by. Because for us, the people of *Nojere*, the Aidersen has fortunately preceded us..."

Indeed, he stressed that thanks to the Aidersen, it has been proven that the mood and state of mind of people during puberty has always been far wiser than the state of mind of those of a more mature age! The young antennas proved more powerful in capturing the world of today.

"Look at me," he said, getting their undivided attention. "You young people have always been more capable receivers of the beauty and importance of the spring, a full moon, love or true freedom!"

He also added that the people of the *Eldrere* thought that "letting go of your dreams" was a result and a sign of life experience and wisdom, and if they saw today's wise men they would consider them and treat them as "overgrown children".

"But our wise men are still capable receivers and much wiser than the ones of past generations because they never let go of their dreams and never forsook their ideals in the face of a belief of dubious origin."

He then spoke of all the different forms of "local states" - namely our nations" - before the *Eldrere*, and briefly looked back on the entire period of their own prehistory: our present and immediate future that is, up until the end of the 24th century. If I'm conveying his words correctly, he said that in terms of state organisation, in conjunction with the corresponding social realities of each time, three were the big turning points of "prehistory": the period of the Athenian democracy, the end of the 18th century (with the North American and French types of states) and the mid-20th century (with the emergence of the welfare states of the North Europeans and the states of social peace, insurance and prosperity of the Scandinavians). He added that while the Athenians had their own type of political institutions, they also had a Plato and a Socrates to complete them.

He also said, however, that our ancestors thought that the answer to every social problem was the ensuring and safeguarding of a high standard of living, in the material sense of the word, that is the abolishment of poverty, unemployment, and insecurity of tomorrow. But such a mentality and tactics ignored the human factor and its internal texture completely because you do more harm to people if you provide solutions to all their economic problems and relieve them of any concern and responsibility regarding living from day-to-day if their souls lack faith in eternal values and ideals and if central moral values and orientation in life are non-existent. The internal balance of these people is more at risk then.

He repeated once again that the distinction between good and evil, right and wrong, is not man-made; instead it has an eternal meaning that goes much deeper than we think and reflects and responds to greater realities, which we now know to exist. This distinction would still exist and remain unaffected even if life stopped occurring or had never occurred on our planet. There would be life on other planets. The so-called innate morality in a worthy man, he says, has incredible depth of origin: it is not accidental or hereditary.

"This awareness has now offered us the consciousness of the destination of human life, which is purely Aidersian and which humans of prehistory or even the *Eldrere* were completely unaware of since they had unilaterally turned all their attention to the economic and industrial culture of the time. Knowledge was incomplete and one-sided. There is no here and there, now and then. Reality is single and multidimensional and contains everything within it."

I remember him saying, among other things, that the duration of this life or the happiness in it doesn't matter as much as the pursuit of excellent experiences, the best reflections of the *Samith* (art, sacrifice, love). The central idea, if I understood correctly, was the rise of the idea of the High, the Divine, the Wonderful, in all their manifestations. He was trying to express in every possible way his worship of the great ideals.

"They gave value to their lives," he said, stressing the words "they" and "value", "regardless of whether the life of those who passed from mortality to immortality was short and full of pain. Their struggle and their sacrifice were not in vain even if what they achieved ended up disappointing them. And not so much the struggles and sacrifice per se, as what they represented in that particular living environment. In fact, the insignificant and humble ones, those who weren't made for greatness, proved more worthy compared to those whose lives were paved with roses, by facing life's challenges successfully against all odds. And when I say 'successfully' I don't mean in terms of profit, but in terms of morals. Tangible happiness, even if we agree it exists, isn't worth as much as confronting misery. Thus life, down here, was earned not by those who were happy and fortunate, but by those who kept a proper moral attitude in the face of challenges as well as joys."

He couldn't stress more that happiness only exists in the form of "potential", which as I found out was a special Aidersian term. I also learned that Lain had lost his only child if that says anything about him…

Another thing he said that struck me was that the inner need for affection and good deeds was capable of giving meaning and value to the life of even the most isolated person, the most underprivileged and alone. Thus, from an early age - and he emphasised this part as a recommendation to his students" - we need to be able to distinguish appearances from the essence of things. He then underlined the need for the modern, enlightened person to fight against the instinct to attain easy happiness and a long life because without the corresponding intensity and high level of spirituality, there can exist neither happiness nor true longevity.

Finally, about life in this environment he said that it is transient and temporary and that's the reason why it's so short and of low quality. The moral and spiritual individuality comes here to live a painful adventure, full of frustrations, a dramatic experience of living in foreign lands, dominated by a constant, painful feeling of absence from its true home; a feeling of nostalgia, thirst and lack of fulfilment.

## ARTISTIC CREATION: ARTISTS OR PROPHETS?

### 19-II

Yesterday we reopened the subject of culture and artistic creation no longer being considered as a mere projection of the human spirit in the outside world. He claims that everything that has been carried out throughout the entire human history in the fields of culture and art does not fall into the category of creation but into that of revelation - a partial one for that matter - a revelation of amazing things, which, however, were "pre-existent", unrelated, that is, to the appearance of man on Earth.

And deep down, he said, everyone preached the same; Plato and Christ, Praxiteles, Da Vinci, Michelangelo, Goethe, Wagner, Einstein and Henry Durant, Agni and Menestrem, Valmandel and Larsen. Except that everyone expressed it in their own language; some with teachings, some with tables, others with sculptures, lyrics or discoveries. They were all prophets without knowing it and they had expressed, though timidly and incompletely, some of the truest, most divine meanings and purposes of this life and of the world in general.

The moments experienced by a cultivated art lover, a sensitive receiver that is, before a great work of visual art, have much in common with the corresponding hours of prayer or reverie of a religious man or a philosopher or with the moments of a poet's inspiration. It is the same "intuition of the glimmer of the *Samith*" revealing itself in many different ways and forms to the capable and worthy receiver; it is the same "feeling of liberation" from the confines of mundane living, the cruel fate of life.

He said that after the acquisition of *Nibelvirch*, dreams and ideals proved to be much more real and tangible than everything that the simple material reality of the natural world contained. And the great poets, the previously regarded as mad, suddenly transformed into prophets! In the end, the creatures of their imagination proved to be real!

He also spoke about religions, saying that the people of the past leaned entirely on the major religions that had been formed over the centuries. But what is more important than the individual religions is the religious feeling, innate to humans due to some turning points in their biological and spiritual development, this "thirst of soul" that makes us consider life impossible without the existence of "higher powers" or "the divine element".

Formerly, people exclusively admired the scientific theories, laws or discoveries of *their* era: Copernicus, Kepler, Newton, Einstein, Astrom, Jergesen, Sioberlef, which had to do with the universe and celestial mechanics. Nowadays, however, said Lain, we know that sooner or later new "truths" will give way to the old ones, disprove them and displace them.

Based on Lain, the same goes for social life. People in the past gave importance to its rules, codes of conduct and its limits. Nowadays, we know that what counts the most is the innate consciousness that exists within each person, which wants justice and morality to reign and gets upset in the sight of unrighteousness.

All these forms of internal necessity are nothing other than that "thirst of soul and spirit" for the *Samith*. It depends on the psychological type of each man. Some find salvation in art and others in religion. This is what we now believe. This is what now leads us; the memory of the Great Reality, the *Samith*, which everyone has now seen with their own eyes…

## 20-II

On artistic creation, I remember him saying that, in the past, by the end of the *Eldrere*, theoreticians believed that art was the process of creating a beautiful and higher world above the real one, an ideal or illusory world, something like a dream. But that wasn't the case. The main goal of the artist is not to give knowledge, but superior experiences, to bequeath to his contemporaries *that* experience which creates and transmits artistic emotion. An artist's job is not to disclose, but to touch the heart.

"Like the genius composer, the great philosopher or the inspired poet, the worthy scientist or the noble founder of a religion, like the leader who sacrificed his life for the sake of his people, choosing his biological self-destruction to save the rest, so does the great artist take on the characteristics of a small god who has the power to give us timid and fleeting glimpses of what really exists: the *Samith*."

**22-II**

Today, in the morning, he repeated that "before the arrival of those great, visionary Aidersian spirits", half of the people agreed that life was unique and unrepeatable and that we were lucky to even experience it once. The other half argued that coming into this life is another experience of biological existence that dedicates itself to the spirit. That type of experience made its appearance on this planet too. Life will be short time-wise - a few decades only - but will be endowed with the full potential for moral and spiritual supply and "broad knowledge", since man will watch the evolution of life and culture unfold on this planet only in a few years, a process that formerly took a whole millennium.

But now they know: the wonderful experiences of life are not an inner issue; they have their external source. The old generations were lured into a hasty and superficial psychophysiological interpretation - a shallow interpretation for that matter. The biological existence on Earth is said to be a "pathway full of pain and glory with an exquisite secret meaning" for the spiritual entity of evolved human beings.

Eventually, he concluded, humans grow to love their body - something that would be incredible if said to them from the beginning - the mortal coil, because it is a fragment of their ego and they have been closely associated with it. They mature with it, they hurt, feel love and pain, enthusiasm and noble passions with it, they go through thousands of inevitable organic adventures, dangers, pain and diseases with it and, at last, they are separated from it amongst tears because it has been part of who they are…

**24-II**

I couldn't follow today's entire lecture. From what I could understand, he was saying that, just like in Tinersen's parable of the tropical land's apple, the "great secret of the world and life", which drew the attention of the curious soul of the Kiils, the creatures living in the apple, was the third dimension, namely something that existed, but was inconceivable to their mental antennas. Likewise, the distance that exists between our world and the *Samith* is for us incredible.

## THE "BEASTS" OF HISTORY AND THE VALUE OF HUMAN LIFE

In another diversion in his lecture, speaking about megalomania and the destructive tendencies of many of the "wild beasts of history", as he called them, he said, "The biggest culprit for the corresponding crimes against humanity, bigger than even the international thugs of the beast of the Apocalypse, like, Clarissa Leyton, the oppressor Tebrief, the bloodthirsty dictator of an era of stifling and intolerable overcrowding and other "wild beasts", was the living environment of those dark times. [Lain used the number 666. Perhaps he meant Adolf Hitler but avoided mentioning his name to Dienach in order to protect him from this knowledge in case he returned to his normal body].For the villains alone couldn't have committed such crimes if life and society had had the foresight to be structured differently."

When it comes to a paranoid man, it is better to control and tame him than to go against him. The proper assessment of things did not escape those paranoid leaders, who supported the doctrine of "action, not thought", but relied even more on the intellect and the spiritual and moral climate of their time. That's what prevented the organisation and proper functioning of institutes.

People of those times failed to maintain a legal order in a context wider that the mere territory of a country, so that it constitutes a "true legal order" that it wouldn't resemble a castle in the sand. The human factor wasn't truly appreciated since people were merely perceived as a number rather than as a moral and spiritual value.

"Today," he added, "such vainglorious maniacs would be considered despicable because, led by their thirst for power and hiding their criminal propensity under the mantle of material power and under the pretext of trying to make a new and better world, they trampled countless beings, each of whom was a whole separate world, as if they were autumn leaves. And now we know the value of each and every being; we don't look at them as living material or as mere organic matter, but as moral and intellectual entities. But back then, the "furious world rulers" and the individual local political leaders had their way to present all our great, current truths and realities as fairy tales, didactic exaggerations and empty moral teachings."

Then, if memory serves, he said that nowadays nobody has the right to "think on behalf of his fellow man, control him or act like a blind force of nature deciding on the bigger or smaller duration of his earthly life." But that's how our ancestral eras prior to the *Nojere* faced life as a whole; they believed that a mere aspect of the *Samith*, our physical universe and the matter and energy contained in it, together with the laws of nature, was everything. The dimension of depth escaped them. Our ancestors suffered the same illusion as the Kiils from Tinersen's parable of the tropical land's apple…

**27- II**

The Reigen-Swage Institute in Markfor can offer you unforgettable winter nights. I've been coming here every day, from the first morning hours, since the beginning of our November, about twenty days now. One can divert and transport oneself in there and think they live in other worlds, other eras.

Here, the art of entertainment has taken incredible paths, unimaginable for our own time, and has invented new, impressive forms of art, entirely different from our ancient theatrical art and our shadow theatre. This amazing art of these times offers you a vivid spectacle that is also accompanied by sound!

Forgive my feeble and clumsy writing, which cannot in the least describe or illustrate any of those miracles I saw with my own eyes. Forgive me, you, who will one day have my papers in your hands. I wasn't even worthy of seeing them, let alone describing them… I wish you could have read them straight from my heart, before expression betrayed them, before my human words ruined their magical beauty…

The sea had its own fragrance while you sailed on board the French triple-decker *Ocean* from the last quarter of the $18^{th}$century, sitting high on its tallest mast, listening to the sounds made by the large sea birds mingling with the officers' orders. The same emotion was generated in the glade of the Tyrolean slope; the same in the country of the aurora borealis; the same in front of the authentic image of the red planet's landscape, which is said to have been sent from our own people hundreds of years ago. Everything looked so real! You think you have been transported to the actual places!

But my biggest passion was history, just like for so many adolescent boys and girls enrolled in the Lain Institute. We sit here and the history of bygone eras unfolds before our eyes.

Even more imperative - needless to say - is my thirst to know the European and world history from the 20th century onwards. And now they have archived all this with remarkable accuracy and in great detail, and they know everything much better than we knew the historical facts of the corresponding time difference from our era.

The disasters and the ensuing losses of valuable material that occurred - especially during that terrible calamity of year - 87 of their calendar *(approximately our year 2300)* - were much larger in size, extent and depth than any other that we had witnessed in our time. Nevertheless, much survived. Apparently the terrible torrent of overcrowding, the unexpected population explosion with the horrific consequent conflicts and atrocities and the new weapons of mass destruction did not sweep everything away. And so today's researchers know about the eras before their 16th century *(our 40th)* much more than we knew about, say, the Roman Empire and the past forms of political and social life. Their representations in particular, contain less fantastic and artistic elements, compared to ours, and many more authentic ones. And that's because they're based on more numerous and better selected documents.

## THE DECLINE OF THE 20TH AND 21ST CENTURY
### Overpopulation shows its face

### 28-II

The 20th century saw the end of European hegemony in the whole world, not only in terms of military, political and economic power and influence, but also in terms of the imposition of authority and ethics. If Lain is to be believed, the whole century flew by in this manner, completing this mournful fall of Europe's civilisation, which had taken the form of a techno-culture of which the main features were the plentiful standardised industrial products, meant mainly for consumption, the unconditional and unlimited admiration of the technical applications of the natural sciences - and all economic values in general - the craving for material comforts in life, the indifference to inner cultivation and consequently, a huge vacuum in people's soul and emotional intelligence.

In the arts, primitivism and abstraction were fashionable and things that used to be considered inconsistent and incoherent, were now considered a new kind of style. In architecture, the era of cubic shapes had replaced the masterpieces of earlier eras. "The unmistakable sign of decline," said Lain, "was not so much the fact that such 'works of art' were produced, but the fact that the second they came out they were immediately welcomed by the public without any questioning or complaints. Mainly this was the great debasement.

During the 20th century, the moral values of the 19th century gradually gave place to the materialistic attitude towards life, its physical "upgrading" through the popularisation of amenities and the "practical" pursuits. The standards of living went up and the consumption of food and industrial products rose to an extent inconceivable for previous times. The "pursuit of the dollar" thereafter became one of the primary motivations of creative action and everyday life. Sensitivity had become old and obsolete. Man's consciousness didn't challenge the circumstances anymore and his capabilities for rebellion - very common in the past - had decreased significantly.

The "Western spirit" expanded in terms of territory, but also lost a large part of its spirituality. It diffused everywhere, throughout the world, gradually overpowering the unique attributes of each nation, like race or language, even in the countries of the Far East. The Anglo-Saxons in general managed to impose themselves on an international level with their currencies and their language, and the North American confederation in particular took on responsibilities of political influence around the world, to such an extent that no one could have imagined at the beginning of the century. But they weren't prepared for it; they lacked tradition and experience.

Along with the economic, political and technological culture that came from across the ocean, Europe was also flooded by the immature American culture, which managed to prevail in almost all areas of intellectual life without the slightest resistance: in aesthetics, dance, music, visual arts, architecture, principles of the youth, attitude towards life. Everywhere! In education, the teaching of the "classics" was significantly reduced everywhere in order to save time for technical training and "more practical" education.

Acts of violence, terrorism and subversion and manifestations of nihilistic attitudes and mentalities occurred every so often everywhere. Long established principles such as solidarity, aid and compassion for the weak and poor and the respect for human dignity started collapsing one after the other, even within families, in front of the new powerful, selfish sermon: "Every man for himself."

If to all that you add the "automation of work" in the new, large industries, which deprived people of time for reflection and moral self-control in the course of their life - something vital for the people of this era - one can understand the poverty of inner life and self, which was one of the main features of the 20thcentury, along with the stressful pace of life and the many manifestations of the "aggressive struggle for survival," as they call it today.

The prevalence of a type of realism, according to which technical progress is not the means to an end but the end itself, was the main culprit for the crisis of intellect and spirit. That's why a new Middle Ages made its appearance in Europe and everywhere else in the world, without anyone realising how or why this happened. They said it was as if it came out the light of the "televisions", out of this blizzard of white light and images…

The democratic ideals were replaced by the "competition of autocracies". The main concern of the entire 20th century was whether the totalitarian institutions should be of right or left-wing ideology. And many conflicts were generated for this reason.

There also occurred several clashes, decades later, when the uncontrollable overpopulation led both the peoples and their unworthy ruling classes to complete deadlock. And when it finally became clear that the necessary preventive measures for monitoring the demographic indicator had been delayed too much, the good old ethical and political demands for "individual freedoms" and for "civil and human rights" collapsed even more to the point where nobody even thought of them anymore.

The Middle Ages had come creeping on the sly. In disguise, they made their way into society through blithe and cheery dances, illuminated boulevards... It was the materialistic century, an era of zero sensitivity, zero concern for human values and zero noble feelings. It was an era of unilateral technological progress without the necessary moral maturity of man.

Everybody was only interested in themselves. Love, straightforwardness, mercy and forgiveness were all swept aside. Within a hard and wildly competitive environment, the value or indifference to the means used by someone for the purpose of attaining wealth was judged based solely on results and effectiveness! The hesitations of conscience were considered as "lack of common sense"! What prevailed was the thirst for power and domination and the smothering of every reaction or emotion that arose by any means possible.

Young people, who were then lacking even the basic moral values, said that "they didn't believe in anything" and, of course, the ones who were to blame were the adults, who had left them alone, without a guide, to "find their own way."

At the same time came what was later to be called "the worthlessness of idols", meaning the observation that, in all parts of the world, young people had started admiring "idols" - actors and mimes, boxers, footballers, scruffy, longhaired musicians, courtesans and heartless tycoons - instead of true heroes!

As a result of the lack of faith in at least *some* ideals, people lost their inner balance. The fall of ideals left a terrible void. People suddenly became incapable of approaching a superior view of life and the world, a deeper interpretation. The world of religion collapsed. A number of physicists argued that the scientific knowledge had come to replace the "naïve faith" in good!

But too much faith in the omnipotence of science did not solve any of the problems humanity was facing, or at least those members of humanity that deserved to be called humans, said Lain. In short, they said that problems didn't actually exist and that questions were posed in vain since there were no answers. "Things are what they are" was their motto. In their view, life was an irrational flow of sequential events, a completely random biological evolutionary process without purpose, direction or reason.

And there came times when this disappearance of all faith and metaphysical havens, combined with the exhausting rhythm of life of the human-robot, resulted in the appearance of distressing mental side effects on a grand scale: severe neuropsychiatric disorders and extensive suicides and then a stage of nihilistic self-abandonment prevailed for many years.

**8-V**

"Nowadays we teach the incidents of prehistory not only for informational purposes but also as a means of exemplification and kind of intimidation," Lain said. So in teaching and on the *Reigen-Swage*, the unwinding of historical facts and events also has an educational mission. Everything is exposed objectively, as it really happened, and students are called to draw their own conclusions.

But someone who has lived in the 20th century, like me, would find remarkable exaggerations in the historical overview of the problematic areas of our times. In any case, what I saw prevailing today is a "sense of liberation" due to the reassurance that "the worst has finally passed" and that those dark times will never come back. This era is characterised by an "exalted soul", a high morale, a deep faith that keeps them morally armed and prepared to fight and sacrifice to defend their current institution if ever such a risk were presented again.

## THE "PHANTOM OF NUMBER" AND SUBSEQUENT BIRTH CONTROL

### 9-V

Tremendous clashes have taken place, especially after the 21st century of the Christian chronology, no longer regarding the world trade and the global industrial supply, the ports and the domination of the seas and the "areas of consumption" or the once sought after "energy sources"- which, up until the 20th century, were the main objective of the foreign and economic policy of the great powers at the time, but for whole different reasons. The cause of those clashes was the criteria that would be established and applied among the various tribes and nations, relating to birth and population control and the "replacement rates" that should be allocated to each race and also the wording of the corresponding legislative texts that were to be voted by international parliamentary assemblies and implemented later by the global institutions of power.

Racial discrimination was, of course, not tolerated by people, at least on these issues, and so they didn't have to keep highlighting the principles of humanity and the value of "equality" in the spiritual entity of man. However, what once existed and was applicable in the years of "comfort of space and number", now had to be desperately fought for since they were well aware of the fact that times had changed and that it was now a matter of survival or extinction. A terribly hazardous situation had now arisen: extensive famines had occurred, mainly in the poorest nations in Asia and Africa, and millions of children were starving and dying, tormented by poverty. But even the industrialised countries of Europe had seen the shadow of malnutrition spreading over them. And because of that, social and political upheavals occurred frequently throughout the world.

The Baltic peoples together with the Slavs, Scandinavians, Germans, Latinos, Greeks, Walloons, Flemish, the Anglo-Saxon and a part of Indians and Israelis had a common front contrasting the above arguments for "humanism" to the "unpostponable need for action" for humanity and therefore shaking the edifice of civilisation their ancestors had carefully built.

This need had become extremely pressing and tight like a noose, a noose more and more ruthless and suffocating and this created a terrible contradiction between theory and practice. As the decades went by, one could clearly see that it was no longer only a matter of food sufficiency but also adequacy of space and that the "phantom of the number", this once unprecedented and unknown terror, this new nightmare that soon came to completely cheapen and demean the value of the human being and to eliminate in its own way–its way being the decline in quality that follows any "inflation" - all hitherto achievements of humanity.

There came times when the ancient law of the jungle defeated the principles of early civilisation. The unfortunate coloured races were finding themselves in a disadvantaged position in all the confrontations, despite their unparalleled numerical superiority, because they once had faith in international laws and had left their strongest weapons in the warehouse of a central federal authority, that is, essentially in the hands of the whites, who always got the majority of votes in global institutions. Another cause of their disadvantage was their inability to effectively cope with new discoveries in the field of mass destruction weapons and the "scientific" conduct of war. Thus, one could see very old, primitive impulses and instincts reviving, even temporarily.

We, the people of the 19$^{th}$and 20$^{th}$centuries cannot conceive how huge and intractable a problem it will be for us in the future to find, an empty and permanent place in that colossal "human organism" called earth and to integrate ourselves into it and manage to live our lives.

The great evil had come as suddenly as a flood and to such an extent that no one had predicted it. Any measure adopted each time gave the impression that it had come too late. And then many scientists who worked on the issue of demographic perspective were accused of incompetence and poor forecasting. Then the public outcry was directed at the Roman Catholic and Protestant Churches, because by "living in the clouds" and by insisting on the old perceptions and the negative attitude, they had contributed to the failure to timely legislate institutions for effective birth control and the monitoring of demographics.

And the days when the whites saw only the person behind the black and yellow skin and preached that "all men were created equal", the days when white people had even gone into civil wars in order to enforce the principles of humanity and respect for life and freedom of every human being, regardless of their colour, now seemed like a dream...

## THEIR DIVISION OF HISTORY

### 12-V

As I have already mentioned, they divide history into two major periods: the "most ancient" *(Eldrere)* and the "new" *(Nojere)*. What is considered as the "New Era" is the last five hundred and twenty-four years, the era of the "enlightened person", the era when the *Homo Occidentalis Novus* appeared. Its starting point was the first *Nibelvirch* and the survival of Alexis Volky. Sometimes they use the Greek words for it: "Nea Epoche".

Before that was the *Eldrere*, the "most ancient age" that had lasted nine hundred and eighty six years, starting from year 1, namely the time of the establishment of the *Retsstat (the "Global State of Law and Order")*, which coincides with the launch of their own, new chronology. Further back was "the dark ages of prehistory" according to their own strange perception. They say that for thousands of years "people had been struggling to survive under the triple scourge of anarchy: economic, political and demographic."

In schools today they paint a rather exaggerated and grim picture of our times, which they call "prehistoric: an image of chaos, brutality, mutual extermination, a "dark world" with criminal instincts and perversions, with "thirst for pleasures in life and indifference to moral acts", with materialistic motives everywhere and disregard for decency.

In fact, their idea of love-making was that of a superficial and heartless act, a mere biological pleasure without spiritual contact, emotion or inner qualities. The influence of "family and school" had been reduced to the minimum. The young people were after "life", "intense activity"; any kind of "dynamic action" rather than thought. The hours of meditation seemed long lost and gone.

The least one of us could say to object to this is that they always "overstated the exceptions", something that I noticed myself and told Stefan as soon as I got home that night from Lain's.

He smiled and told me that the production process of the "economic commodities" was arbitrary and completely lacking in coordination. There were also too many rival, dominant political powers and patterns in international relations, something like states within a state, and last but not least, a lack of any monitoring of demographics. He smiled again…

They too have their own historians and their own methodologies in historical research and historiography. Their own distinction, the border between history and prehistory is not the beginning of writing, as it was to us. Their starting point was the prevalence of law and order. This last one - law and order and its final establishment - they consider a prerequisite for real, spiritual civilisation.

I've been told that attempts to impose control on births had also been made during "prehistoric times" and on a grand scale indeed, but without "united institutions throughout the world." And this lack of appropriate institutions had led to extremely grave historical injustices. And it goes without saying that all the efforts for the establishment of political federations and especially economic unions and all sorts of economic consortiums before the *Retsstat* - the establishment of the Universal Commonwealth with law and order - had the exact same impact on society.

They say that over 450 years of "prehistory" were full of such "experimental institutions" and various "separatist coups", leading each and every time to global crises and collapses before the final proclamation of the Universal Unifying Assembly on March 5$^{th}$, 2396 AD, which later in the future came to be triumphantly justified.

Most of these experimental institutions were regional, taking the form of nationally or ideologically neighbouring racial groups, which were aiming for a simple "balance of power." And although the substantial value of those institutions was essentially negligible - due to the form in which they appeared - it constituted the foundations on which the Universal Commonwealth, in its present form, was ultimately built. That happened more or less around 2390 AD, that is, 477 years after our League of Nations. The dominant figure, as I was told, was an Englishman named John Terring, the first leader of the Universal Commonwealth.

## ELDRERE: THE FOUR-CENTURY STRUGGLE FOR REAL GLOBALISATION
### The first fighters of the new world and global food issues

### 13-V

As I mentioned above, "exemplification" and "bullying", along with the transmission of information and knowledge, were nowadays used as educational tools for teaching prehistory in schools, lectures and the *Reigen-Swage*. Something like showing *our* children the way and conditions of the life of a Roman slave in a galleon, the morals and traditions of the time of feudalism and the extent of the sexual rights of the master over the newlyweds in the villages of the serfs or the pyres of the Inquisition in Spain...

And yet today they honour the people of the 24$^{th}$ and earlier centuries in many respects, regardless of how appalling the incidents of those times are. In their eyes, those people of our times are the "first fighters", who struggled and fought and suffered in order to enable future generations to live a normal, human life. They are the "honoured ancestors", the "pioneers who paved the way." They look back to our era with gratitude! They characterise it as "epic" and "heroic" and strongly believe that it was necessary for the course of history; without it the law and order and the rationalisation of life would never become possible.

Lain says that every era generates its own questions, questions that the elders are called to answer for the youngest. And every era has its own characteristics. He said, for example, that the 20$^{th}$century was characterised by people's tremendous efforts to control forces, such as electricity, nuclear energy or solar energy. People began to dominate nature. In addition, the automation of work, due to the electrical and electronic devices created a problem that was not visible to the naked eye: the workers' extra free time! In fact they argue that that self-determination given to the workers, mainly the industrial ones, was, according to many thinkers, one of the main reasons why human history and civilisation on earth took this course! Because that extra free time of the workers was filled with low-quality spectacles and entertainment in general, like gambling, prostitution, the speed races and sports games and vulgar popular mass media. Music was reduced to simple melodies and rhythms, the masterpieces of literature circulated in illustrated summaries and thought was considered a waste of time! Another characteristic of the time was that people lost their ability to distinguish the good from the bad and the beautiful from the ugly in art and creation...

In the 21st century, the rural economy was put on the back burner. And as if the demographic problem wasn't enough, a new, terrible issue made its appearance: the increasingly smaller area of arable land, which was constantly being eaten away by the increasingly expanding giant urban areas: the so-called urbanisation.

By then, it was already a fact that food was no longer adequate and people started looking for nutrition alternatives and sources outside the boundaries of the food industry, mainly focusing - if Lain is to be believed - on seas and oceans, which gave the impression of an inexhaustible source of food.

Thanks to scientific progress of the era, nutritional and edible substances could be extracted from plankton and the underwater flora and fauna. Artificial photosynthesis, however, had not yet come to the rescue of humanity.

But the most tragic thing of all was still the "phantom of the number". At this point in history was when the sentence "the coming years will be hostile" was first uttered. People lived in very tight spaces, but in colossal residential areas and many times they were forced to move around wearing masks because of the polluted air.

In another field of life, the 21st century was marked by the first test flights with destination to the nearest alien lands…

## *(Lost notes followed)*

At the same time, on our earth, the first serious and somewhat positive universal efforts were made to strike down the monster of anarchy, which tormented human societies for centuries and in many forms: political disorganisation, fights over sovereignty, military rivalries, plundering of national economies, demographic anarchy and the like. And so began a dramatic struggle that lasted approximately four centuries, with many alternating phases and transitions, a struggle between the ancient, but well-founded, beliefs and the new ideas about the organisation and rationalisation of life.

The revolution in political organisation that was based on logic and humanity followed the exact path and time sequence of the two other great revolutions, the French of 1789 and Russian of 1917: first came the philosophers, intellectuals and theorists of the new world order, saying that as the form of organisation of the 19th and 20th centuries with the fully armed dominant nation states, which most positively led to holocausts and annihilation could not continue, and then - after a long period of time - followed the political activists, orators and social reformers.

Mainly in continental Europe and Great Britain, the intelligentsia urged the political leaders of the large and powerful nations to stop their "outdated and unsynchronised course."

They preached prudence and sound reason and told them that the days when "the people had to fight for their rights" were long gone and that, old incentives and slogans like "national prestige", "no compromise, no retreat" and "heroic course of the nation" had lost much of their value due to new conditions of life.

They spoke of a "system of eternal values" that their European ancestors had bequeathed to the new generations and told them that they had to be the guardians of this sacred legacy, which was much larger and deeper than any of different ethnic roots or linguistic differences.

They said that cultural heritage, historical traditions, the course of life and historical destinies were common to everyone. "We must unite both in life and in consciousness!"

There was no need for extensive revolutions to take place in order for the new world order to be built on the ruins of the old regimes. To a large extent, pivotal international treaties were signed, and that was enough, at least initially.

The new law and order followed more democratic paths since the days of the Pax Romana, although it took a long time and several attempts to establish it. The expectations of the proponents of the New Order were often wrong. Many were repeatedly persecuted before the New Order finally prevailed.

While the small nations had no such "concerns about the future" in the 21stcentury, in the large and powerful countries new political alliances had begun to take shape, alliances that had integrated in the program some characteristics of European or universal federations. In fact, it was even reported that the old parties, the Socialists and the Christian Democrats, also added requirements of the new era to their programs.

As the decades passed, these new ideas and perspectives found more and more fertile ground, especially in the hearts of young people and the lower social strata. And so, with the passage of time, the political arena began to acquire its first "great men with global recognition and appeal" for the first time in history, in contrast to the local leaders we had become accustomed to.

Technological advances had eliminated distances and had brought people very close to one another. The world gave the impression of a single region, still politically disorganised, waiting for the "legislators" and the powerful politicians with global authority to permanently lay down the rules for the "organisation" of the planet. At the same time, man now had weapons of mass destruction in his control, unknown and inexistent in earlier times. The rapid technological acme, however, was not in line with the corresponding moral maturity and rationality. There was no "internal law", a law of spiritual culture like the one they have now, which was needed as a guarantor of law and order.

In our times, they said, we thought that ensuring the compliance with the law within each country separately was sufficient. War was for us a natural way of resolving serious disputes between nations. That was the state of mind we had before the 21st century.

The 21st century had to come in order for people to suddenly realise that they were hovering above a frightening gap in the global public sphere and that their institutions were completely obsolete. So, gradually, the once dominant states began to bestow - deliberately or not - part of their previously almighty powers, especially in the fields of foreign policy, international relations and arms, to a central, federal political organisation. They kept their historical memories, traditions and customs, language, legends and their domestic institutions, but they had now realised that in a future war there would be no winners and losers. They would either stick together, or all together they'd lose. They began to see who the true enemy was: the lack of strong and effective global institutions with the preventive mission to control all forms of conflict. They finally realised that what united people - their common biological fate and their shared responsibility for the maintenance of culture - was more important than what separated them.

The smaller nations were rather comfortable with their old social formations and had their own internal problems to worry about, so they were the last ones to adopt the new forms of organisation. The "Great Powers", however, which had come to the fore in the 21st century, were struggling to understand one another. There was constant whining and complaints about the ways and criteria of the distribution of universal income. No one ever believed that their share was fair…

These "reactions" of the 21st century were meant to become the omen of the future "separatist movements", which erupted repeatedly and were incited by the same "political nuclei" of the initial reactions! The requests were the same: demographic regulation and financial interests... For four whole centuries, sometimes the French or the Anglo-Saxons and other times the Germans or the Slavs revolted for "autonomy", all with the same objective: to take the lead, from then on, in the historical course of mankind. "This fiery ordeal will pass," they said, meaning the war they themselves had started. "Whatever happens is for your own good. The democrats are unable to give you the order that you need..."

And the economic wars were usually followed by armed conflicts. In the latter they only used the old conventional weapon since the separatists had no access to the "forbidden ones", but this did not prevent those conflicts from evolving, several times until the 24th century, into real, extensive wars with mass casualties that threatened the universal federation with outright collapse every single time.

Eventually a bearable organisation was created, which, in its final form, lasted for many decades and paved the way for the end of prehistory, the new chronology, the coming of John Terring and the beginnings of the *Eldrere*. However, separatist attempts appeared in the first hundred years of the new chronology as well, that is, almost until the end of the 25th century, as Lain said, but they were too weak and doomed to failure. Mostly, as we explained, they were condemned in the minds of the people of the *Eldrere*, who no longer tolerated political anarchy, coups and the dominance of the strongest.

During the last one and a half centuries of their prehistory *(20th-24th century for them)* the migration waves had been reduced to a minimum and the population had been equally distributed around the world, not only in central and northern Europe any more, but on the other continents too. The Scandinavians had not yet been invited to descend to the deserted southern regions up to the Mediterranean Sea for the purpose of re-colonisation after the debacle they had suffered just 87 years before the definitive establishment of the *Retsstat* and the beginning of the "new chronology". The white race had now conquered all five continents... And from the Semitic peoples, about a hundred and twenty million Israelis - now most of them Christianised - were at the helm both culturally and economically in southwest Asia, having developed there a high level of techno-culture, always with the Holy Lands as its centre.

Latino populations, mainly from South America, had colonised nearly all of the central areas of the African continent - you'd only see black people on very rare occasions. The warm now - thanks to the artificial air conditioning - Arctic regions were dominated by a brotherhood of Russians, Norwegians, Anglo-Saxons and other Baltic nations such as Finns, Poles, Danes and Canadians, while Antarctica - also characterised by a much more temperate climate thanks to human intervention - was colonised mainly by white South Africans (probably descendants of the Boers) and in the east by Australians and New Zealanders.

East Asia was occupied almost exclusively by Slavs, who had come from the north, the descendants of North Americans from the western states and by a medley of Europeans, who could now fit more comfortably in all those fertile valleys, while several millions of Indians lived in the highlands of the centre of the continent and Tibet. In the Mediterranean, the Ottomans had retreated to Lake Van and the Greeks had re-inhabited Asia Minor, since their country as well as the North African coast had been evacuated. The latter was largely resettled, mostly by Italians, as soon as life there was possible again. This is mostly what I remembered and managed to copy from my books.

This was the territorial status quo prevailing in the 23rd century and, in fact, the maintenance of this status quo had been guaranteed at the time - mainly by the white race, which was the big winner of the confrontations - in the ecumenical councils of the federal transnational democracy that had been established, with representatives of both the people and the governments of the member countries.

In fact, I was surprised by the fact that the "civic spirit" of those who served in the armed forces of the now established universal authority was formed by special and long-term educational training. They removed them from their social environment and the environment of their national life at childhood and submitted them to special training in order to consider themselves citizens of the world and have a high level of general education. They handled the new electronic devices of universal legal order excellently and their number was incomparably smaller than the number of the armed forces of prehistory though their term of office was much longer. So it was only natural that there were more young scientists and technicians rather than officers and soldiers.

They were also aware that they wouldn't be forced to use their invincible firepower, on which they had the monopoly, and was only valuable as a kind of guarantee. Nevertheless, they had blind faith in the universal congress and, were taught at birth to forget their ethnic origin and consciously obey the dictates of the two Parliaments and the executive authorities of the federation.

A similar sense of responsibility to humanity also suffused both the military and the members of the collective Executive office and the double parliament (the former elected by the people and the latter appointed by the governments). They all considered themselves devoted to the service of unity. I remember them being called "diplomatic agents of unity" and always "at the service of humanity". Only secondarily did they consider themselves envoys of the people who had elected or appointed them. A type of the local leader still exists, but possesses limited powers because now international law has prevailed over domestic law.

The institution of "unified citizenship" had already been introduced to all by the Anglo-Saxons Verchin and Milstone by the 22nd century. The shaping, however, of a common national consciousness was not directly obtained and in line with the ever more refined version of federal institutions. On the contrary, this formation took centuries and it was an extremely slow psychological process. Much later, after the first two centuries of the *Eldrere*, a new "universal sense of ethnicity" began to mould. People began to realise that they were members of a single, universal, national and political community. Although historical memories had not, of course, died out, as I was told, more universal ideals started taking shape. "This is *our* country," said the representatives of the new generation, looking up at the sky of our blue planet!

At the end of the second century of their chronology - two hundred years or so after the time of John Terring - was the time that politicians had been freed from government responsibilities and replaced by the great technicians and other leading figures in natural sciences, who were now responsible for handling political power in the world over. The new leaders then introduced something that had started a long time ago: the establishment of a global federation of labour organisations - in the form of a political institution and not that of a trade union any more - and, following completely legal procedures, they turned these new cooperative collectives into the basis of economic life on earth. They were also the basis even of political life, I might add, if you consider that people had to participate in the *glothners (their industrial units)*, registering for long-term occupation there, in order to obtain the right to vote. In those times, law and order had prevailed conclusively and convincingly. There was no longer fear of a separatist revival.

However, the first centuries of the *Eldrere*, even after the year 486 and the creation of the Rosernes Dal, was a one-sided era of technical civilisation and a true spiritual man, they say, would not have felt comfortable in such an environment of mechanocracy and materialism. The Valley of the Roses, Rosernes Dal, took a long time to pay off and many philosophers throughout history contend that the 9$^{th}$ century of the great intellectual creation is not itself a consequence of the directions of the Valley, nor exclusively the fruit of its spiritual influences. The Renaissance in spiritual values came late; approximately by 700 of their chronology.

The most characteristic features of the *Eldrere*, their old age, is the prevalence of the ultimate and satisfactory order in the world, "the policy of the compass", as they call it, which resulted in the rational course of collective life, good governance and administration, egalitarianism, universalism in political values - such as universal suffrage, equal rights, social justice, individual freedom, united sense of ethnicity and the highest personal safety - organised global production, abundance of food and all kinds of industrial products in general and generous distributions to the *Cives* not based on their contribution to production, but on each person's needs. In addition to all that, there was also a meticulous birth monitoring for the sake of human dignity. For the first time in history, so far, they had achieved high living standards of the entire population without exception and the participation of all in the positive exploitation of the goods of material culture!

And I, dazzled by the incredible number of images I saw *on the Reigen-Swage*, images of comfort and abundance in material goods, would prefer a thousand times to live a life travelling between Paris and Vienna after the Napoleonic wars... If I were to choose, I would gladly trade the mentally and socially insured restful life of the "master of the *Eldrere*" with those decades. I'd gladly give up such a life of "safety and certainty for the future." The *Eldrere* seemed to me extremely lifeless in its first six hundred years, judging of course from those bits of life that I manage to see, here, on the *Reigen-Swage.*

But Stefan and the others here more or less share the same opinion: that in the early centuries of the *Eldrere*, peoples' ability to experience an inner and more spiritual life was significantly reduced, nearly inexistent. Lulled by the sense of satisfaction concerning the abundance and quality of material goods and under the impression of happiness, as they say, the "thirst of the soul" had dwindled.

That's why they argue that the contribution of the *Eldrere* to the building of the true "inner culture" was minimal. That era only took pride in the quality standard of industrial goods and the more than sufficient production of them. Humans were considered numbers in statistical studies rather than personalities and spiritual entities. By "progress" they only meant economic and technological achievements. They conceived of happiness in terms of life comforts and adequate distributions. Happiness for them was an easy, enjoyable life with modest and limited esoteric thoughts. Prophets and artists no longer existed. Those who spoke of man's metaphysical pain were considered morbid.

In a word, the *Eldrere* was the era of the apotheosis of the technical and economic culture and the downturn of the inner culture, as Cornelius was telling the children of the Lain Institute some time ago.

The *Eldrere*, he said, was an extension of prehistory - after the 20th century and until 2396 AD - an era of technical and economic prosperity. These latter forms of organisation and life spanned from my time until the 7th century of the new chronology. They say that the past generations were aware that no spirituality continues indefinitely with new achievements. After it reaches its peak, it begins to decline, the spiritual and moral foundations bend and in the end, the only thing that remains is the carcass of techno-culture. I think that what Cornelius was doing here was nothing more than telling the old version of our own Oswald Spengler, who spoke about the fall of the Western world.

So, this was the image of life in the *Eldrere*, at least from what I had seen on the *Reigen-Swage* and from what I heard from Lain, Cornelius and Stefan; and all this after the definitive establishment of the *Retsstat* on March 5th of our 2396 AD.

The great intellectual work and legacy of the past were not destroyed. They still existed but only few engaged with them. They were forgotten in libraries and warehouses without attracting the crowds with their old charm anymore…

For this to happen, their own Renaissance had to come, which did between the 7th and 9th centuries, and was followed in the next hundred years by the famous, exquisite zenith of civilisation. That's when the old treasures of the intellect and spirit resurfaced...

# THE "FEAR FACTOR" AS AN EDUCATIONAL TOOL FOR THE YOUNG CITIZENS

## 2-VI

It is a habit here in the Lain Institute - and perhaps not just a habit, but an educational method throughout the world - to exaggerate the weaknesses of our historical eras and to go as far as to scare children, creating a kind of anxiety in them with all the horrible images they make them watch. They want to plant and promote in the children's psyche the faith and devotion to current institutions, universal homeland and the new era from a very early age. I think their goal is to rule out any possible future threat to the universal organisation of all political, social and economic aspects of life, which has been solid for centuries now.

I don't know how effective this process is and to what extent their goal is achieved in the long run, but the means they use to accomplish it are characterised, in my eyes, by an incredible ferocity, an intolerable cruelty; I must admit that it's something quite frightening.

"Will they come back?? Will they come back??" cried the frightened children of the lower classes yesterday at the sight of the "barrage of fire attacks" and the destruction of an unknown-to-me state from explosive and incendiary bombs of our own 20th century, as I was later informed.

The horror painted on the faces of the youth while asking Cornelius, me and Stefan questions, was indescribable. They were under the impression that the green lava that flooded the streets, horrific collapses of buildings and the fire torrents that covered in flames the city blocks - images I saw with my own eyes on the *Reigen-Swage* together with the youngsters - were weapons of aliens that had invaded our planet, weapons that all our defences had failed to neutralise!

When they explained to them the next day that this was not a foreign invasion but actually self-destruction, when they told them that their ancestors literally destroyed their own cities and people themselves, the youths were left speechless. They couldn't believe it! When they finally realised it, they tightened their fists and swore that, growing up, they would never let this horror and tragedy happen again!

"Don't be surprised!" said Cornelius. "Considering the conditions of life back then, there was no other way… The reigning mentality was: 'Kill or be killed'. Atrocity was the rule and the annihilation of others the slogan."

"What others?" a boy asked.

"The supporters of the opposite party or opinion, depending on the occasion. Friendship was not something natural; instead it changed every so often and depended on the circumstances and interests. A mere order was enough to turn yesterday's allies into enemies and vice versa. And don't blame the ordinary people. Even back then they were inherently meek and good. They were tame and cheerful, similar to us. They didn't hate each other. They loved strangers and foreigners, they were hospitable and they liked animals. But sometimes, economic and political power fell into the hands of miserable beings and that's how the wars broke out. Wars didn't come naturally. They were artificially created by their bad and unworthy leaders along with the weapon manufacturers, mainly Asian," he claimed. "They pushed peoples towards hatred and mutual extermination. It is fortunate that our species managed to prevail. The risk was fatal."

Many a time I wondered if what Lain said to the children was objective and fair. Listening to him you'd think that the yellow and black races, which never found vindication in history and which are almost absent nowadays, were solely to blame for everything.

"Isn't it true that war had been a biological need?" asked one of the older children. How would all that immense population of the time fit on this tiny earth without war?"

"Yes, it was indeed a biological necessity," replied Cornelius. "But so was the law of the jungle among the primitives, in the times of savagery. The law of selection and survival of the fittest..."

He continued by saying that the laws of physics have a typical disregard for the moral connotation of any action. That's why all these atrocities had to permanently disappear from human civilisation. The continuation of such events and such manifestations of brutality were indicative of man's failure to establish a regulatory procedure with the purpose of finding a "humane way to resolve any conflicts."

He then said that a few decades before the era of John Terring, war was already being viewed by all people as "a state of anarchy, nihilistic rebellion against institutions, criminal violence, general collapse of values and self-destruction."

This modern, popular teacher said more things on the subject, which, sadly, I don't remember. And I think that no teacher of the past, not even the most skilled and educated teacher of the 20th century, could have been able to even slightly approach the level of spirituality and mentality of a teacher of the *Nojere*.

Although their profession and specialties might unite them, they are divided by a lot more: different cultural circles, different historical eras and a completely different social reality. Cornelius is not just a teacher; he is "a teacher of the *Nojere*". There's a huge gap between him and us.

Another interesting conclusion that I had drawn, concerning the leaders of our time - especially the older ones - was that, from a psychoanalytic perspective, they were often under the regime of unpleasant mood that's quite common in the elderly, and a profound, subconscious bitterness felt due to the organic law of decay. I also think they had an aversion to the youth, which often took the form of spite and that's why it was extremely rare to find the youth in positions of power back then, even though those positions would have enabled them to exploit the qualities of enthusiasm and love for life and people. Very interesting point of view!

## THE NIGHT OF THE "GRETLYS" *(the Grand Light)*

### The events of the September that changed humanity and history

### 3-VI

That same evening Stefan told me, "From now on, don't go to Lain's for history classes any more. In order to be able to deeply experience and appreciate the dawn of the *Nojere* you need isolation, concentration and meditation. Make sure you revise all that you've learnt when you're alone."

I talked to him about the wild scenes that they show to the children, scenes of war and of all the other incidents that had taken place before the *Eldrere*, making them cringe in horror, and I told him that it was both unfair and unnecessary to traumatise children with such images.

"War is not coming back," I said. "Fifteen centuries have passed since the beginning of your historic era and this is the best guarantee that it will not come back! Times have definitively changed; war is something prehistoric!"

### 5-VI

Today I have dedicated myself and my day to meditating devoutly and attentively upon all the great things that my eyes were worthy of seeing last night. I've told everybody that I want to be alone all day. Never in my life have I felt such an excitement, or rather, such awe and holy thrill. Now I'm by myself, locked in my room, remembering it all and I praise God for giving me the opportunity to witness them in this life.

There are moments when I feel the need to fall on my knees and pray. Last night, around midnight, I found myself watching on the *Reigen-Swage* the great days of 986 *(3382 AD)* and couldn't believe my fate that gave *me*, an insignificant worm of the 20$^{th}$ century, the unbelievable chance to see the dawn of the *Nojere* come alive before my eyes! I saw the holy deaths of that September in the Valley, Alexis Volky before me in the midst of the Great Moment, the torrent of the *Roisvirch* that followed and all the major incidents that shortly thereafter opened new pages in the history and spiritual life of those times.

I sit in my armchair, thinking about all that with tear-filled eyes, full of gratitude.

I wonder what power could ever be so powerful as to shed such an unearthly light on those white faces! What was that exquisite thing that those people saw in their last moment on this earth that was so inaccessible to our eyes? They say that all those men and women who suffered the "sacred blows from the unbearable light" those first six days in the Valley of the Roses were beings of significant inner beauty and nobility. Who could have imagined that even their outward appearance would have been beautified, as if all the magnificence of their souls had suddenly spilled over to their faces? And almost all faces there were young. I looked at them one by one. Something like ecstasy and triumph was drawn on each of them. Why do today's people say that they succumbed? I witnessed quite the opposite: every single person there looked as if they had been transformed into the personification of victory, as if they had suddenly been called upon by God!

After all the sudden deaths in the beginning, nothing foreshadowed the glorious things that the future held. Life in the pre-*Roisvirch* Valley flowed peacefully and institutions were increasing and flourishing but, no matter how satisfactory the fruits of long-term reflection and meditation and the findings of thousands of institutes and research centres were, it had never crossed anyone's mind that such an incredible intellectual achievement would ever be a possibility. Even though almost five centuries of self-cultivation and inner development of the intellect and the personality - through many generations of fine anchorites - were about to be completed, it still seemed like a miracle!

For the outside world, the two major events of early September were firstly the huge preparations for the World Exhibition in Blomsterfor, which in terms of global participation and wealth turned out to be by far the most successful one ever, and secondly the election of a new *Lorffe* of the time, whose name escapes me. These were mainly the issues that preoccupied the crowds then.

And the era did not seem to conceal any particular Messianic needs, nor were there any preconditions in the world for the emergence of this kind of group psychology. On the contrary: people lived happily in every corner of the world around that time, with security, law and order, political organisation and stability, sufficiency of goods and comforts, and with moral and psychological balance.

The incredible boom in literature, arts and intellect, which were engraved in people's minds as "the golden age of intellectual and spiritual culture", had only just happened a century ago, in their great 9th century. People still breathed that fresh air of the great and newfound period of prosperity and had incorporated all its creations into their own lives. Anything but a crisis of morals and collective distress prevailed in the world.

And yet, in the midst of such a completely balanced and genial atmosphere, one of the first days of September, the outside world suddenly discovered that peculiar incidents were taking place in the Valley, incidents whose importance could not be explained, but which would, however, go down in history as earth-shattering - if it was, in fact, proven that their content and meaning was actually what many big names of the Valley believed them to be.

Thirty-six hours before the *Gretlys* and the survival of Alexis Volky, four similar incidents occurred outside the Valley of the Roses, in locations far away from each other: one in Lesley Gate, one in the Balearic and two in the North Sea. People turned to God then and began to pray in groups, leaving all of their other jobs and responsibilities!

That reminded me of the times when, every now and then, the approaching of a comet threatened to destroy life as we knew it and everyone sought solace in religion. But this time it was not the fear of death that caused this anxiety in people around the globe. A secret hope had arisen, a hope for some sort of an imminent enlightenment, the discovery of a great secret, completely distinct from the natural world, which was the object of study for the exact sciences.

Nobody could tell what really happened then. Did it have anything to do with what some wise men later claimed, namely, that some unknown, but at the same time friendly superhuman beings from far, far away, had shed their beneficial light over our land? Nobody could say with certainty. Most people didn't want to accept in any way the existence of such external and alien spiritual forces, limiting themselves to commemorating the "200" and repeating the names of Miliotkin, Joel Letonen and Gunnar Nelbarn, the leaders of the first anchorites, the pioneers and settlers who, 486 years ago, were the initiators and founders of the Valley of Roses. They say that the Aidersen Institute "took over" from the descendants of the "200".

During the nights that followed, most of the people throughout the world stayed awake. The bells constantly tolled, calling people to prepare for what was coming.

Inside the Valley now, multitudes of people spent days and nights in the parks and squares of the immense campuses of the Aidersen Institute. In fact, not only were they not giving up, as fatigue must have worn them down, but the crowds were only *growing* in size after the *Gretlys* from September 7 and onwards. For more than 250 years now, this famous institute with the global reputation has been the only one to provide moral and emotional support to the people of a time when the masses were resting in the bliss of ignorance and considered the thirst for metaphysical quest a tyranny, a thirst that in earlier times was considered an honour and a privilege of only a few, handpicked spiritual figures.

Billions of people around the world had put their spiritual hopes in the great wise men who were housed in that glorious city – the Institute. There, in the Aidersen Institute, among the high ceilings of the large central palace, in the auditoriums, next to the semi-circular cluster of statues and accompanied by the venerable figures of the old tradition, those of Pythagoras, Plotinus and Kant, that of Blaise Pascal, Socrates, Plato and Maeterlinck, of Riset, Gustavsen, Rasmathy, Plioskin and so many others, the great Chillerin had spent most of his life, entering the Aidersen as an apprentice from a very young age in the early 9th century, there, in those auditoriums, where he later taught…

Chillerin himself believed that regardless of the finite nature of human knowledge, humans had neither tried hard enough, nor had they selected the right methodology for knowledge acquisition in the past. He didn't have anything specific to say yet, but he did have faith in people's ability to resolve the great mysteries of the world, despite the imperfection of the mind and senses, and he believed that the day when they would finally arrive wasn't far away.

Whilst thinking about all this, I'm now watching on the *Reigen-Swage* the Aidersen Institute, staying alert during those long nights, with thousands of people surrounding it on their knees, keeping a vigil all over the campus, waiting for their spiritual leaders - Chillerin's great grandchildren - to emerge with an answer, an explanation of what was going on, but in vain, for they were not yet in a position to give any.

Inside the vast hall: a crowd of sleepless, overworked and upset wise men, dressed in the official Aidersian garment with the blue stripe on it, the stoat and the insignia. The whole Aidersen was in a state of confusion and distress and plenty of other people from smaller yet related institutes kept arriving, even from the other side of the Valley! The meetings were continuous and successive but without any positive result so far. Even the wise men of the Aidersen themselves were waiting to be informed about what had just happened from those coming from outside.

Yes! Things have finally started to become clearer now and many of them speak of some sort of an incredible reward. The emergence of a new, unprecedented *Virch* had now vaguely become the centre of discussion and the name of the elder Alexis Volky, their old peer who had definitively left the Aidersen Institute several years ago and had gone to become a monk, was whispered in the circles of the wise men with much respect over the next few days. No one had made contact with him yet. The only thing they *had* done is to make the selection of the ambassadors that would be sent to him. They did not even know where exactly in the vast Valley lay the secret retreat where the venerable Elder had withdrawn after "what he saw", spending his days and nights fasting, meditating and praying.

While the crowds waited in devoutness outside, inside, the wise men with their gaze lowered before the busts of their predecessors, the *Lorffes* and *Ilectors*, and with their faces buried in countless piles of miniature books that contained the crystallisation of the all the intellect of the entire human history, carried on discussing and deliberating feverishly. But still no results…

## 5-VI

## (Late at night)
## "But God chose what is foolish in the world to shame the wise"

The *Nibelvirches* had begun to multiply and become more frequent both in the Valley of the Roses and in distant countries, and almost none were fatal after the survival of Alexis Volky. His cry of ecstasy and his subsequent peaceful sermon, which, as the days went by, encouraged other triumphant voices and individual spirits to speak up. But the crowds only recognised and trusted the Aidersen Institute. That's what they had learned to respect and listen to through a long tradition passed from father to child and that's where they had laid the hopes of centuries! But the Aidersen remained silent and cautious. And it would stay that way for weeks to come.

## 6-VI

Nowadays the entire holy place is unfenced. I saw it in the *Swage*. A simple string of white marble, sculpted into small rectangular rings, shields it from careless missteps. Even a child could jump over it if one wanted to. But no one crosses. They all go round it anti-clockwise, starting from the cluster of the small cedar trees. Passing through there, one finds oneself in a large, stark white courtyard - or at least so it seems on the *Reigen-Swage* - with a few columns and walls which, up to a certain height, seem to be made of ivory. In the background, very close to the ancient white wall, beneath the dome with the Novotronium by Nikorski, you can see the seven holy lights and the banners fluttering in the azure light. The entire sanctuary is paved with a single pure white, marble-like slab and the surrounding area is covered with the famous light blue rosebushes, just like in the Pantheon.

Now I'm seeing the same place again, but the way it used to look. It's identical! I saw the white-bearded Alexis Volky dressed in the white robe standing tall - as the septuagenarian elder has always been under - the stars as he experienced his majestic, god-like Great Moment.

How many times had Jaeger and Stefan talked to me about this place and with how much emotion! I clearly see Volky's student Mary-Lea sitting on the stairs at the feet of the great Master, hurt, and now destined for the Beyond, away from the ugliness of this life. You can see her crying with joy. She doesn't hide her face; she keeps her head up instead, as if in the midst of ecstasy and inspiration.

You see the old man standing upright and motionless, with his head up, staring at the vast state. It looks like a white vision. The ecstasy, the awe and the "holy horror" of the first moments are engraved on his face and have left a trace of light, a glow beyond description on it. He is no longer trembling and you can clearly see how he is now, a master of his own emotion. He knows there is no reason to boast; it just happened that out of all people, he proved to be the most prepared. That's all… He's just another one of us, with the exception that he was able to withstand this "sudden stroke of light", because for him it wasn't so sudden. The "exquisite divine spark" had hit on real rock this time!

Always upright and stiff, he looks towards the horizon while a tear rolls down his pale, ascetic face. I wonder what he's thinking… Is he seeing the dawn of the new spiritual day down there on the horizon? Or is he thinking about the past and pondering the incredible outcome of the history of mankind?

You see, he had spent his whole life in the Aidersen Institute since he was a young child. He had had made the dreams of his ancestors and Chillerin's promise his own, and he cared for them deeply…

# THE STORY OF MARY-LEA: A MODERN SAINT

## 7-VI

A few days later he gave his name to Mary-Lea - adopting her posthumously - a long tradition in the Valley among beloved teachers and students who happened to lose their lives prematurely and then attended her funeral in the Aidersen, among the crowds of wise men and the thousands upon thousands of other people, standing strong and proud, without shedding a single tear.

That day was an apotheosis for Mary-Lea, as thereafter she would be remembered in the Aidersian tradition as one of the most popular figures of modern spiritual culture. Her funeral pyre was surrounded by thousands of flowers from all around the world, and thousands of people, all dressed in white, knelt around the ashes of that noble Troendin, whose soul couldn't bear the "breaking of the bonds" and the "nostalgia of the heavenly homeland".

On the 7th and 8th of September, the last two days of her life, after having escaped from the Valley, she wandered in remote lands, somewhat mentally unstable and unable to master her thoughts. The last people that she encountered were left with the impression that she was possessed by obsessive thoughts.

Two gardeners in Doriani said that on the morning of the 8th, a beautiful blond girl with deep blue eyes dressed in a long white dress had stopped them and asked them the way to the sea and actually explained to them that she was heading to the seaside, bringing very good news to a young lad who had been waiting there for a response, patiently, for thousands of years… In fact, she even repeated the same phrase in ancient German: "Er wartet auf ein Antwort", which means, "He's waiting for an answer".

Further down, there was a bevy of workers who were on their way back from work at the break of dawn. To them she spoke normally and with reason. They offered her grapes and she accepted them. Three hours before noon, in the orange groves of East Eliki, she gave her bracelet as a gift to the security guard's little daughter. She sat down in the workshop for a quarter of an hour and asked for some water. Her eyes were red, as if she had been crying all night long, but still, she spoke coherently. What drew her attention were the blooming chestnut trees, and she spoke about them to the guard's wife.

She drowned that same evening. She was found on a desolate part of the seashore at dawn. Two fishermen, father and son - insignificant people, whose names, however, made it into the history pages - dragged her body out of the water. I watched that scene on the *Reigen-Swage*. Her youthful body hadn't been deformed in the least, and the long, white, wet dress clung to her curves. That was the end of this first "Saint of the *Nojere*", the first beloved, immortal figure of the "New Era".

Now every year on the anniversary of her death, fifteen days before New Year's Day, thousands of people, dressed in white robes and carrying baskets with fresh flowers and wreaths, walk on and on along the beach singing hymns, as a sign of remembrance and appreciation. Two hours before midnight, they throw their flowers in the deep blue sea.

Mary-Lea Volky was a good spirit and is now considered a friend and patron of girls and women. All her other contemporaries grew old, succumbed to the laws of biological decay and left this world. But Mary-Lea stayed the same forever: nineteen, uncorrupted and immortal, a peer of every generation! Her name has been turned into poetry and legends; she has become a muse! Thousands of small statues, busts and monuments of her exist all over the world, and she is always depicted with golden hair, lips like cherry, and deep, sea-blue eyes filled with the light of the Mediterranean. Countless of finely crafted amulets and icons are made every year as a tribute to her. Her memory has been linked in people's hearts to some kind of a supernatural bright light that attracts you in such a powerful way that it's impossible to be put into words.

Silvia and Hilda had brought her up in conversation several times before I knew who she was. In fact, I remember one time in particular: one night back in our villas they mentioned her while we were gazing at the stars Arcturus and Vega through a small telescope…

## THE JUDGEMENT OF THE AIDERSEN INSTITUTE
### A new beginning

### 8-VI

On one of the last days of September - when it was finally clear that facts had spoken for themselves - the Aidersen Institute broke its silence. The Institute with the unique global prestige reminded people how, about fourteen thousand years ago, man had managed to become a small God in study of the physical world and the relevant technical applications and, for the first time ever, created a star through the processes of "fusion and division". What was happening now was as "divine" as that scientific and technological breakthrough that had occurred back then, only now it concerned every aspect of life! Again like a small god, man was finally able to tear away the veil of the "Big Secret" and see what was behind it.

What followed? We already know. It was meant for this generation to realise the dream of thousands of years and generations ago and for man to climb high up on the top of the Valley and finally "see". They said that Alexis Volky was the first "chosen one" but that hundreds of others followed the year after, and thousands more the year after that. And that's how now people know. They don't just believe anymore; they've seen it, they know!

"The *Nibelvirch* had to come," said Arald, another Aidersian, a month later, "in order for the true quality, content and meaning of the other *Virche*s to clearly show and shine!"

After people realised what had just happened, some praised God for having been born in this era and being part of this holy generation and others praised Volky for having endured so much and having paved the way for the rest of humanity.

In the beginning and for a considerable period of time, people from all over the world had neglected their jobs and had almost completely given up on all worldly matters and concerns. They were still unable to handle what had happened; they just didn't know how yet.

## MASS SUICIDES AND THE PURPOSE OF LIFE

### 9-VI

Over the coming months Volky and the other great men of the Aidersen felt the need to stop once and for all the "mass exodus" that followed, because they found themselves in front of hundreds and then thousands of cases of people whose motive for life had subsided and what had now replaced it was a new impulse, that of "desertion" and "escape", which most often manifested itself in people as a consequence of the *Nibelvirch.*

This new impulse had emerged together with the incredible feelings of happiness, spiritual peace, a kind of divine joy and a nearly "Socratic" conciliation with death but it had also brought with it a disregard for all worldly things, which now felt insignificant to people, foreign and unworthy peoples' concern.

What they could not handle was not the daily routine, the realities and the small joys and sorrows of life; it was that all their dreams, loves, loved ones that were no longer by their side, the happiest moments of their lives, things that they used to think of as mere memories, had now been condensed into an incredible force that had come back to haunt them.

There came days in 986 and 987 *(3382 and 3383 AD)* when the spiritual leadership of the planet was seriously concerned whether this "early psychological and spiritual maturity", this leap in biological evolution and spiritual progress, had come at a good time, and whether the Valley's centuries-long project would have unpleasant consequences as well. Almost everyone had proven far from being prepared, even the *Ilectors*, with the only exception of a few hundred imperturbable elders, followers of Volky.

Creation, with wise foresight, had successfully hidden its secrets from man, with great zeal and for thousands of years. They recalled that the first two centuries of the Valley many of them were against this enormous spiritual task and strongly insisted on putting an end to the special effort to achieve an advanced spiritual culture and create an intellectually superior man. In short, they wanted to say: This is how things are and they are fine the way they are; let them evolve at their own pace and don't rush them because God knows what any action that accelerates the natural process may awaken…

The solution they came up with in order to stop the "mass exodus" was to highlight the purposefulness and necessity of every stage in human life on earth, including the one they were going through at the time. They convinced people that even that tough phase was a small but essential part of the *Samith* and it was their duty to go through that too. They told them that "we all come to this life with a purpose: to love much and give a piece of ourselves to others, even if that causes us pain, to be thirsty for the beautiful and the true, to get to know the worldly wonders of nature and help the weakest creatures, and to leave this life when our time comes and not before like deserters.

They stressed that what they saw should in no case be linked to the termination of life on earth. On the contrary. They told them that the purpose is for life to go on and take an upward course, each time getting one step closer to perfection, to the truth! "If we become extinct, how is this upward course going to continue? Will you deprive the next generations of your own species of the chance to one day compare themselves to our generation and feel as proud of their progress as we feel today, compared to our ancestors? We are the indispensable link between the past and the future. We are the present and we must not be lost!"

Alongside this argument, commands were given by the Valley for immediate plans that would result in an even better organisation of society, a society that would give its members new life incentives. Major infrastructural projects were initiated, research for new inventions was announced, new institutions were established and better associations were created almost in all areas of social life. Even pan-European music festivals were organised, which served as a distraction, stimulating people's interest in life again.

**10-VI**

All this persistent campaign resulted in a considerable mitigation of the aforementioned escape impulse and in a decrease in the numbers of such incidents. As it was expected, they failed to completely eliminate them during the first year. In fact the Aidersen later said: "It is very difficult to keep those who are dying of thirst from running straight towards a well when one appears before them."

They were right. Because what did people have until then? What did they live on? They lived on little drops of water that evaporated very quickly. However, despite the difficulties faced the following year, the problem gradually subsided until it was completely eliminated. It didn't happen all at once - it couldn't have - but step by step. The world returned to a normal pace of life, but everyone had kept deep inside their soul the memory of what was later to be characterised as "*the* most important moment of the spiritual progress of mankind."

By that time, of course, all of their questions had been resolved and everything had an explanation: the "sense of living in a foreign land", the "thirst for the eternal", the "feeling of deprivation". The *Nibelvirch* had shown people where it all came from.

### 11-VI

From the early 987 and up until now, the Valley has been studying the classics with a new, unprecedented zeal. Everything has acquired a new meaning: from Socrates and Plato to Confucius, Siddhartha Gautama and Jesus. Even the conception of infinity, the incorruptible, the contrast between the present and eternity had become subject to re-evaluation. No one spoke of the "struggle of man against his fate" anymore. No one spoke of the "conflict between the individual and the world" either.

In fact, about the suicides of past times they now say that their cause was neither the "pain of love" nor the "excessive sensitivity." The reason was "the sacred thirst of soul and the longing for the *Samith*."

### 11-VI Again

### (Late at night)

Tomorrow morning I don't have a lesson with Lain, and I'm not planning on writing either. I intend to spend the whole day outside the city. Tonight's starlight is magical. I think that tomorrow we'll have the first sunny spring day with clear blue skies. It smells like spring already.

**Retsstats Aarsdag, MDX**
*(anniversary of the establishment of the Universal Commonwealth)*

Bells, bells, bells, bells ringing interminably since the very first morning hours, as if it were Holy Saturday. If you ask them, they'll tell you it symbolises the "Resurrection of our species"!

The great leaders are absent today. They all have a meeting in the Valley. I'm sitting on the terrace and looking down. There are few people on the streets. The parks and groves are glistening. It gives me such a pleasure to walk in the morning sun… I could do it forever! Today the city is calling you to walk it!

**12-VI**

Markfor is a state that you can very easily fall in love with. Yesterday I felt once again how right these people's way of thinking and living is. And now that our stay here is almost over and we will soon begin a tour of the central European states and then around the Rosernes Dal, I feel an even greater attraction to this place, almost like a craving.

Yesterday morning I discovered the hedgerows of Leouras, while in search of the gallery of the Medici, a green and silent area, too green and too silent to be part of the city centre. But vast contrasts are one of Markfor's best characteristics. You can still see the flocks of *linsens* and *velo* scooters and hear the roar of the crowds flooding the main arteries of the city from half a mile away. But if you stray a little bit, you suddenly come across idyllic landscapes, as if you've travelled to a faraway land on a magical journey; and yet, you've only walked for a few minutes.

## SIGHTSEEING IN MARKFOR

For those who love the tradition of the old state, the most beautiful part of Markfor is found on the other side of the block. Here it's like turning the clock back four hundred years: huge mansions that appear uninhabited, vast schools and classrooms that look desolate and masterful architectural libraries with content that my knowledge and education doesn't yet allow me to appreciate. Westward, inside the huge park, you can see the Rector's Palace with the famous Doric colonnade in the background. Nearby you'll find the study areas of the Laureatis with the statue of Giordano Bruno in the middle, and the auditorium of Milioki, an old founder and facilitator of theirs. And there's their poet, Selius! I've read something of his. His monument is extremely tall compared to all the other marble statues. It is bronze and all six sides of the giant pedestal are embellished with relief representations of his life and quotes taken from his most beautiful lyrical pieces.

Another building that fascinated me was the Church of Alma, which is both the palace and the temple of the spirit at the same time. Built in Gothic style, it is mainly famous for the sculptures on its facade. Its construction began in the $9^{th}$ century by the famous architect Rauschen Torneo, but finished later on because its creator passed away before he completed it. Two hundred meters away is the garden where the great-grandfathers of the present generation had managed to store centuries-old rocks from the pedestal of the ancient statue of Castello Sforzesco, in a rectangular railing with an uninscribed plaque.

Markfor is a state that can be loved dearly since it combines the old with the new times. If you are an art lover, Markfor will welcome you through its three major museums: the Luigi Davide, the Titiano and the Goya, and then the Nibrera and countless other, smaller ones, among which the famous special Tenarelis museum/glyptotheque. If you want to study any field, you won't find a better place to do it. You can choose from simple lectures to large universities attended by the *Cives* and even academies of philosophy and the fine arts.

As far as libraries are concerned, the four largest ones are open, each one dedicated to a different field: the Aidersian is for literature, the Cartesian for philosophy, the Alexandrian for history and the

Laurentian for the history of art. And of course, they also have the famous symphonic orchestras of Markfor, where you can listen to all kinds of music; from ecclesiastical music to the masterpieces of Valmandel, Svelder, Holger Nielsen, Ruthemir and so many others...

If you are a sports fan, Markfor has no wrestling rings and fields and courts for matches to offer because they now detest our sports and all sorts of records, but it has abundant physical exercise centres and swimming pools where, however, no record is ever pursued and no competition is ever held.

If you happen to be sad, a walk through the streets of the city will suffice to make you feel better. And if you still have the heart of a child, then Markfor, the favourite "wildflower", the state with the bright smile, will welcome you with sunbeams streaming through the chestnut trees of the Parco Centrale and its gardens will embrace you!

The way the people face the world and see their peers here is very different from ours. So are the rules of socialising with each other. If you walk down the street no one will bother you. If you're standing still, staring at the ponds in one of the large parks, they will leave you in your thoughts. Never has it happened for someone to speak to me when I'm alone in such circumstances.

It is, however, a completely different case if you enter one of the games centres, sports stadiums, pools, or *larinters*, as they call them. I remember what happened to me one morning, about five months ago, one of the first days that I went and listened to Lain. Early in the morning, before the lecture, I went past a great stadium that seemed to have a vast array of facilities for table tennis and I entered, curious to see up close all the tables lined up. I walked around and, naturally, every once in a while I stopped and stared. But I seemed to have forgotten what Stefan had told me a million times, that is, that "here there are no strangers", until I realised on my own that in *such* circumstances they don't leave you in peace. Therefore, after a while, two girls and a young man in his thirties who was accompanying them - all three strangers to me - came towards me and asked me if I wanted to play with them. I replied as politely as I could and finishing my sentence with the necessary "tank"*(their word for "thank you")* that today I was in a hurry, adding that "perhaps another morning I could have the pleasure of doing so".

I didn't know what else to say. You shouldn't tell your name here, nor do people ask it or tell you theirs. Nevertheless, they might have been strangers to me but to them I was their old, anonymous comrade at the *glothners*, a person worthy of interacting with, a partner, even a friend!

In such conditions of social life, who could ever feel lonely here? The feeling that I had so many a time experienced in my previous life, the melancholy of loneliness, was unknown here!

## THE ANNIVERSARY OF THE "BIG DAY" AND THE EXTINCTION OF THE RACES

Yesterday afternoon I took the *velo* scooter for a ride for the second time. The evening view of Markfor is completely different from the morning one. This time there were thousands of people on the streets and there was plenty of light everywhere. As I heard, all these people had just returned from the Valley, where they had travelled yesterday for the big day, the anniversary of 1510 years since the day of the union, the day when a true state with law and order replaced the political and economic anarchy of the past. I also overheard some young people on the street singing something that reminded me of the words children in ancient Sparta used to say to the elders: "ἄμμες δε γ' εσσόμεθα πολλῷ κάρρονες", which means "*but we shall become much better than you*".

Dear Lord, please help those
Who come tomorrow
Be better than us today
And make them worthier
For the sake
Of the greatness
And the glory
Of our beloved Earth!

The torchlight procession that took place ended in front of the towering statue of John Terring, in the middle of the square, as is the case on this night every year.

Behind that square begins one of the largest main arteries of eastern Markfor. I'm almost home. The skyline of Markfor, embellished with thousands of 100-storey skyscrapers on both sides, seems endless and incredible. And everywhere around them: huge, beautiful gardens.

Passing by here, I feel young and happy too, I feel like one of them. And lately this feeling is very frequent. It seems as if this gap of mine in education and tradition has magically been filled tonight, as if I have assimilated their experiences and made them my own.

Late last night, at the cheerful dinner table of the *Cives* from Riyalta, on the immense rooftop of one of the skyscrapers enclosed with crystal fences the ancestral memories of the common meals of the early *Eldrere* came alive. The celebration of the great day ended with a few touching words, tear-filled eyes and recollections of the glorious personages of their history.

Dinner lasted one and a half hours in a very cordial atmosphere. And for the first time ever, I saw these people, who detest alcohol, drink a tiny bit of wine, especially the ruby-red, sweet wine, served after the meal together with fruit, their famous Lacrimae Rosae, produced by the Grimbole collective. When dinner was over, everyone stood up and observed a few moments of silence for the great day. Needless to say, I did the same. In the end and after the countless wishes for the years and generations to come, they stood up again and began to whisper an ancient hymn, fortunately *sotto voce*, so I could pretend with dignity that I was whispering along…

No meanness nor gloating, no insidiousness nor scheming, no selfishness, no deadly wars, no back-stabbing in social life, nor all those incidents of pointless wickedness. How unhappy we were back then! We spoke of humanism then and they have finally made it come true!

Of course, their historians and educators seem to forget that it was out of necessity that those years were so dreadful and that we couldn't have done anything to prevent it. Not that we didn't want to; we just couldn't…

There are times when I want to tell Lain and Stefan, who so honour the founders and organisers of the *Eldrere*, that when they address the "great" politicians and "defenders of humanism" it would be more correct and befitting to ask them: "What happened to the coloured races?" "At what cost did you achieve the prevalence of humanism among the white and the establishment of your beloved law and order?"

History is now written and read from their perspective because they were fortunate enough to prevail. But history would have been written in a completely different way and their atrocities would have been condemned in the strongest possible terms had the yellow race inherited the earth… They now write history as if it were a morally flawless triumph, a pure heroic path, an exaltation of the soul, a historical perspective possibly very similar to the one taught in the seminaries of the church by a group of Spanish sages in the 18th century: the triumph of the invasion and destruction of the obsolete cultures such as the Incas and the Mayans...

"What happened to the ancient civilisations of Asia, you hypocrites?"That's what I should ask them! On the *Reigen-Swage* I saw that only until the mid-24th century of our own chronology were there still some "yellow pockets" scattered here and therein the vast territory of Asia, which is now inhabited by the French, Anglo-Saxons, Slavs and Latinos. I also saw that at the same time on the "black continent" it was tremendously rare for one to encounter any blacks.

Fate was very cruel to these races and quite ironic as well, because while they had just ceased to be slaves and were emancipated politically in autonomous territories, the brutal attitude of their "old colonial oppressor", who had meanwhile panicked by the "nightmare of the number," returned to haunt them for another 150 years. The earth must have witnessed horrid atrocities of inhumanity after the 21st century, which lasted for hundreds of years. Ultimately, the black and yellow races, as well as all other races of Asia, paid the price with the termination of their own history on earth.

## AIDERSEN RIVALRIES AND THE ATTEMPTS AGAINST THE NEW REALITY
### Gled and Ossen Institute and Lesley Gate

### 13-VI

### (Very late at night)

I had already heard a lot from Lain about the crisis that the Volkic preaching had undergone for decades towards the end of the first millennium of their new chronology, before it triumphantly prevailed later on. And such a crisis was anticipated since the *Nibelvirch* was never a given to the wider public in any of the eras that have ensued since its appearance. Nowadays, however, the Valley says that it is much more tangible and accessible to the people - even outside the circles of the *Ilectors* - than it was in the past.

I didn't go to the Reigen-Swage Institute today. I haven't been there for eight days. I stayed at home all day. Wanting to rest my eyes for a bit, I ordered books that are specially designed and printed to be heard instead of read! I put one of them in the special device that came with it and heard a short, popularised, historical narration of those years, from 987 until 1030 *(3376-3419 AD)*. What is most difficult for me to understand are the many technical terms of the peculiar old language of their most ancient texts, terms that have been preserved and are still used even in the simplest and shortest books of today, because they claim that the youth of today know them and understand their meaning. In any case, I write down whatever I've understood and in the way I've understood it, trying to convey these new terms and concepts in the language of our time, and deliver them the way we would. I honestly don't know what's harder: trying to assimilate them or transcribing them using the lexical formulas of our own, old way of expression? Anyway...

One would expect that the main subject of controversy in the Valley of the Roses would be Volky himself, since, based on our own saying, "No man is a prophet in his own land". But quite the opposite happened.

In the Valley he was worshiped and deified. Instead, the biggest reactions came from the major intellectual centres of Gled, Ossen,

Vikingegnist and the Skolkin Institute. They mostly attacked his fans and students and the biggest names of the Aidersen, that is, the first ones to write about the "Great Revelation", having previously lived the *Nibelvirch* themselves, for Volky didn't write anything himself after the year 986 and for the last ten years of his life, as was the case for Jesus, Buddha and Socrates.

The Gled and Ossen Institutes in particular, fought against the *Umoddelbare Oplysning (Direct Knowledge and Instant Enlightenment)* and highlighted the dangers of any road to the perception of reality that exists outside the framework of capabilities of the human cognition. Ratziskin of Ossen believed that the senses were imperfect, but the human mind was a *mirabilis organum* that substituted their imperfection and remedied the wrong sensory data transmitted to the brain. "Everything that actually exists," he said, "can be reduced to cognition. *Nihil in mundo, nisi in intellectu.* Anything that does not comply with intellect and reason does not exist. Or better: it is impossible to be sure of its existence."

It was impossible for the Gled and Ossen, especially during the first few decades, to admit the "new intellectual abilities" of the man of Rosernes Dal, the new knowledge and capacities and the supernatural experience of the Aidersen (overforstandige empiria). What the Aidersen argued was for them unacceptable: namely that man had acquired a new "instrument of knowledge" that on the one hand gives us findings so palpable and data so positive that would satisfy even the most conservative early believers in sensory data, and on the other hand proves that its texture is "beyond cognition" and "beyond reason" (ratio).

Two scientists, Milliakof and Durant, took advantage of the "confession" of the Aidersen, namely that it was possible that the original, remote ancestor of the "new antenna" of the *Nibelvirch*, had been the "intuition" of the old times and distorting that confession by omitting the part that the first Volkists added to that idea - that nevertheless that intuition was denatured into something completely different - they stressed with all the power and authority that the Ossen gave them, how precarious and dangerous this road that leads to mystical flights of fancy was.

Milliakof did not live to see the utter defeat of his rationale and the triumph of the Volkists. In the mid-11$^{th}$ century, the *Nibelvirch* was at its peak and, led by the first major Aidersians, the Valley of the Roses had become part of the intellectual vanguard of the human race and was making history!

Another attempt against the new preaching was made by some circles of physicians - though with limited impact - about a thousand years ago, which tried to find weak spots in Volky's psyche and say that "he was the first victim of a mass delusion, which has persisted through time." The leading role in that "movement" was held by the Lesley Gate Institute, with its world-famous medical school, followed by five or six other groups of wise men from all over the world, and the whole debate lasted for about a decade.

What was their theory? More or less the following: Make no mistake; everything that you now feel comes from within. All these wonderful things you want to say are nothing but a vivid reflection of your own ideas. Their source is not external; they derive from your own depths. So come to your senses and realise that you are walking the tightrope between sanity and illusion!

The Gate of Lesley said, of course, a lot more than that against not only the Greats of the Aidersen but also the entire Valley. They scrutinised and criticised the entire five centuries of the Valley's existence, adopting the opinion of the old reactionaries, who supported that they would have been better off without that enormous spiritual endeavour. They turned against "the 200", the founders of the Valley, and strongly denounced the whole project aimed at the premature evolution of our species, arguing that in order to get there, hundreds of thousands of years were needed and that the Valley was a danger to the mental balance of our race. They also insinuated that "many great and wise men are born in our time, but many of them are not entirely mentally stable."

Finally, they said that no artificial leaps forward were necessary *or* welcome, and that the simplest of their recommendations to the Valley was that they should be careful because "apart from predisposing future generations to a higher intellectuality, they were also predisposing them to severe psychoneurosis."

Neither the Aidersen Institute nor anyone else from the Rosernes Dal ever responded to these accusations and insults. As I heard, throughout this decade of debate and controversy, the Valley was defended by both their colleagues from the Elders of Lesley Gate -

those specialised in the same sectors and fields of studies as them - and by great spiritual personalities from outside the Valley, major intellectuals, foreign to the field of medical sciences, most of whom were graduates of the great universities and institutes of the 9th century, ranging from those of Grand Torneo and Blomsterfor to those of New Upsala.

I remember what Atterman of Blomsterfor once said: that for a new species that's still in its prime, like the human species, it is ridiculous to express fears of its degeneration and eventual downfall. "Only during the last few centuries have we slightly begun to find our way," he used to say, "and we have no connection to the ancient spirit anymore. Our decline is still very far away."

However, it is said that the venerable metropolises of the North and, above all, the alma mater of the modern spirit, the eternal Norfor, stood as the most powerful defenders of the Volkists. Carstens, Orlik, Vera Brandes and the Ekersborg Institute condemned those few scientists that were "searching for pathological causes in order to explain and simultaneously spoil the kindest and truest discovery of the human spirit in history." They even reminded them that countless times in the past great universal truths and discoveries in science and other areas of the human spirit had seemed completely improbable and were severely criticised. And countless times in the past the pioneers had been unfairly blamed and scorned and had suffered a very "unhappy" ending.

As far as the accusations that the Valley "doesn't give birth to very robust animals" are concerned, the defenders argued that "that's not supposed to be its purpose at all; plus such a mission wouldn't be very honourable. We abound in beings with spiritual mediocrity that are only useful for their own well-being and not worthy of doing anything more. But we also abound in beings with true spiritual superiority and faith and real capability for global contribution, and yet, none of those beings who have lived among us, from ancient times until today, would fit your measurements of the ideal psychological type of human being, the robust animal that you preach about."

Then came the great days of 1050 *(3439 AD)*, with the priceless confirmatory work of Gibling, Eric Gord and Tervalsen. The literary movement of the Minores, from the Aidersen, about which

Jaeger and Stefan had talked to me quite a few times in the past, came later, in the late 11th century. The works of this school of art and thought remained classics throughout the entire Volkic history. In fact, in Lain's library, I saw with my own eyes some of Fletchius's relevant writings, dating from that era. But after many unsuccessful attempts to study them, I concluded that they just weren't for me.

During the next few years, Alexis Volky found global recognition as the "greatest intellectual hero of the human race." And only after the initial excitement had subsided did many descendants (MC-MCC) realise that a figure such as Volky had no need to exaggerate, lie or embellish facts. Facts were enough by themselves. He was the first one who was able to bear to see and tell the world, without adding anything of his own. They said that he truly *was* a magnanimous and extremely gifted spirit; but that's all. Some, however, went so far as to unsuccessfully compare Volky with the greatest representatives of their natural sciences: Astrom, Vilinski, Jergesen and Sioberlef and even with our own Newton and Einstein!

Nevertheless, despite the admittedly weak efforts to reduce Volky's value and contribution to the development of global culture, he stands here among them as one of the dominant figures of history and, based on their beliefs, he will remain so for centuries to come.

Hundreds of thousands of biographies have already been written about him up to the present day, not counting the ones on Volkic preaching. Each and every one of his ancestors - all of whom lived in the Valley - have been studied, from the most ancient one to the most recent Volky who, as a matter of fact, was one of the 200. Tinersen - the one with the parables - was one of the many, maybe even one of the greatest, who popularised and taught the Volkic preaching after 1200, with the year 2396 AD as year 1, so around 3596 AD.

The spiritual preaching of the Volkists had the same immeasurable influence on the world in the visual arts, prose, poetry and philosophical thought, but also in the shaping of the moral conscience and moral education of young people, that is, the contemporary view of human life and the world in general.

## LAST DAY AT MARKFOR

### 14-VI

Today is the penultimate day of my stay in my favourite city. In the morning I went to the centre of Markfor, ancient Magenta, to... vote! Nobody here asks if you live permanently in the city or if you are entitled to vote and such. This perfect lack of control by the Committee of Technical Agency Partners of the broader Markfor area, the region where they are assigned as election representatives, is owed to the fact that there have never been any incidents of any kind of trickery or fraud for many generations now.

The elections concern the construction of new buildings in the centre of Markfor and the maquettes have been displayed to the public for two months now. The main ones are maquettes of three large buildings, meant to be constructed for educational purposes, but there are also some floricultural project suggestions for the decoration of the parks and squares of the state and any *Civis* who is a permanent resident can go and vote based on their preferences. So I, too, employed my mediocre sensory abilities, carefully chose the ones I liked the most and voted. In my head, my love for Markfor atoned for my "fooling" them by pretending that I live here permanently, but deep down I know that "one of them" would never do such a thing; they would never get carried away and lose their self-control. At least through these pages I can confess. But apart from that, I don't think I would even tell Stefan...

### 18-VI

I don't think I could ever experience such a thrill, such a lovely anticipation for the journey anywhere but in this new life of mine! It's now the third day of our journey and despite all the fatigue - now we don't only fly all the time - despite the countless crowds and the amazing variety of new images and experiences, tonight I found some time to write a few lines, not so much to describe what I've seen - which is impossible - but to say how happy I've felt throughout this whole trip, much happier than in any of my previous trips, and especially the one to Norfor.

This time I found it easier to get in touch with these vast states, whose size and noise scared me to the core seven months ago. I remember that I couldn't shake the feeling that, at any time, they would fall on me and crush me. Well, to be honest, another reason why I don't feel that way now is because neither Torneo nor New Göteborg, nor Anolia appear that big or crowded when you're coming from Markfor…

They're much smaller and much more beautiful and they don't have any immense underground illuminated states. Their population is less than a million and their sky is free from the dense steely nets of the overhead bridges that create a huge weight on your chest when you're unaccustomed like I was.

And their names are easy and calm: Rosa Azzura, Maribor, Liebach, Lilienborg, New Scaldia, Rosenborg, New Christiania, Sotsiana, Bozen, Nymalmoe… They're all garden cities, continuous and successive in most cases, around the areas of Ancient Tyrol, Slovenia and now old city of Stirlen, as I noticed on the map.

But no matter how beautiful everything I've seen these three days is, I know that nothing would seem as beautiful if I wasn't filled with this amazing thrill of the journey itself. And this sweet joy of the journey, just like every other kind of joy, comes from within; it's a gift from my inner self! To have the fortune to travel with Stefan, Hilda and Silvia is a precious feeling! So, how can the endless rains of yesterday spoil your mood, when the sun lives now in your soul?

**20-VI**

Thousands of nature's signs, more and more every day, foreshadow the arrival of the spring. Yesterday was a lovely sunny day. In a couple of weeks everything will be blossoming here.

## THEIR AMAZING MOTORWAYS AND OTHER MEANS OF TRANSPORTATION

**New Göteborg, 21-VI**

The distance between Assilia and New Göteborg is approximately 70 kilometres and this part of the motorway runs all the way through dense plane trees and silver poplars. Stefan said that we were approaching major centres of production and that behind these idyllic landscapes, deep inside the earth, there were huge, powerful pipelines and power converters that bring titanic forces to the *glothners* of New Göteborg, all the way from the Atlantic coast, thus providing the young people that are doing their two-year service there with the necessary energy.

The total length of the motorway is 2500 km if I'm not mistaken. It is the same autostrada with that of Anolia and Torneo, the famous Taussen *bilvej*, as they now call it, and it connects far bigger states than the ones we're going to visit. Stefan didn't know much about the wide, ancient old road surface when I asked him. He never does when it comes to issues of contemporary art and technology... It seemed like it was made of a synthetic, light green crystal, without, however, being transparent and it is said that its maintenance won't trouble but the very distant descendants of the present generation.

Seeing the width of this motorway you cannot believe in your eyes! Something less than half a mile! But they say that this is now common for their major intercity motorways. But it's not just the motorways; dozens of roads and streets spread all around them and among them lawns, flower gardens, flowerbeds. From above, the green lawns look like strips embroidered on the landscape, stretching thousands of kilometres.

The widest motorways are the ones used by the *ragiozas*, these personal, multi-storey, transcontinental wheeled vehicles, which resemble articulated vehicles. There are also roads for pedestrians, *velo*s, and all sorts of today's transport means.

Something else that struck me is that their roads are divided according to speed: there are separate roads for all the different speeds of all the different vehicles! We had taken the special road designed for very low velocity because we wanted to enjoy the views and the trip as a whole. "There's no hurry; we can go at our own pace," Stefan had said.

On the route we've chosen there are hundreds of *larinters*, fitness centres, swimming pools, resting spaces, health stations and numerous shops scattered all around, housing the always available and willing "partners of *Bilvef*", those in charge of this giant motorway.

Countless signs with instructions and directions make the life of even the most distant and unknowing visitors easier and a whole crew is ready to help the romantic *Cives* that still prefer land travel even if these roads are now considered impractical and quite old-fashioned. Of course, *they* chose air travel for the significant trips. No other means of transport can match air transport in either speed or safety. Even the heaviest shipments of materials in huge quantities are today effortlessly executed via air travel.

According to Stefan, we are now crossing a countryside that only seems to be uninhabited, but isn't! If you go deep inside, behind the dense rows of trees you will see a fairly dense settlement. After all, I've said it before: there are no uninhabited places here today; only sparsely populated or densely populated ones.

An endless array of giant, artificial, white and pink rhododendrons cuts now the road in half. I heard Silvia calling them with their, familiar to me, ancient name: "Albaspines". It is obvious that people have played their part here as well, interfering with the metabolism and altering organic matter, in their own way. It looks like the small earthly God has once again worked wonders, making the rhododendrons stand still, greeting the passers-by!

I also want to note the only ugly thing I saw this morning. About half an hour before we reached the city, three rhododendrons in a row were trying to keep their old and parched branches a few meters away from a busy road and no one seemed to notice or even care. The only reason I was impressed by that gap in greenery and by the ugliness of the dead trees was because I know how much attention they pay nowadays to such details.

## TECHNOLOGICAL ADVANCES, CLIMATE CONTROL AND "RETURN TO THE BASICS"

As acknowledged by Stefan, in a short talk we had, their technical and technological culture has been in decline for several centuries now. Their ancestors had succeeded in much larger and more complex projects. Of course, they now claim that they no longer need to repeat such colossal ventures. For example, I haven't been to Australia, but I saw on the *Reigen-Swage* that it has been converted into a huge generator that supplies on its own almost the entire globe with energy!

Now, as far as agriculture is concerned, they have returned to harvesting crops, which now no longer grow periodically, but do not depend on the weather any more. During that terrible period of overpopulation, people had abandoned their land and their flocks and had sought the solution of the global nutrition crisis in laboratories. People of today do the opposite: they go back to the old ways, not out of necessity, but out of nostalgia, improving, of course, the previous methods and procedures by employing their perfect technological advancements. Thanks to this shift in lifestyle, there are again meadows and grasslands in the picture; thanks to the partners of the *Lansbee* (rural areas) and, mainly, thanks to the flocks. You can't even imagine the incredible technical training today's shepherds and farmers have. The combination of diligence and attention to the monitoring and control of the "technical instruments"- which now have their own, individual kind of memory and judgment, similar to the human mind, is their recipe for their success.

At the same time they also control the climate, as did their ancestors during the era of advanced technology, and therefore have expanded their practices to areas that, in the past, we couldn't believe could be inhabited. Where there once were glaciers and deserts you now see thick, lush meadows, experimental nurseries, pastures and new crops. The same goes for the endless plains and plateaus of Central Asia that are now inundated with this unheated diffused light that they have managed to create. Yet another Herculean feat!

The current population in the immense state-countries has risen to several hundreds of millions under this controlled and pleasant-for-humans climate, especially around the major nuclear production units, where an incredible number of settlements have accumulated. Augerinia, the Star of the East, the Steel Castle, Terringa, New Tashkent, Mata Uralia, Samarkanda, Nova Tuguska (the Nygusca of the Europeans), ancient Irkutsk and Omska, Boldieno, Nysuomi… Huge human beehives of ten, twelve, even fifteen million people, and at the same time industrial cities that made use of the inexhaustible energy reserves of the vast continent of Asia (gas, hydroelectric potential, solar, wind).

The fact that almost the entire globe is flooded with white people doesn't surprise me as much as the fact that they've found the way for all these people to live and prosper to such an unexpected degree! That I could have sworn was impossible!

## THE MASSIVE COLONISATION OF MARS AND THE GREAT DESTRUCTION

Even that frantic colonising expedition on Mars from the year 2204 and onwards, which lasted about sixty years, is the work of their ancestors at the time of their technological acme. They actually managed to build and maintain entire villages and housing estates on the "interplanetary colonies" of the red planet. In fact, the colony thrived for several years even under very adverse conditions for humans. Now, however, the majority of their settlements is in decay. On that planet, nature was the one that prevailed! Twenty million souls perished within a few months - mostly Anglo-Saxons and Slavs, but also many settlers from the mainland of Europe - due to the harsh and unexpected change of climate and atmospheric conditions that no human technical device was able to restrain. The indiscriminate, natural forces were the cause of the massive holocaust of 2265. But still, even for just a few years, man's great dream and ambition to colonise another planet came true! The few survivors of the terrible doom of the "Columbuses" of the ether, who managed to return to Earth, bequeathed future generations with plenty of stories about another fabulous human feat.

In conclusion, from what I saw in the *Reigen-Swage* Institute in Markfor during the winter, one thing is certain: about a thousand years ago, there was unimaginable progress in science and its applications. They had acquired a civilisation so advanced that, when you saw its works of art, you wondered if they had been made by human hands! If that progress had continued uninterrupted, I cannot even imagine what today would have been like. But the so-called period of "suspension" intervened and it played such a key role in history that today it feels like their time is only a couple of hundred years more technologically advanced than ours.

Their inner culture, however, is thousands of years ahead thanks to the experiment of the Aidersen Institute and the Valley of the Roses. That's why these people are so incomparably different from me in terms of mental and moral life issues; much more different than *we* were from the people of two millennia ago.

Thus, their lives are now steeped in serenity. The first peaceful days became peaceful years, and those, in turn, peaceful centuries. Man was redeemed from violence, fear for the future, poverty, exile and mutual destruction. Thanks to the "Aidersian lifestyle, culture and tradition", human value and dignity found vindication.

## EXTRATERRESTRIALS: BRIEF ENCOUNTERS

But today's people are also at a major disadvantage: with the disappearance all risks whatsoever, humans' ability to fight and cope with difficulties has been dulled. It's incredibly unlikely to find warriors nowadays; they're like a defenceless species on the brink of extinction. Therefore, in case of a potential external danger, nobody would know how to react. But if you argue that to somebody, they'll reply that there are no longer dangers and more powerful neighbours and all that are a thing of the past. In fact, they explained to me that the destruction of civilisations always takes place immediately after a sudden boom in culture when hardships have yielded to art and inner cultivation. That's when the uncouth invaders make their appearance and ruin everything.

But the most incredible thing I've been told is that they don't even fear their extra-terrestrial neighbours! They've told me that they know all about the neighbouring planets and that the few that have life on them (!) are inhabited by intelligent and spiritual beings that lack the instinct of domination and the concept of conquest and expansion. They have a much higher view of and respect for life and they are completely harmless to humans! They could have pursued contact with us thousands of years ago if they had wanted to. They already had the necessary technology to do it, but they didn't, because these creatures did not want any contact or relationship with us, not even a peaceful one. They preferred to watch us and study us from above, thus satisfying their thirst for research. It was in their nature; that was their mentality.

The only times that they tried to contact us were when they felt that man was in danger of extinction because of his immaturity and his inability to handle the tremendous power of nature that he had unlocked. "Then," they told me, "they approached us, taught us, and disappeared again..."

# TERRINGTOWN: THE BIRTHPLACE OF JOHN TERRING, THE FIRST UNIVERSAL LEADER

## Marienborg, 26-VI

Large in size but sparsely populated, Marienborg in Central Europe has probably got more museums - mainly historical ones - Reigen-Swage Institutes and theatres than housing estates. It was built right next to the big motorway that connects Blomsterfor with Terringtown and it was destined to become exclusively a city-museum complex, without any residents. That explains why its current, permanent residents are all descendants of the old art critics, historians, musicologists, students and art lovers who settled here centuries ago. Along with them, a large number of scientists and artists from Terringtown had also come here to do research on major works of their own renaissance, the $9^{th}$ century. When these people moved here, they also brought with them their way of thinking, their morals, lifestyle, and style of dress; even the air of the venerable metropolis and birthplace of John Terring.

It is said today that the work of John Terring was far superior for the history of humanity than the legend that the descendants of his generation had created around the "first great publicly active man".

When he was young, he was a big dreamer. During his childhood he had spent two summers in his very old, ancestral villa with the beautiful gardens that today has become the central square of Marienborg. By the time he died, the only thing that had survived from the villa was its walls and yet they found a way to restore it - staying as true to the original as possible - and transfer it here, all the way from Terringtown, along with his notes of "mad, grandiose plans", mementoes of those two summers, which revealed the restless heart of a child that would later achieve great things. There still exist historical pictures of his parents, his two sisters, who were almost the same age as him, and his adopted little brother, Charles Terring.

This morning, I sat and stared at the towering statue in his memory, located in the square bearing his name. Mondstein, the sculptor, has portrayed him with his right hand raised, pointing far in the distance. Further down, you see the smaller-sized statues of the four other precursors: Spaak, Verginus, Milstone and Trodalsen.

For all present-day people, Terring is the most charismatic public figure in history. For his contemporaries, the *Cives* with the universal national consciousness and the uniform civic education, Terring, one of the protagonists of human history, does not only live inside the history pages; he's still here, living among each new generation. This modern-day Woodrow Wilson enabled new paths to be created by leading the way to the establishment of the new chronology. Thanks to him, his charm and persuasion and the impact he ultimately had on so many different cultures, the necessary trust in a universal social and political life that was worthy of and equal for all the inhabitants of Earth was built. He lives among *them* and *they*, all the inhabitants of today's universe, love him as deeply as he had once loved humanity and shared the pain and sorrow of billions of people. They love Terring, the political figure, "the first ever to essentially and effectively escape the shackles of the local ruler", Terring the inspirational orator who mesmerised the crowds around the world, with the deep wrinkles of mental concentration engraved on his forehead and the characteristic grey stole of the "Great Year" *(their year 1, our 2396 AD)* draped around his neck, a very frequent accessory of his. But even more, they love the Terring of the portrait by Knut Valdemar, making a speech at the 2394 European Convention, the year after which the Universal Commonwealth was established.

**Blomsterfor, 27-VI**

**(Shortly before midnight)**

It makes you wonder: which is that ingenious race that managed to defeat the monster of overpopulation and the relentless lack of space? Which are those miraculous generations that did not fear that they would suffocate among those billions of people and instead managed to build layers of ground, like floors, one above the other? Who are those people who managed to produce abundant food for all from their laboratories through artificial photosynthesis?

I asked Stefan why people choose to crowd together in overpopulated cities when there's so much nature in the countryside that could host them, offering them a much more comfortable and quiet life. He answered that they prefer to densely populate their cities in a rational way - a way that seems to me, the inexperienced and unfamiliar, more like insanity - than to spread out to the farmlands and other unadulterated parts of nature. That is why they build the city upwards instead, stretching incredibly wide air bridges they call "kroom", high above their skyscrapers. You can even see their technicians shake them like whips when they fix them! If you look up, you'll see them hanging above your head like a net or an enormous spider web!

Truth be told, the modern face of their megacities is, in my eyes, an incredible spectacle! That doesn't mean, however, that they don't intimidate me still. This morning, a flock of countless giant flying saucers, thicker in the centre and thinner at the periphery, coming one after the other without stopping, shook me to my core. I was sitting on a bench, calm and unsuspecting when suddenly I felt the sun disappear so I lifted my head. When I did, I saw the giant flying discs flying above my head, spreading a horrifying shadow over the waters of the river and the cottages!

"Why be afraid?" Stefan later asked me. "There was no reason to be frightened just because you happened to be alone." He later explained to me that those discs were headed to their artificial moons, thousands of kilometres upwards, in the densely populated colonies of their scientists. That's how the scientists and technicians alternated shifts. At lunchtime and again in the afternoon, Stefan gave me some special binoculars and I saw for myself quite a few of these artificial "human moons", situated very high up in the sky above Blomsterfor. Some were larger, others were closer to us, and you could see them gleaming in the sun rays.

## FEELING LIKE A STRANGER

### Blomsterfor, 28-VI

A brief tour around the central arteries of Blomsterfor left me with a completely different impression from the one I had yesterday, watching it from afar. I think I should change quite a lot of what I wrote in my hasty notes last night; my conclusions were frivolous. In fact, had my initiation to the fast-paced Markfor not preceded, I don't think I would have even been able to stand on my feet without the aid of Stefan here in Blomsterfor, among the millions of people that crowd together and bustle about the city, under the shadow of these unbelievably huge buildings.

Stefan stood by me as much as he could throughout our morning walk. But we also had to make sure that Hilda and Silvia, who had come along, didn't notice my perturbation. And the truth is that in one of the central districts of the megalopolis, in the middle of Toeplitz 1812 square, I was almost irreparably exposed, so much that they afterwards started asking me if I had suddenly fallen ill. Holding Stefan's arm, I barely managed to cross the square. And not because of the urban mintels - something similar to our tram - which at that time weren't even moving, but because of the sudden, overwhelming vertigo I felt, caused by the incredibly vast, flat, open area with an oversized bronze sculpture in the centre.

Later on, I regained my composure. To my understanding, the cause of my transient collapse was more psycho-neurological than physiological. I sat in the shade for a while, calmed down, had a sip of an orange juice I was offered and when we started walking again, I begged Stefan not to make me cross that immense square again. Nevertheless, I saw much beauty and majesty this morning; I saw it with my eyes, but not my heart... My soul was empty once again, helpless, incapable of reaching any new depths of perception, appreciation or understanding. I am aware of that emptiness inside me. And if I don't write anything of substance, anything deeper than the fleeting external impressions of my everyday experiences, it's not due to a lack of interest in asking and learning about all those great things, nor to my idleness or commitment to my relationship with Silvia; it's because of this awareness of mine. You see, the essence, the soul of all these things is not just offered to anyone, to a stranger, an outsider, a temporary visitor like me. I'm lacking in preparation and knowledge of tradition. At least the tourists from my era knew something about the places they visited. I, on the other hand, know nothing. My vision functions perfectly, the desire exists, but fate had planned it so that everything would be superficial to me. I cannot digest all these things, I cannot make them my own; I try, but I fail every time…

I know that what I see is the visible condensation of a long, profound reality, foreign and inaccessible to the uninitiated, the synthetic image of a beautiful life in which I am not entitled to take part. A centuries-old tradition, mature in meaning, in institutions, in the organisation of life and culture, gets in the way and separates us. These centuries knew how to guard their secrets…

With each step I take, the bitter awareness of my gap in education and tradition grows stronger. A few hours ago, I sat by the riverside, by that incredible, over 200-feet-long *quay*, and looked at the monumental, wrought iron doors of those enormous buildings that seemed crafted with great care and attention to detail, like lace. Above me, *linsens* and *vigiozas* quietly followed their usual trajectory while I was trying to figure out to which world I ultimately belong…

## FLOWER DECORATION AND THEIR TRANSPORT NETWORK

### Blomsterfor, 29-VI

This megalopolis is now the biggest in population among the states around the Rhine and, apart from its exceptional technical and spiritual culture, it is also famous for its love for flowers. I saw cascades of flowers everywhere: on the facades of palaces, on the streets, in central squares. Gladiolas, carnations, purple lilacs, geraniums in a number of wonderful - new to me - hues as well as climbing roses and periwinkles that covered the walls. In the arcades, which serve to protect them from the rain, you feel like you're in a museum; the ceilings of those dreamy arcades are decorated with their favourite pastel colours and gilt frames. It seems that in other states of Central Europe with a population of twenty to thirty million, they are also accustomed to similar artistic decorations in the arcades. This seven-lane avenue is called Von Gottes Gnaden and I don't know if it's the only boulevard of Blomsterfor. Maybe Stefan sent me here deliberately to amaze me. If that's the case, he has succeeded!

In the evening, I spoke to Stefan about these incredibly expensive roads they have in their gigantic states and asked him how on earth they can afford such reckless overspending. He laughed and told me that they hadn't cost anything and that thousands of young artists-*Cives* had offered to build them, or connect their name with the decoration of the arcades of their homeland. That reminded me of the case of Lain, who carries on with his educational and pedagogical work solely out of emotional and intellectual inclination and moral satisfaction.

Stefan told me about the current redistribution of human effort and talent, a programme that has been implemented by the new economy and technical advancement and seeks to address the boredom that would plague a great number of the prematurely demobilised workers, if they have not found new objectives after their twenties, a new purpose or a noble mission in their lives.

He then explained the procedure of decorating the city to me: first, the office partners estimate the number of designers and decorators that will be needed for a two- to five-year period. Then they send the names of those who have offered to help to the leading contemporary specialists *Lorffes* of the Valley. After that, the *Lorffes*, with the assistance of worthy delegates - all great artists - compile the list of candidates and then the permanent residents of the area where the artistic intervention is going to take place vote effortlessly online, and the electronic vote-counters in the municipal facilities announce the shortlist.

Another thing that struck me in Blomsterfor is the fact that this huge state, with its *linsen*-filled sky, did not hesitate to also build a terrestrial transport network with central ground stations in its major districts-cities, which enabled access to greater Europe and the rest of the world, as well as those huge terraces, bases of their civil air transport network. Now only the major ports for the *daners* are located several kilometres outside the capital.

So let me paint you the picture: pedestrians and wheeled vehicles dominate the streets while high up above, thousands of flying vehicles circulate and land on the terraces of towering buildings. From there, using high-tech lifts, people descend to street level and continue their journey. All surfaces are, of course, incomparably larger than what we're used to, as is the incredible number of visitors that perpetually - albeit quietly - go up and down.

Through the central stations of Norstat, on the outskirts of Blomsterfor, pass the large intercity motorways, the Eurasian autostradas leading to Arlenhom, New Trondheim, the Big Bergen, Terringtown, Varsava, Harkovo, Tobolsk and all the way to Siberia and the Pacific coast.

Here I saw for the first time one of their huge *ragiozas* parked, because until now I gaped at them on the move, speeding at an incredible rate for their size. With its multiple floors, it looked like a fallen skyscraper from afar.

It's enough to see just one of these intercity wheeled vehicles with the incredible dimensions, these enormous moving cities with restaurants, spas, lounges, and specially designed car parks - *furgos* they call them - where they store the small *linsens* and all sorts of individual flying vehicles for the roughly 500-1000 passengers, to understand why their large universal arteries that link Portugal to the metropolitan states and capitals of the Far East were built so incredibly wide.

**Blomsterfor, 30-VI**

Two professional film directors of my time made their own films about the Great War, one focusing on London called *Waterloo* and the other one on the Balkans with his film *The Last Bridge*. If only they knew that due to a number of coincidences their works would survive after so many centuries while millions of other films - possibly much better ones and not as commercial - have been long lost, they would have been so proud!

Now that I mention *Waterloo*, I remember the derogatory way they spoke of Napoleon who, after his army was almost completely destroyed, said that "one night suffices for the French women to rebuild the great army," reducing human beings to mere flesh. Stefan told me: "Every person is a whole world. Do not touch it. Do not interfere with it. First of all, you can't, and second of all, you have no right to! The esoteric person is independent of the physical aspect of the individual, completely irrelevant to their material or biological existence. They are made up of a vast moral universe of dreams, ideals, moving life stories of tenderness and affection, love, humanism and sacred human suffering. And no Napoleon can ever destroy that."

## ART AND 3D THEATRES

In their museums and galleries, next to the exhibits of their most famous works - mostly the masterpieces of their 9th century - they also display some artworks of our 19th century, mainly from the fields of music, poetry and the Art of Discourse, as well as several works of the plastic arts of the Renaissance. I wonder if anything from the 20th century, the "times of decadence and darkness" as they call it, has survived. Probably nothing that is related to art, but perhaps something from our technology.

Last night they took me to the centre of Blomsterfor, to the famous outdoor theatre of Arlington with the artificial air-conditioners that sufficiently covered every inch of that huge, amphitheatrically-designed open space. They call it an "arena", but the meaning of this word has changed throughout the years and has now come to mean "open-air", without referring to the shape of the theatres, which is, however, usually circular or ellipsoid, or their architecture, and without implying any connection whatsoever to the ancient Roman amphitheatres. And the truth is that it looks nothing like them. That monumental complex of buildings truly amazes you from the moment you see it, at first for its size and its elegance and then for the unlimited possibilities of its stage. Every single minute in that theatre makes you feel like you've entered a magical parallel universe; it gives the impression of a legend or a fairy tale brought to life, in the service of mankind!

The scenes alternate with the same ease as on the *Reigen-Swage*. And in both cases, directors can use all their genius and talent. Although in the *Reigen-Swage* you know that everything you see - including the characters, who are nothing but actors - is artificial, it all feels completely real; as if you're living among them, as if you're part of the story. And even if you turn your head in any direction, the action continues to unfold uninterrupted, apparently thanks to some kind of miraculous combination of "laser beams", offering the spectator these magical panoramas. Here, too, the plot unfolds before your eyes stereoscopically, enhancing the illusion of depth, only now, you're not a part of the spectacle. If you take a look around, you can see the stone-built tiers of the amphitheatre as well as the thousands of other spectators that fill them.

Here the actors are real and so are their voices. The dialogues and noises are live. However, the technical resources have reached such a level of perfection that the clouds you see, the sky, the rivers, the houses, the stones and all sorts of landscapes, seem as real as the ones around you, below you and above you! Of course, if you went closer and tried to touch them, they'd disappear. Here all viewers, regardless of their position or their actual distance from the stage, see and hear the actors through the transparent rectangular crystal in front of the seat, which is flanked by a magical tape that reproduces sound! A spectator in the upper tier seats sees and hears them with the same ease as a spectator in the front row seats.

In short, with the exception of the dynamic vividness of the actors' performances and the vibrancy of their voices - voices here just need to be clear and with correct articulation, the volume isn't important, like in our era - everything else feels like the stuff of dreams and fairy tales, just like in the *Swage*. That's probably why these colossal, hollow theatres of current times have been designed with such unlimited possibilities: to create that dream-like atmosphere.

The incredible impact that the Arena of Arlington has on the foreign spectator is mainly owed to the superb coordination between the actors and the technical means used also by the *Reigen-Swage*. And that technical capability makes it possible for plays that were initially made for the *Reigen-Swage*, to be performed here as well, using the same sequences of alternating scenes and without losing any of their magic!

As for the name of the amazing director who won the audience's applause in the end of the play, it's Helmut Krotiner.

The great majority of the population of Blomsterfor originates from the north. I heard people say that, apart from the millions of descendants of the Teutons and the Germans, there are also numerous distant descendants of the Finns, Swedes and Norwegians here, who had been asked by the leaders of the era of Trodalsen, Verhin, Vohlbach, Delaroche and Baldini, 15 centuries ago, to descend to the Rhine, to the Danube and all the way down to the Mediterranean. And they obeyed, without initially wanting to, in order to prevent further conflict.

The great disaster of -87 was still relatively recent at that time and so this conscientious migration to the South, which was triggered by the South itself, coincided with the enactment of the Magna Carta of Altekirchen when hope for a better life, politically, socially and demographically speaking, was reborn from the ashes. At the same time, the unions and the independent, self-reliant cooperative organisations of all kinds of partners, precursors of the *glothners*, had started to become institutionalised.

## CEREMONIES AND THE USE OF RELIGION

### Blomsterfor, 1-VII

It's the first day of the month today and here in Blomsterfor they have the custom to celebrate it as a Christian holiday, like Christmas and Easter.

I have noticed that they have no icons or statues, but thanks to their magical technical means, the scene of the Annunciation appeared today, in the first morning hours, in the crystal clear sky, outshining the nearest stars…

Lost as I was in the huge crowd, I couldn't even see the main body of the procession, but Stefan told me afterwards that the procession was led by the VIPs in snow-white robes and representatives of the Valley of the Roses by their side and by several *unge*, as they call them here, from the Order of Mary-Lea, dressed in their official uniforms and wearing their traditional silk scarves. Beside them, children dressed in white with golden belts around their waists carried wreaths of light-coloured flowers.

Despite the luxury of the uniforms and the flowers, the solemnity of the atmosphere was undeniable. From the prayers that they chanted, I recognised *Ave Regina Caelorum* and later they sang "*Sancta Dei genitrix, ora pro nobis*". During the latter, thousands of people sang along "*Pra pro nobis... Miserere nobis…*"

Never in my life had I been a part of such an evocative, such a solemn ceremony, until now. And what makes me draw this conclusion is the incredible devotion and consistency of the crowd during the procession. What gave rise to this feeling of uniqueness was not the spectacle itself or the wealth of the procession, but the fact that they experienced it so sincerely and deeply!

Once again, I realised that religion is, above all, an experience and an emotional attraction to the Divine and to the ideal of Sanctity. It is a question of "heart and intuition" rather than rationalism in this sacred "bond" between man and Spirit.

If you asked Stefan whether there is anything truly rational underlying, say, the "Virgin Mary", or if it corresponds to something real, my friend would have the answer ready: "I don't want to hear anything about rationality when it comes to these things."

But this time I insisted. I asked him if what he and Jaeger had told me was true, namely that after the Volkic Revelation, religions, or at least their dogmatic aspect, turned out to be something like children's fairy tales.

"Yes," he replied patiently, trying to make me understand. "What you say *is* true, but don't forget that the substantive content of the *Samith*, its true texture and structure, still escapes us entirely. So long as we're still humans, it is inaccessible to us. In other words, we use religions as a substitute; they serve to comfort us and alleviate this deprivation of ours…"

I felt for him because he was clearly struggling to express himself in the way he wished. It hurt him to try and put all these beliefs and ideas he had in his head into a logical sequence of thoughts. Every attempt to rationalise those "great things" made him sad and agitated, because for him such things can only be perceived through faith and intuition.

**Annelud, 2-VII**

Lysborg, Cologne, Rozenholm, New Scone, Koblenz, Mayentia, Mannheim: pearls of the modern Rhine, which is now four times wider than the ancient one. It took us all day to traverse it but we became witnesses to a parade of such indescribable beauty that any signs of fatigue or boredom are not even worth mentioning. New Radviko, Karlsruhe, Annelud, Strasborg, New Karelia… If I had twenty lives, I'd spend them here and nowhere else!

Oh my, what colours, what lights, what incredible beauty in those fir-covered areas! Flower cities and water cities alternate as we proceed. In front of us, a kind of canal with entire garden cities built on its banks, dream-like, and now inhabited riverside locations, artificial waterfalls that perfectly imitate the work of nature, *gestalads* of monumental grandeur, modern temples of the spirit, conservatories with immense concert halls, countless hostels, *Civesheims* and villas surrounded by vast green areas.

But all of this was for me nothing but a fleeting vision. I can't say that I truly saw any of these miracles, that I got enough of them, that I know them, that I truly experienced them.

I arrived in Annelud with the impression of a big, recent loss, an unreasonable and unfair void inside me. I was left with the thirst to go back to those dreamy places as soon as possible, to walk them one by one! But Stefan says we can't go back. We've got a different destination: we're headed southeast. There are moments when the circumstances of life, which have basically been imposed upon me, make me feel that Stefan doesn't see me as a friend and companion but rather as an "equal" who has suffered a traumatic experience and still struggles with his injuries. He sees me as the "Cive of the *Nojere*" who, however, still depends on other people to take care of him, the mentally crippled "prisoner of his amnesia", the only man in today's world that isn't free to fly to wherever he wants, whenever he wants…

## 2-VII Again

## (Very late at night)

Spring has come for good now and the nights here in this beautiful city of the South are magical. The days are longer and the evenings are now quite warm. Now I'm on the terrace of the *gestalad* where we're staying, lying in my chaise lounge, facing the garden. I'm sitting wrapped in the thin but warm coat that was given to all of us in the *Forening* distributions, staring at the sky. It's a bit chilly but the starlight is marvellous. Plus, the soft wind that blows carries scents from the nearby gardens.

I think about what Kant used to say: "Two things awe me most, the starry sky above me and the moral law within me." The sky is my most loyal friend, the dearest companion of my soul because it is the same as in my own time. And no one can deprive me of the magic of this clear night sky!

# THE NEW RENAISSANCE OF 3300 AD
## Visual arts and their techniques

### Nysalzborg, 4-VII

The aesthetic pleasure offered by the "United Museums" in Nysalzborg and the state galleries, which are said to be some of the most representative galleries of central Europe, could only be compared to the deep satisfaction the art lovers of our time felt when visiting our major temples of art: the Louvre, the Prado, the Hermitage, the Borghese Gallery, the Pitti Palace and the museums of Rome. Because if there is one field of culture in which the current civilisation matched, but didn't actually manage to exceed the achievements of our time - at least the ones up until the 20thcentury - this is the visual arts. In every other aspect of life and culture I strongly believe that this world is far ahead of our own. Any attempt to compare them would overwhelmingly be to our detriment.

And by "current culture", of course, I mean mainly their great 9th century and not so much the 600 years that followed. In that century, art reached its greatest peak in the history of the new civilisation. As for the exact period that I lived in, the history of their art classifies it, unconditionally and without further debate, as a period marked by the decline and fall of art, describing those years as a kind of a new Middle Ages that elapsed between the beginning of the 20th century and their regeneration. Not to mention the time when gibberish and nonsense were conceived as a new kind of "style", "originality" and "art".

Now, when I say that these people managed to match us, I'm talking purely artistically and aesthetically and not in terms of technical means. In the field of technical means and advancements, their superiority is unmatched since they are capable of creating effects that we could have never even conceived. Here are some examples: the way their colours and lines are maintained, their "photochromata", all the different methods and types of shading, the topographers' dimension of depth, and the famous "colourlight", which is also known as the "skylight colour of Anolia" - an innovation of the school of Stiernsted, a great painter of the 9th century - and is specifically used for the depiction of the sky in landscape paintings, and other such technical achievements that are independent of the purely artistic value of works. Luckily, they know exactly to what extent they should use these technical means without ever sacrificing true beauty for the sake of technical progress; their undeniable and unmistakable aesthetic prevents them from losing control.

**Youthsmile, 5-VII**

**(Late at night)**

March is almost over and there's no place like the old Austrian Tyrol to welcome April. The lyrics of a poet from my time come to mind when I think about it: "O primavera, gioventù dell' anno!" ("O Spring, youth of the year!")

We arrived here yesterday, late in the morning, along with the tens of thousands of people travelling in the gigantic caravan of *daners*, mainly from the countries of the far north, from Olesud, Trongemi, Bergen, Scavanger, Norfor and even from the Polar Regions. Their faces were beaming with happiness. Most of them were going to embark on individual means of transport and continue their journey to the Mediterranean shores... Oh, how I wish we stopped here for a while too! I could not imagine a greater personal desire at the moment. Spring afternoon and sunset in Youthsmile!

**7-VII**

**(Outside Youthsmile)**

Silvia and I - just the two of us this time - passed numerous rural areas called *lansbees*, whose names I didn't bother asking. I didn't feel like asking anything, neither yesterday nor today.

Happy days... Blissful days! Who were these people that managed to convince us that pain was "a prerequisite of life" and that man's destiny is to suffer? How wrong I was! Oh, how wrong I was to believe them! How wrong I was to think and live that way! How much of my youth and zest for life have I squandered? I wish I could pass the time I have left here with Silvia in this lovely artificial Tyrolean valley, which today has a population of over four million. How I wish I could spend my days and nights here, and only here, in Youthsmile, living the dream, the fairy tale!

True happiness does not cost anything. It nestles in the smallest things. Youth - not chronological youth or the youth of the body, but the youth of the soul - and love are enough to make your heart capable of perceiving all this happiness that surrounds you, all these divine messages that you daily miss.

Today, as Silvia was walking through the gate wearing her hair down, the expression of her eyes and her arched eyebrows reminded me of the features of Villi, Anna's son. I only saw him once in the central square of our little village, but his image was indelibly etched in my memory. They looked so much alike in everything they said and did, not just their features; they were like two drops of water! It was as if she would never be lost, as long as he walked the earth, as if she would always live on through him, as if miracles happen in this world and human science does not know everything, as if there are things that exist outside of our own sphere of possibilities and concepts, as if the determining factor of one's personality, along with genes, also conceals some ineffable spiritual element that doesn't know limitations of time and space, that defeats the poor, transient nature of human life, that crosses the abysses of time, a spiritual element inconceivable by human reasoning, but always present.

## STROLLING THROUGH THE LANSBEES

### 8-VII

Today I rose from my armchair early in the morning when peace and quiet still embraced the *lansbees* that were sleeping beneath the crystal clear, blue sky. I took quite a long walk until the time that I know Silvia usually wakes up. Gradually, the *lansbees* started to wake up as well. Men and women, but mostly young *Cives*, boys and girls with thick hiking boots and small, soft hats in their hands, some alone, others in pairs and others in larger groups, headed off to the wooded slopes. The majority wore the insignia of their group on their lapels.

On the way I met a well-formed young woman with blonde plaits, who was heading to the mountain on her own. I stopped and looked at her. Although she realised that I had noticed her, she didn't lower her gaze. Neither did she make eyes at me, of course. She didn't have the slightest intention to provoke and that was reflected in her expression. It was characterised by a child's innocence without any passing hint of coquetry whatsoever. It revealed confidence in front of the stranger she had just encountered that she had no reason to keep at a "distance". But she did not give me the slightest perceptible encouragement. She was probably wondering why I had stopped and if I needed something, her glance was an unpretentious, friendly one that exuded an air of equality.

I knew that if I asked her something, let's say for directions, she would answer me with much courtesy and dignity and with the necessary, here, "*tank*" *(thanks)* at the end of each phrase. And that if I tried to walk side by side with her she would not get suspicious of my intentions, nor would she start having any similar psychological reactions. She would find it polite, friendly and guileless, as if we were old friends. And if later I met and kept company with her friends, they would also treat me in the same way: like an old and regular member of their group.

I hadn't forgotten though, that Silvia would be expecting me shortly, so I didn't talk to her at all. I put an end to our encounter by nodding goodbye, as is now customary in such circumstances - that is, between an unknown young "citizen" and an older man who has no reason to talk to her.

At the entrance of the green meadow that leads to nearest motorway, there's a marble sculpture of Mary-Lea Volky, one of the most famous ones of the old Tyrol, work of their 12th century sculptor Ottermanden. The statue lends its name to the sylvan road that lies ahead. The *Bilvej* motorway runs outside Youthsmile and the artificial valley. No motorways of theirs run through the states or cities. That's why they have built smaller, ring roads to connect the two.

The first impression that a foreigner has of Mary-Lea is that she is somehow a "saint of Christianity", proclaimed by the spiritual leaders of the Valley of the Roses, at a time when the Christian Church had stopped proclaiming saints for centuries. At least that's what I felt while sitting at her feet. Regardless of the historical reality, one could easily characterise Mary-Lea as a kind of "Christian spiritual figure", and that because of the "inner relationship" between the preaching of the *Nojere* and our own ancient religion, which is considered today a universal tradition.

I'm taking one last look at the sculptural masterpiece by Ottermanden. The smile of Mary-Lea slightly resembles the enigmatic smile of our Mona Lisa, and somehow manages to bring an indescribable happiness to your heart. It is a symbol of regeneration and hope: after the fall of faith and beauty, the worship of incoherence, the disregard for moral principles and the absence of ideals in life, the defeat of humanism, the political anarchy and the terror of a nuclear disaster that permeated life eventually proved powerless and transient. It is the living testimony that the new Middle Ages that elapsed were also transient, since the Great Reality erased that shameful past and turned a new leaf in human history, by defeating all evil and righting all wrongs.

I'm just sitting here, staring at the sculpture. The sight of her is so soothing and so comforting; it gives me a deep, internal, aesthetic satisfaction. I rejoice to see that the spring of Youth and Life are still present here, unmoved and unaltered, after thousands of years. It's nice to see that, in reality, nothing has ever been lost; it's all here, stronger than ever!

## THE "WALK OF VIKINGS"
## Dareja - the centre of automation - and Eliki

### 12-VII

The huge motorway that connects New Christiania with Ejastrem passes across the wide plain with the enormous crystal-fenced *quays* built for the *daners* and the thousands of other travel facilities of the *Biltur* partners that stretch up to the Alps, provides scenic views of the glaciers, which were the product of obsolete technology from many centuries ago that had managed to control the climate of the mountain ranges in order to enrich the Silea, an artificial river that flows just behind them.

It's called "The Walk of the Vikings" and, according to Stefan, it's the largest motorway in southern Europe. It was first paved a very long time ago, around the time when the Silea was created.

Seeing that junction of major arteries and the *ragioza* with all those huge and heterogeneous vehicles, I felt like I was saying goodbye to all those idyllic suburban cities and the beautiful landscapes forever, only to return once again to the large, industrial city-centres of modern life. Trying to hold back my tears, I waved goodbye while the other three did not seem to mind leaving all this behind in the least. They were so overwhelmed with joy and anticipation for our arrival at the Rosernes Dal that they couldn't think of anything else!

I asked Silvia if she was feeling tired due to the very few hours of sleep she had had the night before. "Not at all!" she answered. "I only wish we could get to the Streets of the Palaces sooner!" The Valley of the Roses was the only thing on her mind at this point.

We stopped over at the junction of Dareja for a while. If you take the "Walk of the Vikings" southwards, stopping at this junction is compulsory. We're a mile's distance from the hill behind which Silea is hidden. We are now very close to the artificial river that flows through the other side of the valley. As a matter of fact, we reckon that at dusk we'll be seeing it flowing on our left-hand side.

I didn't know that Dareja was such an important transport hub. It is necessary to stop here if you want to take one of the *ragioza* to travel either eastward towards the Hungarian plains, westward, towards the Swiss lakes, southward, towards Liguria, or even if you want to cross the Adriatic or the Aegean Sea.

The population of Dareja is about 3.5 million, with two-thirds of it being permanent residents. Not at all big, that is, considering its world reputation as "the state of the great technicians" and the crucial role it plays in transportation worldwide. It is true, however, that its technical and technological civilisation is unparalleled. Its old laboratories and institutes keep operating with the same pulse and vitality as before. Polytechnics still attract hundreds of thousands of students from all parts of Europe and their settlements and considered the embodiment of taste and moderation.

The Naira and the Fierlan, two artificial tributaries of the Silea, which basically look like canals, run through the oldest part of the city in symmetrical lines. The buildings are majestic but perhaps too symmetrical and uniform both in terms of construction and colour, since they're all painted in alternating shades of yellow ochre.

Dareja is the centre of automation. It is the Mecca of southern Europe, in relation to its technicians. It was with Dareja's own designs that the Silea was created, and it was Dareja's wise men that made the construction of the glaciers of Small Giostendal possible. It is the city whose schools gave the world a Yarl, a Boyer and a Karl Hornsen - something like our Curie, Lavoisier, Fermi, Max Planck and De Lesseps.

Hilda told me that, in terms of purely spiritual civilisation, Dareja can't compare to Markfor, Anolia or Blomsterfor. It never had the same long tradition of spiritual creation. And she said that the changing times and the downturns in technology often hurt the pride of this great and glorious state. Dareja is now a follower rather than a leader…

It's breaking dawn. The huge bronze Vikings that have given their name to the motorway flank the road. The sight is spectacular! Throughout the whole trip the *ragioza* hasn't touched the ground! It's going so fast that it feels like it's flying! Stefan says that the *ragioza* is only three inches above the asphalt of the autostrada, but that's enough to protect it from any contact and therefore any friction with the road surface of the Viking motorway. That's like magic considering the weight of this "flying-boat" that speeds like lightning!

It is now morning. If it were up to me I'd stop for a while. I noticed that the vegetation had been gradually changing, an indication that we were approaching the Mediterranean Sea. "And yet we are still far away," Stefan corrected me. Sometimes I forget how different everything is from what I remember, how much it has changed...

Cypress-apple trees, linden trees, elms, jujube trees, then fruit trees, then century-old plane trees beside the streams and further down endless rows of azaleas and tall, silvery poplars. The smell of the air brings back memories from my childhood field trips. They so dearly touched my soul back then that I remember every detail and I swear that the air smells and tastes exactly the same as then! I can't put in words what a magical feeling it is to know that I have been here before and that I've been given the chance to return to this life: it's a feeling of triumphant happiness, awareness of my unique destiny, a divine feeling of gratitude!

At the junction of Eliki the all the passengers exchanged the *vigioza* for several small-wheeled *Cives* mintels that had been waiting for us there. All four of us got into one of them and continued our journey.

After exiting Eliki, the first thing I saw was around a hundred priestesses of the Rosernes Dal awaiting the arrival of the *vigiozas* so they could continue, in turn, their own journey. I remember having come across a few of them in Markfor too, but never so many of them together. They didn't look like travellers. The small, soft handbags they were carrying were the only thing that gave them away. Quite a few of them were encircled by children - two or three around each. I counted about a hundred and fifty of them, but they must have been even more! Was it considered as some kind of an "honorary escort" for priestesses or had they been entrusted with the children's care? You couldn't tell. They stood there motionless in contemplation and the obedient children stood quietly by their side.

At the flower gardens of the junction of Eliki I saw for the first time what is probably the most absurd luxury of these times, something that I had not seen in any of the major cities so far - not in Markfor, not in Blomsterfor, not in Anolia, not even in Norfor: enormous artificial baskets with a diameter of 15-20 meters decorated with flowers and plants hung from everywhere, magnificent artworks of some virtuoso florist-painter- and wonderful tableaus with themes from the "Advent of the 200" and the creation of the Valley of Roses.

The flowers and plants here are not geometrically or lace-shaped like in Markfor. Here what prevails are the myriad, totally natural looking shades of green, from the light, silvery olive green to the black-green of the fir trees, in forms and shapes exquisitely crafted and daily tended to by specially assigned "florist-supervisors", so that the work of the "teacher" does not wilt or get damaged in the slightest. From afar they look like gobelin tapestries laid on the ground as if to welcome the travellers. Of course, no one touches them.

In the afternoon we were on the road again. It had become a lot more obvious now from the surrounding landscapes that we were approaching the Valley. Big temples and institutes spanning hundreds of meters and all sorts of *kierketaarns* - perfectly round or ellipsoid little temples with snow-white, circular colonnades - had now taken the place of the giant blockhouses on both sides of the road and the shades of pastel colours had given way to a soft rose colour light.

The sky here is completely free of those dense, dark flocks of enormous flying vehicles and the thousands of platforms and terraces of the *linsens* here are scattered among parks and flower-gardens instead of the giant airports of northern regions.

Every now and then, you could see up on the hill the manor houses of the *Lorffes*, the leading representatives of modern spirit - still locked for this season - which, however, belong to the Rosernes Dal and not personally to them, and which later will be passed on to their spiritual successors, as Stefan informed me.

Beside them you could see the hermitages of the *Ilectors*, deserted red granite monasteries built with severe contours, the personal silent retreats of the Emeriti.

What mesmerises the people of today even more than the beauty of nature, even more than the magnificence of the environment, are the toponyms and the childhood memories they evoke.

Silvia and Hilda had come to the Valley on Christmas Eve many years ago and Stefan had visited the great spiritual centre a few times a while after them, but all of them already knew the history of every inch of this land from when they were still at school.

If you take a glance behind the poplars that line the creek, behind the light pink wall of the monastery of the *Ilectors* in Delfia, you can distinguish the complex of the one-floor communal facilities of the hermits of Naade. Astrucci and Lain had told me about them in Markfor: four hundred years ago their predecessors were the original "founding fathers" of the Valley, the earliest scholars, interpreters and editors of the oldest texts of the Aidersian tradition. They still call them by the Greek word "eremites", which means hermit.

## SILEA, THEIR ARTIFICIAL MOTHER RIVER

While the hazy sun was slowly setting, Stefan, who up to that point had been calm as always, suddenly grabbed my armed to show me a large river that had popped out from the West in the far in the background. "Look! Look!" he cried and simultaneously Silvia and Hilda started screaming in excitement "It's Silea! Silea!"

I turned and clearly saw a very wide strip of water even from this far away. Had these shrewd people then changed the entire continental map? No river of this size had ever existed in these latitudes in my time! But Stefan told me that the Silea did not only belong to southern Europe and that it ended here after a long meandering, starting from the Mont Blanc in Savoy.

One of the oldest symbols of technological and economic consortium and political cooperation in Europe, the Silea passes through a number of countries and its waterfalls, dams and artificial bends - since it is an artificial river to begin with - had once given the peoples of Europe great prosperity thanks to the immense production of hydropower that supplied the entire continent for more than a century.

Later the discovery of new, significant energy sources undermined the importance of the Silea, at least as a source of energy. Nevertheless, in the hearts of the Europeans, the moral and political significance of its construction, its smooth operation for about a 130 years as well as its overall contribution stands as a reminder of the cooperation and solidarity that replaced the strife between nations, a symbol of the survival of the spirit of Altekirchen and of the importance of its articles of association, with the Charter of Nations being the emblem of the first, original, federal union of the Europeans.

And so the Silea remains intact, with its ports, its bridges and its stations of the Paneuropean Hydroelectric Energy Consortium - now of historical importance only - still located on the outskirts of the cities that the super-river runs through.

Wonderful colourful balconies decorated with all sorts of flowers continue to impress you for hundreds of kilometres, hanging above the bronze statues of the pioneers of the original federation: Milstone, Grueberg, Rickenmat, Vergina, and the hero and martyr

Gustav Siovogia, who didn't get to see his vision realised since he succumbed to the pressure too early and, one autumn night, tore his chest open with his own hands and died betrayed, persecuted and isolated.

We crossed the inconceivably long and wide Silea bridges once or twice. Thousands of people were gathered on the incredibly wide pavements of the bridges, either sitting on benches and talking or leaning on the railings and gazing at the water beneath them.

From the Albielle bridge, while staring far into the distance, along with the crowds of *linsens* that were ahead, for the first time I saw quite a few ancient small, hovering boats meant for private use- which looked like they had been plucked from very old garages or museums - flying velos and amphibian tricycles, wingless nano-helicopters, incredible *vigiozas* with old style turbines and all sorts of other comic flying vehicles that were trying hard to keep up with the newer and quicker *linsens*.

No matter how many times Stefan has reassured me that the transparency of the *Forening* - a kind of consortium or partnership - is solidly established and that the cooperative associations of the partners are guarantors of the safety of its products, I have unintentionally come to believe that even these perfect times may have some weaknesses. Those *Cives* - and they are many - who travel in such vehicles must either be capricious or unfairly treated, temporarily at least, by the *Forening* distributions, having to wait patiently for quite a while in order to get the vehicles that they deserve, vehicles that the rest of the *Cives* already possess.

The night had already fallen when the Silea, after an absence of half an hour, reappeared in front of us, illuminated, at the turn of the road. Only the night-time hours do justice to the true beauty of this river. "At this time of day, the Silea gains the sanctity of the Ganges in our eyes; we see it as the sacred river of Europe," said Stefan.

Apulia, Erika, Terranova, Rodope, Great Poplar, Emerita, Fata Azzura, Teskera, Nydelfia, Egeria, Villafranca, Filiatura: dreamy outskirts of the Valley filled with *Mindre Skoles* (their primary schools), *Vilenthens* (their secondary schools), historical and ethnological museums, planetariums, conservatories and institutes, "serenity centres", lecture venues, libraries and study rooms, temples, complexes of hermitages and huge amphitheatres. The greater surroundings of the Valley create an incredible spiritual atmosphere.

Stefan was striving to inform me about the history of each of these wonders and explain their deeper meaning to me as well as he could. He never left my side and didn't stop answering my questions - even questions that I hadn't asked yet. I noticed that he never once spoke to our friends. But they weren't talking to each other either; they were both focused on their thoughts.

We continued travelling during the night without stopping anywhere. Thousands of people in their individual vehicles passed us by on that extremely spacious motorway, all overwhelmed with the same excitement and anticipation about their arrival at the Valley. In the middle of the night, in a true cascade of white light flooding the horizon, we arrived at the Valley of the Roses…

## VALLEY OF ROSES: STARING AT THEIR SACRED CITY

### Rosernes Dal, 13-VII

I sit and stare at the "holy" city of these times, exhausted from the charm of this mesmerising view, which can only compare with landscapes of dreams and fairy tales.

From the densely populated hill with the small and gentle gradient where we had settled in at midnight of the night before last, I cast a glance and realised that we had finally arrived!

An artificial basin that I had seen before on the *Reigen-Swage* stretched before us, full of rose bushes, temples and countless monuments, palaces with the famous crooked domes of Gratia Dei and Lysicoma: a giant garden city with a resident population of six million souls - including the regional *lansbees* that surround it - cut in half by the river.

There are no stars in the sky and this faint, diffused, cool light, that doesn't seem to stem from anywhere in particular, gives you the illusion of daylight. I think I've said it before, but this artificial light of the current times looks like the aurora borealis.

I was mesmerised! I couldn't take my eyes off of it! Fabulous treasures of topaz, amethyst, rubies and sapphires sparkle under this brilliant light! Each and every one of the semi-circular lines on the horizon was a wonderful, floodlit temple of art, a monument to the spiritual history of the last centuries. This is how they use most of their gemstones nowadays; to decorate their large cultural centres! They don't belong to anyone! Their purpose is to satisfy the eye of their beholders!

"Look Andreas, look!" Silvia turned her face towards me and looked at me, fascinated by the image of the Valley that lay ahead. "Look! This is our earth, Andreas, our globe, our own planet even if we don't believe our eyes!"

From up here you have a great view of the countless palaces of the *Ilectors* and the *Lorffes*, their observatories and all sorts of "radio wave stations" that carry the glorious names of the old researchers that they honour - like Striberg, Tegner or Feridi - the galleries that host their masterpieces, the temples of the Franciscans in Cordei a municipality of the Valley, and the Madonna of the Roses. And if you turn around, you'll see a great number of planetariums, conservatories, gyms and swimming pools, everywhere on the periphery of the Valley.

Here are the galleries of Iberia, Latium and New Sabina with the famous ninety-eight heterogeneous but so fittingly matching capitals, each of which occupies several pages in the history of art. And there's the temple of Human Suffering and the altars of Maternity, Research and Sacrifice, built in the memory of the thousands of scientists who were persecuted or crippled by radiation and their struggle against bacteria and viruses. And there are the premises of the Aidersen Institute - an entire city in itself - and the temples of the "dead religions", each built in their respective style: Buddhist, Hindu, ancient Greek temples, synagogues. I even saw a temple for Zarathustra!

There in the background I can see the temple of Love and Peace, the construction of which lasted for three whole generations, as I was told. Designed by the great Niemorsunt - a project of the 9th century, finished in 876 - it was the fruit of sincere cooperation between the architects Olaf Keirl, Hilda Normanden and Alicia Neville.

To the east stands the Pantheon, with the arch-shaped halo that bears the famous here inscription "Honora Praecursoribus Aeternus", written in golden light! There's something magical about this inscription, apart from the golden light with which it was written; no matter where you are and from what angle you look at it - from above, below, far away or up close - you can see it as clearly as you would see it should you be standing right in front of it!

Next to it, the Temple of Poetry by Kekonen, also from the 9th century. Between the Pantheon and the Streets of the Palaces stands the temple of Damon and Phidias, a special project inspired by Yalmar and Rinarschield - the most renowned *Lorffes* of the 12th and 13th century, whose names and friendship marked their era - that was assigned to the architect Heimerstam for the perpetuation of the idea of friendship as a whole and not his own personal friendship.

To the west, temple-palaces devoted to Justice, Freedom and Culture and Virtue and Humanism and beside them the monument by Igor Bodurof that will forever recount the sacrifice of the twenty million people that took part in the unsuccessful attempt to colonise Mars. And here's the invisible and intangible temple of God! You seriously cannot see anything! It is a place of religious trance and concentration, for the *Lorffes* alone, which only takes form if you are in it!

I also saw the temple of the Unsung Martyrs by Dean Kersteen made of synthetic ivory! Oh, I had read so much about him in the books that I was given! He was one of those who, back in the dark ages, had "inadvertently prophesised" what was coming. Most of the temples were built in the first two centuries of the *Nojere*, but their meanings were interpreted considerably differently after the *Oversyn* was obtained.

When in the 8th and 9th century the now famous, prophetic words of Bramsen and later of Nyttenmat were heard, it was as if the Aidersen also knew, deep down inside: "Everything that excels will necessarily defeat everything that doesn't; the superior spirit and truth will prevail, sooner or later." Or "It is the law of nature and creation that thousands of planets inhibited by living, thinking beings meet their 'great destiny'. Some already have." As for our little earth, they said: "Don't let insufficient time intervals cloud your judgment; if you want to make comparisons, choose a bygone era. For example, compare our times to the Stone Age."

The great elders, predecessors and precursors of Chillerin, the wise ones who waited for death to open up new horizons of superhuman knowledge and mental development, never, not for a second, believed that they would ever just cease to exist. As if they knew…

I've concluded, therefore, that virtue is eventually rewarded, that a moral compass is a prerequisite for bliss, that consciousness is ultimately the "God within us"! Even philosophy was vindicated when it highlighted the ideal of moral personality in a cruel world. And in that temporary, marginal and transient world, within a context of finite human fate, people had spoken of "the eternal" and "the indestructible", and had conceived infinity as a notion.

For me, even Wagner, who in his opera *Parsifal* presented the idea that purity can defeat all temptations and achieve redemption, was vindicated.

I've been sitting here all night trying to make out all the temples that are scattered throughout the Valley of the Roses, with my eyes glued either to one of the many powerful telescopes that they have here on the *gestel's* balcony or to the night vision binoculars that Stefan gave me.

It's after two a.m. It's been hours since my companions went to bed and I'm still roaming uncontrollably on the terrace, amid an ecstasy of the senses, not even thinking about fatigue, not even having the need to let my feeble body sink into my armchair.

A thousand things that I've seen on the *Reigen-Swage* and the map of the Rosernes Dal pop into my mind and I want to find as many of them as I can. I even managed to discern a few dozen statues and monuments, out of the millions that are erected outside the temples. Names, dates and all sorts of artworks and significant achievements are spinning inside my head.

If Stefan were here right now, I would ask him, "What is the deeper meaning of the Valley? Is it true that nothing is ever really lost?"

Myriads of personal memories and thoughts are flooding my mind and soul.

The magical diffused light fades away and the light of the new day takes its place in the crystal clear blue sky. It's the twelfth today. I didn't think I'd make it here. I didn't think I'd get the chance to see the Valley with my own eyes; but I did, and now I want to see everything!

"Did you stay here all night long?" asked Stefan, suddenly breaking the silence. He was up very early, around ten past six, right on time for the sunrise. The girls were still asleep. He looked a bit worried about the fact that I hadn't lain in my armchair at all, but I calmed him down saying that I was feeling very refreshed and revitalised.

"I don't think anyone slept last night," he said. "But at least we lay down for a few hours." Hilda didn't get a wink of sleep all night. Her heart was beating like crazy and at three a.m. she got up and took a pill to calm her down. She was overexcited, much like a child that can't wait for the dawn of Christmas Day… You see, here no one wants to leave this life without having seen the Rosernes Dal at least once."

Stefan spoke to me about the universal capital with the usual, for the times, pride that stems from pure excitement, love and experiences of their childhood.

"Tomorrow afternoon we'll go down to the Valley," Stefan told me before he left. "Did I tell you it was tomorrow afternoon? It's important. You have to prepare the *troje*, the formal piece of clothing designed for the occasion, but that should be the least of your worries. Above all, prepare your heart! Take a retrospective look at your life and pray from your heart. You're one of us now. Just make sure that your thoughts are pure. Everybody is praying these days. You should pray too; for mother earth, for the institutions, for our dead, for the final deliverance from barbarism, for the end of prehistory."

I'm sitting on the terrace with Silvia, waiting to hear the bells. Stefan told me that it's been a week now since the regular, morning bell-tolling started from the spires of the Unsung Martyrs. These days are known as the twelve days of prayer before the memorial service. Silvia is sitting next to me holding my arm. "Sometimes, our inner being is in need of a gentle sense of solitude and tranquillity, accompanied by a caring and loving presence, away from the bustle of the world, an isolation that serves as a sign of respect and appreciation for all these beloved places ..." she whispered.

I told her that I honestly couldn't agree more and squeezed her hand warmly when the first bells rang. There is something about these sounds that reminded me of Christianity even though their intensity and aesthetic value is greatly enhanced.

With eyes closed and both palms pressing her temples, Silvia listened in silence, lost in her thoughts and focused on her prayer. "Oh, let me hear the bells," she had said shortly before, when I tried to express my excitement in a few words.

We shouldn't be talking here. After the holy bell-tolling, Stefan told me that no one, in no other circumstance and nowhere else in the world, could ever hear a melody as divine as the one that comes out of the spires of the Martyrs. It's incredible that it has no match around the globe.

## AN AMAZING RESEMBLANCE

In the afternoon we are scheduled to descend to the Rosernes Dal. And this is the day and time you chose to visit me Anna? And in this way?

On June 29, 1906, while we were lying on the grass of the small, joyful valley of our homeland, dreaming about our future together, you told me verbatim: "How thirsty the human soul is for solitude sometimes! How thirsty for a sense of peace, for a view like this, alongside your loved one…" I remember that five days later I was leaving for Rome. Oh, my dear Anna, you deserve all the happiness of the world, wherever you are…I used to say that the purpose of my life was to protect you and guard you from all evil. On July 8, I had similar thoughts in Piazzale Napoleone at sunset, on the long terrace of Valanie overlooking west Rome. "We should see this together," I had told her.

In the summers of 1913 and 1914, just before the Great War, when my life had already taken a downward spiral, I went back to that part of the south, to that same terrace of the French architect.

Oh my! The case is so similar… Of course, Silvia hasn't got the slightest idea about that since I'm being fanatically cautious, hiding it very well from all three of them; Silvia, Stefan and Jaeger. Does my destiny have any *more* surprises in store for me? My soul bows before this miracle that managed to annihilate the abyss of memory and time.

### 13-VII Again

### (Quite a while later)

I think that what made my love with Anna so divine wasn't the intensity of the erotic passion, but the quality of our emotions. What we lived has become "holy" precisely because it was so pure and kind, a genuine reflection of what today is called the *Samith*. And that's why the possibility of our love was not extinguished by physical death. Time failed to erase it…

# DOWN TO THE VALLEY
## Sightseeing in the city

### 14-VII

### (2 a.m.)

From five p.m. to midnight I spent my time with Stefan, going from terrace to terrace, ascending and descending their famous and fantastic elevatores, a kind of public lift we would call them, and using all their new *vindebros* - bridges designed for mild hiking - without the slightest effort, among countless thousands of late-nighters, like us, pilgrims all dressed in formal, mandatory uniform of the Valley. Stefan was striving to explain to me, in the best possible way, everything that we saw in the oldest part of the sacred state.

Unlike in Norfor and the other cities we've visited, I never felt the need to lean on Stefan while in the Valley. You can never feel lost or terrified here. The river and surrounding villages always give you a clear sense of direction. The feelings of indisposition, helplessness or hesitation that I've experienced elsewhere do not apply to this place.

We're wearing a pair of short, dark-coloured trousers with black stripes that stop slightly below the knee, green silk high socks, a white double breasted vest with white lapels and special white boots that make no noise whatsoever when they touch the ground. And I forgot the green stole-belt that decorates the uniforms of the standard *Cives*.

At first glance, there are two or three things across the region of the old, central Rosernes Dal that make a strong impression on the traveller: the clarity of the sky due to the lack of traffic, the absence of purely residential areas across the great state, and the lack of the "aura of a capital city", contrary to the other megacities I've visited, mostly in terms of lifestyle and pace of life. I´ve only seen individual means of transport here, and still, they were very high above, personal *linsens* or *vigiozas* that don't scare you and don't affect the clarity of the sky.

Here you'll see no *daners*, no gigantic, hovering satellite islands, no underground cities or any other sorts of hidden urban extensions and no steel overhead bridges resembling streamers like those in Blomsterfor. And instead of residences, there's an incredible ocean of monuments and parks and arcades and altars and flower beds. And I wonder, where do these six million people live? I'm quite sure they live on the remote, light blue slopes and hillsides that surround the Valley-excluding of course the *Lorffes*, the *Tilteys*, the *Ilectors* and the great artists.

And then, exactly what sort of capital is this? Rosernes Dal, equal in size to Norfor, seems more like an idyllic haven of the intellect rather than a real capital city to me… I would accept a term like "the capital of dreams and beauty" to describe it, but it certainly doesn't feel like the centre of their current universal political and economic community.

It may be the ultimate supervisory authority and the coordination and alignment of their few institutions emanates from here, but none of this becomes obvious to the outsider. A key element in the life of this vast city is what could possibly be called the worship of a mixture of things, like religiosity, art, meditation, and other great spiritual endeavours, which no one tries to hide. In my view, the Valley of the Roses could be described as a kind of Lhasa and Medina of the current "Western" world.

This is, then, where the great-grandchildren of the Europeans who survived the ravages of the wars live: Anglo-Saxons, Slavs, Germans, Greeks, Latinos, Scandinavian, Walloons and Flemings, Dutch and Swiss, Finns and several more nations of European descent.

**15-VII**

Once again, I'm staying up late writing after having spent the entire day sightseeing, from seven in the morning until nine in the evening. The four of us took a walking tour of the city centre. The early April heat was toned down by the cool breeze and the scented air that wafted with it. You have to walk to most places; otherwise you don't have time to see anything.

On the way back, our excitement gave way to fatigue. A good shower and a light dinner accompanied by refreshing frozen fruit juices - they don't touch anything that has alcohol in it and I'm not even sure they're familiar with its use, except maybe wine. But the girls remained silent the whole time. I noticed that they sat away from each other at the table, both immersed in their thoughts; shortly after they retired to their rooms misty-eyed.

"You keep on with your books and your writing. Don't bother comforting them," Stefan whispered to me with a smile. "They'll be fine… Nobody ever knows why a woman cries. Are their minds gripped by memories? Are they feeling a sense of dissatisfaction despite everything that they saw today? Are they tears of joy? Or are they tears of boredom caused by the lack of employment since all of the main problems of life are solved?"

He was in a somewhat inappropriately good, for the occasion, mood, and although he was trying to be discreet, one would think that he was mocking them for their excessive sensibility. He reminded me that one of the many names used to describe the Valley of the Roses was "the Kingdom of Human Suffering", referring to the longing of the soul and the deep human element of inner pain, but I think that this name has a more profound and historical meaning; it's a tribute to the bloody centuries of prehistory.

I didn't know what to say so I didn't reply and a few minutes later I withdrew to my room as well. For the first half an hour after dinner I leafed through two compact travel guides about the Rosernes Dal, which, to be honest, were aimed at children and then I settled down to write.

All sorts of images swirled through my head. The face of this great city has been completely changed these days. You bump into thousands of foreign pilgrims, who have travelled from all different parts of the world, everywhere on the streets and massive motorways. They've come for the big procession scheduled for the day after tomorrow. They seem to be very comfortable in the *slaabroks*, the mandatory uniforms that I described above, which they only take off when they go to sleep in the luxury hostels, the *gestalads* and the *civesheims* located on the surrounding hillsides.

These days the Valley is full of *Tilteys*, *Ilectors* and *Lorffes*, as well as representatives of the clergy. They walk around the city just like everyone else, simple and modest, making people feel equal. I've never seen so many of them gathered in one place, but I've also never seen such a lack of interest from the people around them. It seems that the concentration, the devotion and the reverential mood of each visitor leaves no room for acclamation. Or better that their common worship for the *Nibelvirch* is so dominant in their hearts that it leaves no room for any other sort of enthusiasm.

In fact, even the outfits of these great men do not differ much from those of the ordinary *Cives*. The only thing that changes is the colour of the socks, the stole and the belt. And yet the final visual effect is not at all monotonous since their insignia complete the outfit - golden chains with emeralds, pearl cumberbunds - lending a very quaint and charming tone to the boulevards, mainly at night-time.

Stefan tells me that this year's participation is unprecedented, and yet it seems that all these crowds were housed adequately and efficiently in no time in the endless urban extension built on the surrounding hills. In fact, he tells me that there's still more space in the *larinters*, the hostels and the apartments. They have a long tradition in organisational capabilities and, once again, they've done a wonderful job.

At 5:30 in the afternoon, John Humphrey and Ulfink Enemark in the flesh, walked by, a few meters away from where we were standing. Stefan pointed them out to me. I barely noticed the famous creator of "Fabiola" and the poet of "Dream on the Riverside", "Forgotten Promise" and "Irenaeus". My eyes were fixed on the statues. I'm less interested in real people. The same goes for the priestesses. We encountered several of them, some older, other younger, dressed in the typical snow white robe. As I have read, the patrons and protectors of their faith are the *Lorffes* themselves even though, in practice, they rarely take part in the rituals. The greatest of them possess the undisputed social primacy in contemporary life. Even nowadays, history seems to repeat itself in many ways. For example, the current social ranking resembles that of the Egypt of the Pharaohs, but without the violence and the flaunting of power.

## THE PANTHEON

I noticed that the current language is richer than ours. Here's an example: while they've always had separate words for "prophet" and "poet", since after the time of Volky, they also have a third word that means both. The same happens with the words "priest", "thinker" and "philosopher"; they now have a word that expresses all three.

I knew that in the Pantheon I would find thousands of works by all the great spiritual men that have existed from my time and onwards. But the area of the Pantheon is extremely large; it's an entire town in itself. I only spent a few hours there when it would take years for someone to study this entire cultural and spiritual heritage. One can find the names hosted there in school textbooks and read about their work. The guidebooks of the Valley are there to help you find content by a specific author or the exact shelf location of a specific book in that vast library. Poets, philosophers, researchers of the natural sciences, music composers, thinkers, humanitarians, public and political figures, mystics, artists, social reformers, educators: they're all here, as long as their work has stood the test of time. Einstein, Newton, Pythagoras, Homer, Milton, Virgil, Socrates, Plato, Confucius, William Tell, Gautama Buddha, Matteotti, Bach, Handel, Rousseau, Tolstoy, Kierkegaard, Seneca, Pascal, Bergson and Rilke are some of the historical figures from the eras before mine that are hosted there.

Their life-size marble, brass, copper and synthetic ivory statues, most of them decorated with scenes from their work, that stand on equally tall pedestals, symbolise, at least in my own mind, a triumphant vindication of the cultural legacy of the "prehistoric and uncivilised", as they call them, times. It gave me considerable pleasure and satisfaction to see some of our great men come alive everywhere around me! Something that really struck me was that I even saw crowned ones, like Codrus, Numa Pompilius and Marcus Aurelius!

No discrimination existed between our men and theirs, from the beginning of the *Eldrere* and onwards, neither in the position of the statues, nor in their dimensions, nor in anything else. The only thing that slightly changes is the interpretation of the "Source" of thought and inspiration of each of them because today there is no contradiction between the real and the ideal.

Everything that was referred to as "spiritual worlds and concepts" by past generations is now considered real. They claim that the source of all inspiration and all manifestations of the spirit in many different cultural fields from the beginning of time is one: "the unconscious thirst of the soul for the *Samith* and the pain caused by the lack of it". The alleged conflict and opposition between real and ideal is basically nothing more than "the incredible contrast and distance between this earthly world that we live in and the Great Reality". That is what causes both the holy pain of inspiration and that conflict.

If our people heard all that, they would secretly laugh at them, but *they* are so proud of this "direct perception" they have of reality and the world, so proud of what they've seen and what they so firmly believe and support, that they wouldn't even care…

The exhibits here are not classified based on the origin, school or era of their creators. All those significant figures come from the great motherland, earth, and belong to the great era, eternity, thus becoming immortal. You see Chopin not far from Tchaikovsky and Rachmaninoff, Goethe next to Hugo and Schiller in the same room as Alfred de Musset. As a matter of fact, a young *unge*, Lyla, told me a few days ago that a number of students, pilgrims from the neighbouring secondary school, the *vilenthens*, had put laurel wreaths and fresh flowers on their heads to honour them. I think about how many tears must have been shed by those great artists at the time of creation and how many tears they must have brought to their innumerable sensitive admirers and I can't help but shiver. At least today they don't consider poets crazy dreamers…

I have just realised how much noble suffering is incorporated in the worldly form of redemption called artistic creation. And when you see, hear or touch a true work of art, it is the closest you can get to seeing, hearing or touching the Great Reality; its memory grows stronger and so does the thirst and nostalgia for the *Samith* that's hidden within all of us. And it is happiness that causes this pain full of spiritual joy!

I remembered something that Lain used to repeat in his lectures: that with the passage of time, our species reached a stage of biological and spiritual development that gave us the privilege of pain! Man has become a "sensitive receptor". All great artists, like Lamartine, Praxiteles, Lessing, Klopstock, Chateaubriand, Phidias, Ribera and Mendelssohn were some of those who saw the light in obscure times, when nobody else could see it. Compared to the average person of their times, they seemed to have had supernatural mental inclinations.

"The greater the artist, the more unsatisfied he is with his own work," Lain once told me. "All artists know that art has no boundaries, no limits, no end." If I'm not mistaken, Beethoven had said something similar long before Lain did. And, as I was informed, what they both meant was that what artists are trying to express cannot be conveyed either through pens, paintbrushes, chisels, or musical notes… Its essence cannot be captured by the human mind nor can it be rationally explained.

In one of his pieces on artists and Art itself, Tinersen says: "Like the fluttering of swallows on an iron-barred skylight of a prison, their purpose is to remind us that it is spring outside, the air is fragrant and the blooming valleys await us. We belong to the bright blue sky as much as it belongs to us."

A while ago Stefan told me: "I wish that all these great men from the ancient times could join us here to experience this salvation, to experience the highest form of spiritual happiness." The *Roisvirch* they call it here. And he said that because, according to Tinersen, "Nobody knew back then the answer to the question: 'Why do we suffer?'" That's the reason why all great artists couldn't find happiness in the outside world. They were still unaware of "the reflections of the *Samith*".

## LATHARMI

At 6:00 p.m. I wandered through the city trying to find the statue of Valmandel. Last fall, I got the chance to listen to quite a few pieces from his oratorio *Prayer Among the Stars' Golden Spheres*, in many of Lain's classes. I knew from the *Swage* and from my autumn studies in Markfor that the statues of Jesus and Volky were more or less in the same location.

"Valmandel's not too far from here," said Stefan. However, we were still inside the Pantheon and we needed to go to the Blue Roses, in Latharmi. That's where Jesus, Volky, Larsen, Domenicus Albani - the "Plato of the *Nojere*" - and Axel Jenefelt - a leading thinker of their 9th century - were located.

We only saw them from afar. I noticed that in this part of the city the statues were more thinly scattered as if the great men that they depicted were entitled to more space! We didn't get up close to them because dozens of *Ilectors*, priestesses and other VIPs were paying homage, most of them kneeling in prayer at the pedestals of the statues. In fact, at the pedestal of the statue of Valmandel I saw a couple of *Tilteys* lying down, dreaming with their eyes open! Stefan didn't want to go near them. He said that we had to wait for them to finish their meditation and prayer first, but we didn't have enough time, so we left.

I couldn't possibly describe the atmosphere that prevailed in the flowery streets of Lagrela. I couldn't possibly put down on this lifeless paper the feelings that I experienced there, in the navel of the Pantheon, breathing that air of deep piety. It was completely different from any other part of the Valley that I've been to. I felt something more when I was there: I felt the faith!

I saw some "guides", dressed in grey uniforms and bearing the insignia of their class, whose job was to lead some groups of foreign pilgrims. They passed by us. What reverence and solemnity! I could barely withhold my tears…

When I heard Stefan saying that we were heading to the Blue Roses in Latharmi, I was expecting to see something like the pastel-coloured rosebushes that I've come across so many times and in so many places up to now. But upon arrival there, I was stunned to find evergreen rosebushes, different from the rest I've seen, almost equal in size with small pine trees! But what leaves you truly speechless is the incredible colour of their rose petals. This wasn't just a colour; it was light! It looked as if the petals were a canvas of an artist, a mirror reflected the colour of the sky, an image of incredible clarity!

We walked past "The Seats of the *Ilectors*". There was only one *Ilector* there now, but he wasn't sitting; he was standing, his eyes fixed on the horizon. We went closer, as close as we could. They say that the greatest *Ilectors* were once here, taking up these seats, those who once found the inner strength to speak their minds "each in their own era and in their own language", those who spoke out more clearly than others, who centuries before the first *Nibelvirches*, had been trying to prepare the people for what was coming. They were said to be half-human and half-celestial creatures, supernatural spirits that had been humanised in the environment of our world. They perpetually startled mankind, and they still do. They cause many conflicts in their time. They all took spirituality to another level…How exactly? Nobody ever knew; perhaps not even them…

"For as long as we remain humans, we are not entitled to know either our origin or our destination," said Stefan without looking at me. "Death is not true oblivion; life is! Life, which limits our cognition, speech and understanding, life which limits us to our senses… So-called death is a redemptive light ..." he added. And he honestly believed it.

As we moved away from the statue of Christ in the direction of Labejona and fatherland of Alexis Volky, I saw, coming from the opposite direction, processions of hundreds of very tall and robust adolescent boys and girls, all from the nearby *vilenthens*, symmetrically lined up in octads. I commented to Stefan on their height and he smiled and said that it's normal after two thousand years of evolution to be a few inches taller…

The small white candles that many of the children were holding in their right hand illuminated the dark. Nearby, I saw several rows of yellowish canisters full of blue and white rose petals, also inexplicably sparkling and shiny. Thereby, I had the opportunity to see for the first time, another miracle of the present times: without the use of phosphorus or any similar material, as Stefan assured me, current technology is able to make a few species of the plant world and the kingdom of the flowers now seem self-luminous and even shine brighter than they do in daylight.

Suddenly, out of the absolute silence, hymns started sounding. Their melodies are divine and, although distinct, they are somewhat similar to ecclesiastical music. Later, the hymns started alternating with invocations, and I had the pleasure of hearing quite a few phrases of our own times. Among them, the ancient Latin "*Gloria in excelsis Deo*" and the incredibly touching "*Miserere*".

One had to have a heart of stone to manage to withhold tears in the sight of that venerable centuries-old tradition coming to life, here, now, after it has touched the souls of so many generations before us.

I couldn't help myself telling Stefan that all those around me looked like Christians, dropping a hint about what he told me about the fall dogmatism, which had started in the 20th century along with the progress in scientific research. "And this dogmatism has continued up to now," I pointed out.

"You're not entirely right," he replied patiently. "Modern life is deeply religious, far more than it was in your own time." He told me that the outburst of disbelief that had prevailed during the centuries that were marked by an extensive and one-sided technological advancement, were succeeded by the deep faith of the *Nojere*. "God exists; Only his essence - what he is and what he's not - is not up to humans to define. And the relationship between creator and creation cannot be conceived by any of the biological forms of organic matter."

I found it impossible to follow all his thoughts. Sometimes I don't even understand what he means, especially when talking about the "undiagnosed element of a mental entity that comes and infuses the higher organic forms of life, without being life itself" or when he says that "there are many more worlds and dimensions of life that escape us, apart from the three-dimensional world in which we perceive something as real."

# THE VOLKIES
## The story of the first "200" and the early years of Alexis Volky

### 16-VII

This morning we found ourselves in Nayatana again and later in the Pantheon, more or less in the same places as yesterday. After going down an anonymous pebblestone street, we ended up in the long paths of Labejona and the orangery. Everything has been preserved exactly as it was 525 ago, in the exact same state and in the exact same place. This is where Alexis Volky walked around as a child.

The first Volkies were of Slavic origin. In fact, their great ancestor was among the "200" who founded the Valley. Much later, after the year 700, three of Volky's direct ancestors married French and Scandinavian women hence the mixed origins.

Initially those first Polish and Ukrainian families were settled in another region, in the northern outskirts of the Valley, but according to history books, after the 6th century *(circa 3000 AD)*, they moved to this area. They were pious, frugal, kind and enlightened people, who dedicated themselves mostly to fruit growing and crafts and in their free time lived a practically monastic life and in many cases ascetic, with a strong inclination towards spiritual meditation and reflection. They lived like that for hundreds of years; their lifestyle became a family tradition that was passed down from generation to generation.

The guide, Viktor Gorms, leads us and ten pilgrims, to a simple, three-storey house-museum of which he's been the caretaker for forty years. However, Stefan informed me that Gorms is not a mere caretaker and guardian of this house; he is also a rare spiritual person and a research scientist.

In this ancestral home, this small farm and the surrounding gardens, Alexis Volky's father, Eugene Volky, spent almost his entire life. Son of the caretaker of a great library of the time and famous in his time for his finest monographs on aesthetics, Eugene Volky was a worthy thinker of the Chillerin School during their 10th century. They say that he never travelled outside the Valley. He was a humble and modest man, a lecturer devoted to his studies. He never aspired to become famous. The more he felt the need to improve his inner self, the more indifferent he became towards recognition of his work and acceptance from others. He was also unconcerned with building up a "career" or climbing the social ladder. The only thing that mattered to him was the maturity and the richness of his intellect and spirit.

At the age of thirty-two he was married for love to his twenty-year old student, Inga Keiry, a sweet brunette with dark grey eyes. Her family tree was of insignificant historical value, but her parents were virtuous people with a spirit of self-sacrifice, which they managed to bequeath to their daughter, along with fine education and excellent manners. "She is worth the risk," the library caretaker had told his son before the marriage was decided, "there are very good chances that she will make you happy and give you a wonderful family!"

But Eugene would have married her even if his father had disapproved; he loved her very much indeed. She was his invaluable assistant at work and his life companion; he was very happy. Unfortunately his librarian father, and grandfather of Alexis Volky, didn't live long enough to witness the miracle of life when she gave birth to his grandson, Alexis Volky, on the third floor of this very house with the bright rooms and open view, the second month of 911, a year after the marriage.

Now the young *unges* show to the visitors what's left of this place, the place where this omniscient man, the promoter of direct knowledge, had spent his childhood. And the venerable old and wise man, Viktor Gorms, is there to welcome you whenever he's got time.

In order to step on the well-preserved wooden floors they give you some cloth shoes to wear. The general atmosphere of silence in the inside of the house makes you want to lower your voice. Stefan hasn't uttered a word since we entered and the *unges* began to talk to us about the few things that are in the house and Alexis Volky's personal belongings.

Here in the Valley you will encounter many famous names that date back to the 6th century and have a long tradition in meditation and inner life cultivation, hence the dynasties of the Chillerins, the Volkies, the Royalsens, the Borges and many others that have passed through the Aidersen Institute. They could probably be paralleled to our own Curie and Strauss dynasties of the 19th and early 20th century.

But apart from the power of heredity, it has been historically recorded that many of the great men and women that have left their mark on our earth have also had exceptional upbringing by their mothers. And it seems as if Inga Keiry-Volky was a very loving, dedicated, selfless and overall wonderful mother to her son for more than twenty years. When the "exquisite mission" of raising a son was finally completed, Inga saw a very different person when she looked in the mirror, but she did nothing but smile in the face of the law of physical decay…

However, the contribution of education, heredity and family tradition was less significant than the inherent values of young Alexis. The boy was born with mental and spiritual gifts and a big, sensitive heart. Just as Mozart was born with the divine gift of harmony, Alexis had an inherent and profound sensitivity and great affection toward people, which he was said to have acquired in some sort of "pre-existence".

At school, that child with the high forehead and the black, soulful eyes always knew a bit more than what was taught in each class. At the age of eight or nine, as he was later told, he had his little moments of rebellion against the unfairness of life, meaning the injustice of human destiny and not that of everyday social life though he hadn't even been slightly touched by this "unfair destiny". His heart was full of compassion. He was meant for many and great things, but happiness was not one of them.

There were moments when Inga fought against this oversensitivity and urged him to come back down to earth and stop agonising over other people's problems. His caring mother thought that her child's candle would eventually burn out if he kept making "the holy suffering of the people" his own.

But everything went well and he turned out just fine. According to his biographers, at the age of sixteen, Alexis had a somewhat strong leaning towards solitude, but at the same time he was also joyful and enthusiastic about life and the world. He loved nature and he used to take long walks around the Valley. The change of seasons alone was enough to fill him with incredible joy.

Throughout his adolescence, Alexis used to choose his extracurricular books by himself. He was inclined towards spiritual communication; he was seeking some sort of "companionship" with the spiritual treasures of the past that had preceded him and thus escaped him. Those wise men "spoke" to him, but the adolescent weighed their words very carefully; he didn't agree with everything they had to say…

In 927, shortly before noon on New Year's Eve, while Alexis was taking a walk with his father Eugene among the orange trees, and they were reviewing their year, the young man said, among other things, that he believed in a "possible identification of the path of knowledge and the path of love" and he talked about "a point where they converge, a point lost in the abstraction of nature and creation, something that the human mind cannot grasp." The proud father listened with rapture and a secret anticipation arose in him…

In his twenties, young Alexis was thinner and his face was full of light. In physical terms, he looked somewhat like Chopin, judging from some photographs of the era. He was undergoing some health problems at the time and his mother worried again. She couldn't shake the idea that her son might not be meant to live a long life, and that idea overwhelmed her.

And the truth is that, between the ages of 19 and 22, Alexis seemed to be one of those fine souls who depart this life too soon to get where they truly belong faster. And yet this did not happen. He was not meant to die young. He was meant to grow old and grey and give to the people that he so much loved the greatest spiritual gift in the history of humanity!

"He was neither a God nor a prophet," said Stefan, "and yet he was the chosen one to see things divine and eternal and show them to his equals." And he continued, "He didn't prophesise the future, but he did see and show the things that always have and always will remain unchanged and untouched since the beginning of time and he proved to people just how much they had overestimated not only the findings of science, but also the spiritual potential of their 'antennas'. He saw, not with his physical eyes, but with the eyes of his heart, and taught in such a way that nobody ever asked for evidence or doubted him. Because what he showed people, what he taught them, was one of these things that can't be proven empirically, like God or love… In order for someone to understand it, a whole different path must be taken and a whole different level of faith must be attained…"

I recall what Lain told me one day: "The further people remove themselves from such values, the harder it becomes for them to one day find a way to comprehend them. If you forget it, it will forget you."

From what I understood, the path that leads to the understanding of these things has to do with the inner evolution of our biological species. It is a path that was completely inexistent in my era - the era of one-sided science and technology - a path that could have only been paved by those insightful and visionary men and women of the Aidersen Institute, which is exactly what happened, around the year 790 of their chronology.

# THE STORY OF COSTIA RUDULOF

## 17-VII

## (In Latharmi again)

I didn't go anywhere else today and I truly wish I could stay here longer, to lose myself among the rosebushes and find shelter in the shade. I'm by myself. Every once in a while I see passers-by and foreign pilgrims make their way through the flowers, looking for some solitude. I hastily jot down my impressions. I'm taking it all in: this beautiful view, this amazing feeling, this magical colour of the rose petals, this wonderful fragrance so generously wafting in the wind. All this makes me relive the moments of my past life, my normal life…

Parents narrate to their children the story of 1086 *(3482 AD)*, the story of the old man, Costia Rudulof, and that spring morning when the leaves of this incredible plant opened for the first time and human eyes saw that rose petals reflecting the "pale blue sky".

The little *unge*, Lelia, knows the true story of Costia. According to her, the seventy-year-old florist was a holy man who adored children and flowers. Birds used to land on his shoulders and drink water from his hands. He lost his only child when it was only five. After that tragic incident, he dedicated his life to relieving human suffering. The mature now florist once had the vision to create the blue roses, which now decorate the streets of Latharmi, for the first time in rose-breeding history.

For several decades, says Lelia, this holy man gathered seeds and planted them, trying thousands of different combinations in order to achieve the desired result. For years and years he planted and replanted, he changed soils, he changed countries, but in vain! Eventually he despaired of trying…

Half a century had passed when, one day, two bright rosebuds attracted the attention of three passers-by in Generali. "Who does this garden belong to?" the passers-by asked some *Mindre skole* children who were playing around there. A couple of them were startled at the sight of the blooming roses. It had been drizzling all day and the sky was full of heavy black clouds. Before you knew it, a crowd of people, teachers, florists, gardeners, craftsmen, ordinary people who happened to be passing by the garden, had gathered around the rosebush and were staring at its blossoms. The children played truant, the passers-by ignored the rain; no one could stop staring at the miracle. It was as if the light that had been hiding behind the threatening clouds had found shelter in the petals of these roses.

Some people went to call Costia Rudulof. The crowd had surrounded the rosebush but none would get closer to it until old Costia arrived. They showed him the rosebuds. He didn't say a word. He stretched out his trembling right hand and, as soon as he touched them, he burst into tears. It was the dream of a lifetime for the florist. A little girl said: "Mary-Lea sent them to us for the 100$^{th}$anniversary of her death!"

After that day everyone tried planting those seeds in different combinations in their own gardens all around town, but in vain; they never bloomed. A few months later, the same seeds bloomed in a random place.

The legend says that these roses can only grow in places where great spirits have lived and where great loves have blossomed... The petals of these roses don't open anywhere else no matter how favourable the weather conditions and no matter how hard one tries; following all the rules, using the best materials or taking care of them every day are to no avail. Not even the specialists in floriculture have managed to discover the "secret" in growing these magical roses that reflect the light of day and the colour of the sky.

## STATUES OF THE FUTURE

### 18-VII

Today I left at dawn and walked around by myself all morning. I spent most of my time at the Pantheon, looking for the statues of the "moderns" this time.

I still remember several names from the ones I came across in there. In the corners of the Pantheon I discovered significant figures of the 20th century that were still unknown in my time. I'm trying to recall what each of them did that made them famous from the stories of Lain, Astrucci and Cornelius. While looking at the inscriptions on the pedestals, I was struggling to find the missing pieces from the puzzle that had been created in my mind from all the books that I had read and all the classes that I had attended in the capital of today's Loggovardia.

Each of those men and women must have made a very important contribution to the civilisation of this world in order for them to be honoured in such a way: words that hadn't been heard, melodies that hadn't sounded, artworks unappreciated by us back then, something important enough to give them a status, a spot in this temple of art and the chance to be reincarnated into immortal bronze, marble and synthetic ivory gods!

"Who knows what the human societies would be like today if it wasn't for Alex Jenefelt, a leading figure of Direct Knowledge and thinker of their 9th century *(circa 3200 AD)*, they wonder nowadays, similar to what we thought about Plato, Socrates and, above all, Christ.

## THE WISE MEN OF THE PALACE STREETS IN KONGEBORG
### Lorffe Gunnar Hiller Jr.

Around noon, Syld came to visit and sat and chatted with Stefan for hours. Apart from being a renowned painter and a person profoundly appreciated by everyone, especially by Stefan, he was also one of Stefan's oldest friends. Jaeger told him that we'd be here and he came to find us on his own. Among other things they talked about, Syld suggested that they went to the Streets of Palaces on the 22nd of this month - just the two of them - to hear Gunnar Hiller Jr., one of the two leading *Lorffes* of the year, speak in a lecture intended for a wide circle of participants. "You might even be able to meet him, talk to him," said Syld.

Stefan told him that he was most likely to have left the Valley by then, but Syld continued: "He is an extremely simple man, despite the very 'official' life that he's been forced to live lately. Deep down, he doesn't really like it that much. The most precious thing in his life is his granddaughter. Last year, he asked the board to enter the crystal square with her, holding her hand. He resented the fact that they didn't allow him, claiming that something like that was impossible. He's simple like that: benevolent and with a loving soul. Of course, you can't just go and talk to him first... He'll find something to say to you if he isn't too tired. Come on, join me, and with a little self-control everything will be fine."

Stefan thanked him but once again replied that he would probably leave in four days and added that it was good enough for him to have seen the palaces from above, which we had already done, on the first day of our arrival.

We had actually flown there, beyond Fgelen, to the Southeast Valley, and we hovered above the Streets of Palaces in Kongeborg. It is an endless state with crystal boulevards in the shades of amethyst, an entire city made up of the palaces of the *Lorffes* and surrounded by vast parks, with the famous purple roses.

Many of the great spiritual men of today have not been sent to live in Kongeborg, but that doesn't mean that the public admires and respects them less; they idolise them all the same! Their value is defined by their contribution, not by their rank. It's just that the other ones, the annual or biannual officials are there either because their predecessors had appointed them as a result of publicly acknowledging their intellectual superiority or because they had requested elections themselves. Sometimes they did this in order to let people judge whether or not they had progressed spiritually in the meantime or because their predecessors were simply tired and wanted to retire, live more privately or even work, especially when their term of office in the Palaces had been extended to more than two years.

If the term of office in the Palaces (Paladser as they call them now) and in Kongeborg also gives some sort of power to the holder of the title and what kind of power that is, I never truly understood. What it certainly gives to the person is great, but symbolic, honours and it is also considered a proof of excellence and prudence. Even though the *Lorffes* and *Ilectors* had found everything tidy and organised from the old times of the *Eldrere*, from the times of the governance of the great technicians, they never wanted to "break with protocol". The *Nojere* for some reason wanted to maintain the old hierarchy and "titles" and to express through them the new evaluative beliefs, beliefs that were in complete disagreement with those of the "old age", the *gammel epoke*, that is, the times of technocracy.

In many cases, these temporary officials haven't really renounced the secular joys and material goods even though they know how to hide it. Most of them however, and especially the top leaders, want nothing to do with all that; the spirit is all that matters for them.

Several months ago, Aria and Syld had talked to Stefan and Hilda about Knut Niversun and how he felt the day he was given the blue and white ribbons… His concern was that someone better had been wronged! "If that's true," he said, "I have a way to fix it next year." And when someone asked him what he would do if it turned out that he was the one that had been wronged, he answered that he didn't care one iota and that someone would right that wrong sooner or later. "Do you think that when children are loved either they need to be declared *Lorffes* to enjoy this love?" he asked them. And I was told that he then made a hint about the *Roisvirch*, saying that "everything wonderful that exists or happens around us we should make part of our lives: the arrival of spring, the distant sounds of children's songs, the love for people, nature and the forest…"

The way their wise men think is very… wise! Even though they are considered superior to all spiritual men of all times, they come to add to what has been told in the past, not to refute it… Never has a Volky tried to discredit Christ. Never has a Valmandel *(860 or 3256 AD)* or a Ruthemir *(1014 or 3410 AD)* ever tried to invalidate a Bach or a Beethoven. They were in favour of enrichment, not demolition.

Something similar is now happening with Gunnar Hiller, says Syld: the highest title that he could ever ask for was that of a grandfather. The greatest joy that he has ever experienced was when his little angel called him "Grandpa" for the first time.

A while back he had been asked if he aspired to see his son taking his place one day. As a matter of fact, his son had shown a very significant inclination towards philosophy and has also written an excellent three-volume work on ethics.

"I cannot know what the future holds," replied Hiller, "but I will tell you one thing: I will strongly hesitate to urge him to expose himself despite his innate talent and prolific vocation…Chances are that for now my successor will be a complete stranger, son of another complete stranger, one of the thousand students of the Aidersen Institute. I do not dream to see my son in my position, and this is not the point. I only dream that my son too will bow down to that future, unknown for now genius, whoever that is…"

## FAMOUS WOMEN OF THE FUTURE

About the famous women of that time, after the 20th century that is, I didn't know much. I can now only recall three names: Erika, Anna-Flaisia and Ariana. I asked Stefan up to whom it is to decide who will be turned into a sculpture and who not, and he vaguely replied that nothing happens without the knowledge and consent of the *Ilectors*. What I noticed was that even sinful people or non-existent, fantastic, characters from poetry, literature or music had been turned into sculptures. I have the opinion that the selection wasn't that careful... Stefan spoke of "the element of the wonderful" in these big hearts, an element that perhaps hadn't been appreciated in all its glory in earlier times. That's why you now see sculptures of fishermen and hawkers, depressed suicides and even women who, in our time, would have been characterised as being of loose morals."This is because at that time no one was aware of the importance of all those people and all the different and sometimes extreme expressions of their inner self; nobody knew that about the common Source of all these expressions," Stefan explained to me.

I can hardly remember any of their artists' names, but you can see clearly in all artworks how genius blended with inspiration and gave birth to an exquisite expression of ideal beauty and pure, noble love.

Stefan also talked to me about De Lamartine's *Graciela*, whose statue we came across at some point, among the rosebushes of Umliani.

"It was a glimpse of the *Samith* that made her heart flutter. She couldn't endure it. That was enough to cause her death… Back then nobody could have thought that at some point in the future her statue would be erected in the largest intellectual centre of the world. Centuries had to pass in order for people to grasp the true meaning of her painful story. Not even Graciela herself realised what killed her. But such kinds of deaths are a beginning, not an end."

Indeed he believes that such deaths have something in common with the deaths of Christ, Socrates and Giordano Bruno. "And I don't want to sound disrespectful or blasphemous," he felt the need to explain himself. He doesn't ignore the enormous differences between the cases. The "thing in common" for Stefan is the fact that in the past such deaths were considered the end, "the terminus", either via suicide, execution, the stake, hemlock, crucifixion or torture, but now the judgment of history has demonstrated the opposite: those ancient "losses" marked new beginnings, not endings. They were a start of something more real, something divine; they were a passage to eternity and immortality.

In front of the statue of another prematurely deceased young and beautiful lady, Vana-Aregia by Thoralsen, Stefan recited the verses that were engraved on the pedestal. He remained motionless in the same spot for several minutes looking at this marble masterpiece, immersed in his thoughts.

"Look at the expression on her face," he said "there's no need to read about the Valley in history books and guidebooks: everything you need to know is here, as long as your eyes and soul are open."

He then explained to me that this particular artwork is one of the rare masterpieces of their 9$^{th}$ century, all of which they're very proud of. Immediately after he added, "Here in the Valley of the Roses, for the first time in history, all hopes and dreams and ideals now have a face, a purpose. They have come true! They have substance! In fact, they are now more real and tangible than our own lives."

I couldn't help revealing my thoughts to Stefan: I told him that perhaps they should be more careful, that perhaps they have mistaken the mere evolutionary progress of the human species for something sublime and transcendent. He found my mentality one of an unenlightened man of the old age with little faith in the wonders of life, constantly suspicious and deprived of emotion. Without scorning me, said, "A true *Homo Occidentalis Novus* would never have articulated such a concern because he knows that all concepts and instincts that exist beyond reason, like intuition, faith, poetry, philosophy or motherhood, have a common source: the *Samith.*"

We walked around those densely "populated" residences of the statues tirelessly until the late evening hours, and, unintentionally, Stefan conveyed his unprecedented excitement to me. Those enormous figures looked as if they come to life when no one is around to see them. We passed by the statue of Mother Renard, Teresa Beren and the wonderful plastic composition of Brigitte Enemark, works by Erksen, Greneval and Ileana Virmpach respectively.

The Brigitte Enemark by Virmpach bore no expression of affection or tenderness on her face, as one would expect. She has depicted her as a hardy, robust working-class woman, powerful, decisive and determined. In her hands she's holding a little boy, who looks either sick or exhausted from all the endless walking. One by one the kilometres that she has walked in exhaustion for the sake of her child are engraved on her forehead. The signs of anxiety and insomnia are obvious around her eyes. But you can see the maternal instinct prevailing; she's always willing to sacrifice herself for her child, after she has surpassed all limits of human endurance.

"So no, the Great Reality isn't based on the ancient instincts that have evolved through time," said Stefan. "It is not a human invention. It is that divine element that lies beyond the realm of reason, the element that philosophy, art and undogmatic religion have been stressing for thousands of years now. But we were too blind to see it. We should have seen it before the *Nibelvirch*. Even the people of your time could have and should have become aware its existence."

On our way back I asked him if the Christian faith and the Volkic direct knowledge were almost the same thing, because the similarities were many.

"Deep down they both preach and aim for the same thing, with the exception that the former is a faith in religion while the latter is a faith in knowledge," Stefan explained, "and religion became extremely dogmatic and anthropomorphic, striving to solve all problems and answer all questions with human means and in human terms, thus disproving its divine nature. Religion lost touch with reality and strayed from its original purpose. It gave the right to any random materialist to claim that scientific research was disproving religion and God as a concept more and more every day. The religious feeling is now on the rise because it was rid itself of its dogmatism, of the Holy Synods and the Holy Scriptures. The current scientific understanding of the world is far from materialistic."

## THE TEMPLE OF THE UNSUNG MARTYRS AND THE GREAT PILGRIMAGE

### 20-VII

Yesterday we dedicated the entire day to visiting the Temple of the Unsung Martyrs. All four of us went there twice; the first time early in the morning and then again at night. It is located on the western side of the Valley, eighty kilometres away from our *gestel*. We arrived there in four minutes of course, thanks to their air transport.

I had read a great deal about yesterday's holy day and seen some bits of this grand procession this autumn on the *Swage*. This procession takes place here and around the Valley in the vast gardens of Terringa once a year with the participation of millions of pilgrims from around the world. Experiencing all this was one of my greatest desires. To walk in the gold-paved square, to see Kersteen's masterpiece and the evening procession from above, through the huge openings of the towering roof, had always been a dream of mine that finally came true! If I hadn't seen it with my own eyes my imagination could have never conceived such a spectacle! Over the last six hundred years, the *Lorffes* had achieved a degree of organisation, grandeur and wealth, both material and spiritual, which was unimaginable in ancient times.

Once again, the girls were sitting by themselves in the dining room in silence, watching pictures and videos from last night. Stefan approached me with the hint of a smile. "So what did you think of last night?" he asked me, now smiling broadly. I didn't know what to tell him and so I avoided his gaze. Had everything I saw last night been for real? I had heard the words "rivers of gold and light" being used to describe last night's event, but I had never dreamt of such grandeur; millions of people, countless lit white candles, such incredible organisation, no fuss, no noise, not even the slightest whispering. And now I had Stefan, who was of course anticipating my surprise, standing in front of me with this grin of satisfaction, asking me what I thought of last night! What do you answer to that?

## SYMPTOMS OF AGORAPHOBIA AT THE GOLD TEMPLE

This morning, at the beginning of the pilgrimage, I had clear symptoms of agoraphobia again, like I had in Blomsterfor last month, in the Toeplitz 1812 square. It happened when Silvia suggested we crossed the Golden Square. Little Lasia, the second *unge* that was sent by Jaeger, hadn't left our side all these days. Many times she'd sit and tell me stories about the Valley in great detail when Stefan didn't have time to do so. We wanted to go see Davis' statue *Christ with the Children*, which was on the opposite side and, truth be told, I would have preferred to get there by going *around* the square instead of through it, but Stefan stood by me and held my arm to help me manage.

The golden, circular square with the elaborate decorations on the floor was about half the size of our St. Peter's Basilica in Rome. It did not, however, have any chapels or pulpits enhancing it. The huge curvilinear pilasters of chiselled marble, twelve in total, supported the thick, carved stone roof, built in the shape of a coin. On the interior, the pilasters were decorated with masterful murals by their famous 9$^{th}$century painter, Fabius Sigra. Its construction was not metal-based. It was built in such a way that even if you removed all the metal bits, the twelve towering pilasters wouldn't be affected at all; they´d still stand proud and tall.

"Let's go to *Christ* on the opposite side of the square… Let's go to *Christ*…" I kept whispering to Stefan, begging him almost while desperately clutching his arm. "That's where we're going," he replied gently, trying to calm me down, "but we're taking a shortcut, much to your disappointment…"

My friend looked somewhat embarrassed as if he had been entrusted with the care of a defenceless child deprived of judgment. "There is no sin in the use of gold, "he says. "Why would you consider it a sin? It serves no purpose nowadays." I felt guilty for my unreasonable attitude. Several days ago he told me that "temple" here also means a commemoration place. "You need to learn how to distinguish the places of religious faith and worship from the mere memorials. Gold is not even considered wealth nowadays. Our *glothners* and our institutions are our gold. This is the true wealth of today. The gold here in the temple is the entire amount of the world's remaining gold, which now has no benefit for the economy, but which during the "dark years" was the main source of human suffering. The gold in this temple is nothing but a symbol of peace."

I asked him if it was true that the forefathers of today's ruling class were industrial workers. He confirmed it saying that the ancestors of today's *Ilectors* and *Lorffes* worked in the *glothners* of the time, just like *they* all do.

I look around me and I see that, thanks to Kersteen, numerous real tragedies of the "prehistoric" for them years have survived and are commemorated here. As in the work of Thoralsen, Vana-Aregia, here the skilful artists have managed to breathe real life into synthetic ivory.

Soon we had to leave; it was other people's turn. I barely had time to see a few parts of Fabius Sigra's frescoes. I happened to see quite a few scenes from of our own Hans Christian Andersen's "The Little Match Girl", perfectly depicted on the curved interior walls. The text was written below in small, gold letters. It was the original text in the old Scandinavian language!

## THE OATH AND THE GRAND PROCESSION

We stayed for two-three hours in the *gestel* in the afternoon to rest. When we flew back to the temple in the evening, the crowds throughout the Rosernes Dal were unprecedented; people filled the vast squares, the wide streets and the numerous parks.

Thanks to Jaeger's help, Stefan and I managed to climb up to the peripheral outdoors halls of the domes, where one has an unobstructed view in all directions. The plan was to stay there for about half an hour, while our friends would view the entry of the *Lorffes* underneath and would save us seats in the tiers of the large golden square.

When the last rays of the sun had faded, the oath began to sound. People were gathered there and in three more locations around the Valley. A great number of *Ilectors* along with the highest representatives of the Ministry addressed millions of young people who would soon begin their two-year service. They addressed *them* directly, but also the rest of the people indirectly. Thanks to their incredible sound systems, each phrase of the oath resonated across the Valley, but without hurting your ears. The oath was recited in the sui generis old language of the *Ilectors*. Nevertheless, I did understand a few words: "For the homeland!", "for the soul of the nation", "for the pride of our ancestors", "for our institutions", "for the rise of the human spirit", "for our culture". And the young men and women repeated: "I swear!"

My lifeless pen is powerless to describe the power and energy of the moment. Following the oath, the children began to sing:

Beloved children from the distant past,
From those old times,
Join us today in the spring meadows
Let us free you from untold pains...

Deeply satisfied and with some kind of a secret pride, I grasped Stefan's hand, striving to hide my emotion from others around me. They also sang two of Johannes Brahms's compositions; "Lullaby" and "Sisters"! I secretly wiped a tear away before it rolled down my cheek. Then we all descended down to the ground floor hall-square, leaving in the middle of that magnificent spectacle.

We found our friends easily. They were watching some friends of theirs perform, female poets from Blomsterfor, the painter Nichefelt, Syld and their old friend Aria, all of whom were taking part in the ritual.

The magnificence of the entire ritual exceeded all expectations. It was a fabulous spectacle and experience overall, not only for the luxury of the costumes and the unimaginable number of precious and semiprecious stones that adorned every object and every corner, but more for the spiritual tradition of centuries that was honoured by all these venerable people in the famous establishments of their universal now capital.

All the great minds of today were present in the temple for the anniversary. Most of them had come from Norfor, Blomsterfor and other European regions, especially from northern Europe. And there, in the sea of gems that adorned the uniforms of the *Tilteys*, the *Lorffes* and the *Ilectors*, there, close to the complex of chapels that constitute the Temple of the Unsung Martyrs, Stefan showed me two elders, the only ones without a diadem on their white-haired heads.

"Look," said Stefan, pointing in their direction, "It's Nicolas Lajevski and beside him Gunnar Hiller Jr.!"

I caught myself staring at them; their shadows were the only ones that didn't sparkle in that golden congregation. So it is them then! They're the ones that Stefan talked so much about this autumn. They are the ones whose life and work he admires so much and constantly exalts to others**AND**! These are the poet and the philosopher that have been holding the top positions in the modern spirit for eighteen months now. They are considered to be the greatest among the living. Little Lasia revived me from my momentary trance, asking me when the fluttering was going to be heard and pointing at the interior domes that weren't lit tonight.

"Once a year," she said, "on the evening of this anniversary, billions of little souls come to the temple to present themselves at the memorial." The pure, the chosen ones, the ones "whose souls have sensitive antennas", might be lucky enough to even hear them fluttering when they enter the temple.

I asked Stefan - silently so that no one heard me - who had told such fairy tales to this child and why they were in the habit of making children believe things that aren't true. He casually, almost indifferently, replied that she must have read it in some children's book. And the truth is that I wasn't that surprised. Besides, it's not the first time that I witness this. It's not the first time that I feel like these people do not particularly care for reason and critical thinking and that they deliberately cross the line between reality and dream world...

Meanwhile, the first hundreds of the four-part procession, which arrives at the city-centre in the shape of a cross from the four different points of the horizon, had begun to arrive at the four gates, one in each of the four sides of the temple. But as I had been informed, all that gigantic torch lit procession would remain outside of the temple. The processional banners and the flower floats would only enter from the west gate. No one uttered a word. They had all turned their attention to the procession, looking with respect and pride as the girls, who were to begin their service in the coming days, silently laid all the ancient emblems of the trade unions, that date back to their 2nd century, under Kersteen's plastic composition in the Golden Square. Everyone was looking at them, from the most prestigious *Lorffe* to the last *Civis*.

The songs could still be heard outside the temple. And then, six by six the flower floats started to enter the temple. The flowers that were meant to cover the emblems had been symbolically sent from all around the world.

"For the children that died every day," said the girls while depositing the flowers. "For the people who were dying of hunger while others threw away their food", "for the homeless who breathed their dying breaths on icy streets", "for the sick who died because they had no money to pay for their treatment", "for the crippled children, the children that were burned alive, buried in groups, died for no reason" were some of the things people exclaimed when paying their tribute.

I felt a shiver run down my spine… We never paid such a tribute to the victims of our lifestyle...

The depositing of flowers - the old flowers, our flowers, not their modern floricultural achievements: hydrangeas, violets, begonias, mimosas and carnations - continued for hours in the same solemn atmosphere. The ceremony would end with prayers. The first break was after the twelfth group of six with flower canisters had entered. We benefited from the opportunity and left because Stefan also wanted to visit the area of New Karelia before it got too late and we had to go back to the *gestel*.

On the way back, I thought about the wall paintings of Fabius Sigra, these 9$^{th}$century masterpieces. I remembered the golden letters on the wall, narrating the story of "The Little Match Girl".

I wonder, all you great artists, you "prophets" of the past with the shining faces, do you know where all your inspiration was coming from? Or did you think your spirit was the source of everything? Did you believe you were making a better world from nothing? Yes, that's what you thought; that's what we all thought at the time.

# THE SNOW WHITE SANCTUARY

## 22-VII

The snow-white sanctuary with the walls made of synthetic ivory that I was told to visit was not far away from the Pantheon after all. I came here today believing that I would see the navel of the Valley, but there are neither temples nor statues here. They have maintained the place almost exactly as it was; they've respected the charm of the past. With the exception of the luminous clarity of the rose petals, fruit of the newly planted rosebushes that surround the area, the lined up banners of Rosernes Dal and the thousands of candles burning on the golden candlesticks, almost everything else has been kept exactly as it was on the day of the big event, in its old simplicity. It's like time has stopped in the year 986, giving you the chance to feel the atmosphere of that era.

There are only a few pilgrims here at this time of day and the peace and quiet that prevails is priceless. One breathes an air of ecstasy, prayer and deep faith here, an air that purifies all surrounding things.

I can't help thinking about the past, about Volky, or the way I have imagined Volky from the stories of Astrucci and Lain, and I've reached the conclusion that the greater the temporal and historical distance that separates us from this huge figure, the more we appreciate it and the more his preaching, the preaching of the "greatest hero in the history of human spirit", illuminates all sides of the mental and spiritual lifestyle of our own humanity.

It's been now over five hundred years that man has been following the way that *he* paved. Thousands of years after the creation of the concept of the exquisite panhuman love of Christ that shaped humanity, and the treasures of emotion that followed it, thanks to Volky, there came that much sought-after moment when the borders of the "existent world" finally opened to such an extent that even the most spiritual and open-minded men of the 20th century wouldn't have dared to imagine.

That spiritual "revolution" was something incomparably greater than what religious faith had ever dared to preach even when it had hit its highest peak. It showed people the truly important things in life; it vindicated ideas and values that had unjustly been the subject of mockery for far too long and clarified the important role they played in the Great Reality even if we did not have an inkling about it.

**24-VII**

**(Back in our villas late at night)**

We flew back here directly from the Valley. My eyes couldn't get enough of the marvellous views of the countryside. From up above I could discern some of my favourite places from last year's travels. They brought back so many memories from our meetings with the group and from the first days of my love for Silvia… Just like I used to every night ten months ago, I sat and gazed again tonight at the beauty of the distant countryside. It felt like yesterday…

**25-VII**

This is the house where Silvia grew up and the thought of her running around this house as a child moves me deeply. I feel like this environment somehow heightened my responsibility to make her happy - a feeling that has pervaded me over the past few months.

**26-VII**

**(At dusk)**

The form that our love has taken is now completely different. That first thrill and enthusiasm has now given its place to feelings of immense affection. When I'm with her, I completely forget about myself. Never in my life have I cared so much about someone else; a dear friend, a neighbour or a beloved person. I think that whatever I do in life, I could never stop being her faithful and devoted friend; I could never stop being "hers", ready for any sacrifice if needed. I profoundly experience the pain and concerns of her parents, their anguish and their yearning for her happiness. I feel as if I have a heavy responsibility towards them, as if I had been chosen among thousands of others to make her happy…

## BACK TO HIS HOMELAND

### 30-VII

Home, sweet home! I flew back to you again! This time, my being here brings me neither sorrow nor regrets, like the last time I was here with Stefan, nine months ago. Today I arrived here all by myself, flying above the old familiar landscapes of my childhood.

Who says that I have nothing of my own in this new life? I have one of the richest galleries of the world, right here, before me! These sights, these incredible images, are more mine that anyone else's! For the rest of the world they're just harmonious lines and colours.

Oh my dearest homeland… Tomorrow when I'm back, will be a double joy for me! I'll ask Silvia to come with me and share my great joy, a world of vivid life memories and familiar places.

They're right when they say that there's no place like home! I've often virtually travelled back to the places where I grew up, I've often let my memories consume me and take me back in time for a while, but there's no feeling in the world like when you're actually there, no matter how long it took you to return and no matter what you had left behind, even if what you had left behind is not there anymore… I feel so blessed, so privileged to have the chance to be here again and I thank Lord for that, for I've never done anything to deserve such incredible fate, such luck and such divine gifts. I feel as if I belonged in the truly enlightened elite, as if I were one of the chosen ones of the Rosernes Dal.

## CONFESSING EVERYTHING TO SILVIA

### 1-VIII

I allowed my enthusiasm and spontaneity to take over, and I really shouldn't have. It wasn't her fault; it was my duty to restrain myself for her sake. I had managed to hide my old life and my true identity from everyone, including Silvia, I had managed to keep it buried deep down inside me for a whole year, and in ten minutes I ruined it all! My heart was pounding with joy, I lost control and I revealed everything all at once… She was startled and at once, all the doubts and hesitations that she's had until now turned into certainty… She had conquered all her fears and suspicions, she was always on my side, she had faith in me, she trusted me. Her faith and trust was what had built such an unshakeable moral foundation for our love, and that unshakeable foundation I managed to demolish in the blink of an eye, just by telling her the truth... The tone of sincerity in my voice left no room for doubt. Her suspicions were confirmed…

I know that at some point it'll pass; she will forget everything and we will go back to normal. People can become used to anything. I speak from experience. I'm hers and she is mine and that will never change! In fact, I'll speak to her tomorrow. Over time, she'll make her peace with the fact that she was destined to connect with a man that is a foreigner in her world, her era and her circle, with a man from a bygone era.

When I told her about my flight over the Swiss Alps, she was the one to suggest that we went there together the next morning, just the two of us…

We departed this morning, with crystal clear blue sky, two hours after the sunrise. She was incredibly fun and vibrant throughout the journey, as if our relationship had just started. She was playful like a child! When I asked her if she was feeling dizzy she replied, "On the contrary, I have never felt dizzy in my life; I don't even know what it feels like!" But I pretended not to hear that and told her not to look down, to look at me instead. I wanted to be helpful somehow, to take care of her. She playfully replied that if she looked at me she'd experience a different kind of "vertige". I noticed how she used the French word for it, just to add to the playful nature of her words. She kept joking until we arrived. She was in very high spirits.

Upon arrival, I felt so proud seeing how thrilled she was with the amazing views, with the wonders of nature that my homeland had been blessed with. I talked to her about everyday things, our friends, our lives, trying to hide how overwhelmed with emotion I was from seeing again the scenery of my old life.

We walked for quite a while until we decided to stop on a hill and lie among the wildflowers to rest. It must have been around noon.

"You're right", said Silvia after a long pause of silence, "this place is magical; I feel reborn!"

We talked about a thousand things and she was very cheerful. In fact, at times I caught her humming while she was tying a dark green silk thread around the windflowers that we had just gathered together. She was making a little wreath. Then, I remember asking her which part of all that we had seen and experienced over the past few months she had enjoyed the most. The words she uttered next made me even happier than I was: "It's beautiful everywhere, as long as we're together." Then she talked to me about her love of nature. "I think it runs in my veins," she said with a smile. And then I was reminded of the meaning of her name: it means "of the forest".

I sat and enjoyed the light falling on her forehead, the arc of her eyebrows and the golden roots of her hair and I felt immense happiness to have my beloved of my youth at my side after so long. But at the same time I felt the grave significance of this boundlessness was not limited to the narrow confines of my poor heart, the confines of my own individual existence. It went beyond me and became a sacred promise for any person wanting to be worthy of something like this - something so unique that it defies the limits of time and space and reason itself. For it truly was a divine gift to see her, a relieving salvation from the ravages of time. It gives hope for an ultimate triumph of life over the fate of death.

And to think that without this awareness of the strangeness of my fate, without the vivid memories of my past life and the deep appreciation I feel for my new life, this relationship, along with all the other situations that I have experienced here and all the incidents that I have witnessed-might have seemed merely normal, even mundane I dare say, to me too, just like it seems to Silvia: the simple joining of two souls that share a close bond.

The next time she spoke, she said something that rendered me incapable of holding back any longer and that's when I revealed everything.

She stretched out her hand, handing out to me the wreath she had finished making and asked me, "Will you put this wreath on my head? I think it's time we headed home. Enough for today… Put it on my head and let's go… I want to be wearing it on the way back…" To her, these words might have been as simple and unimportant as a drop of water in the ocean, but she had no idea what effect they had on me!

Lost as I was amidst an unprecedented thrill and surprise, I took a look around me and couldn't believe it! I had only just realised that all this time we had been sitting at the very spot, on the very hill where thousands of years ago Anna had talked to me about a wreath of windflowers. I remembered exactly what she told me that day: "Enough for today... Let's go back... I have to be home early. Next time we're here I'll make a wreath of windflowers. Will you place it on my head?" She then promised, she swore to me that we'd come back; and yet that was one of the last times I ever saw her alive…

And then I felt a spark inside me ignite and explode!

"What happened? What did I do to you? What did I say?" she asked me worried, seeing a flood of tears streaming down my pale face. I held her clasped in my own, squeezed it tightly and started kissing it all over.

"Oh my dear Anna, my lovely Anna! How many years you take me back with these words! So it wasn't a lie then! We've kept our promise; we came back!"

I realised what I had just said just by looking at Silvia's reaction; her facial expression was simply indescribable! She grew pale and unintentionally - I want to believe - she tried to draw away from me. She looked as if she was frightened of me! Initially I didn't do or say anything because I was frozen to the spot; her spontaneous reaction had left me speechless. After I overcame the shock, in vain I tried to convince her to look around her. In vain I talked to her about her mother, her brother, her friend Amalia and the environment of her home, narrating as many facts and details as I could remember from her previous life, in order to convince her…

"Don't you remember the orchard? The travel book? The tall poplar tree under which we sat for hours? Don't you remember when we climbed the Two Peaks? Nothing?"

I tried everything; I called upon all my memories and all my powers to make her believe me… I mostly talked to her about the last time we met, when I sat at her bedside, in her room, a few days before she died… I urged her to make the greatest effort possible to bring back those memories, memories that I was sure still existed somewhere deep inside her; but nothing… She couldn't remember anything. She didn't speak at all. She only looked at me; it was a worried and searching look that she gave me. The only words she managed to utter were, "I'm cold." And then we left…

Employing all the faith I had in her, I spoke to her as logically as I could and tried to show her that there was no reason to be so startled at hearing this true story. I explained to her that many people were aware of my situation and had thoroughly studied my case, including Stefan, Jaeger, the physician, Professor Molsen, people from Norfor, like Valdemar Esklud, Miss Koiral and many others, and even more people from the Rosernes Dal. There was no reason therefore to be scared. I even encouraged her to go find Jaeger and ask him herself whether or not I was out of my mind…

"It was true then… I knew it! I had felt it… But then again I tried so hard not to believe it…" she whispered.

Little by little we both calmed down. She came close to me, stroked my hair and wiped my eyes, just like a mother does to her child when it's upset. But then she drew away again and sat alone, lost in her thoughts. It had been a while since someone had spoken when she whispered, "It doesn't seem to be God's desire for people to remember." And she wept. Overwhelmed with emotion, we both hushed. I got up first and helped her to her feet.

"Let's go," I said. As we departed she told me she believed me and then she reassured me of her love for me.

"Only don't expect from me to feel like I have come from another era, like you," she said, "I completely believe and respect everything you've told me about your life, but I am not like you. I am a woman of my era; I'm just like everyone else."

We barely spoke throughout the entire trip back. The cheerfulness of the morning had been completely brushed aside by the incident with the wreath of the windflowers. Silvia was wearing the wreath on her head, which I had placed there, and was wrapped up in the usual blanket made of synthetic fur to protect herself from the wind. She no longer seemed anxious or worried; just moved… Every now and then she'd say a word or two. And I noticed that she never said the name "Andreas" again, since that moment up on the hill…

## BACK TO THE PAST

### 1-VIII Again

### (Late at night)

A little while ago I sat Stefan down and told him the whole truth about my old love story with Anna, and then I told him about today's incident with the windflowers. His reaction was nothing like Silvia's: no surprise, no horror, no terrified looks. He believed me straight away, he didn't doubt me for a second! Excited by the spiritual power of the great love that had defeated time, he gripped my hands and smiled at me. He had found nothing out of the ordinary in my story, nothing that was breaking the limits or the laws of life.

"I've told you before," said Stefan, "the human perception of time and space is not infallible. It could be that what our minds conceive as yesterday, today and tomorrow within the Great Reality and believe them to be distinct from each other is nothing but an eternal present that is not aligned with the standard, human conception of time."

So that's why you made me go through all this pain, my dear God? Maybe Stefan is right; this transcendental love between two people, a love that has been through thick and thin, has now almost been sanctified. Destiny had reserved a special place in this world for such a love, even after thousands of years. And this marvellous work of destiny goes beyond the narrow confines of my own personal case. This wonder deserves a place among the highest and holiest achievements of the human soul! This is the epitome of true love!

It is truly worthwhile for one to come into this world as a human being and live this life. If things are so different from how our eyes and reason conceive them, if such a divine fate can be reserved for a human being in this world, it's really something worth living for. We don't know exactly what life is all about or how it unfolds or what it contains, but those worthy of finding out are in for a wonderful surprise! It is a reality impossible for our mind to understand and our words to express.

What is this feeling now? My eyelids are getting heavier and heavier! Am I feeling sleepy? Yes, yes, it is sleep that burdens my eyelids! This is the first time this happens to me in this new life of mine! Oh it's such a sweet feeling! Does this mean that I'll be able to rest at nights from now on? Oh I've missed this… I'm starting to feel so relaxed…

**THE END**

*(At that moment, Andreas Northam falls asleep for the first time in a whole year. As soon as Northam sleeps, Paul Amadeus Dienach's consciousness returns to his natural body back in Switzerland in the year 1922 and he recovers from his coma.)*

*Rector Georgios Papachatzis on 3 October 1964 at Panteion University doctorate degree awarding ceremony of Jean Lesage.*

*©Photographic Archive of the Pandemos Digital Library-Panteion University*

# TRANSLATOR'S PREFACE TO THE FIRST EDITION (1972) OF THE *VALLEY OF THE ROSES*

*(Pre-introductory and Critical Note, a kind of Preface, to Dienach's published remnants. It was written six years prior to the first edition of The Valley of the Roses [1972]).*

Dienach's "Chronicles From The Future" *("Pages from a Diary" was the original title of the first edition)* offers the essence of the cultural development of Western Europeans in the distant future. More specifically, here, right after Dienach's "First" and "Second Diary", the continuation of Western civilization's history, from the 21st century onwards, is illustrated over a long period of time. Outwardly, however, these prophetic manuscripts are very simple in form: they appear to be passages of travel fiction, a time travel to the countries of our continent, to those distant future times, a panoramic view of social and spiritual life, within that distant future cultural development - pieces of a vivid and real life as seen and known by the author, who hereby narrates it as a traveller-narrator. It was, he says, his own fate that his life be bound, as he writes, with one of the rarest meta-psychic and spiritualistic phenomena. It was thanks to this that he managed to experience all he describes.

Paul Amadeus Dienach left neither a name nor, most probably, the slightest publication in his homeland. In autumn 1922, he arrived from central Europe in Athens and later on, in winter, started tutoring students of limited financial means in foreign languages, namely French and German for a small fee. Having spent, as he said, his childhood in one of the various districts of Zurich, where his parents had settled after his birth, he went on to spend his adolescence in a village, close to this big cultural hub of Germanic-speaking countries. Afterwards, he pursued humanistic studies, with a particular flair for history of civilisation and classical studies.

In 1906, he briefly worked as a teacher, in a private school most likely, perhaps in one of the towns surrounding Zurich. Being of weak and delicate constitution - he had the appearance of an intellectual - he travelled, though rarely and as much as he could afford, to the West and South. Of his travels to Paris and Rome, I gather he has written about it somewhere in his manuscripts.

I remember his deep affection for his mother, who appears to have been a saintly woman from all that he told me and, above all, a wonderful mother. When I met him, she had already passed away.

As he was leaving the manuscripts in my care, he had called me "his most appreciated one in his small circle of students" and I remember him using the phrase "my young friend". It is nothing but obvious that feelings of loneliness and desolation flooded his soul at the time of writing the note. None of his family was left. At some other point, he had told me: "He who has not experienced isolation cannot know its meaning."

He passed away, I gather, in the Athenian suburb of Maroussi or perhaps on his way back to his homeland, through Italy, in some town of our neighbouring peninsula, most probably during the first six months of 1924, after suffering an attack of tuberculosis, which manifested in Athens and did not last but a few months. Over the course of my twelve recent summer trips to Zurich, from 1952 to 1966, I did not manage to locate his relatives or other traces of the Dienach family. Maybe, however, he has distant relatives of the new generation on the outskirts. It could be, nevertheless, that the young anti-Hitler reserve officer of the German Occupation army was right - I shall write about his version further down, at the end of this pre-introductory note - that my teacher "suffered from the complex of his people's guilt" of the imperial era. In this last case, one would search in vain outside the German ethnicity to find him based on a "borrowed" surname.

Had Paul Amadeus happened to be born in the Indies, he would have expressed himself without a second thought. He would have talked, even as early as 1922, about his two lives, the self-cognisance of the ego, the reminiscences of incomparable richness, his *other* existence, which had developed in such different periods. However, Dienach was born a European, a Central European in fact, the offspring of a highly educated German-speaking Swiss man and his Salzburgian exceptional mother. He was always careful with his words, cautious not to let slip things that went beyond rationality and scientific, cognitive thinking. He strongly believed, all the same, in a spiritual element of an undefined nature in man, which eludes the law of biological decay, surpassing the barriers of time and space. He believed this was true not only for our own biological species, at least in the finest cases of individuals, but also in a variety of superior species of beings endowed with thought, language and feelings, with emotional wealth he meant to say, on millions of planets, unknown to us for the time being. It is thanks to this, Dienach says, that cultivated man, individuality enriched with values of inner culture, rises above confined and cruel biological fate. It is thanks to this element, which could be, as he said, much different from the one-sided view of the soul-unit of religious faith or other established spiritual preachings and convictions, that free spirit continues to exist unfettered by the law of biological evolution and decay. Regarding the course of the individual's spiritual being, the time-space continuum is not an obstacle - he *saw* it and he *lived* it - as he writes in his manuscripts.

"It was only in the field of celestial mechanics and generally of research of the natural universe that we humans managed to become Copernicans," I remember him telling me when he talked to me about the course of the human spirit through the centuries. "Our entire philosophy and our worldview continue to be Ptolemaic: geocentric and anthropocentric."

He would often speak of the triple blinders of time, space and biological species - the finite, that is, cognitive sensors, inherent spiritual abilities and knowledge potential of the human-receiver - which prevent us from acquiring a superior perception and view of the world and life. At the same time, he believed - something quite astounding given the times - in the possibility of a future expansion of the limits of the worlds of existing things, the worlds of Being.

He often talked about a majority of spiritual civilisations and a parallel upward course of myriads of biological species within the cosmos, of myriads of species of rational beings existing on a large number of golden celestial spheres, about a progress and evolution of a moral rather than a technological nature. He would not concede that our planet is the only inhabited celestial body or that our biological species is *unique,* the crown of Creation. He disapproved of excessive technological development and the forms of techno-economic societies, considering them of secondary importance, and believed that what mainly served the great purposes of Creation was the elevation by means of noble pain, abnegation, kindness, love, self-sacrifice - inner cultivation in general.

However, he had never talked about the rare fate of his private life - so much rarer in our European, geographical and intellectual sphere. Neither had he told me much about the content of his manuscripts, which he had decided to send me upon leaving. He had given me quite a few pages and I had read them while he was still alive, causing me to experience an indescribable thirst to read these manuscripts. Nonetheless, when he spoke, the many wonderful things he talked about seemed to be his deepest beliefs, but not experiences he had truly lived.

Up to the day I lost track of him, I recall that he did not strike me as a type of mystic, endowed with elements of the exceptional or the supernatural. He appeared to be a very cautious, careful and reserved Western European, a restless philosophical spirit of the 20th century, like the "next century's Faust", but without the latter's versatile education; Dienach seemed to be a simple educator, who had, however, burning questions, with that longing of the heart that honours the human race. He possessed an irresistible longing in an age of materialism and pragmatism, which the final decades of the 19th century had passed down to the first decades of the 20th. It was perhaps in this intellectual clime, where he was born, raised and became a man, in this exact context of intellect and scientific perception of the world where his education lay. It was perhaps precisely to this that he owed his great hesitance and cautiousness about even hinting at anything that lay beyond what was established, what was accepted on the basis of rationality or facts of the positive sciences.

Ever since the day the handwritten translation of his manuscripts resurfaced, his distant remembrance returned unintentionally and insistently occupied my thoughts. This time, I took the final decision to have them published as soon as I saw them emerge from the old drawer one morning while looking for something else. Among them, I also discovered with some excitement some favourite yellowed letters and a notebook with notes from when I used to study along with other students whom I remember fondly.

A strange thing happened to me with Dienach: in those days of old, he was for me just an acquaintance of a few months. My carefree spirit at the time and, besides, the big age difference would not allow for a bond to develop between us worthy of being called friendship. But the more years went by, the more I realised that, when leaving for Italy in 1924 - going there to die - Dienach had bequeathed a huge part of his soul to me. Thus, my spiritual connection with him flourished upon his death. A simple earlier acquaintance with this man of unique and unprecedented personal fate in life slowly became compassion and friendship over time.

As I later understood, he had formed the impression that from our entire group, a lively bunch of young students, I had somehow treated him better. The truth is I found him less boring that the rest did and, besides, I had set my mind on learning a foreign language at the time. Therefore, it is not strange that we happened to spend entire evenings together talking about all sorts of things. I shall always remember that cautiousness in his words as I mentioned before, even though he liked to exchange views with me - more than with the rest - on various philosophical and historical issues.

During the first years after his death, every time I read his manuscripts - I had since started translating them as best as I could and that was the case from 1926 to 1940 - I would always say to myself: "Look, Dienach was set on writing literature. He attempted to portray a mentally ill character and by inventing a myth, a plot, he found the way to write his own ideas on all sorts of things."

At the time, I was infused with scepticism, something very common for students of my time. I refused to believe anything defying the accepted laws of nature. I actually remember finding that religiousness flooding Dienach's thinking, evident in the pages of his *Diary*, somehow exaggerated. As time went by, I realised how little we humans know of these laws and how thoughtless it would be to entirely exclude phenomena regarding psychological functions that defy the ordinary, rare as they may be.

But even more so, the more years went by, the better I pondered on some incidents from the time of my acquaintance with Dienach, some of his reserved words, which only now could truly interpret. In this way, my conviction that all these manuscripts written by a dead man, the sad man with the deep-set eyes who seemed so tedious to the rest of us - as one companion of ours had said not entirely unfairly one day - was actually his *Diary*. I have now come to believe that this man, who was probably not highly educated or intelligent, this practically unemployed man in his final years, who was neither a craftsman of language, as is evident from his manuscripts *(futile were the translator's efforts to simplify the style in some cases, without betraying the meaning; to present the phrase less presumptuous and not so brightly coloured and ornate with all kinds of adjectives - as Dienach was given to waxing lyrical quite often, which he actually admits somewhere in his manuscripts)*, nor had professed having any other job in his homeland, apart from teaching, did not write of figments of his own imagination and nor could he have all those things he wrote about within him. He did nothing but narrate what happened in his life and what was meant for him to *see* and *live* by a strange turn of events.

One more thing: Dienach did not invent a mentally ill character, but was ill himself, even before the attack of tuberculosis, I mean to say. He was an aloof and whiny hypochondriac, to say the least - notice his never-ending complaining in his writings - and hypersensitive almost to a pathological degree. He did not wish to speak of his two past illnesses (in 1917 and 1921-1922). Still, I recall him vaguely telling me at some point that "lethargic sleep is not an enigma for science anymore" and that "this reaction of the neuro-psychological system, this defence mechanism can be beneficial at times when neural cells are overcharged. It contributes to regulating their alternating current flow and protects them from impending collapse". In either case, had it not been for his illness, he would not have encountered such fate in his life, which nowadays astounds us.

Who, indeed, could have predicted that this man's illness would take such an incredible and unique turn? Much has been said about the unknown powers hidden within the human soul. It is true that we are unaware of thousands of things that exist and that thousands of things happen around us about which we are clueless. Nevertheless, who would ever speak of such potential of the human psychodynamics that resembles a miracle? Of course, this does not mean every emotionally overloaded psychological state bears such incredible potential, as was Dienach's case. However, certain similar states - few among the many - may appear to lead to such parapsychic (or metapsychic) wanderings, as was the case of the spirit of these manuscripts' author.

I recall that in 1923 we only saw Dienach as a man whose life was crushed by incurable sadness. Back in those days, the phrase "some great love affair" would frivolously come to our smiling and slightly sarcastic lips. Indeed, the writings in his "First Notebook" show that he was a man who had failed at his job and ended up being good at nothing in life due to his morbid predisposition of the incurable romantic and his unfortunate love affair *(See e.g. Dec. 6, 1918 [First Edition]: I was telling myself to be strong, pull myself together and go out - but I couldn't. Jan 17, 1919 [First Edition]: I feel guilty towards my mother, etc.).* That exaggerated purple prose and those repetitions here and there, along with quite a few redundancies, retained by the translator, as well as that excessive sentimentality are everywhere to be found in his manuscripts.

It is true, however, that every time he was not absent-minded or lost in his never-ending daydreaming, it was interesting to talk to him. He would often like to ask us about our studies. In fact, during one of our conversations, he told us that he had also pursued history and classical studies in his homeland when he was young, but a few years later, an illness forced him to permanently leave his job.

Another time, when someone asked him about his choice to come and live in Greece, he told us, revising his first strange answer that he did it "for reasons of nostalgia", that he came motivated, as many others, by love for this renowned city.

"And besides," he added with that hesitance in his voice - the same voice he used every time he had doubts whether his words would come across as right and rational - "I had this wish to see a place that lives two lives, divided by *twenty entire centuries.*"

The fact that a kind of nostalgia was dogging him once again here in Greece as well was evident to anyone spending time with him. As every ailing person, he would also blame the place and the climate. In fact, I believe that this man, who felt at times, as we would say about him then, that "life was too short for him" wherever he went, he could not manage to get these thoughts out of his head: "Where could the exit be?" In the end, he had stopped teaching and spent, as we found out afterwards, the final months of his life in a somewhat dismal financial situation.

He was not interested in material needs. Instead, he was tormented by the thought of dying young - as it finally came to be before he had turned thirty-eight - and that he would not have enough time to write, as only he knew how, the history of European culture, which was his lifelong dream. "In two volumes," he would fervently say. He was convinced he could. The only thing lacking was time. When I asked him about how he would divide the historical periods and he told me that the first volume would reach up to our great 19thcentury, he felt my puzzlement at that moment. He immediately hinted, hesitantly and vaguely, that he had his own personal methodological convictions and that the second volume would be more of a critical work. However, it was obvious there was something more to this. It was only when the *Diary* reached my hands and I started reading it that I realised that Dienach intended to reach up to spring 3906 in that second volume. He had been hiding this from me during our conversations. How bright his face was, I recall, how bright… Every single time I bring that moment to mind, I feel the faith that kindled and inspired him stronger - the conviction that he *knew* all that came later and that he could narrate it - if only, he said, he had been given health and available time by fate. He had the courage to do so. "There are," he said, "occasions, very rare, to be honest, when we already know what the future holds for us. We have so many incidents where forward knowledge clearly manifested itself."

Last night *(The "Pre-introductory and Critical Note" was written in 1966)*, I was once again skimming through the pages of the translated version of the *Diary* and my mind went back to him. Many old things have since been lost, but I had never forgotten that I had these manuscripts in my possession. In fact, the more the years went by and the carelessness of youth faded, the more the thought of them would haunt me with pangs of guilt.

I have pondered on their publication for a long time. Not only for reasons of the natural respect on behalf of a student towards the memory of his old teacher, but also due to the latter's very rare case. It was thanks to the unprecedented fate of his private life that Dienach was lucky enough to be aware of many of the things that would occur many years hence - via the science of the space age - accessible to the wise and, in fact, via the methods of scientific research which natural sciences hold dear.

Many will say: "Is it possible for cases of such detailed memories of pre-existence to occur in the middle of Europe?" However, one should ask the following: "Why have people with such living memories of a previous existence only appeared in the East Indies?" The prevalence of materialism in the European lifestyle has reached exaggeration and positivism has infused the spirit of the European man to the extent of unbearable one-sidedness. The more you let go of these things, the more they do too.

Nowadays, the name Dienach is still unknown. It is natural to be absent from every index of writers, every encyclopaedia. However, there will come a day when he shall be an honoured and glorified name. The distant descendants of modern Western Europeans shall utter it with respect. There will come a time when one shall see all things he so thoroughly describes in his texts come true in Europe. He so vividly portrays them because he has seen them with his own two eyes. He has actually lived all that he narrates.

Just like the night they brought me the manuscripts, so it was two days ago, that I read until nightfall. Just like that time, I did not wish to turn the lights on. Just like that time, I thought I would suddenly see the figure of my distant friend in the still of the night, appearing between the two window panes that shone milky white in the darkness, as milky white as I remember my friend's complexion from those times of old…

For all those who do not wish to hear anything about parapsychology, extra-sensory perception and cases of metapsychic phenomena, for those who do not accept anything beyond the limits of scientific thinking and data, Dienach did not *see* and *live* his writings, but invented them. He envisioned, that is, the course of future cultural developments of our species and more specifically the white race and as a matter of fact - daring to courageously and lastingly address - for a rather considerable period of time. Besides, he recorded his own convictions in each field of philosophical thinking (especially moral and cognitive-theoretic convictions), his own metaphysical beliefs.

According to this view, Dienach had put his own thoughts in the mouths of his heroes (Jaeger, Silvia, Lain, Cornelius, Stefan, Astrucci, Hilda, Syld and so on) of a rather novel narration. This, however, is hardly believable by anyone who had the chance to meet Dienach in person and was aware that he was not some exceptional genius and that his level of education was not so unique. This Central European, and he alone, assigns such a sublime meaning and such exceptional content to the world and life that he not only beautifies life, but he also even exceeds the conceptions of ancient Greek classical education and humanistic tradition, which does not, however, correspond to anything inexistence.

If one accepts the more rationalistic of the two explanations, one must say that Dienach's texts are pages of applied futuristic sociology and an optimistic perspective in metaphysics. Some of the writer's convictions are quite characteristic. We present them directly below.

Dienach does not foster the slightest appreciation for human cognitive abilities. He even considers *a priori* perceptions of the mind, for instance, time, space and classifications, too narrowly human. He says that the succession of time periods, yesterday, today, tomorrow, and even the concept of space are what is apparent. They appear to us in this form because they correspond to the perception sensors of human-receivers, to their mental capacities, that is, to their cognitive potential, intellect and rationality. The objective reality of time eludes us. It may very well not be our familiar linear time, with the sequence that we consider rational, with its rational flow, but deep down be an everlasting present. Similar is the case with space. It is impossible for man to perceive anything existing beyond three-dimensional space. There are, however, huge realities, which are included in this notion. For example, the dimension of depth eludes us. According to Dienach, underlying Kant's simple moral demands of practical reason are excellent and unperceived realities, quite real, even though they are not accessible to human intellect. The new faculties, which the *Homo Occidentalis Novus* managed to acquire, added, as Stephan would tell Dienach, an endless ontological depth to reality, where the once moral demands of the old cognitive-theoretical version are included.

Objective ontological reality suffers no harm - it is just *we* that are incapable of perceiving it - because the perception sensors, the mind, human reason happens to be finite and imperfect. An objective being suffers no harm because the entire cognitive and psychic human structure, the entire rational organisation, happens to be weak by nature. In exactly the same way, for instance, ultraviolet and infrared rays suffer no harm regarding their objective existence and reality because the perception abilities of the human vision sensors happen to be inadequate.

He disapproves of the rise of rationality to an almighty cognitive power. He does not agree that human intellect is the only safe origin of spiritual life or that the cognitive function is the highest or that only what is acceptable by means of rational proof is related to ontological reality.

Regarding all science, if one excludes mathematics, as he says, Dienach has doubts about whether it gives us the real, objective picture of the natural universe. He stresses its fluid nature and speaks not of one natural science that is the most objectively valid - as it was believed in the 19th century - but of many subjective natural sciences, one for each different period. He considers the achievements of physics very useful to our empirical knowledge, their technical applications in the various fields of natural sciences and to the progress of material culture, but not to the knowledge of the true nature of beings. Fate has not provided us with the key to perceiving their objectivity. Our knowledge of all this is too human by definition. The proper knowledge of actual Being goes beyond our potential. As was the above mentioned case of the colour rays in the solar spectrum, such is the case here as well with the perception of the natural universe: for the living beings that humans are, senses are tools within nature, but also barriers. Our mental capacities, our knowledge potential, intellect, rationality, are tools within the worlds of existing things for the biological species of rational beings to which we belong, but they are also obstacles.

Dienach considers even the distinction between physics and metaphysics entirely human. It is the sensory perception of this particular biological species and its finite cognitive potential that limit them. We no longer live, he says, in the times of Aristoteles, Descartes or Kant, the times of worshipping human intellect and reason, as if these were something unattainable, unique and incomparable. The distinction human intellect has made between physics and metaphysics are subjective (for humans), but not objective. It is impossible, he says, to perceive how much reality (a reality of incredible grandeur and superb beauty), how much ontological validity may underlie all that we have become used to calling "spiritual worlds" a long time ago. The correct definition of this term is, according to Dienach, neither that which has no real ontological substance nor that which only exists in our spirit, but that whose objective existence and nature human-receivers lack the ability to perceive.

For thousands of years we believed humans to be the only species of living beings to have a higher spiritual life, inner cultivation, inner culture and a free spiritual personality. This erroneous conception of our uniqueness is, according to Dienach, the main reason we consider human cognitive abilities such as intellect and reason so satisfactory - almost infallible according to intellectuals and positivists. He says that this is the main reason we consider the human mind to be omniscient and rationalism to be absolutely valid and we say that if something truly exists, then it is impossible for our intellect not to perceive it.

The level man occupies among myriads of species of intellectual and rational beings is, Dienach says, quite superior. However, man is not the Crown of Creation unless, of course, we limit ourselves to the spiritual and intellectual life of our planet. All humanistic tradition, religious faith, the Greco-Roman spirit and Renaissance had, our author says, passed down to our Western Civilization the unshakable conviction that man is the spiritual centre of the universe. Our whole thinking is egocentric, anthropomorphic and geocentric. Myriads of different biological species are higher than our level and myriads of others are lower. In fact, the utterance "the heavens declare the glory of God" has, he says, meaning and content incomparably broader and higher than the one intended by those expressing it and generally by what people thought at those times. Positivists, intellectuals, empiricists, rationalists and critical philosophers are all mistaken, he says, in considering human perception sensors of imperfect and finite potential to be infallible. They are also wrong to hold that nothing exists apart from what is given and tested by the intellect, rationality and experience. A higher, truly higher, view of the world and life is not feasible, Dienach writes, as long as we continue to look at things exclusively from the human point of view, our own perspective and in light of our own mental capacity.

Another point worth noting in Dienach's writings is his belief (he *saw*, he says, and *knows*) that the cognitive abilities of many other biological species provide an equally subjective image for all that exists - though much more perfect and complete than ours - even if these species are on a higher level than us in the scale of the myriads of species of rational beings. The finite element, he says, is inherent to the inevitable fate of organic matter, no matter how endowed the latter is with the divine spark beyond certain stages of its spiritual development and biological evolution. When the spirit comes to embrace matter, you cannot, he says, ever find perfection. There is no perfection in any of those creatures that are superior to us, in any of their functions corresponding to what we are used to calling 'mind', 'reason' and psychic-intellectual functions. They are also burdened by the fate of understanding only the apparent facets of reality, he says. In other words, they also have their own worldview, which they supposedly consider real due to their limited ability of ontological perception; in the same way, we have our own physical-scientific worldview, which we owe to Copernicus, Kepler, Newton, Einstein, Max Planck, Werner Heisenberg and the rest of our wise personages.

The most wondrous thing he writes about is that actual Being exists, the deeper essence of Being, that is, the objective and no longer the apparent reality. This Being exists beyond the thousands of subjective images in the field of ontology and generally in the sphere of knowledge and beyond all kinds of perceptions, which vary incredibly on those myriads of inhabited spheres and in the incredible breadth of time periods spanning millions of centuries. They vary, he says, depending on the level of the species of logical beings and even on the particular stage of their biological and spiritual development along with the various developmental stages of their psychic-spiritual functions. Human language cannot express this inconceivably large ontological reality, of course. Dienach, however, employs a term: the *Samith*. He actually believes that this term is not conventional, but it is a specific word of a peculiar language of the wise of those distant future times he discusses.

Let us suppose that one of the superior species of rational living beings somewhere in cosmic space could ever grasp the entire true nature of this objective ontological reality, its essence, its structure, its entire ontological content. Then, he says, we would immediately solve all the big and unknown problems of the world, a small part of which constitutes, also here on our Earth, an objective of our metaphysical pain, an object, that is, of unbearable spiritual thirst, of irresistible nostalgia of spirit and soul. These problems are the natural universe in its objective nature, the existence of God, the beginning and the end of beings, the deep mystery of life and its purpose, all sorts of teleological opinions, eternity and infinity. Moreover, the thousands of questions in metaphysics, the origins and the destination of people as well as their place in the entirety of Being, everything we hopelessly strive to understand, everything inconceivable but existing, of ontological substance, no matter how much it eludes the abilities of human intellect and the perception sensors of rationalism.

Dienach believes that it is feasible for superior living beings to have knowledge, not of the *Samith's* essence, of course, which is impossible, but at least of its evident existence. He even says this could be feasible by people, though in the very distant future, upon long-lasting self-cultivation of the psychic-spiritual abilities of our species and an evolutionary course of a more moral nature.

This knowledge of *Samith's* existence would suffice, according to Dienach, to put an end to man's metaphysical angst and save the human spirit from the eternal fate of pain and doubt. Despite its inaccessible essence, the all-so-clear knowledge of the existence of that large ontological reality, which objectively exists, could not come to the chosen ones among us, to those whom fate would have given the divine grace of actually witnessing its existence. It could not come but in connection with that meaning of incredible and inconceivable grandeur and with the feeling of hyper- cosmic beauty it encompasses.

"Do not take these last words with their human meaning," Dienach writes in some footnotes. "Alas," he says, "upon hearing the word 'grandeur', we think of space, of range. The same applies for hyper-cosmic beauty, which is something beyond the limits of human psychic tolerance to great aesthetic joy and superb spiritual happiness and besides, something entirely inaccessible to the poor and finite perception potential of human aesthetic consciousness. Maybe, however, it is an unintentional foretelling. Maybe it is a distant reflection of it, which had once feebly shone in Goethe's or Beethoven's dreams and in those of other masters of artistic creation and philosophical thinking during the heyday of the European civilisation.

I recall Dienach writing somewhere else in his manuscripts, which were later lost, about Kant's distinction between the *beautiful* (for example, in the great and immortal works of artistic creation and the perception of beauty by the cultivated lover of the arts) and the *sublime* (for example, at the sight of the starry dome and at the perception of the sublime by the sensitive religious person of advanced inner cultivation and rich spiritual culture). I also recall Dienach writing further down about Kant's observation that the former causes deep aesthetic stirring while the latter brings about a sense of wonder and profound religiousness as well as a feeling of awe and veneration.

I remember Dienach not admitting to such a distinction, but, on the contrary, giving a single explanation for all this: he writes somewhere that an unbearable thirst of the soul pushes us towards these concepts. The *Samith*, however, is, deep down, the object of our nostalgia. Lacking it, we resort to all those things that give our spiritual world the impression of its worldly forms. They somehow grant us - though temporarily - some salvation from the unquenched thirst for the *Samith* within our own ambience of life. That is all we have in the cruel fate of our world.

Besides, Dienach continues, this need for salvation is the reason religions were established in the first place. Men feel that life is impossible without a religious feeling. This salvation is also pursued by artistic, and generally, creation in its various forms (composition of symphonic music, lyrical poetry, visual arts, treasures of the spirit in general). The same reason led to the construction, through the millennia, of an entire spiritual edifice of meritocratic convictions and high ideals (such as humanism, love, justice, altruism, freedom, education, and the spiritual urge towards moral completion). This need for salvation is the reason men became capable of expressing sublime moral demands to their Creator and suffering, fighting, sacrificing themselves, dying - without an ulterior motive, in the spirit of voluntary sacrifice - for high emotional and moral values. All this to quench, as much as possible - even temporarily - that unsatisfied, sacred thirst of the spirit and soul. The deepest reason, the true origins of the entire civilisation throughout history is this unrelenting spiritual tendency, this urge for salvation from the pain from the lack of the *Samith*, unconscious though we may be of it.

According to Dienach, the enlightened and worthy thinker should thus actually address the problem of the origins of civilisation. All that has ever been taught about it is, as he writes, superficial. Instead of considering the ever-evolving course of civilisation an expression of people's strife and tendency to return to God, from whom they have been separated by sin (Gianbattista Vico), the essence of people's social life (Auguste Comte), an outcome of the competition among social classes of conflicting financial interests (Karl Marx), the manifestation of biological evolution by means of youth and decline (Oswald Spengler), the fruit of older suppressed and repressed sexual desires, which return transformed and idealised and are externalised indifferent forms upon long-lasting unknowing processing in the depths of the subconscious (Sigmund Freud) or, finally, the manifestation of a tendency towards domination, supremacy and distinction, for the sake of reacting to the feeling of inferiority and weakness during childhood (Adler and other proponents of individual psychology), it is better, he says, to admit the deeper, truer reason. Even if Carl Jung, Dienach writes elsewhere, searches for the origins and the cause of works of civilisation in the vast richness of noble and high inclinations and tendencies encompassed in that hidden area of the psychic organism, man's subconscious, it does not explain enough regarding the origins of this richness. They are not only hereditary features and refined instincts. This may also be the case, but these features are "absolutely secondary". This interpretation lacks depth. Without the *Samith*, without the sacred thirst of the spirit and soul and our nostalgia for it, there could be no noble urges of the man's soul towards things that are desirable, undiscovered, impossible and inexistent - inexistent and impossible in our meagre ambience of life - towards eternity, infinity, the divine, perfection and ideal beauty. Neither would the great acts of moral beauty exist, nor the attraction to sacrifice or anything beyond reason, to the beautiful, sublime, unexpressed and divine.

Dienach later talks about man's future efforts to make a leap forward in the process of evolution, a gain of millennia in the long psycho-spiritual and moral maturity in a way to accelerate, as much as possible, the ability of acquiring direct knowledge. Men shall be able to do this when they have overcome this stage of technical-economic civilisation and once satisfied and satiated with the cultural achievements thereof, they shall turn to pursuits that are more spiritual. Dienach writes that if he understood correctly, the evolution of the intuition and second sight of the old times from their past embryonic state shall generate the acquisition of this new human spiritual ability. The new cognitive potential, the new experience, which shall render the knowledge of the *Samith* crystal clear - despite the inaccessibility of its essence - and shall also give that feeling of the incredible and inconceivable grandeur and hyper-cosmic superb beauty that is connected to It.

This astute species is restless, he writes somewhere. After its insane achievements in the technical universe, it suddenly enters new paths. It puts its hand to artificial development, reinforcement and activation of extremely old abilities, which had been lying dormant in the deepest parts of the psychic organism. It aspires to see this elusive secret light of no cognitive processing become evident, stable and conscious. What was once considered transcendent *(In all his texts, Dienach uses the word transcendent in the meaning of metaphysical and hyper-cosmic. Throughout his manuscripts, Dienach calls transcendent the high realities, which stand above man's perception sensors while fate has not given man knowledge thereof. The 18th and 19th centuries had doubted whether they corresponded to something existing. Dienach thought of them as realities in connection with the great metaphysical problems. He stresses the validity of their ontological substance.)*, what was true but inconceivable, real (existing) but unthinkable and inexpressible, our species wants to make them the object of evident knowledge here and now. Since intellect and reason have been proven unsuitable *(he means to say insufficient)* for this, this new, astute species acquires new cognitive potential *(he means new perception sensors)*.

One of the main reasons Dienach was so hesitant to reveal himself to his friends at least and did not wish, as long as he lived, to have his manuscripts published, was the new terms, the neologisms he had to use at the time of his writing. *(Generally, new words are one of Dienach's greatest obstacles in expressing himself. He had found himself, he says, before thousands of new terms of another age of superior spiritual life, before thousands of new verbal expressions of a richer language, which was the linguistic instrument of a civilisation superior to our 20th century one. In many cases, he had to use these new words in their original form. However, he prefers using a periphrastic wording by means of our words where it is possible. Thus, for instance, the great rooms of teaching [5 of VI], the unions of willed competences [30 of VI], the office partners [14 of VI], the partners of herds, the service, the boulevards of the settlement [26 of VI], etc. constitute a German periphrastic rendition of the original one-word term. The same applies for the ambiance of this life, which intends to express the opposite of the concept of life after death or the opposite to the transcending course of the individual's spiritual entity after biological death. The same applies for the peripheral far rooms of domes [20 of VII] and the established officials [Gretwirch Aarsdag of September 6 for us] and many others.)* The *Nibelvirch*, which attributes man's acquisition of that new superior spiritual ability, above intellect and rationalism, that new perception sensor (knowledge potential) cannot, he says, be expressed in any of our languages by any term. Intuition and second sight are simplistic compared to it. Besides, hyper-vision very much reminds us of one of our own material (of the experience) senses. Still, that distant future age that Dienach's manuscripts refer to frequently employs the term *Oversyn* or *Supersyn* as near synonyms to the *Nibelvirch* or actually as its outcome. Elsewhere it uses the terms direct knowledge, direct view and experience beyond reason interchangeably.

Vain were the attempts of an acquaintance of his to tell him that he was not right to be so hesitant. Besides, *concept* was unknown as a verbal term before Socrates and *idea* was never uttered as a word before Plato. In vain. He could not bear, he said, the thought of comparing himself to men of such gigantic stature.

Either way, Dienach writes that the *Nibelvirch* inaugurates a brand new stage in the evolution of the spiritual life of the human race. This new superior spiritual ability and knowledge potential is, he says, a frontier, a limit separating the *Homo sapiens'* life, which lasted millennia, from the dawning of a new life for the enlightened man, the *Homo Occidentalis Novus*. Besides, he writes that he heard it said that anatomic variations had been observed in the main connective brain centres afterwards.

The entire multi-millennial age of articulated speech, intellect, ability to reflect, all these cognitive functions, with the passage from naive faith to knowledge and positive sciences and even with the entire content of the *affect*, the emotional and co native urges and with all that psychic richness, is, Dienach says, a single age: Stage B. Regarding Stage A, he says that particular stage is reserved for the early, primitive man, whose senses and instincts were the only content of his mental life). From the *Nibelvirch* onwards, Stage C dawns. It is an element which is added to the so far psycho-spiritual functions, which is not just new, but also superior in merit. None of the previous ones can compare to this, to direct enlightenment, even though they were a *sine qua non* condition of the latter in terms of continuity. This new element - the possibility of direct view thanks to the *Nibelvirch* - did not come to demolish, reduce or weaken older mental functions. It came to add to them. It came to complement the entire cognitive human structure with something else, something more powerful.

One of the most characteristic of Dienach's observations was that only once Stage C dawned did the right explanation and the deeper meaning of thousands of things during the previous stage become evident and only in this way did they receive proper interpretation. During Stage C, man became conscious of the deeper meaning of all those earlier things. These were the noble emotional urges, the high ideals, religious awe, the unbearable need of the soul of the greats for artistic creation in its highest expression, the inner need for justice, even if it concerned others and not oneself. Other noble sentiments were deep and true love and the attraction to voluntary sacrifice, the thirst for the final justification of virtue and the lofty longing for immortality, the ever misunderstood - as a base concern for mortality - spiritual inclination for a lease of life, that tendency to overcome the barriers of our biological fate and, generally, an entire universe of high moral and spiritual values. In one word, they were the most solemn and sacred ideals of the human soul. It was made clear that all those were nothing but diversiform manifestations of an unknown thirst of the spirit and soul, an ever unappeased nostalgia. It was only thanks to the *Nibelvirch* that it became possible for men to see its most profound object (the *Samith*), to gain, that is, knowledge of what lies beyond the worldly manifestations of its apparent directions (the *a posteriori* interpretation, as he writes).

This thirst of the spirit and soul is the origins of the entire civilisation. He says that the higher the level of the moral and psycho-spiritual civilisation on a given sphere (inhabited planet) during a specific age, the more intense and noble shall the thirst of the soul be. In other words, it is the unknown spiritual and moral pain for the colossal difference - in beauty and grandeur - between the ambience of life and the *Samith*; between the apparent, that is, and the large ontological reality, which is multidimensional, and objectively existent.

One of the basic common features and common points between our biological species and the thousands of other species of rational living beings on myriads of celestial spheres is, according to Dienach, this common deepest cause for every sublime spiritual offering and generally for every creative inspiration for cultural achievements. Such is the unquenchable thirst of the spirit and soul, the nostalgia for the *Samith* even if we do not always feel it, even if it is not a conscious yearning.

Beyond a certain stage of evolution "of the psychic and spiritual life" this deepest cause starts, he says, to appear imperative, invincible and unappeased. The forms of organic matter may greatly vary compared to ours, depending on the terms governing the appearance and the ascent of life to those very distant spheres. If these terms, however, have actually happened to meet with the "divine spark", if they encompass something to which we owe our intellect, rationalism and emotion, then they cannot but approach our species in everything pertaining to the higher spiritual realms. Something similar to our own unquenchable thirst for research and knowledge shall exist, something similar to our own "worries of the heart", something similar to our unbearable inclination towards the indestructible and eternal, the inherent warm emotional attraction towards a supreme existence of unknown nature and with our honest faith in "higher powers", something similar to our own great artist's imperative inner voice, the inevitable psychic urge to give the ideal of beauty a visible form, to grant the work a lease of life, beyond the model's biological decay, to defeat time and the law of decay. Dienach concludes that the deepest, radical cause of all those civilisations and their historical realisations is common; it is the thirst of spirit and soul for the *Samith*.

For Dienach, this common feature has, apart from the primary importance of the common cause and also the common purpose, the importance of time duration and even validity (*Geltung*) in the vast cosmos. He writes that every species' mission on every inhabited sphere and the task assigned by fate is to erect the spiritual structure of its civilisation as beautifully, perfectly, highly and completely as possible. This common trait has greater importance than the historical cultural achievements themselves. Civilisations, he says, come and go. However, their deepest origins remain eternal and unalterable.

The great aesthetic civilisation of Classical antiquity, the thousands of statues and temples in Athens and Corinth, the high level of common aesthetic consciousness of those times in ancient Greece, which created man's inner need to live in such an ambience of beauty, came and went. However, the cause remains. The thirst of that soul, the nostalgia for the *Samith*, shall create, he says, something new - never entirely the same, something new with original elements. This is actually the case with the new great miracle of creation in symphonic musical compositions in central Europe during the $19^{th}$ century, which is the worthy equivalent of the Greek miracle of the Classical Age.

Discoveries regarding the laws that govern the natural universe come one after the other and the ever new celestial mechanics prove the teachings of each previous version mistaken. However, the cause remains. It is the thirst of the spirit and soul, the nostalgia for the *Samith*, which is manifested in this field in the form of that longing for research, which honours our species. It is the spiritual yearning and invincible inclination to learn something more each time and discover something more correct regarding the great secret that surrounds us, to extract nature's secrets, to diagnose the laws that govern natural phenomena.

Religions, with their doctrines, the stories of their sacred history, their teachings and their rituals of worship, come, go and vary depending on the places, spheres and times. However, their deepest cause remains. In this field, the cause in question is manifested via the feeling of religiousness. This is an unbearable need of the soul for both our humanity and for every deserving species of rational and emotional living beings on other inhabited planets.

The specific forms often assumed by high ideals, the eternal moral values and values of spiritual life, come and go. However, their deepest cause remains. Their effect on our spiritual world does not depend on each ephemeral form. The cause never varies. The inner need is always as intense, the feeling of worship, the frenzy and the competitive tendency are always as intense and the same applies for the force of spiritual longing and unbridled enthusiasm. No price seems high enough for their sake, regardless of the particular form each of those great ideals assumes every time.

This profound cause - the only thing that does not change - is, according to Dienach, the thirst of the spirit and soul for the *Samith*. He considers the latter similar to the Kantian "*das Ding an sich*" as a verbal expression. Regarding its essence, he considers it the objective Existent in its entirety, the whole of Being at its deepest essence, regardless of finite cognitive abilities, knowledge potential, which the various species of biological beings share on the millions of the celestial inhabited spheres. In other words, he considers it the all-existing ontological reality, which is multi-dimensional and of objective substance.

Reinforcing and activating all these inherent human spiritual abilities, once done extensively and for a sufficient amount of time (faithful and persistent self-cultivation for thousands of years), could, according to Dienach, exercise decisive influence on the forms of spiritual life and generally the cultural life for very long periods of time. It could also gradually form a peculiar civilisation, which would leave, one would say, its own distinct mark. That distant future age of civilisation that he narrates - which he *saw* and *lived* for those of us who believe him - has its own individual nuance due to the very deep influence of the Aidersen Institute, the *Nibelvirch* and the Volkic spiritual preaching, the Volkic teaching, as he narrates in his manuscripts, along with a variety of other factors, which he reports as an eye witness in his *Diary*. The same is true in the years before our existence, starting from ancient history: every single age of civilisation has its own character, which matches its cultural identity. This is also largely due to the very intense and deep cultivation of certain human spiritual and intellectual abilities.

For instance, the ancient Chinese civilisation, monolithic and isolated, was mainly characterised by its excessive devotedness to tradition. The Egyptian civilisation of the time of the Pharaohs and high priests had focused on life after death. The ancient Jewish civilisation, as well as the later Islamic one, was of evident religious nature. The Greek civilisation of classical antiquity centred on the worship of natural beauty and was infused with unparalleled spiritual elements, thanks to the Socratic teaching of self-discipline, morality, virtue, mutual respect and the incomparable principles and convictions of the Platonic Ideal. It was a civilisation with a sense of proportion and beauty, an artistic and aesthetic civilisation above all.

The civilisation of the Italian Renaissance had certain characteristic features such as the revival of classical texts, the thirst for free thinking, the elevation of aesthetic consciousness and artistic creation using themes principally taken from the Christian tradition. The 19th century German civilisation created an entire universe of harmony and, besides, brought Europe an unprecedented development and acme in scientific thought and philosophical thinking.

Generally, within the millennial turnings of the wheel of history, various tendencies prevail. At times, it is rationalism, the materialistic ideas and the mentality of research, observation and experimentation on behalf of natural sciences - the almightiness of the laboratory. At others, it is aesthetic consciousness, the sense of beauty, the development, that is, of the sense of good taste. In other moments in history, it is the conquests of the technical universe, the comforts and the mass production of standardised industrial products (the popularisation of the application of inventions, the material abundance of means and the democratisation of comforts). Then, some other times, it is fanaticism, intolerance and the ideological prejudice against spiritual or political preachings or even religious past ones. Finally, there are times when it is intellectualism in thought and in every other expression of social life.

A possible one-sided reinforcement of cognitive functions - only of the mind and not of the emotion - could, Dienach somewhere says, create a materially almighty race, in the course of millennia, of incredible technological achievements, of a remarkable progress in natural sciences and their technical applications. However, such one-sided progress would generate a barbaric race in terms of inner cultivation, with no gentleness of mores, with no inner culture, with a massive void regarding the soul, moral values and emotions.

The opposite paths lead elsewhere: for instance, the age of Romanticism in Western Europe gave a major voice to emotions during the first three or four decades of the 19th century. They were the principal motivation of creative inspiration, not only in literature, lyrical poetry, painting or sculpture, but also in musical composition, philosophical thinking and metaphysics. Moreover, they motivated the course of political life, the convictions based on merit, the trends of ideas, the start of social reforms, enthusiasm, high ideals, the morals and in social life, in general, in almost every sphere of cultural activity. Spontaneity and sentiment drove artistic creators and poets to produce works of unparalleled aesthetic inspiration, with the element of the marvellous and the mythical and they also made them disapprove and shake off the old "rules of technique". Vis-à-vis the established logical forms, in every field of creation, affect prevailed throughout those times. The surrounding material reality was being put aside and ignored, yielding to emotion and imagination. The perception of life and the world beyond reason prevailed everywhere, on every sphere of the known and in every field of achievement.

Dienach also makes the case of other spiritual courses and directions. For instance, Western man has shown complete disdain for the profound mysticism of the East. Based on the latter, the Hindus, for example, had developed their own peculiar primeval spiritual civilisation up until the 19th century. Within a life which was materially frugal and a strictly agricultural economy, disapproving of every attempt for social climbing and ignoring all the achievements of science and technology, these deeply philosophical religious tribes had focused their attention on Brahma and his teachings. At the same time, they strove to embrace and realise the fusion of man's individuality with the spirit of everything, the identification of the human soul with the One and everything.

He also says that the intensive and somehow one-sided cultivation of human psychodynamics, once done extensively and for a considerable amount of time, could form an entire civilisation of another form of its own individual mark. This cultivation can be done by means of telepathy, reading and transferring thoughts, foreknowledge and foretelling of future events, perception beyond senses, invocation of spirits, and so on, within a spiritual ambience that would be very different from ours, within a beatified ambience of social co-existence. One would there observe a noticeable fall in the positive sciences and rationality as well as in pragmatic judgement and materialistic life in general along with faith in data perceived by the five senses, in the experience of material and real life around us.

Either way, Dienach disapproves of any one-sidedness in the course of civilisation. He condemns, that is, any exaggeration in any exclusive and one-sided direction, which would result in the weakening of certain fields of human abilities. The truly high purposes of culture, the teleological opinions which hold most merit, are connected to a parallel, balanced, harmonious and almost equilateral cultivation and development of the best human abilities and the worthiest tendencies, according to this version. His perspective embraces, as much as possible, the prevalence of higher ideals, the experience of unparalleled spiritual and emotional treasures encompassed within the real and deeper spirit of Christianity and the realisation of humanism and freedom in social life, among the peoples of the world. In fact, Dienach considers these two last ideals, humanism and freedom, the highest one could find in the system of moral values formed within our Western civilisation by classical education, humanism and Christian tradition with their marvellous union, their incomparable marriage.

During the four years of the German Occupation in Greece - all Dienach's manuscripts were still available up until the events of December 1944 and the days when I found shelter in a friend's home, in Thisseos Street, on Christmas Eve 1944 - four people had read the original two "Diaries" and the *Diary with the Chronicles From The Future*: they were the respectable Greek Macedonian friend and colleague, highly educated, whose favourite occupation was, as I can recall from then, his involvement in the Masonic and theosophical movement - he ranked high in Freemasonry; a theology professor from the Greek island of Tinos, who was quite renowned in his time; and two German friends of the latter, father and son. The father was a history professor of liberal ideas while the son was a young reserve officer of the Occupation army with great aversion towards the Hitlerites, which he did not hesitate to share with me.

Each one of them had kept Dienach's actual manuscripts for several weeks and months and had read them to the end. However, their impressions of the manuscripts varied.

The German history professor told me, upon returning the manuscripts, that Dienach was not a simple professor of mediocre education, as I thought at the time. He was, he says, a great personality of the Western European spirit, a true spiritual leader of the white race, a prophet inspired by God, inspired by the love and thirst to contribute to the survival of the Western civilisation. He also added that Dienach foretells the Yellow Peril and the terrible wars of the 23rd century and calls upon Europeans to be infused with the need of a single national consciousness and a pan-European political community. In the case of Dienach, the German historian told me, the time succession between theorists and pragmatists is repeated as it had occurred in both great revolutions: the French one of 1789 and the Russian one of 1917. Twentieth century Dienach stands, he says, before the great fighters of the following centuries, before the European political leaders and the warlords of the 23rd century as their ideological and theoretical forerunner. In other words, he is what Voltaire, Rousseau, Montesquieu, the Encyclopaedists and other 18th-century thinkers more or less were before the orators of constituent national assemblies and the military leaders of the bourgeoisie during the last ten years of the 18th century in France.

"You Greeks have the term 'teacher of the nation'," he said. "So, Dienach was a true teacher of the nation, but with a different meaning from yours, a much broader one: a meaning regarding the ethnological, territorial and mostly cultural scope of the Western European spirit."

However, I remember the German professor being on a different train of thought on another day:

"In Dienach's texts one can distinguish two opposing ideological tendencies. On the one hand, the voice of the 19th century onwards, the centuries of a materialistic view of the world and life, the centuries of technocracy. On the other hand, there is the voice of *the Nojere* as Dienach would call it (3382 AD). This former's motto is that the proper pragmatic viewing of life, the world and scientific thinking succeeded the immature time period of naive faith. Our 19th century," he says, "introduced us to science and put an end to the 'theological prejudices' of past times. Research methods in natural sciences led us to the knowledge of things as they truly are. It also showed the true nature of man (a biochemical laboratory of marvellous hereditary mental abilities) and the world (the natural universe with its material elements, with matter-energy and the powers they encompass as well as the laws of celestial mechanics). It also became evident that men, prompted by the fear of death and the bitter realisation of their ephemeral biological fate, created religions, God, the Beyond, the distinction between bad and good as well as life after death as a justification of virtue.

The *Nojere* (986 of the 'new chronology') proves these things to be faulty. They are, he says, on a merely human scale. They are only what the finite cognitive potential of human-recipients has the ability to perceive. It is only what is perceived by this particular biological species on this grain of sand of the divine strand, which encompasses countless inhabited spheres. The conviction of this 'new age' is that the ontological reality, as objectively existing, is entirely different. It has such a hyper-cosmic and superb beauty and such a cognitively impenetrable and 'unlikely' grandeur that it finds something very different before it - another 'side' of it; only a simpler one. It is the natural universe and life in its entirety along with whatever falls under our cognitive abilities: the senses, the intellect, rationality etc. Before it, all that was said by the greatest religions in their dogmas, the most 'undoubtable' truths in natural sciences - via the method of 'scientific' research - and the highest cosmic-theoretical conceptions as well as the most valued expressions in metaphysical faith all seem naive and childish. This reality is 'something inconceivably big'."

The German historian's son was of a different opinion:

"Dienach's main idea was to continue the love story with his dead beloved," he told me. "This intense thirst of his soul was what made him write the *Diary*. This secret longing for such a possibility, his deeply human burning heartache breathed into him the desire to narrate all that. Using his pen, he gave his constrained human biological fate the time extension that real life would deny. All this happened in order to write the continuation of the ongoing story of a great love, which was prematurely terminated, and to pursue it. He did not actually live his writings. It is all 'made up by himself', artificial and imaginary. Dienach is an 'incurable romantic', 'a poet with quite a few delusions' and in fact 'a psychologically ailing individual who lives inside 'his own' reality."

The young anti-Hitler reserve officer of the German Occupation army later asked me to swear that those manuscripts were authentic and that Dienach had actually existed. I did so with pleasure, since I knew it well enough to be true. I tried to figure out his character: the content of the *Diary* had excited him, literally overwhelmed him. Anyone could speak with him freely. He was an honest humanist and not that ideologically distant from us Greeks.

"He doesn't exist anymore," he told me later on in the conversation, "but how wonderful it is that his mode of thinking has survived through these manuscripts..."

He confessed to me that many sections of the *Diary* had brought tears to his eyes.

"Are you sure that only his mother was Austrian?" he later asked me. "My personal opinion is that his father was also Austrian and that he had participated in World War I. He had nothing to do with Zurich and it will be pointless for you to search there when Europe is at peace. He was Austrian and a Catholic and he had experienced the terror of the 1914 War."

At first, he showed me in the 'First Notebook" the words written about Father Jacob that he "had gone out for a walk with three Protestant priests on August 14, 1922". Then he showed me another phrase of the *Diary* Pages at the end of the 12th - VII: "How happy would I be had I been relieved of every feeling of disgust and shame, away from the smell of mustard gas," he says where I have now put the title-header on the pages "The Valley of the Roses" *(original title of the First Edition)* in my translation.

"He was a Catholic and his father was German or Austrian," my interlocutor continued. He had a guilt complex, which could not be justified in his individual case. It is highly likely he had participated in the war. He was hypersensitive. He suffered from "the complex of his people's guilt" of the imperial era. He literally writes anti-war literature in many parts of his texts. He was not Swiss. He had kept his real self secret from you and most probably his real name. He did this while trying to "find students" because he knew that half the Athenians of that time - in 1922 and 1923 - were sympathisers of the Entente Powers."

The university professor from the Greek island of Tinos and an outstanding man of intellect of those times found the *Diary*'s central meaning elsewhere.

"What is most essential in Dienach's manuscripts," he said, "is his perspective that an incredibly great and beautiful solution to the great metaphysical problems shall be found after a long, long time. These problems are the problems of the world, God, the origins, the course and the end purposes of men, the beginning and the end of beings. This shall be an incredible interpretation to the deep mystery of life, a brilliant answer to all those great questions that have taunted man as a thinker in the most noble and valued of individual and group cases. It would be so great an explanation that the human mind 'cannot perceive its grandeur and exquisite beauty for the time being'. He believes that there will be a time when what happened with the field of celestial mechanics and the natural universe in general at the beginning of the 20th century shall also happen in the field of a more universal worldview. In other words, true, ontological reality will prove to transcend to an incredible degree the highest dreams of the human spirit and the boldest expectations of the human heart. Dienach envisions that what people will once know about these issues shall be superior in terms of grandeur and beauty to what we know today, even more superior than the scientific knowledge of the beginnings of the 20th century of the issues of the natural universe in comparison with the times before Eudoxus, Aristoteles, Aristarchus, Hipparchus and Archimedes."

I remember him telling me on another day:

"Dienach reminds me of William James *(William James, an American thinker, 1842-1910)*, Renan, Huxley and other thinkers of the central and Western Europe of the end of the 19th and the beginning of the 20th century, who feared that Christianity no longer satisfies - namely in its dogmatism - an increasing number of the modern educated people of the Western world. Christian doctrines have more and more difficulty, the aforementioned thinkers say, staying in touch with what is already known of existence, as this is revealed to us by the course of the world and the development of knowledge during these last two centuries. From then on, their roads part. These crypto-materialistic thinkers have the tendency to replace religion with an infinite admiration towards science and even towards evolutionary humanism. They also hold that religions that place themselves 'above worldly matters' speak of things that do not exist and that it is high time the West adopted a religion taking the course and direction towards the fullest possible development of man's spiritual and moral abilities, towards the harmonious and fullest realisation of the highest and most beautiful predispositions and worthy tendencies. Dienach is of the opposite mind. He does not only believe that there are realities that are characterised as 'metaphysical' and 'otherworldly' by man. He also believes that what 'objectively exists' is of a grandeur and beauty which is inconceivable by the human-receivers. It also stands higher and escapes ('exceeds') all that was said so far by the greatest religions, the most valued philosophical teachings, the most ambitious cosmic-theoretical conceptions and, generally, the highest spiritual preachings on this planet throughout the history of the human spirit. Dienach envisions a great new spiritual preaching, Volkic Knowledge as he calls it. The latter shall be a spiritual teaching of unprecedented level, excellent and wondrous, which tends to replace the already known accepted dogmas of Christianity and its theological basis in the ontological field with a broader, higher and more universal view of the world, life and every sphere of existence. This shall be done without offending the established values of the Christian tradition and its incomparable moral teachings in the slightest."

My educated Greek Macedonian theosophist and respectable friend was of another, totally different, opinion.

"I am totally convinced," he told me upon returning the manuscripts to me "that the *Diary* has not been written by Dienach in Athens in 1923-1924. It has been written in northern Italy and other European regions in 3905 and 3906 by Andreas Northam. He was its real author. Dienach's personality and life are a simple 'strong memory of pre-existence', which occupied for many months, almost a year, Andreas Northam's thoughts, emotional world and generally his spirit and his whole thinking. Dienach is 'a simple copyist from memory'. He did nothing but write 'for a second time' in 1923-1924 what was written by Andreas Northam 'for the first time" in 3905 and the following year. The temporal antinomy is clearly set on the human scale, so this whole story seems incredible from the start. One may say that I am being irrational. However, this antinomy in the flow of time only exists for human standards, for human perception potential, only for human standards, which can only understand the meaning of aligned time with yesterday, today and tomorrow. Extremely rare are the cases when the human spirit overcomes the obstacles, transcends human standards and acquires means of perception beyond the senses, telepathy, clairvoyance and a great number of things beyond the 'established' kinds of psychic potential. Time may very well actually be - in its objective nature - different from our own human perceptions thereof, which are subjective and anthropomorphic."

The Greek Macedonian theosophist had obviously worded the above thoughts in impeccable purist Greek (since he was infused with this linguistic tradition). I, however, transcribe them here in the vernacular, since it is the variant of this entire pre-introductory and critical note. He was assisted in reading the manuscripts by a young German-speaking reader, a relative or a friend of his - a student of the pedagogical academy or an archaeologist if I remember correctly. He was the only one among the four not to have mastered Dienach's mother tongue. He had not read the entire manuscript, he said. Nevertheless, he talked to me about them. He believed that only the "First Diary" and the "Second Diary" were actually written by Dienach himself. He attributes the *Diary with the Chronicles From the Future* to Northam. Regarding Northam, he also believed that at the age of twenty-eight he was meant to be - upon some very serious injury, which had temporarily led to his clinical death - Paul Dienach's reincarnation, which is, he says, "a totally rare case of reincarnation since it occurred in a European region of our own sphere."

I remember that in one of our meetings this theosophist and Mason and respectable friend formulated the thought that all those who had happened to meet Dienach in person and then read his *Diary* would have made. The thought that the author of these texts bore in mind the same facts, the same things, the same incidents, the same "material" in a word, on which the future historians shall work after a very long time. The difference is that the latter shall give this material the form of historical research and historiography and their methodology shall be totally different. Here, Dienach handles that same material as a traveller-narrator and assigns it the external form of "travel fiction" of a somewhat literary nature in the wording of the text and with that embellishment which was so familiar to his mentality and did not fit with the usual style of our times. I remember my respectable friend added that the most interesting element underlying these texts is the retrograde perspective of times not too far from us now (the 21st and the 22nd centuries) that can be adopted by someone recording historical impressions in those very distant years in the future.

George M. Papachatzis

August 1966

# LIST OF PROPER NAMES

## NAMES OF PEOPLE

**AESTHETES AND ART PHILOSOPHERS**

**MEN**
Close
Lestrem
Lucifero
Nimotti

**WOMEN**
Lelia Nopotkin

**ACADEMICS**

**MEN**
Volky
Milioki

**PUBLIC FIGURES AND POLITICIANS**

**MEN**
Baldini
Verhin
Grueberg
Delaroche
Milstone
Franklin Montague
Rickenmat
Gustav Siovogia
John Terring
Torhild
Trodalsen
Vohlbach

**FLORISTS**

**MEN**
Costia Rudulof

**LORFFES (leading officials of the intelligentsia)**

**MEN**
Yalmar
Ulfink Enemark
Nicolas Lajevski
Knut Niversun
Rinarschield
John Humphrey
Gunnar Hiller Jr.

**ILECTORS (High-ranking leaders of the intelligentsia)**

**MEN**
Buren
Jaeger

**WOMEN**
Tatiana Baclyn

**GREAT SPIRITUAL LEADERS**

Alexis Volky

**ARCHITECTS**

**MEN**

Olaf Keirl
Kekonen
Igor Bodurof
Niemorsunt
Rauschen
Heimerstam

**WOMEN**

Vada Lastrem
Alicia Neville
Hilda Normanden

**ASTRONOMERS – NATURAL PHILOSOPHERS**

**MEN**

Striberg
Tegner
Feridi, father and son

**BIOLOGERS**

**MEN**

Jacobsen
Jansen

**SCULPTORS**

**MEN**

Greneval
Eriksen
Dean Kersteen
Albert Kingsman
Sweeny Koniemark
Levertin
Arald Mayen
Melsam
Mondstein
Gutorp Nilsen
Davis
Nurberg
Ottermanden
Pradelli
Feinrich

**WOMEN**

Ileanna Wirbach

**GREAT THINKERS (with no specific object or specialty)**

**MEN**

Durant
Olaf Esklud
Esterling
Zalmar
Milliakof
Ratziskin
Runerborg
Matjei Svanol
Viktor Gorms

**GREAT THINKERS CONTEMPORARY TO ANDREAS NORTHAM**

Axel Jenefelt

**AIDERSEN THINKERS**

**MEN**

Bramsen
Borge
Nyttenmat
Royalsen
Chillerin

**THINKERS, FORMER EDUCATORS**

**MEN**

Johan Geyer

**ASCETIC THINKERS**

**MEN**

Aloisius Nilson

**ANCHORITE THINKERS**

Joel Letonen
Miliotkin
Gunnar Nelbarn

**DRAMATISTS**

**MEN**
Evelyn Cornsen
Bjornsen
Borudin
Ignatio Walmine

**PUBLISHERS**
Dupont

**INTERPRETERS OF AIDERSEN INSTITUTE THOUGHT**

**MEN**
Tinersen

**EDUCATORS**

**MEN**
Astrucci
Cornelius
Lain
Gunnar Bjerlin

**INTUITIVE SPIRITS**

**MEN**
Atterman
Gibling
Eric Gord
Carstens
Orlik
Fletchius

**WOMEN**
Mary-Lea
Vera Brandes
Tervalsen

**INTUITIVES FROM THE VALLEY OF ROSES (ROSERNES DAL) AND AIDERSEN INSTITUTE**

**MEN**
Arald
Gustavsen
Poliotkin
Rasmathy

**SCIENTISTS**

**MEN**
Astrom
Vilinski
Yarl
Jergesen
Karl Hornsen
Boyer
Sioberlef
Eilensleyer
Erlader
Valdemar Esklud
Esterling
Sabba
Stirlen
Holberg

**WOMEN**
Coiral

**PAINTERS**

**MEN**
Knut Valdemar
Svansen
Nichefelt
Fabius Sigra
Stiernsted
Syld

**WOMEN**
Dora Vilen

**DOCTORS AND RESEARCHERS**

**MEN**
Molsen
Diseny
Kirchof
Flessing

**PREACHERS**

**MEN**
Knut Dieter

**SCIENCE HISTORIANS**

**MEN**
Rondelli

**WOMEN**
Brigita Luni

**ART HISTORIANS**

**MEN**
Nymark
Pierri

**WOMEN**
Inga Pearson
Ludmilla Sikorski

**MUSIC HISTORIANS**

**WOMEN**
Dalia Keetly

**PHILOLOGISTS AND CRITICS**

**MEN**
Koralsen
Duilio Markmatt
Felix Diemsen
Oaken

**CRITICS AND PHILOSOPHERS OF CULTURE**

**MEN**
Anerholm
Kershey

**GREAT COMPOSERS**

**MEN**
Valmandel
Ruthemir

**OTHER COMPOSERS**

**MEN**
Holger Nilsen
Wesley
Svelder

**MUSICIANS**

**MEN**
Olaf Ledestrem

**POETS**

**MEN**
Jonas Geerlud
Thoralsen
Kronen
Kirsten Larsen
Munsven
Alexis Rogen
Pradelli
Selius
Sulsnik

**WORST POLITICIANS**

**MEN**
Tebrief

**WOMEN**
Clarissa Leyton

**SCANDINAVIAN POLITICAL LEADERS**

**MEN**
Grofel
Lennrot
Gunnar Morgensen
Dinoyer
Sioberg

**PHILOSOPHERS**

**MEN**
Domenicus Albani
Axel Engelmeier
Regialsen

**WOMEN**
Rosa Vernley

## PLACE NAMES

**A**
Aarl
Albielle
Alicante
Alimaje
Almetta
Altekirchen
Annelud
Anolia
Apulia
Ariana
Arlenhom
Arocaria
Arona
Artenfor
Assilia
Augerinia
Aurizio

**B**
Bellagio
Bellinzona
Bergen
Biarritz
Big Bergen
Big Oak
Big Torneo
Bignasco
Binenborg
Blomsterduft
Blomsterfor
Boldieno
Bolzano
Bordeaux
Boston
Bozen
Brixen

**C**
Castalia
Castelnuovo
Cernobbio
Christiania
Clarens
Como
Cordei
Coridalli
Cyprus

**D**
Dareja
Delfia
Denia Vallia
Diana
Doriani

**E**
Egeria
Ejastrem
Eliki
Emeriti
Erika
Eroica

**F**
Fata Azzura
Fedkirche
Fgelen
Fiammarosa
Fiammazzura
Fiammetta
Filiatura
Flabia
Flora Maris
Florence
Flower Nest
Foyia

**G**
Gallarate
Generali
Geneva
Genova
Geteborg
Gianna Terringa
Gled
Gratia Dei
Graz
Grimbole

**H**
Harkovo
Heidelberg

**I**
Iberia
Igmor
Irkutsk
Ischia

**J**
Jomfru

**K**
Karlsruhe
Koblenz
Koln
Kongeborg
Konigskind

**L**
Labarene
Labejona
Lagrela
Larilud
Lassa
Latharmi
Latium
Lauri
Leag-Aud
Legnano
Lesley Gate
Liebach

Ligont
Lilienborg
Lilla Funka
Locarno
Loggovardia
Loikito
London
Lugano
Luino
Lysborg
Lyseblaa
Lysicoma

**M**
Magenta
Majorca
Malta
Mannheim
Margellina
Maribor
Marienborg
Markfor
Mata Uralia
Mayentia
Mayerlink
Mecca
Medina
Mediolano
Menaggio
Mendrisio
Meran
Midnight
Diamondstone
Minorca
Montreux
Monza

**N**
Naade
Nayatana
New Christiania
New Eliki
New Göteborg
New Helsinburg
New Karelia
New Loria
New Marniano
New Narvika
New Orleans
New Retvik
New Rimalgee
New Sabina
New Scaldia
New Scone
New Tarracona
New Tashkent
New Torneo
New Trodheim
New Upsala
New York
New Youthsmile
Nielud
Noghera
Norfor
Nostadt
Notiburg
Nova Tuguska
Nyborg
Nydelfia
Nyfor
Nygusca
Nylienborg
Nymalmoe
Nysabel
Nysalzborg
Nysuomi
Nywien

**O**
Ojford
Olesud
Omska
Orta
Ossen

**P**
Paridisi
Paris
Parma
Pretoria
Procida

**R**
Ragrilia
Resenfarvet
Rho
Riegen
Riyalta
Rodope
Rome
Rosa Azzura
Rosenborg
Roselukin
Rosernes Dal
Rozenholm

**S**
Salerno
Samarkanda
Scagen
Scania
Scavanger
Seaside of Joy
Sesto Calente
Sgelen
Silea
Slesvich Holstein
Small Anolia
Small Blomsterfor
Small Scania
Small Terringa
Smirilud
Sorrento
Sotsiana
Sproja
Star of the Dawn
Star of the East
Stella Maris
Strasborg
Stresa
Svanelud
Svendoni
Swansval
Sydney
Syracuse

**T**
Tebelen
Terranova
Terringtown
Teskera
Tholosi
Tobolsk
Toeplitz
Torneo
(same as Big Torneo)
Trassilea
Tuplin

**U**
Umliani

**V**
Valearides
Valheim
Varennes
Varese
Verbania
Versailles
Viborg
Vien
Vikigruder
Vikingaand
Vikingegnist
Viliana Villafranca
Villach
Vina
Visenje
Vokamvyl

**W**
Waren
Warsaw
Washington
Weimae

**X**
Xanthi Fedriada

**Y**
Youthsmile

**Z**
Zakantha

# CHRONOLOGICAL TABLE

**2204 AD**: Colonization of Mars (the colony thrives for sixty years before it is totally destroyed killing twenty million people)

**2309 AD**: Medium scale nuclear war destroys most of Europe except Scandinavian and Baltic countries

**2320 AD - 2350 AD**: Repopulation of Europe. Peaceful settlement of Northern populations to Mediterranean Sea

**2394 AD**: Final European Constituent Assembly

**2395 AD**: Final World Constituent Assembly

**2396 AD (YEAR 1)**: Official Establishment of the "*Retsstat*" (a world nation with law and order). End of "Prehistory" and beginning of "Historical Era". Year ONE of the new chronology. The first 986 years (2396 AD-3382 AD) was the ancient period of history (*gammel epoke*). From 3382 AD, when the Volkic preaching was of global consensus, begins the new era and the new man, "Homo Occidentalis Novus", succeeds Homo Sapiens.

**2596 AD (YEAR 200)**: The top scientists from around the world are now the new world leaders, responsible for all global governmental actions. At the beginning they were given the order by politicians with global influence, like John Terring.

**2823 AD (YEAR 427)**: Leader Torhild asks symbolically if there is an adequacy (in fact, total global adequacy) in the "distributions" of every industrial good. There is adequacy, now every person has what he needs.

**2846 AD (YEAR 450)**: The city of Norfor begins operating as a Global Spiritual Life Centre

**2894 AD (YEAR 498)**: The "Beginning of the 200 Hundred" and the building of Rosernes Dal (Valley of Roses)

**3000 AD (7th Century)**: The New Renaissance in spiritual Values.

**3100 AD (8th Century)**: The Renaissance goes on.

**3126 AD (YEAR 730)**: Establishment of the Aidersen Institute at Rosernes Dal

**3200 AD (9th Century)**: The "Golden Age" for arts and spiritual achievements.

**3226 AD (YEAR 830)**: Aloisius Nilson predicts the upcoming rise of the "Spiritual Civilisation"

**3253 AD (YEAR 857)**: The greatest poet of all, Larsen, dies and passes to immortality…

**3256 AD (YEAR 860)**: Valmandel's Oratorium "Praying between the Golden Spheres of the Stars" is heard for the first time. It is the best piece of ever written.

**3273 AD (YEAR 876)**: Architect Alicia Neville finishes her masterpiece: the "Temple of Peace and Love" at Rosernes Dal

**3307 AD (YEAR 911)**: Birth of Alexis Volky.

**3382 AD (YEAR 986)**: On 6th of our September Alexis Volky is hit by the "*Nibelvirch*" and survives. Instant Enlightenment. A new "antenna" of perception is added to the human brain thanks to *Nibelvirch*. It is called: "*Oversynssans*" (supervision). This day (our 6th of September) was later announced as the first day of the NEW ERA (Ny Epoke).

**3392 AD (YEAR 996)**: Alexis Volky dies at the age of 86.

**3396 AD (YEAR 1000)**: Crisis of the Volkic preaching

**3410 AD (YEAR 1014)**: Ruthemir's masterpiece "Glorifying Service" is played for the first time

**3546 AD (YEAR 1050)**: Final prevalence of the Volkic Ideal as "consensus gentium".

**3482 AD (YEAR 1086)**: The first Blue Roses (roses that physically radiate blue light). The masterpiece of gardening by Costia Rudulof.

**3600 AD (13th Century)**: Tinersen and his "parables".

**3905 AD - 3906 AD (YEAR 1509 and 1510)**: Andreas Northam writes his "Diary Pages". He will have vivid memories of pre-existence for a period of twelve months, before he dies at the age of 29.

# CALENDAR BOARDS

The calendars were formed by George Papachatzis, the one and only translator of Paul Amadeus Dienach's manuscripts. The "New Calendar" was established in the 2nd century of their chronology (year one=2396 AD) and was kept until the 40th century. Their creators were the best scientists of the world, responsible for the world government at that time. Valley of the Roses (Rosernes Dal) kept the same calendar, regardless of the fact that many astronomers argued that it wasn't 100% accurate.

**New Year's Day**
**(intercalary)..... 23 September**

### MONTH I

1 ............... 24 September
2 ............... 25 September
3 ............... 26 September
4 ............... 27 September
5 ............... 28 September
6 ............... 29 September
7 ............... 30 September
8 ............... 1 October
9 ............... 2 October
10 ............... 3 October
11 ............... 4 October
12 ............... 5 October
13 ............... 6 October
14 ............... 7 October
15 ............... 8 October
16 ............... 9 October
17 ............... 10 October
18 ............... 11 October
19 ............... 12 October
20 ............... 13 October
21 ............... 14 October
22 ............... 15 October
23 ............... 16 October
24 ............... 17 October
25 ............... 18 October
26 ............... 19 October
27 ............... 20 October
28 ............... 21 October
29 ............... 22 October
30 ............... 23 October

### MONTH II

1 ............... 24 October
2 ............... 25 October
3 ............... 26 October
4 ............... 27 October

5 ............... 28 October
6 ............... 29 October
7 ............... 30 October
8 ............... 31 October
9 ............... 1 November
10 ............... 2 November
11 ............... 3 November
12 ............... 4 November
13 ............... 5 November
14 ............... 6 November
15 ............... 7 November
16 ............... 8 November
17 ............... 9 November
18 ............... 10 November
19 ............... 11 November
20 ............... 12 November
21 ............... 13 November
22 ............... 14 November
23 ............... 15 November
24 ............... 16 November
25 ............... 17 November
26 ............... 18 November
27 ............... 19 November
28 ............... 20 November
29 ............... 21 November
30 ............... 22 November

**MONTH III**

1 ............... 23 November
2 ............... 24 November
3 ............... 25 November
4 ............... 26 November
5 ............... 27 November
6 ............... 28 November
7 ............... 29 November
8 ............... 30 November
9 ............... 1 December
10 ............... 2 December
11 ............... 3 December
12 ............... 4 December
13 ............... 5 December
14 ............... 6 December
15 ............... 7 December
16 ............... 8 December
17 ............... 9 December
18 ............... 10 December
19 ............... 11 December
20 ............... 12 December
21 ............... 13 December
22 ............... 14 December
23 ............... 15 December
24 ............... 16 December
25 ............... 17 December
26 ............... 18 December
27 ............... 19 December
28 ............... 20 December
29 ............... 21 December
30 ............... 22 December

**MONTH IV**

1 ............... 23 December
2 ............... 24 December
**Christmas Day**
**(intercalary)......25 December**
3 ............... 26 December
4 ............... 27 December
5 ............... 28 December
6 ............... 29 December
7 ............... 30 December
8 ............... 31 December
9 ............... 1 January
10 ............... 2 January
11 ............... 3 January
12 ............... 4 January
13 ............... 5 January
14 ............... 6 January
15 ............... 7 January
16 ............... 8 January
17 ............... 9 January
18 ............... 10 January
19 ............... 11 January
20 ............... 12 January
21 ............... 13 January
22 ............... 14 January
23 ............... 15 January
24 ............... 16 January
25 ............... 17 January
26 ............... 18 January
27 ............... 19 January
28 ............... 20 January

29 ............... 21 January
30 ............... 22 January

**MONTH V**

1 ............... 23 January
2 ............... 24 January
3 ............... 25 January
4 ............... 26 January
5 ............... 27 January
6 ............... 28 January
7 ............... 29 January
8 ............... 30 January
9 ............... 31 January
10 ............... 1 February
11 ............... 2 February
12 ............... 3 February
13 ............... 4 February
14 ............... 5 February
15 ............... 6 February
16 ............... 7 February
17 ............... 8 February
18 ............... 9 February
19 ............... 10 February
20 ............... 11 February
21 ............... 12 February
22 ............... 13 February
23 ............... 14 February
24 ............... 15 February
25 ............... 16 February
26 ............... 17 February
27 ............... 18 February
28 ............... 19 February
29 ............... 20 February
30 ............... 21 February

**MONTH VI**

1 ............... 22 February
2 ............... 23 February
3 ............... 24 February
4 ............... 25 February
5 ............... 26 February
6 ............... 27 February
7 ............... 28 February
8 ............... 1 March
9 ............... 2 March
10 ............... 3 March
11 ............... 4 March
**Retsstat Aarsdag [Universal Commonwealth's Anniversary] (intercalary)...... 5 March**
12 ............... 6 March
13 ............... 7 March
14 ............... 8 March
15 ............... 9 March
16 ............... 10 March
17 ............... 11 March
18 ............... 12 March
19 ............... 13 March
20 ............... 14 March
21 ............... 15 March
22 ............... 16 March
23 ............... 17 March
24 ............... 18 March
25 ............... 19 March
26 ............... 20 March
27 ............... 21 March
28 ............... 22 March
29 ............... 23 March
30 ............... 24 March

**MONTH VII**

1 ............... 25 March
2 ............... 26 March
3 ............... 27 March
4 ............... 28 March
5 ............... 29 March
6 ............... 30 March
7 ............... 31 March
8 ............... 1 April
9 ............... 2 April
10 ............... 3 April
11 ............... 4 April
12 ............... 5 April
13 ............... 6 April
14 ............... 7 April
15 ............... 8 April
16 ............... 9 April
17 ............... 10 April
18 ............... 11 April
19 ............... 12 April

20 ............... 13 April
21 ............... 14 April
22 ............... 15 April
23 ............... 16 April
24 ............... 17 April
25 ............... 18 April
26 ............... 19 April
27 ............... 20 April
28 ............... 21 April
29 ............... 22 April
30 ............... 23 April

**MONTH VIII**

1 ............... 24 April
2 ............... 25 April
3 ............... 26 April
4 ............... 27 April
**Day of Universal Altruism (intercalary) .... 28 April**
5 ............... 29 April
6 ............... 30 April
7 ............... 1 May
8 ............... 2 May
9 ............... 3 May
10 ............... 4 May
11 ............... 5 May
12 ............... 6 May
13 ............... 7 May
14 ............... 8 May
15 ............... 9 May
16 ............... 10 May
17 ............... 11 May
18 ............... 12 May
19 ............... 13 May
20 ............... 14 May
21 ............... 15 May
22 ............... 16 May
23 ............... 17 May
24 ............... 18 May
25 ............... 19 May
26 ............... 20 May
27 ............... 21 May
28 ............... 22 May
29 ............... 23 May
30 ............... 24 May

**MONTH IX**

1 ............... 25 May
2 ............... 26 May
3 ............... 27 May
4 ............... 28 May
5 ............... 29 May
6 ............... 30 May
7 ............... 31 May
8 ............... 1 June
9 ............... 2 June
10 ............... 3 June
11 ............... 4 June
12 ............... 5 June
13 ............... 6 June
14 ............... 7 June
15 ............... 8 June
16 ............... 9 June
17 ............... 10 June
18 ............... 11 June
19 ............... 12 June
20 ............... 13 June
21 ............... 14 June
22 ............... 15 June
23 ............... 16 June
24 ............... 17 June
25 ............... 18 June
26 ............... 19 June
27 ............... 20 June
28 ............... 21 June
29 ............... 22 June
30 ............... 23 June

**MONTH X**

1 ............... 24 June
2 ............... 25 June
3 ............... 26 June
4 ............... 27 June
5 ............... 28 June
6 ............... 29 June
7 ............... 30 June
8 ............... 1 July
9 ............... 2 July
10 ............... 3 July
11 ............... 4 July
12 ............... 5 July

13 ............... 6 July
14 ............... 7 July
15 ............... 8 July
16 ............... 9 July
17 ............... 10 July
18 ............... 11 July
19 ............... 12 July
20 ............... 13 July
21 ............... 14 July
22 ............... 15 July
23 ............... 16 July
24 ............... 17 July
25 ............... 18 July
26 ............... 19 July
27 ............... 20 July
28 ............... 21 July
29 ............... 22 July
30 ............... 23 July

**MONTH XI**

1 ............... 24 July
2 ............... 25 July
3 ............... 26 July
4 ............... 27 July
5 ............... 28 July
6 ............... 29 July
7 ............... 30 July
8 ............... 31 July
9 ............... 1 August
10 ............... 2 August
11 ............... 3 August
12 ............... 4 August
13 ............... 5 August
14 ............... 6 August
15 ............... 7 August
16 ............... 8 August
17 ............... 9 August
18 ............... 10 August
19 ............... 11 August
20 ............... 12 August
21 ............... 13 August
22 ............... 14 August
23 ............... 15 August
24 ............... 16 August
25 ............... 17 August
26 ............... 18 August
27 ............... 19 August
28 ............... 20 August
29 ............... 21 August
30 ............... 22 August

**MONTH XII**

1 ............... 23 August
2 ............... 24 August
3 ............... 25 August
4 ............... 26 August
5 ............... 27 August
6 ............... 28 August
7 ............... 29 August
8 ............... 30 August
9 ............... 31 August
10 ............... 1 September
11 ............... 2 September
12 ............... 3 September
13 ............... 4 September
14 ............... 5 September

**Gretvirch Aarsdag**
**[Nibelvirch's Anniversary]**
**(intercalary) .... 6 September**

15 ............... 7 September
16 ............... 8 September
17 ............... 9 September
18 ............... 10 September
19 ............... 11 September
20 ............... 12 September
21 ............... 13 September
22 ............... 14 September
23 ............... 15 September
24 ............... 16 September
25 ............... 17 September
26 ............... 18 September
27 ............... 19 September
28 ............... 20 September
29 ............... 21 September
30 ............... 22 September

**(New Year's Eve)**

# GLOSSARY

***Aarsdag:*** Anniversary.

***Biglys:*** The Great Light.

***Biltur partners:*** Travel agency workers.

***Bilvej:*** Colossal motorway running through Eurasia.

***Bigvirch:*** The great ***Virch***.

***Civesheim:*** Luxury inn or permanent residence for citizens ***(Cives)***.

***Civeshostels:*** See ***Civesheim.***

***Civis:*** [pl. ***Cives***] Citizen who has completed the two-year service.

***Civesgard:*** The crimson palace.

***Consumfiorinin:*** Consumer collective.

***Daner:*** Immense oblong aircraft named after the man who invented them.

***Eldrere:*** Old times.

***Forening:*** Collective or union. In northern Europe they are called ***Brugsforening.***

***Furgos:*** Specially designed car parks.

***Gammel epoke:*** See ***Eldrere***.

***Gestalad:*** Luxury hotel.

***Gestel:*** Luxury inn similar to a ***Gestalad.***

***Glothner:*** Vast state-owned industrial cities.

***Gretlys:*** The Great Light.

***Gretvirch:*** The Great ***Virch*** (see ***Virch***).

***Ilector:*** High-ranking officials of the intelligentsia with a special position in society.

***Kierketaarns:*** Round or ellipsoid temples with white, circular colonnades.

***Kjole:*** Ritual robe.

***Lansbee:*** Rural area.

***Larinter:*** Sport centres.

***Lilk skole:*** Primary school.

***Linsen:*** Flying vehicle for private use, named after its inventor.

***Lipvirch:*** True love, sharing many similarities with young love. It is considered a glimmer of the ***Samith***.

***Lorffe:*** High-ranking officials of the intelligentsia, leaders of society.

***Lys:*** Light.

***Mindre skole:*** A smaller school of primary education.

***Nibelvirch:*** Term coined by the Aidersen Institute of unknown etymology meaning the new cognitive ability attained by people, a new antenna of comprehension. Thanks to the *Nibelvirch*, the human brain was able to perceive new fields of reality.

***Nojere:*** New times.

***Oversyn:*** Enlightenment due to the *Nibelvirch*, a new dynamic in cognition.

***Oversynssans:*** see ***Oversyn***

***Quay:*** Airport runway.

***Ragioza:*** [pl.] Transcontinental, multi-storeyed, articulated vehicles used as public means of transport.

***Reigen:*** see ***Reigen-Swage***.

***Reigen-Swage:*** Projection device named after its two inventors combining sound and image in varying sizes ranging from small personal devices to wall-screen. Something like our television.

***Retsstat:*** The establishment of the Universal Commonwealth with law and order.

***Roisvirch:*** Spiritual happiness of a higher level, a very intense emotion similar to ecstasy often beyond what humans can bear. In the latter case, it may lead to suicide.

***Samith:*** Term coined by the Aidersen Institute of unknown etymology meaning the whole of all existence. Its essence is incomprehensible to finite human capabilities

***Slaabrok:*** A uniform of short, dark-coloured trousers with black stripes that stop slightly below the knee, green silk high socks, a white double breasted vest with white lapels, a green stole-belt and special white boots.

***Swage:*** see ***Reigen-Swage***.

***Storlys:*** The Great Light.

***Tilteys:*** [pl.] Officials of the intelligentsia but not the highest ranking ones.

***Troende:*** Term used to define the man of Northam's era, the citizen of the future.

***Troje:*** Work uniform.

***Unge:*** Youngster up to the age of 17 who voluntarily participates in the 'following' of the intelligentsia greats.

***Velos:*** Bicycles.

***Vigioza:*** Private flying vehicles.

***Vindebros:*** Bridges designed for mild hiking.

***Vilenthen:*** Secondary school.

***Virch:*** Term coined by the Aidersen Institute of unknown etymology meaning the valuable new intellectual and spiritual capabilities added to human cognition and psyche after the appearance of the new species Homo Occidentalis Novus in 3382 AD.

***Werksted:*** Factory

# Acknowledgements

Special thanks to my wife Tonia Tsoumi, my brother John Sirigos and his wife Jo Gillan, owners of ancient-origins.net. Without their support this publication would not have been possible.

Also, I would like to thank from the bottom of my heart Greg Papadoyiannis for his wise comments, Vassilis Tsakiroglou for his immediate response to my requests, Eleonora Kouneni, Thalia Bisticas and Matina Chatzigianni for their precious help in the translation of the Diary, and Radamanthis Anastasakis, without whom, this life changing book wouldn't have survived.

Achilleas Sirigos

This Way Out Productions
info@thiswayout.gr

Made in the USA
Middletown, DE
07 August 2020

14716184R00234